Since he was in charge of the amphibious operations in the Falklands War in 1982, it goes without saying that there is no one better qualified to tell the story of that aspect of the campaign than Commodore Michael Clapp. Here he describes, with considerable candour, some of the problems met in a Navy racing to war and finding it necessary to recreate a largely abandoned operational technique in a somewhat *ad hoc* fashion. Some of the facts revealed in this book will come as a surprise to many, both among those who 'went south' and among the armchair historians who think they know exactly what occurred. In this clear and incisive account, Michael Clapp, aided by Ewen Southby-Tailyour, has provided a major contribution to the history of the Falklands War.

Michael Clapp was educated at Marlborough College. He joined the Executive Branch of the Royal Navy in 1950 and after service in Korea and Cyprus, was sent to become an Observer in the Fleet Air Arm, becoming the Senior Observer of 801 Squadron, the first operational squadron. This was followed by command of HMS *Puncheston*, a minesweeper, during the Indonesian confrontation where he was mentioned in dispatches. His service then included a period as a lecturer, Command of 801 Squadron, two frigate commands, two tours in the MOD and an appointment as Executive Officer of HMS *Norfolk*. He was appointed Commodore Amphibious Warfare in 1981 and found himself in Command of the Falkland Islands Amphibious Task Group. He was made a Companion of the Bath before retiring as a Captain in 1983. He is married with three children and lives in Devon.

Ewen Southby-Tailyour spent much of his childhood on board a 30-ton Bristol Channel Pilot Cutter. He was commissioned into the Royal Marines in 1960 and spent most of his career commanding units within Commando Forces or detachments of the Royal Marines at sea. He was awarded the Sultan's Bravery Medal for gallantry during the Dhofar War and received the OBE for his distinguished service in the Falklands. He is the author of two previous books on the Falklands, *Falkland Island Shores* and *Reasons in Writing*.

AMPHIBIOUS ASSAULT FALKLANDS

THE BATTLE OF SAN CARLOS WATER

Michael Clapp
&
Ewen Southby-Tailyour

ORION

An Orion Paperback
First published in Great Britain by Leo Cooper in 1996
This paperback edition published in 1997 by
Orion Books Ltd,
Orion House, 5 Upper St. Martin's Lane,
London WC2H 9EA

A CIP catalogue record for this book
is available from the British Library.

ISBN: 0 75281 109 6

Typeset by Deltatype Ltd, Birkenhead, Merseyside
Printed and bound in Great Britain by
The Guernsey Press Co. Ltd, Channel Islands

DEDICATION

We wish to dedicate this book to the people of the Amphibious Task Group, TG 317.0, be they ladies, men or officers, Chinese or British, Merchant, Royal Fleet Auxiliary, Army, Civilian, Royal Air Force, Royal Marines, or Royal Navy and especially to the staff. We jointly shared an experience which we hope will never have to be repeated and this book can in no way express our admiration and gratitude for their cheerful, willing and courageous support.

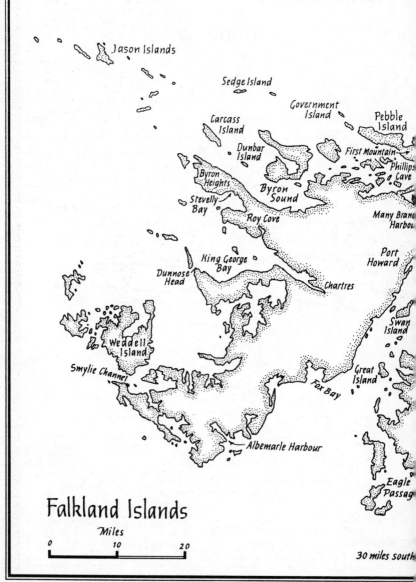

SOUTH ATLANTIC

Jason Islands

Sedge Island

Government
Island

Pebble
Island

Carcass
Island

First Mountain

Dunbar
Island

Phillips
Cave

Byron
Heights

Byron
Sound

Stevelly
Bay

Many Branc
Harbou

Roy Cove

Port
Howard

King George
Bay

Dunnose
Head

Chartres

Swan
Island

Weddell
Island

Great
Island

Smylie Channel

Fox Bay

Albemarle Harbour

Eagle
Passag

Falkland Islands

Miles

0   10   20

30 miles south

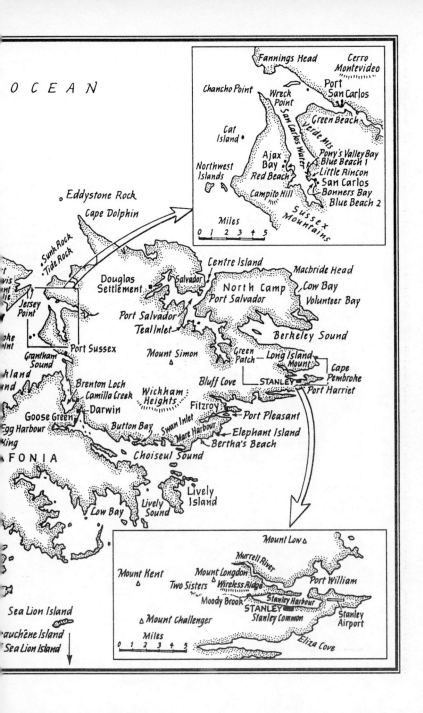

CONTENTS

AUTHOR'S NOTE

Admiral of the Fleet Lord Fisher once wrote that 'Sailors are not remarkable as dialecticians. They are more given to making decisions and acting upon them.' This is still largely true and it has therefore been with some trepidation that I agreed to work with Ewen and put down the story of the Falklands Amphibious Task Group on paper.

Firstly, we are grateful to our wives and families who have lived with this book which has rekindled memories of a campaign in which they had much less pleasure than we. Their support in both events has been remarkable and deeply appreciated.

While largely written in the first person, Ewen has done most of the writing, and collating the huge amount of information we have been offered. Some of this has already appeared in other publications but none has been explained through the eyes of the Amphibious Task Group Commander who at various stages in the campaign was the jam in the sandwich, in pole position and then the piggy in the middle.

Without this mass of information the story would have been hollow but we both feel confident that it will stand the test of time and is as historically correct as we could reasonably hope to achieve. Sadly, two key figures, Admiral Fieldhouse and Vice-Admiral Halifax, have since died and we have not, therefore, been able to discuss this story with them.

The views expressed are, of course, our own and cannot in any way be held to represent those of the Ministry of Defence or others. The story attempts to give one person's interpretation of events, rumours and instructions during a tense, exciting and exhausting period. Despite relatively modern communications for that time and the Royal Navy's expertise at writing carefully drafted and apparently precise signals, misunderstandings and alternative points of view were inevitable and not uncommon.

After so many years, it is difficult to avoid the accusation of hindsight but we have tried hard not to fall into this trap. Many conversations, signals and events remain clearly imprinted in our's and other peoples's memories while, inevitably, some others have not been as clearly remembered.

We are, however, enormously grateful to everyone who contributed, to Leo Cooper for his patience and to Tom Hartman who has cheerfully corrected our scripts. The collation, writing and publishing have therefore been almost as 'joint' as the Falklands campaign itself.

FOREWORD

by Admiral of the Fleet Lord Lewin

Britain is an island nation. For over a thousand years Britain's military expeditions have depended on ships to transport men and materials, with warships to defend them and ensure the continuity of their supply. The Falklands War was a classic example of this eternal truth. This was the war that for fifteen years Governments of both persuasions had been telling the Services they would not be required to fight. Priority was on nuclear deterrence and readiness for war on the Central Front. Only the doubtful prospect of timely reinforcement of the Northern Flank kept the art of amphibious warfare alive. If the Chiefs of Staff had suggested that flexible forces would be better equipped to cope with the unexpected they would have been paid scant attention. Yet, as so often throughout history, the unexpected happened.

From his key position in the command chain Michael Clapp gives a detailed account of the operation which, while fascinating to the general reader, will be of value to future historians and should act as a handbook for practitioners of amphibious warfare. Many lessons emerge: the importance of logistics, a dull subject compared to the excitement of battle and so often ignored – yet without food, fuel, ammunition and so many other bits and pieces from spares to mail the battle cannot begin, let alone be won; the availability of merchant shipping, the vital factor in both world wars, indeed in every war Britain has fought; the need for a clear chain of command and unambiguous directives, and reliable communications. Above all, the narrative demonstrates that high morale comes from tough training and good leadership.

This book concentrates on the mechanics of war and evinces a healthy disrespect for 'Them' – the politicians and those in Whitehall. It was ever thus, but in defence of the High Command all members of the Chiefs of Staff Committee had fought at the sharp end in World War II and had no illusions about the dangers the Task Force would face. It is understandable – indeed desirable – that the impact of political events should not have been bothering those fighting the battle down south. But politics had an all-pervasive influence. The legal basis of the whole operation depended on United Nations Resolution 502 which condemned Argentine aggressions and Article 56 of the UN Charter which permits action in self defence.

The immediate international political support, and, in the case of the United States, material support, were essential and had to be fostered. First there were attempts to negotiate a peaceful settlement, but after the first Haig shuttle it was clear in London that this could not be achieved. After the sinking of the *Belgrano* international support was fast draining away and there was strong pressure in the United Nations for a cease fire. Because a negotiated settlement was never a starter, this could only have resulted in a temporary cessation of operations, say six weeks. With winter coming, this delay would have been disastrous for our forces, just established ashore with no shelter for our ships exposed to the antarctic gales. Such a delay could not be countenanced. It was this political background that caused Admiral Fieldhouse, the operational commander, to order the attack on Goose Green against the judgement of the man on the spot. In the event the risk was justified and this early success provided the springboard for ultimate victory.

The Chiefs of Staff would have had good grounds for advising that recapture of the Falklands was an operation the forces were neither equipped nor structured to carry out. Thanks initially to the confident and positive advice of Admiral Sir Henry Leach, a determined Prime Minister took a difficult decision and the Task Force was launched. Many factors contributed to success but foremost were the professionalism and determination of all those who went south. The defeat of an evil military dictatorship had wide repercussions: democracy was restored to the Argentine people, Western deterrence was strengthened by this strong response to unprovoked aggression, Britain's position in the world was enhanced. It is perhaps not too far-fetched to suggest that Britain's resolute action presaged the break-up of the Soviet Union.

CHRONOLOGICAL ORDER
OF MAIN EVENTS

1981

9 July   Joint Intelligence Centre report to HMG.

1982

11 March   Scrap metal workmen leave Argentina for South Georgia.

19 March   Argentines land at Leith.

24 March   *Endurance* despatched to South Georgia.

26 March   *Operation Azul* ships sail from Argentina.

31 March   Reports reach Whitehall that the Falklands would be invaded on the 2 April.

1 April   'War' Cabinet meets. *Hermes* and *Invincible* stood to.

2 April   Falklands invaded.

           Clapp appointed Commander Task Unit.

5 April   *Hermes and Invincible* sail from Portsmouth.

6 April   First 'amphibious' ships sail.

10 April   Clapp appointed Commander Amphibious Task Group.

           Woodward appointed Commander Carrier Task Group.

           Thompson appointed Commander Landing Force.

12 April   Maritime Exclusion Zone established by submarines.

17 April   Meetings at Ascension Island chaired by Admiral Fieldhouse.

18 April   Carrier Task Group sails south from Ascension.

25 April   South Georgia retaken.

27 April   Plans for landings presented to 'War' Cabinet.

30 April   Carrier Task Group reaches exclusion zone.

           General Moore briefed in Ascension Island on landing options.

1 May	First landings on Falklands by Special Forces.
	LSLs sail from Ascension.
2 May	*Belgrano* sunk.
4 May	*Sheffield* hit.
7 May	Exclusion zone extended to Argentine 12 mile limit.
	Main Amphibious Task Group sails south from Ascension Island.
10 May	Decision taken by Clapp and Thompson that San Carlos was the AOA.
	Alacrity transits Falkland Sound.
12 May	*Queen Elizabeth II* sails from Southampton with 5 Infantry Brigade and Major General Moore embarked.
	Amphibious Task Group ordered to: 'Repossess the Falklands as quickly as possible.'
13 May	Thompson gives 3rd Commando Brigade Orders for San Carlos landings.
14 May	SAS attack on Pebble Island begins.
15 May	Clapp holds Pre-Landing Conference.
18 May	'War' Cabinet presented with (and approves) the San Carlos option.
	Clapp and Thompson ordered to redistribute troops prior to landings.
	Amphibious Task Group meets up with Carrier Task Group.
	Clapp confirms timings for landings.
	Clapp ordered to 'Go' subject to final confirmation on 20 May.
20 May	Clapp receives orders to land from London.
21 May	3rd Commando Brigade establishes beachhead at San Carlos.
	Ardent sunk.
23 May	*Antelope* sinks.
25 May	*Coventry* sunk.
	Atlantic Conveyor hit.
27 May	45 Commando and 3 Para begin march eastwards from San Carlos.

	2 Para advances towards Darwin.
	Queen Elizabeth II arrives South Georgia with 5 Infantry Brigade.
28 May	Battle for Darwin and Goose Green begins.
29 May	Moore, Woodward and Clapp meet on board *Hermes*.
	Clapp becomes Commodore Falkland Islands.
30 May	Moore arrives San Carlos in *Fearless*.
	Mount Kent secured by SAS; 42 Commando begins occupation.
2 June	*Canberra*, with 5 Infantry Brigade embarked, arrives San Carlos.
	2 Para begins advance along southern flank.
5 June	Harrier FOB opened at San Carlos.
	Scots Guards sail for Bluff Cove.
7 June	Welsh Guards sail for Fitzroy.
8 June	*Sir Galahad* and *Sir Tristram* attacked off Fitzroy Settlement.
11 June	3rd Commando Brigade's battles for Stanley begin.
13 June	5 Infantry Brigade's battles begin.
14 June	Argentine land forces surrender in Stanley.
17 June	Argentine Junta collapses.
18 June	*Canberra* sails for Argentina with Prisoners of War.
19 June	*Norland* sails for Argentina with Prisoners of War.
23 June	Clapp and staff move ashore to Stanley.
25 June	Clapp officially appointed Commodore Falkland Islands (COMFI).
	Canberra sails for United Kingdom with bulk of 3rd Commando Brigade.
10 July	Clapp appointed Chief of Staff to Commander British Forces Falkland Islands.
13 July	Clapp and majority of staff return to United Kingdom.

GLOSSARY

We regret the need for such a long glossary. While trying to put naval and military jargon into civilian English we have found that it is not always possible without over-complication or losing the flavour imparted by service language. We hope this glossary will help!

For entries marked * a fuller description will be found in the text.

AAC Army Air Corps.

AAF Argentinian Air Force.

ABU Amphibious Beach Unit.

ACOS Assistant Chief of Staff.

AD Troop Air Defence Troop, 3rd Cdo Bde, RM.

AEW Airborne Early Warning.

AGI Russian spy trawler; principally electronic intelligence collection.

AMTRAC American-designed, tracked, amphibian landing craft.

AN/TPS-43 Argentinian, long-range, radar-controlled air warning system.

AOA★ Amphibious Objective Area.

AOR★ Amphibious Operation Room in an LPD.

Area Air defence An air defence system capable of taking on targets which are not flying directly at the missile launcher or unit to be defended.

AS12 British, air-to-surface launched missile (helicopter).

Assault Ship See LPD.

ATG★ Amphibious Task Group.

ATP★ Allied Tactical Publication. Handbooks for doctrine and practices.

*Awkward** Operation to deter underwater attacks by swimmers against ships at anchor.

Azul Argentinian operation to invade the Falkland Islands.

BAOR British Army of the Rhine.

BAS 3rd Commando Brigade Air Squadron. (3 BAS).

Bde Brigade.

Blowpipe British, hand-held, optically-guided anti-aircraft missile.

Blues and Royals Cavalry Regiment. An amalgamation of the Royal Dragoons (The Royals) and the Royal Horse Guards (The Blues).

Blue-on-blue Accidental engagement between forces on the same side.

BMA * Brigade Maintenance Area.

Bn Battalion.

Bofors 40mm Anti-aircraft gun fitted to most HM ships, LSLs and MV *Elk*.

Broad Pennant A white swallow-tailed pennant with St George's Cross and one red ball which is a Commodore's personal insignia. Technically it is not a 'flag' which is rectangular and reserved for Admirals, but the term flagship is used.

Camp The Falklands countryside anywhere outside Stanley.

Canberra Elderly bomber used by AAF for night bombing and by the British for photographic reconnaissance (PR).

CAG * Commander Amphibious Group (i.e. Commander of the ships, landing craft and support helicopters (the naval elements)) – COMAW.

CAP * Combat air patrol of fixed wing aircraft.

CAS Chief of the Air Staff.

CASEVAC Casualty evacuation.

CATF * Commander Amphibious Task Force. (i.e. Commander of the amphibious group and landing force (the whole gamut)) – COMAW.

CBG Carrier Battle Group – FOF1.

CDS Chief of the Defence Staff. The Chairman of the Chiefs of Staff committee consisting of CDS, CNS, CGS and CAS.

Cdo Commando.

CGRM Commandant General Royal Marines.

CGS Chief of the General Staff.

CinC Fleet Commander in Chief of the Fleet – during *Operation Corporate* he was also Commander of the South Atlantic Task Force (CTF).

CinC UKLF Commander in Chief, UK Land Forces.

Chaff Strips of metallic foil shot into the air by rockets or guns to decoy radar-guided missiles or confuse the enemy's radar picture.

Chinook RAF and AAF twin-rotor helicopter capable of carrying ten tons.

CLFFI* Commander Land Forces, Falkland Islands – MGRM Cdo Forces.

CLF* Commander of the Landing Force – Com. 3 Cdo Bde.

CNS Chief of the Naval Staff.

Com Commander (in the control sense and not rank).

COMAW* Commodore Amphibious Warfare.

Corporate* Operation to recover the Falklands.

COS Chief of Staff.

Coy Company. Usually a rifle company in a RM Cdo or army battalion.

CTE* Commander Task Element – directly responsible to a CTU.

CTF* Commander (of the South Atlantic) Task Force – exercised throughout by CinC Fleet.

CTG* Commander Task Group – directly responsible to a CTF.

CTU* Commander Task Unit – directly responsible to a CTG.

Dalek Robot in children's television that speaks with a metallic, disjointed and staccato voice.

De-gaussing Method by which the magnetic field of a ship is lessened.

DOE* Defence Operation Executive.

DSSS* Defence secure voice satellite communications system.

EOD Explosive Ordnance Device – UXB.

Exocet French-designed ship-ground or air-launched anti-ship missile.

FBMA* Forward Brigade Maintenance Area.

FCDT Fleet Clearance Diving Team.

FCO Foreign and Commonwealth Office.

FEBA Forward Edge of Battle Area.

FIC Falkland Island Company.

Flag Captain The Commanding Officer of the Flag Ship.

Flagship The ship in which the Commodore or the Admiral and his staff are embarked and which flies their respective broad pennant or flag.

FMG Fleet Maintenance Group.

FOB Forward Operating Base for either helicopters or landing craft away from their parent ships.

148 FOU Commando Forward Observation Unit, Royal Artillery. Used especially for controlling naval gunfire against shore targets (NGS).

GAVO★ Group Aviation Officer.

Gazelle Light helicopter deployed with BAS.

Gemini Small, rubber, inflatable boat deployed with HM ships and used as a raiding craft by the Landing Craft Squadron.

GH Government House, Stanley.

GPMG British General Purpose Machine Gun. 7.62mm calibre.

GR3 Harrier. RAF VSTOL aircraft used for ground attack and photographic reconnaissance.

GSO1★ General Staff Officer Grade 1.

HEALT★ Helicopter Employment and Assault Landing Table.

HEGFI HE. His Excellency the Governor and Commander in Chief, The Falkland Islands.

JTP★ Joint Tactical Publications laying down doctrine and practices.

LCU Landing Craft Utility, capable of carrying two main battle tanks.

LCVP Landing Craft Vehicle and Personnel, capable of carrying four tons.

Log Logistics. (Cdo Log Regt – 3rd Cdo Bde's Logistic Regiment.)

LPD★ Landing Platform Dock. HMSs *Fearless* and *Intrepid*.

LSL★ Landing Ship Logistic of the RFA *Sir Lancelot* class.

Lynx Light helicopter used by RN and RM for anti-submarine, anti-tank and communication duties.

Malvinas Current Argentinian name for the Falklands.

Marisat Maritime Satellite Communications carried by some STUFT.

MCM* Mine Counter Measures.

Mexeflote Low, flat, self-propelled rafts manned by the RTC capable, in their longest version, of carrying 120 tons. Carried by the LSLs.

MGRM* Major General Royal Marines.

Milan Infantry, wire-guided, anti-tank missile.

Mirage French-designed, delta-winged supersonic aircraft capable of launching Exocet. 'Dagger' version for air to ground attack.

M&AW Mountain and Arctic Warfare Cadre, Royal Marines.

MN Merchant Navy.

NAAFI Navy, Army and Air Force Institutes. On board, shop run by civilians.

NAS Naval Air Squadron within the Royal Navy's Fleet Air Arm.

NBCD Nuclear, Biological, Chemical Defence and Damage Control.

NGS Naval Gunfire Support for ground troops from ship offshore. See 148 FOU.

O Group* Military Orders group.

Oerlikon 20mm quick-firing light gun used for close-in defence.

OP Observation Post.

Opgen Mike* Operation Order issued by CATF bringing together all the maritime aspects of a landing.

OTC Officer in tactical command of a specific naval operation.

Para Parachute Regiment.

*Paraquet** Operation to recover South Georgia.

PC82 Small, lightly armed, Argentine patrol craft.

PNG Passive Night Goggles worn by a selection of helicopter pilots.

Point Defence An air defence system only capable of taking on targets which are flying directly or almost directly at the missile launcher or gun.

*Porcupine** Operation to counter Argentine surface threat against shipping in San Carlos Water.

PR Photo-reconnaissance by aircraft.

PR* Public Relations.

PLC* Pre-Landing Conference – the COMAW's 'O' Group.

Pucara Argentine-designed and built, twin-prop, twin-seat aircraft designed for counter-insurgency operations in a ground attack role.

QHM Queen's Harbourmaster.

RA Royal Artillery.

RAMC Royal Army Medical Corps.

Rapier British point defence ground-to-air missile system with a limited area air defence capability.

RAS Replenishment At Sea. Liquids and solids by pipe, jack stay or helicopter between ships.

RCT Royal Corps of Transport.

Red Button* Operation to clear civilian ships to the east during a surface engagement.

RFA Royal Fleet Auxiliary. The Royal Navy's civilian-manned fleet of logistic support ships.

Rgt Regiment.

Rhienmetell Argentine 20mm anti-aircraft gun.

RM Royal Marines.

RMAS Royal Maritime Auxiliary Service.

RN Royal Navy.

RNLMC Royal Netherlands Marine Corps.

ROE* Rules of Engagement given by the British Goverment ordaining, in advance, the appropriate responses to an enemy's expected actions. (And amended as required, depending on changing circumstances.)

Roland French surface-to-air missile employed by the Argentinians.

RRC Rigid Raiding Craft. GRP – constructed, outboard-powered, fast, open craft deployed with the Task Force Landing Craft Squadron.

SAS Special Air Service. (Army).

SAS* Surface Assault Schedule.

SACC* Supporting Arms Co-ordination Centre in an LPD.

SACEUR Supreme Allied Commander Europe.

SACLANT Supreme Allied Commander Atlantic.

SEAO Staff Air Engineer Officer.

SATCOM Satellite Communications.

SAVO* Staff Aviation Officer.

SBS Special Boat Section. (Royal Marines)

Scare Charges Small explosive charges dropped overboard at irregular intervals to deter underwater sabotage swimmers while a ship is at anchor.

Scimitar Small, light tank deployed by the Blues and Royals. 30mm Rarden Gun as main armament with 160 rounds. Crew of 3.

Scorpion Small, light tank deployed by the Blues and Royals similar to the Scimitar.

Sea Dart Naval, medium to long-range surface-to-air missile with a good area air defence capability.

Sea Harrier Naval VSTOL aircraft used mainly for air-to-air combat.

Sea King RN helicopter with various configurations. During *Operation Corporate* these included anti-submarine duties and medium lift troop carrier.

Sea Skua Short-range, helicopter-launched air-to-surface missile.

Sea Wolf Naval, automatic, short-range, point defence, surface-to-air missile.

Seacat Naval, largely manual, short-range, point defence, surface-to-air missile.

Seaslug Naval, medium-range, surface-to-air missile with a limited area air defence capability.

SF Special Force. The SAS, the SBS, M&AW, 148 FOU, RA.

Sidewinder U.S. air-to-air guided missile carried by Sea Harriers.

SHAR Sea Harrier.

*Shutter** Operation conducted by submarines to give an early warning of air attacks.

SMCDO* Staff Mine Countermeasures and Diving Officer.

Sky Hawk American A-4 attack aircraft used by the AAF.

SMEO* Staff Marine Engineer Officer.

SNEB British helicopter-launched anti-tank missile.

SNO Senior Naval Officer, in particular those embarked in STUFT.

SOG Special Operations Group.

SOO* Staff Officer Operations.

*Springtrain** Exercise by First Flotilla in Mediterranean at the time of the Argentine Invasion.

Sqn Squadron.

SS11 British helicopter-launched, wire-guided anti-tank missile.

Stinger U.S. hand-held, anti-aircraft missile, used by the SAS.

STUFT★ Merchant Ships Taken Up From Trade.

Sutton★ Amphibious operation to establish the beachhead at San Carlos.

SWEO★ Staff Weapons and Electrical Officer.

SWO(D) Staff Warfare Officer (Aircraft Direction).

TA★ Transport Area.

Tab Parachute Regiment slang for Yomp

TACHQ Tactical Headquarters.

TEZ★ Total Exclusion Zone.

Tiger Cat Argentine-operated anti-aircraft missile system.

Tornado★ Operations to deceive Argentine forces in the Falklands prior to *Operation Sutton*.

Tp Troop.

TRALA★ Tug, Repair and Logistics Area.

UXB Unexploded Bomb – more formally, EOD.

Wasp Light helicopter used by RN for anti-submarine and communication duties. Military equivalent is the Scout.

Wessex RN medium-lift helicopter used for support tasks afloat and ashore.

WRNS Women's Royal Naval Service.

VSTOL Vertical, Short Take Off and Landing. e.g. Harrier.

Vulcan RAF, elderly, long-distance, conventional and nuclear bomber.

Yardarm Clearing 'The process of taking precautionary steps to ensure that no blame will attach if something goes wrong.' (*Jackspeak* by Rick Jolly, published by Palamando, 1989)

Yomp Commando slang for long march with full load. (From sailor's slang 'to eat').

PROLOGUE

> To a war are required, a just quarrel; sufficient
> forces and provisions; and a prudent choice of
> design.
>
> Francis Bacon 1561–1626
> Considerations Touching a War with Spain 1624

IN THE SPRING of 1982 the Royal Navy was reeling from yet another series of cuts which to many of us in the service made little sense. It would, however, be wrong to suggest that we did not appreciate the need to try and improve efficiency and to save money in order to reduce the burden of taxation, but to continue to reduce our capability with few obvious reductions in commitments did not seem to make military sense.

A growing weight of political opinion had dictated that the Central Front was all that really mattered. Even though intelligence suggested that there was no known intent by the Soviet Union to attack the west there was the perception that the United Kingdom's tentative moves towards greater participation in the European Union required a firm display of British military power on German soil: military strength that could not be reduced for fear of political repercussions.

At sea we could only wonder at these decisions, especially as the cuts fell more heavily on the Royal Navy than on the other services. Computer-aided analysis had favoured air power at a time when new shipborne weapons systems were turning the tables in favour of ship defence. Such analysis was intended to be objective, but was not able to take account of training, dash and determination, each of which is a war-winner. At the same time new anti-submarine systems (such as the towed-array sonar system) began to offer a long-term enemy submarine detection capability far superior to any airborne method. We were indeed still the Silent Service, apparently unable to make full use of public relations or the media to awaken the support of public opinion or that of politicians: the public seemed scarcely to know of our improving capabilities. It was little better within the Ministry of Defence itself, for while we continued to keep our doughty reputation for tactical argument intact our ability to explain and influence more strategic and long-term thinking was withering.

It was all too easy for sceptics to write-off the Royal Navy as having no role in 'the next' NATO conflict which, they argued, would be over in a matter of days and certainly before we had ships and submarines in the operating areas. Any argument suggesting there would more likely be a considerable period of tension and therefore warning was counted as simply a means of justifying otherwise somewhat useless ships and too expensive to countenance in terms of sono buoys, etc.

While there was no indication of Soviet intent towards the strongly defended central region there was acceptance that the 'softer' flanks could (and probably would) be absorbed by the Soviets for they offered so little obvious and immediate economic or political loss to the west. The question of the Soviet Union's undoubted advantage of safer access to the World's oceans for trade and influence was often discussed but all too easily, and just as often, put aside. It was the central economies of Europe on which British politicians concentrated and wished to support and the other two Services were not slow to take advantage of this mood.

Hardly surprising, therefore, that it was easier to dismiss the Royal Navy for apparently wanting to hold on to ties of Empire and Commonwealth as a means of maintaining its size, structure and capabilities. It had, after all, seen out the last soldiers and airmen on a large number of occasions when colonies, protectorates and dependencies received or won their freedom. A reduction of its ability to either patrol world-wide or project power ashore (the *raison d'être* of the navy almost since its birth) would inevitably lead to the death of such 'out-moded' pillars of British defence policy: yet these very aspects were precisely what was still needed by so many countries, for whom we retained defence commitments.

Within the Ministry of Defence a favoured expression was 'salami slicing', a policy whereby selections of the capability and a few expensive men would be shaved off little by little from a number of capabilities so that any hurt was either not noticed or well spread. Seldom were these cuts balanced by a similar reduction in tasks. This technique was often justified as being the result of increasing efficiency but it saved civil servants and staff officers the task and consequent risk of conducting a fundamental review while continuing to dangle the carrot that implied that as each cut was small it could be added back quickly if it was necessary or if the money was suddenly available.

Over the years this tactic had created imbalances and inefficiencies. Ships and staffs were seriously undermanned and equipment was often incomplete. All this only served to increase the strain on Naval Servicemen and their families. The 'can do' attitude which the Royal Navy had for so many centuries adopted as an unofficial and proud motto was now working against it. It had been an admirable but risky attitude; at times in stark contrast to that of the other services who seemed incapable of action until the exact numbers of staff and men had been joined with precisely the correct equipment; only then apparently could they or would they accept any specific task.

Thus, in the circumstances, it should not have surprised anybody who understood and believed in sea power in general and the Royal Navy in particular that morale in the Fleet flagged at all levels. Our 'can do' bluff was about to be called and this positive approach was about to face its greatest test in recent years. Yet, as before, this attitude appears not to have benefited the Royal Navy wholly in the long term.

At that time, the very early 1980s, the politicians continued to accept that the role of the Royal Navy was mainly in support of the Supreme Allied Commander Atlantic (SACLANT) by providing submarines with which to engage Soviet ballistic attack submarines and surface ships, while at the same time providing our own nuclear missile deterrents. British ships (including our new small aircraft carriers) would be provided for anti-submarine support to the Striking Fleet Atlantic as well as convoy protection in the Atlantic, Channel and North Sea. Protection of the northern and southern flanks of NATO would be provided by an integral amphibious task force. Our small mine counter-measures force would attempt to keep open the major United Kingdom ports and supply routes to the continent.

The only United Kingdom naval force having, then, any real contact and experience with the forces of the Supreme Allied Commander Europe (SACEUR) was my small (brigade level) United Kingdom/Netherlands Amphibious Task Group (UK/NL ATG) with its landing force of the British 3rd Commando Brigade Royal Marines supplemented (for NATO tasks but not national ones) by elements of the Royal Netherlands Marine Corps. The main role of the UK/NL ATG was to land the Commando Brigade, or part of it, on the flanks of SACEUR's territory to assist in holding land, ports or airfields which might be of maritime use to an enemy. Its tasks included not only SACEUR-held territory such as Norway, the Baltic Approaches, Denmark and parts of Schleswig Holstein in the north and the Bosphorus in the south, but also islands of vital interest to SACLANT such as Iceland, The Faeroes and The Azores. This Amphibious Task Group was expected to sail early in a crisis and certainly early enough to be received by the 'host nation' before hostilities began. By reacting so soon, a display of NATO solidarity would be shown that might, before it was too late, deter an enemy in its actions.

It was to me an immensely interesting and challenging task but one that raised little excitement with the Royal Navy as a whole who expected the role to be subject to the next series of cuts and who were more interested in purely naval tasks such as submarine or anti-submarine warfare.

There was sufficient shipping within the Royal Navy's influence to land part of the Amphibious Task Group in a number of pre-planned operations but if the full force was to be deployed from sea then considerable extra shipping would need to be 'taken up from trade'. At any moment those ships could be far-flung making advance planning for shipping manifests almost an impossibility if time was short.

All this was fairly obvious and straightforward but the flexibility of naval power meant that the need for operations out of the NATO area was always a possibility whether or not the ships could be spared.

The Royal Navy was, therefore, organized with such possible tasks in mind. Outside the Ministry of Defence there were two full Admirals (4 star level, in NATO parlance), one to operate the complete British Fleet as its Commander-in-Chief (CinC Fleet) and the other to command the training and all shore-based functions, Commander in Chief Naval Home Command (CinC NAVHOME). Below CinC Fleet were four junior Admirals commanding the sea-going forces. Their tasks had only recently been reviewed and clarified: Flag Officer Submarines, Flag Officer First Flotilla (FOF 1), Flag Officer 2nd Flotilla (FOF 2) and the Flag Officer Third Flotilla (FOF 3).

FOF 3's earlier title had been FOCAS or Flag Officer Carriers and Amphibious Ships and although the title had recently changed his duties had not. He was responsible for all aircraft carriers and amphibious ships and, as such, had a special responsibility not just for the ships but their businesses themselves. He held the national titles of Fleet Aviation and Fleet Amphibious Warfare Authority. He was also responsible for integrating the Royal Fleet Auxiliaries (RFA's) that provide tanker and stores ships in support of the fleet at sea. He was also unusual among the Flotilla Admirals for he had a NATO role (the only other was the Flag Officer Submarines) as the Commander Anti-Submarine Group Two under the NATO command of Commander Striking Fleet Atlantic. It was a big task under one title but he was supported by an unusually large staff (for a sea-going Admiral) and, unique among his fellow flotilla Flag Officers, he was usually a Vice-Admiral.

FOFs 1 and 2 commanded groups of destroyers and frigates but could also include within their force ships normally belonging to FOF 3. Sometimes it was an uneasy relationship with the two smaller Flag Officers openly squabbling over FOF 3's wider role. Misplaced jealousy in practise, for FOF 3 would invariably need to call on the destroyers and frigates as escorts for his own task force of major warships and there was a need for a sea-going authority in these specialist operational areas.

I was included in FOF 3's staff as the Commodore Amphibious Warfare (COMAW) tasked to command the United Kingdom/Netherland Amphibious Task Group and also be his Chief of Staff (Amphibious Warfare). This appointment was the only other sea-going Royal Naval one to have a specific NATO role within the Striking Fleet Atlantic. Clearly I provided the Amphibious advice in support of the Admiral's title of 'Fleet Amphibious Warfare Authority'.

The Royal Marines provided the majority of the trained landing force within this UK/NL Amphibious Task Group: others with 'specific to task' duties could be drafted in to add to the men of the Royal Netherland Marine Corps who, for NATO duties, were part of the 3rd Commando Brigade's Order of Battle.

Despite being part of the 'Naval Services' and depending on the Royal Navy for their role as 'sea soldiers' the Commando Brigade units were organized largely independently with the Commandant General (CGRM – a Lieutenant-General) being their operational commander as well as their representative in the Ministry of Defence. Beneath the CGRM were two Major Generals one in command of all Commando Forces including the 3rd Commando Brigade and the other responsible for all Training, Reserves and Special Forces. The first equated, largely, to CinC Fleet and the second to CINC Nav Home.

A 'Trident' Committee of FOF 3, MGRM Cdo Forces and

the Flag Officer Naval Air Command met at intervals and was attended by me but not, surprisingly, by the Brigade Commander of the 3rd Commando Brigade: my 'opposite number'. Points of mutual interest were discussed, many of which had specific relevance for the Commando Helicopter Support Squadrons manned by Royal Navy Fleet Air Arm personnel.

Already the position of COMAW had become yet another pawn in the game of cuts. It had been disbanded about four years earlier, only to be resurrected about two years before the Falkland crisis. The reasons for disbandment were, by the time I reached office, obscure. The file said little but a Brigadier Pringle had commented to the effect that 'now that the amphibious group had to use merchant ships, the need for a Commodore seemed to him to be even more essential'. This Brigadier was now the Commandant General and had made me most welcome on my appointment. He had expressed concern at the long-term role of the Royal Marines as it was becoming increasingly more difficult to justify their retention in small ships and the Corps was therefore finding itself inevitably moving away from the Royal Navy and more towards the arms of an army who were suspicious of specialist units in principle and may not choose to accept their services, if it came to that.

The story appears to have been that without the Strike/Attack Carriers and without the Commando Helicopter Carriers the Royal Navy had, not unreasonably, concluded that there was now no amphibious capability. We were unable to provide air defence over a beachhead or the close air support that might be needed by the landing force. Without the Helicopter Carriers we could not land the marines by helicopter tactically as they had come to practise, nor could we land many of the stores that were normally carried by these ships.

To some, therefore, the role of the Commodore and his staff was no longer required. On the other hand, the commitment to reinforce the NATO flanks and islands continued, but, inevitably, we would have to use merchant ships. The Navy did not seem to believe, at that time, that the job required a dedicated officer and staff, presumably as convoy procedures existed. Since we would never carry out an opposed landing, any such amphibious operation would be 'administrative' as part of a major NATO operation under the defensive umbrella of the United States Navy and host nations. We would simply land the troops and stores on to secure jetties and beaches where they would be welcomed by local people and facilities – the host nation principle. All that would be needed was an officer to take charge of a mixed bag of ships and simply deliver them to their destination.

Command during an amphibious assault under opposition was certainly not envisaged and a permanent Commodore and staff would not therefore be required. Time had shown that Brigadier Pringle was correct and my Admiral, Derek Reffell, had been appointed to set the job up again, but on a more limited basis, with the staff integrated with that of FOF3. Having redunded the job, it was probably difficult for the Navy to justify full reinstatement so soon after its disbandment. The Treasury would not approve!

While the Commodore's position had been given new life, it was under rather different circumstances. My Admiral, FOF 3, no longer had the Light Fleet Aircraft carriers or Commando Helicopter Carriers upon which much of the concept of projecting naval power ashore depended: but he did have two Assault Ships (as they were originally styled) later re-named as Landing Platform Docks (LPDs).

These two LPDs, HMSs *Fearless* and *Intrepid*, were commissioned in the early and mid-1960s respectively. It is not generally remembered that they were procured primarily for the use of the British Army, as were the Landing Ships Logistic (LSLs) of the *Sir Lancelot* class who were largely bought out of the Army vote. The LPDs' main roles were to provide Headquarters facilities for both the Commodore and the Brigadier, and to transport and land the headquarters of the landing force and the initial waves of tanks and heavy equipment. These would command and support the Royal Marines' Commandos with their light guns which would have been landed in advance from the helicopters

8

and small landing craft carried by the two light fleet aircraft carriers (later to be known as LPHs or Landing Platforms Helicopter) *Bulwark* and *Albion*. Once the beach and immediate hinterland were secure the LSLs would beach (or use their Mexeflote self-propelled rafts) to disgorge the heavy stores and back-up *matériel* required for operations ashore.

This had all enhanced the Royal Navy's capability and certainly its flexibility. At that time, too, we manned four aircraft carriers each with a nuclear and conventional strike attack function via Buccaneer, Sea Vixen and later Phantom aircraft flown by the Fleet Air Arm.

Each of these carriers also had its own anti-submarine helicopter squadron, all-weather air defence fighter squadron and airborne early warning flight. They possessed a formidable range of self-defence armament. While this capability made them a high priority target for a sophisticated enemy they were, too, a strong opponent to weaker nations with their land-based air forces and small, coastal navies.

Both the strike-attack and all-weather fighter squadrons could provide 'tanker' and photographic reconnaisance support: facilities we needed, but were denied, in 1982, due to earlier defence cuts. These attributes make a 'carrier-navy' a most effective, power-intensive force in a nation's armoury and one able to influence events, with flexibility and surprise, out of all proportion to its comparatively small size.

By the spring of 1982 the LPHs and all but one of the light fleet and aircraft carriers had gone. All that remained to support amphibious operations (themselves under threat with the planned demise of the LPDs) was the *Invincible* class – not much more than small helicopter and Sea Harrier platforms and the ageing, and threatened HMS *Hermes*. With no airborne early warning or tanker capability and the much reduced range and weapon load of the otherwise remarkable Sea Harrier, and with the running-down of the amphibious shipping we were close to impotency in our ability to project power ashore which has arguably been the primary role of Navies over the centuries.

Defence being needed only as the result of a threat and offence being the best form of defence.

To assume, as was the case at that time, that future NATO operations would have a 'host nation' supplying welcoming facilities such as prepared beaches, jetties, docks and transport at the start of an amphibious operation was naivety on a large scale: the one 'war' that Britain had not yet fought since 1945 was a 'NATO' one, with or without a host nation. Given the likely location and time-scale of British unilateral operations the chances of achieving a landing without some degree of opposition despite the host nation offering 'welcoming' facilities were minimal and in the Falklands, of course, out of the question.

Perhaps, the best example of why we, in the Royal Navy, felt frustrated is summed up by Mr John Nott's Parliamentary Statement made when Secretary of State for Defence. On 25 June, 1981, he said, in part: 'It is for this reason that, while we shall complete the new carrier *Ark Royal* we intend to keep in service in the longer term only two of the ships of this class with their heavy demand on supporting anti-submarine and air defence escorts. The older *Hermes* will be phased out as soon as the second of the new carriers is in operation ... We shall maintain the three Royal Marines Commandos, since we place great value on their unique capability, but we shall dispose of the two specialist amphibious ships (*Fearless* and *Intrepid*) rather earlier than planned ... We envisage resuming the deployment of naval task groups – centred sometimes around a carrier, sometimes around destroyers or frigates – for substantial periods on visits and exercises out of area.'

What politico-military influence such out-of-area anti-submarine groups would have is hard to guess. Any intelligent country could see clearly that the UK was advertising that it no longer had the capability and, by very simple deduction, the will to project power ashore. The message must have been uncomfortably clear to members of the Commonwealth and Colonies, while being welcomed elsewhere. At least it helped recruiting and retention, but few sailors were deceived. The lion was thought to be an amiable pussycat.

In particular, our amphibious landing force (the Royal Marines' 3rd Commando Brigade) was to continue in being but without the specialist amphibious ships from which it could land – they were now gone, or would be very soon. As one cannot exist without the other, and one leg of this defence policy was already earmarked for scrapping, clearly the Royal Marines were about to be next. Fortunately John Nott appeared to have a temporary change of heart in November, 1981, after a visit to HMS *Fearless* on exercise in the Solent where I and my Landing Force Commander, Brigadier Julian Thompson, the Commander 3rd Commando Brigade, met him. This was followed directly by a visit to Royal Marines, Poole. The two LPDs were granted a limited reprieve from Death Row as late as February 1982: nevertheless it was just in time.

The 'unique capability' status of the Royal Marines referred to by John Nott was, in large measure, due to the flexibility afforded by the doomed 'specialist amphibious ships': Landing Platforms Docks and the Landing Platforms Helicopter.

Perhaps, in fairness, it was the Royal Navy, still by nature a Silent Service and at that time still a monastic and inward-looking organization with little contact with society, who never managed to explain its case satisfactorily or in sufficiently strong and unambiguous terms to the politicians and the press – and thus the public. Basically, few of us saw the need to. We knew and that was what mattered! This opinion was strengthened by my discussion with Mr Nott who showed a remarkably uninformed view of naval operations and priorities. The risk to the nation of reducing the Royal Navy (for budgetary reasons only) was quite simply deemed to be low; providing no one called our bluff.

Now to the Falklands crisis in particular, which was doing just that! The last intelligence assessment to cover Argentinian aspirations in the South Atlantic before April, 1982, was presented on 9 July, 1981. It highlighted, not surprisingly, nor for the first time, the staunchly pro-British attitude of the Falkland Islanders (of whom by far the greatest number were of British descent) and the growing impatience of the Junta to the 'sovereignty issue'.

One of the Junta's declared aims was to 'teach the Islanders a lesson', probably to hide their disappointment (indeed, failure) over the lack of a satisfactory solution of the Beagle Channel dispute with Chile; they were also suffering continuing internal economic and political dilemmas from which attention needed to be diverted. One of the report's conclusions suggested that the issue might be brought to a head by Argentinian economic sanctions and various commercial restrictions: the Islanders relied heavily on Buenos Aires for communications and domestic oil, among other commodities and services.

The intelligence assessment ended by expressing the view that if there was no hope of a peaceful settlement to the main issue – sovereignty – then there would be a high risk of Argentina resorting to more forceful measures. They might act swiftly and without warning. In such circumstances military action against British shipping or a full-scale invasion of the Falkland Islands could not be discounted.

Despite the findings of this report a mere nine months before the invasion, the positive signals from the Governor of the Falkland Islands during the previous years and Captain Nick Barker's warnings (which were seen in some quarters as a thinly disguised ruse to save his ship, HMS *Endurance*) the Foreign Office, and, in consequence, the Cabinet appeared to have done little, if anything, to prevent (or prepare to meet) the 'officially perceived' threat. On the other hand there was perhaps so little hard evidence of real action (there was always much posturing by Buenos Aires) that to 'call out the navy' every time the Argentinian fleet put to sea might, understandably, have been seen as over-reaction to what was in effect a long-standing and on-going problem. Also understandably, the senior members of Cabinet and the various 'interested' Ministries had much to occupy their time and, without stronger reasons for them to be alerted it is, unhappily from a Falkland Islander's point of view, hard to see that much could have been done at their level.

What does seem odd is that no specific contingency plans

appear to have been made by the British Government, plans that could have been drawn up entirely 'in house' without causing alarm or rumour. No plans, as far as I know, were drawn up by the Royal Navy either, despite it being the only service able to have taken useful action at such a long distance from friendly ports and airfields. No doubt, in the political climate at the time, any inclusion of the Falkland Islands as a specific operational requirement by the Royal Navy would have been met with the customary suspicion by the other armed services and the civil administration as a blatant attempt to maintain an 'outmoded and expensive naval capability more suited to empire building and gunboat diplomacy than the demanding requirements of a NATO war.'

From the mid-sixties on the British Government had always said, publicly, that it could not and would not negotiate on sovereignty: yet it seemed willing to do so providing the Islanders' wishes remained the paramount decider. That the Islanders would never waver in this view seems never to have entered the Government's equation. Any such commitment to 'sovereignty talks' was a hollow gesture – and probably seen as such by the Junta.

It certainly appears that, privately, the Foreign Office was happy to be rid of the Falklands enigma and by default if that was necessary and in the absence of any more honourable method. One cannot help wondering, not for the first time when considering the South Atlantic and the Foreign Office, what parts of the intelligence briefings and reports were omitted and what were presented for discussion by Ministers.

While unexpected by Mrs Thatcher and her Government, when it came the invasion surprised neither the Islanders, the Intelligence Committee nor the Royal Navy. In the Ministry of Defence there were still no plans for dealing with a 'Falklands Crisis' although there had been talk in Whitehall, before 2 April, of copying Prime Minister Callaghan's 1977 actions of sending a token deterrent force of at least one nuclear-powered fleet submarine. This had been dismissed on the grounds that an overt deterrent had to be large enough to impress. In that case, it might have been seen more as a provocative move forcing the Argentinians into the precipitate action we did not, then, expect them to take. On the other hand if the deterrent was covert it might not deter. With hindsight, however, it seems surprising that some method of 'political or diplomatic signalling' could not have been determined earlier, but, the Foreign Office may well have opposed this.

In the Ministry of Defence a September 1981 paper (written as the result of July's intelligence assessment) was updated in March, 1982. This was to have been the basis for the Ministry's contribution to a Foreign Office paper on the Falklands to be discussed in Cabinet during early April. However, the paper suggested few new measures for dealing with any renewed tension and certainly did not propose boosting the intelligence effort nor increasing (for instance) the length of Stanley's Cape Pembroke airport runway. It was neither an optimistic nor useful contribution to what could (or should) be done in a crisis and was not even presented to the Cabinet when the South Georgia 'scrap metal' scare was in full flow.

This latest incident came to light on 9 March when the British Embassy in Buenos Aires was informed that forty-one workmen would leave for South Georgia on the 11th in the naval transport *Bahia Buen Suceso*. Their job was to remove scrap metal from Leith. On arrival on the 19th they raised the blue and white Argentine flag before defacing various areas with notices warning against any 'unauthorized' landing. On that same day the Argentine navy conducted a full-scale practice invasion landing on the mainland of Argentina. HMS *Endurance* sailed on the 21st from Port Stanley with an augmented Royal Marines detachment, thereby depleting the garrison in the Falkland Islands. She arrived at Grytviken, South Georgia, on the 23rd, the day after the departure of the *Bahia Buen Suceso*.

On the 24th an Argentine corvette sailed to intercept HMS *Endurance* between South Georgia and the Falkland Islands but they 'missed' each other, thankfully, for on that day *Endurance* was ordered to Grytviken with firm rules of engagement including instructions to prepare to use force if negotiations for the removal of the scrap metal team did not result in its peaceful departure. Just before this, another Argentine naval supply ship, the *Bahia Paraiso*, had been despatched for Leith with reinforcements of marines and two helicopters. Clearly the Argentine navy had suddenly seized the opportunity to capitalize on the (originally innocent but tactlessly conducted) scrap metal affair. On the 26th the Argentinian Foreign Minister stated, publicly, that the men on South Georgia would be given all the 'necessary diplomatic protection' they needed and added, ominously, that, 'With the *Bahia Paraiso* stationed fifteen miles north of South Georgia any protection could also be military'. It is highly probable that it was on this day that the decision to invade the Falklands on 1 April was confirmed by the Junta.

Also on 26 March an Argentine fleet sailed, ostensibly for a joint anti-submarine exercise with the Uruguayan Navy. That this unusual and suspiciously well-publicized exercise went unnoticed, or unremarked, by intelligence sources, is strange, for, not only was this an unlikely time in the annual conscription cycle to be conducting such affairs, but the exercise never took place anyway! Even more unusual (had it been released to the press) was the full composition of that 'anti-submarine' fleet. Embarked in the Tank Landing Ship *Cabo San Antonio* was the 2nd Marine Infantry Battalion boosted by a platoon of the 25th Infantry Regiment and 16 American-designed, amphibious, tracked landing craft (AMTRACS). Their ice-breaker, the *Almirante Irizar*, carried another two platoons of the 25th Regiment, while the British-built Type 42 destroyer *Santissima Trinidad* carried a 'commando' of 70 men. Task Force 40, as it was called, also included another Type 42, (the *Hercules*), and the ex-French Type A 69 frigates *Drummond* and *Granville*, all of which were ordered south-east to intercept *Endurance* if the British decided to take military action.

The third Type A 69 (*Guerrico*) sailed for South Georgia with 60 marines embarked and accompanied by the submarine *Santa Fe* carrying a small group of 'commandos/under-water swimmers'. The ex-British aircraft carrier *Veintecinco de Mayo* sailed in company with a further destroyer escort and a tanker. Admiral

Anaya, the Argentine Chief of Naval Staff, was about to put into effect his promise that it would be the navy that would liberate the 'Malvinas'. His view was that *Operation Azul*, the code name for the operation, was likely to be more of a transport exercise than an assault; provided action was quick and effective little opposition was expected. The Junta assumed that the kelpers would be ready to welcome them with, if not open arms, at least a friendly wave while Britain was not expected to do anything serious to evict them once established ashore, despite rumours of the despatch of a nuclear submarine and 'some' surface ships. The worst that Galtieri and his advisers waited for was an initial 'wrist slap' in the United Nations before the world was seduced by (from the Junta's point of view) more bloody examples of aggression.

The Argentine press statements (such as they were – incomplete) were passed to Whitehall. The only real conclusion was that Argentina did not intend to quit South Georgia – to which, unlike the Falklands, they had never laid claim.

On 27 March the Royal Fleet Auxiliary tanker *Appleleaf*, then *en route* from Curaçao to Gibraltar with a full load of fuel, was ordered to collect general stores before diverting to the South Atlantic in support of *Endurance*. Also on that day the British government despatched the submarine HMS *Spartan* to the South Atlantic and Rear-Admiral John (Sandy) Woodward, commanding the First Flotilla's exercise, *Springtrain* based on Gibraltar, was told that he might have to prepare his ships for operations. The RFA ammunition ship *Fort Austin*, commanded by the redoubtable Commodore Sam Dunlop (who had served at sea for the whole of the Second World War) was also sent south to support *Endurance*.

Fleet Headquarters in Northwood had been alerted to the possible need for a properly constituted and balanced Task Force on the 29th and was, by the next day, well into achieving a 'war footing'. A twenty-four hour watch-keeping system was initiated and certain specialists (none of whom, unfortunately, had amphibious training or experience) were co-opted to Fleet

Headquarters with the staff of the Maritime Tactical School soon being employed as a 'think tank'.

It was not until 9 April that the Commander-in-Chief's staff was to be augmented by a team from Headquarters Commando Forces with their commander, Major-General Jeremy Moore, as the Land Deputy. This provided an excellent team to advise on land operations in particular. They could not, however, be expected to give the full advice needed to cover the naval aspects of an amphibious operation.

On 30 March the situation had reached the point where the Assistant Chief of Naval Staff (Operations), Rear Admiral Tony Whetstone, felt it necessary to form a two-star Defence Operations Executive (DOE) to brief the acting Chief of the Defence Staff, Air Chief Marshal Sir Michael Beetham, on the central direction of military operations. This committee met twice again (on 31 March and 1 April) before the MOD assumed a rather more formal war configuration. It was a measure of how seriously the MOD then regarded the future, but particularly it was a pointer to how concerned was the Royal Navy.

The Commanding Officer of 40 Commando (Lieutenant-Colonel Malcolm Hunt, Royal Marines) was ordered to stand by to fly his Commando to the Islands, as was the Officer Commanding the Commando Brigade's Air Defence Troop, although no one explained how they would get there in what appeared to be a rather short space of time left. (By sea it would have taken thirteen days at twenty five knots and there was no possibility of flying!) In fact the CO of 40 Commando was told not to tell his men that they were now on a shorter 'notice to move' nor even that this was a possibility.

Not only did these orders not emanate from, or via, HQs 3rd Commando Brigade nor COMAW but neither headquarters was warned, formally, of such a need. Indeed neither the Brigadier nor I were to be given any formal notice that our forces might be needed until 2 April.

By late on 31 March intelligence confirmed that the Argentinian South Georgia operations, which had started off innocently enough, were now being used by the Junta as a cover for more dramatic events: an invasion of the Falklands themselves was now not only certain but actually under way. Reports reached Whitehall that day that the Islands would be invaded on 2 April (bad weather had delayed Argentine plans by twenty-four hours).

The scrap metal crisis now took second priority to meeting the invasion of the Falkland Islands. Deterrence had failed: different plans would have to be drawn up to prove that any invasion would be pointless, but there was not much time. An added factor was the view held by the Secretary of State for Defence, John Nott, who, paraphrasing a report from his Army and Royal Air Force Chiefs of Staff, gave his opinion that 'the Falklands once taken could not be re-taken.' (*The Downing Street Years*, Margaret Thatcher, HarperCollins.) In fact Sir Michael Beetham while exercising caution, had suggested that the announcement of the despatch of the three SSNs (*Splendid* and *Conqueror* had sailed on the 30th and 31st, respectively, to join *Spartan*) would be a deterrent, but even their fast underwater transit times meant that their arrival would be too late to deter. Actually, HMS *Superb* had been reported, wrongly, but conveniently, by the British press, to have sailed some days earlier. She had, but not for the south. This dis-information was allowed to stand without denial and, of course, HMS *Endurance* had been on station with an enhanced Royal Marines Detachment since the 21st. On the 31st, too, 40 Commando and the Air Defence Troop were stood down from any possible move south, the Commando Brigade being told, 'no units are required'.

The decision to face up to the invasion was made at last by the Prime Minister during the evening of Wednesday, 31 March when, at John Nott's suggestion, she gathered together her closest advisers in the Houses of Parliament. This was to be the most crucial meeting of all, fortuitously attended by the Chief of Naval Staff and First Sea Lord, Admiral Sir Henry Leach. Originally uninvited, he had actually gone to the House to seek out Mr Nott for a discussion on a pessimistic MOD brief which, in essence, argued what could not be done rather than emphasizing what could be done. Admiral Leach felt he should make it quite clear that, while nobody could now prevent an invasion, the Royal Navy could (in isolation of the other two services if necessary) despatch what he called a 'retrieval force'.

In the words of Mrs Thatcher's memoirs, Admiral Leach (who had been ushered into a rather more senior meeting than he was expecting) 'was quiet, calm and confident'. When asked what he could do, he replied, 'I can put together a task force of destroyers, frigates, landing craft and support vessels. It will be led by the aircraft carriers HMS *Hermes* and HMS *Invincible*. It can be ready to leave in forty-eight hours.' This was the first positive opinion received by the Prime Minister. Events and decisions occurred in rapid succession after that.

On 1 April, HMS *Hermes* and HMS *Invincible* were stood to for operations but paradoxically not yet HMS *Fearless*. It was confirmed to the Brigadier that his 3rd Commando Brigade was to remain at seven days' notice. By chance that day, too, Jeremy Moore, the Major General Royal Marines, Commando Forces, was handing back the command of the Corps to the Commandant General (Lieutenant General Sir Steuart Pringle who had been severely wounded by the IRA) on the seventh floor of the MOD while on the fifth floor the Naval Staff were planning the deployment of an amphibious force; neither general knew anything other than that elements of the Commando Brigade had been stood-down the day before. Britain's Amphibious Landing Force, extraordinarily, were not yet 'in the loop' – nor was the Royal Navy element, my amphibious staff and I, whose task, it had only recently been reaffirmed, was to load and command the ships of the Amphibious Group and execute any landings.

During the evening of 1 April the Prime Minister convened a meeting of what was to become, effectively, the War Cabinet, with an invitation, this time, for the First Sea Lord to attend. The decision to shorten the 'notice to move' of ships to four hours and the Royal Marines' Commando Brigade to seventy-two hours (at last) was taken at this meeting.

At the same time Rear-Admiral Woodward, fortuitously further south at Gibraltar, was ordered to head covertly towards

Ascension Island with his 'Springtrain' Group: HMSs *Antrim, Glamorgan, Glasgow, Sheffield, Brilliant, Arrow, Plymouth* and the RFAs *Appleleaf* and *Tidespring*.

The main armament of an amphibious task force is its landing force. It is, therefore, nothing without troop ships and preferably troop ships that can each carry a Group of upwards of 800 men together with the helicopters with which they can be landed. Britain possessed no such ships since HMS *Hermes* had been converted to anti-submarine duties in 1976. The first priority therefore was to re-build the required amphibious fleet to meet this latest threat. There were just four days in which to do so.

Only one 'amphibious' warship could be stood-to immediately for this operation. Of the Royal Navy's two Landing Platforms Dock (LPD) HMS *Fearless* was in Portsmouth Dockyard at operational readiness having converted back to her periodical and more permanent role as the Dartmouth Training Ship carrying cadets and midshipmen. Extra classrooms had been fitted for this role over the years in the form of 'porta-cabins' welded to the decks abaft the bridge. These were to remain, as in practice they always did, and were to be used as Special Forces planning and intelligence offices. Her slightly younger sister HMS *Intrepid* was de-stored and entering what was euphemistically known as 'preservation by operation' but better understood as 'mothballs' in case *Fearless* irretrievably broke down and needed spare parts.

Fearless was the only ship available to provide the essential command facilities for only she and her sister ship, *Intrepid*, possessed an amphibious operations room designed to control the landing force, the landing craft, and to a lesser extent, helicopters in an amphibious assault. This is a jointly-manned naval and military operations room from which the Commodore Amphibious Warfare conducts the assault and the Brigade Commander commands his Brigade before he establishes his Headquarters ashore either after or while his forces secured the beachhead. In practice the communications and general facilities available to both staffs came from the 1950s era and were scarcely adequate, but better than in any other ship.

Fearless then had no strategic satellite communications and only one secure voice VHF set able to talk with the Brigade ashore and one to talk to warships. Her communications in all senses were outdated. She lacked, for instance, a satellite weather reporting system and a modern Naval Operations Room. Reliable command of a Force, in modern warfare was not really practicable. Furthermore as they are not fitted with stabilisers the LPDs roll heavily, especially when loaded; 35 degrees either side of the vertical in one continuous movement being unusual but certainly not unknown. One good roll and the complete force disposition was liable to slide off the plot in a jumble of plastic models!

An LPD is, in basic design, a floating dock fitted with a bow and suitable engines to enable her to keep up with the fleet. Above the dock is a small flight deck from which two medium support helicopters can operate at any one time, but more can be carried and flown off. In the dock itself she carries four Landing Craft Utility (LCU) each capable of carrying about 100 tons of vehicles or stores. These craft were originally designed to lift two main battle tanks but successive naval architects and some strange re-writing of the stability criteria have reduced this payload to less than 60 tons – a restriction we were to ignore often.

The LPD's dock remains dry while on passage but prior to a landing is filled with water before the huge stern 'gate' is lowered to float out the LCUs. The ship also carries four smaller Landing Craft Vehicle and Personnel (LCVP) on davits, each capable of carrying four tons. This could be (as far as bulk is concerned) a light vehicle and trailer or 32 men with temperate climate equipment.

The sea-state operating parameters for dock operations is low but with the insides of the dock lined with heavy wooden battens to absorb some of the shock a moderate sea can be accepted especially if the ship moves slowly ahead to create a slight 'calm' off the stern. With a long swell this is not so easy even if the sea state itself is light, for when the ship rolls and pitches the water is 'free-flooding' or, in layman's terms, sloshes about in the dock.

In extreme conditions it has been known for the LCUs to hit the under side of the flight deck and ground heavily on the dock bottom in the same wave. The LCVPs can only be lowered in a relative calm and hoisted in even less sea, although, again, the ship can obtain some form of 'flat' water by conducting a slow turn into the side along which hoisting operations are taking place; the same 'slick' technique that was once used to recover spotting seaplanes.

Fearless's armament (the landing craft are often described, quite correctly, as her 'main' armament) is entirely defensive and consists of four Seacat mountings and two 40/60 single-barrelled Bofors, hardly what one would have expected for such a politically and militarily important vessel. Undoubtedly her safety was, as John Nott's statement suggested, even more dependent than ever (as was the original concept of amphibious operations) on supporting escorts and aircraft carriers with all the associated air and submarine defence that they imply, but this defence had been whittled away. Her potential in other respects was clearly still enormous and unique.

Even allowing for these obvious disadvantages – old equipment, calm-weather operating parameters, poor self-defence, slow speed – these elderly LPDs were still remarkably capable in amphibious terms; able to carry a squadron of main battle tanks or the equivalent in wheeled vehicles and an embarked force of more than 400 men without going into 'overload'. They were originally designed from a British concept (that was then taken up by the Americans before we built our first LPD in the early 1960s) not long after the Second World War.

Of the Landing Platform Helicopters (LPHs) there were potentially two, HMS *Hermes* and HMS *Invincible*. The facilities of both had been studied prior to the Spring of 1982 by my staff with help from the Major General Royal Marines Commando Forces' staff: the intention had been to assess them in terms of the numbers of marines they could carry and the amount of bulk military stores they could lift. Their command and communications systems were also tested against the day they would be needed to conduct a limited amphibious operation if the LPDs were unavailable due to their age and, of greater likelihood, their disposal.

Invincible's inspection for this unaccustomed role had been completed before Christmas, 1981, while *Hermes'* was carried out in late February 1982. Their potential as assault platforms was reasonable and certainly better than nothing but they could not match the old *Bulwark* and *Albion* in terms of lift capacity. As command platforms they lacked the space as well as the communications fit for a joint operation in a small commando-size raid, but, off Norway perhaps (a host nation) they might just about manage.

The Amphibious Task Force did have call on the LSLs. These ships, starting with *Sir Lancelot* in 1964, were procured through the army vote to the order of the then Ministry of Transport. With their beaching, roll-on, roll-off and flight-deck facilities, coupled with their ability to carry two 120 foot Mexeflote powered lighters to assist in landing their tanks, men and bulk stores they are an invaluable addition to amphibious operations away from formal ports and dockyards. They began service with the British India Steam Navigation Company and transferred to the RFA in 1970 but were always tasked by the army, who, after all had very largely paid for them. British officered with Hong Kong Chinese crews they had special problems.

Of the six LSLs all except *Sir Bedivere* were available, or nearly so; she was abroad supporting an army exercise and could not join until the end of April. *Sir Geraint* was already in Devonport; *Sir Galahad* was due into Devonport on 4 April and *Sir Percivale* was at Zeebrugge unloading army stores for BAOR. *Sir Percivale* was ordered to complete her task with the utmost speed and return to the Royal Corps of Transport's military port at Marchwood (near Southampton) where *Sir Lancelot* was already berthed. *Sir Tristram* was in Belize and so it was easy for her to be directed to Ascension Island to load. Thus five LSLs were instantly transferred from army control and made available for amphibious duties. It was rather convenient, administratively, and could, certainly, have been worse, as far as a speedy departure was concerned. From an operational point of view it was not quite so straightforward and their communications fit, which complied with Board of Trade rather than Naval requirements, was to be a major drawback.

Clearly to embark just the 3rd Commando Brigade further ships would be necessary and with the force expanding rapidly as the numbers of the Argentine troops ashore in the Falkland Islands became known the necessity for more transport ships became an imperative. One battalion of the Parachute Regiment, a squadron of light tanks from the Blues and Royals, together with a Rapier air defence troop joined many other smaller but no less vital organizations such as the Royal Marines' Special Boat Squadron, a squadron from the army's Special Air Service and explosive ordnance demolition parties.

I too was to embark extra staff and experts such as mine-clearance divers and others. On 1 April SS *Canberra* was earmarked but it was doubted at the time that she would form part of the actual assault force.

Other ships would be needed and they would be found from the Merchant Navy and thus manned by civilians. When the SS *Canberra* was earmarked as the most likely candidate for a troop ship, a telephone call was made to the Peninsular and Oriental Steam Navigation Company asking for their representatives to attend a meeting 'within the hour' in Whitehall. Questions to be asked: 'What is the ship's best speed and her most economical? What type of fuel does she burn and how much can she carry? Can she refuel at sea and if not can she be converted to do so? Can helicopters land on and, if not, is there a flat deck that can also be converted?'

Canberra would never be an LPD nor an LPH but it was clear that she could certainly help. Mike Bradford, the Second Captain of the *Canberra* came to my office in the Royal Marine Barracks Stonehouse, near Plymouth, to be briefed and quizzed.

Up to now there had been a series of 'normal' Cabinet meetings, at which the forming and then despatching of the Task Force had been authorized, but on 6 April the War Cabinet (although it was, apparently, never to be known officially by this title) was convened, holding its first meeting the next day. The

Chief of Defence Staff (Admiral of the Fleet Sir Terence Lewin, now back early from visiting the Far East) was a permanent member of the team that was to meet at least once, and often twice, a day over the next fifty-five days. This group was fully responsible for operations in the South Atlantic and required all military decisions with political 'undertones' to be referred to it. The 'ordinary' Cabinet was to meet sixteen times during the operations, occasionally to discuss nothing but the Falkland Islands crisis.

From the military point of view various planned war committees were set up on 1 April with the Chiefs of Staff meeting at least once a day. This committee included briefings on Public Relations and Press matters – a subject that was to occupy much of the members' time. The work of the DOE was found now to be largely superfluous although it continued to play a useful part with non-controversial decision-making at single service (but inter-related) level. It was to meet nine more times.

As is standard procedure the MOD Defence Situation Centre (DSC) was to be active throughout the operation with the largest proportion of participants coming from the Royal Navy. To form a link between the DSC and all other interested agencies a Naval Staff Advisory Group was established as a liaison body. It was, after all, to be a navy-led, and commanded, operation.

A Special Operations Group was also established in the army's operations cell reporting direct to the Assistant Chief of Defence Staff (Operations).

All this then was the prelude to Britain's largest amphibious operation since Suez and, in matters of execution, probably the most complex since the Second World War. Several adverse factors were relevant from the start: one such was a strategic defence policy (which must be seen as the nation's and its dependencies' insurance policy) which placed greater emphasis on central Europe with its stockpiles and huge defensive-barracked forces than on a flexible, internationally-minded expeditionary force concept which had stood this country in such good stead for centuries. While trying to maintain some influence in Europe we had turned our backs on our kith and kin in the

Commonwealth. In consequence, Britain had failed to ensure it possessed an adequate amphibious capability or a coherent plan. This meant that not only was this war inevitable but once joined it could be won only by the tenacity and professionalism of its volunteer, armed servicemen with the courageous support of unarmed civilians caught up in the campaign through no choice of their own.

Si vis pacem, para bellum.

CHAPTER ONE

THE CYCLONE STRIKES

> There must be a beginning of any great matter, but
> the continuing unto the end until it be thoroughly
> finished yields the true glory.
>
> Drake in the *Elizabeth Bonaventure* riding at Sagres,
> May 17, 1587, to Sir Francis (later Lord) Walsyngham

FOR ME IT was a particularly inauspicious start to a campaign
that was to become of world interest.

On 2 April, 1982, I was in my tenth month as the Commodore
Amphibious Warfare (COMAW) and had returned the evening
before from an intensive recce of Denmark and Schleswig
Holstein for a forthcoming series of amphibious exercises.

At about five o'clock that morning I was shaken by a rather
grumpy hall-porter of Portsmouth Royal Naval Barracks wardroom: 'There is a telephone call from some Major Yeoman, Sir.'

Guy Yeoman was the Royal Corps of Transport major on my
staff and a man with an engaging grin, known as 'Roger So Far'
because of his idiosyncratic radio procedures. I asked whether
the signal that he told me was waiting in my office at Fort
Southwick (an old Palmerston fort guarding the eastward,
landward flank of Portsmouth) was so important that I should
forgo the planned haircut that morning. He replied, 'No, Sir.

There is plenty of time for that.' I returned to bed. Drake and his bowls die hard!

On my arrival the signalmen and staff officers seemed preoccupied. There was no sign of any signals let alone the one that might have needed my prompt and early attention. While I waited for my staff to bring me up-to-date Rear-Admiral Derek Reffell (then Flag Officer Third Flotilla – FOF 3 – and my immediate superior) put his head round the door. 'You're looking very relaxed. Have you any idea what is going on?' I replied, 'No, I am waiting for my signals, Sir.' Whereupon, and much to my surprise, he rushed off to collect them himself. When he returned the reason for the alarm was clear: one of them was the one for which I had been shaken early that morning. Among many items it was clear that a Task Force of two CV5s (aircraft carriers) and one LPD (assault ship) escorted by at least four DD/FF (destroyers and frigates) and appropriate support were being brought to immediate notice for operations. The force would be required to transport three Commando Groups and the Commando Brigade Headquarters with combat and logistic back-up to the South Atlantic.

The Ministry of Defence (Army) was requested to make at least two LSLs available as soon as possible. The provision of additional lift from ships taken up from trade was being investigated urgently.

More escorts and supporting RFAs from the returning Springtrain group were to be despatched towards the South Atlantic, but were not to go so fast that they arrived in the area of interest before meeting up with those ships sailing from the United Kingdom.

Clearly something major was afoot as this was a Ministry of Defence Signal addressed to the Commander-in-Chief Fleet (CinC Fleet) at Northwood. The Falkland Islands were not mentioned but the newspapers were reporting stories. There was no formal command structure nor clear aim but by reading between the lines the Admiral's and my imagination had plenty of scope for intelligent guesswork. He, of course, knew more.

Having given me time to absorb the bare facts contained in the

MOD's signal Admiral Reffell returned to ask what my plans were: I replied that it might be best if I went to my offices in the Royal Marines Barracks, Stonehouse, Plymouth, where I would be closer to the Royal Marines. But, on the other hand, if as expected, he was to be involved directly in charge at sea he might prefer it if I stayed closer to him at Fort Southwick.

Some of my staff were still in Denmark, but others with me had flown direct to the West Country from Gatwick. I had returned to Fort Southwick to brief the Admiral on our recce for exercises in the Baltic approaches over the next few years.

Sending my driver, Leading Airman Park, ahead to Plymouth with the staff car a helicopter was ordered for later in the day. This gave me time to talk to Admiral Reffell who had much greater amphibious experience. He had already been the Commodore Amphibious Warfare but at a vital time in its 'new' existence for he had been appointed with the express purpose of regenerating the post some three years after its disbandment. He had also commanded the Commando Carrier HMS *Bulwark* and was well known by the Royal Marines, knowing many of them personally. I liked working for him very much and found him delightful, calm and intelligent and by using those attributes that morning he helped me dissect and choose the essential questions we needed to have answered: we also speculated how the operation might develop.

During my months as COMAW I had witnessed one amphibious exercise in Norway and commanded two more, one in the Baltic and, only weeks before, one in north Norway. I knew enough about amphibious warfare to have one or two bees in my bonnet, but also to realize how very small my experience and grasp of the subject was.

My main concern was that over the years the Royal Navy had been required to develop operations in support of SACLANT protecting Atlantic convoys and seeking submarines but, as a result, it was ill-equipped for operations in the fjords and close to the Baltic coastline. Neither the amphibious ships nor their escorting frigates were fitted with radars suitable for operating near land masses and we had few point-defence weapons capable of deterring an air attack. Both were available if the cash could be found for them. The Royal Navy had developed excellent weapon systems but these were designed to take on the long-range Russian missiles we then saw being launched against carrier groups and convoys. What was lacking were 'close-in' weapons for a warship stationed inshore that were capable of dealing with conventional bomb- rocket- and machine-gun-equipped aircraft.

Most of the frigates were therefore equipped for offshore operation with very limited inshore close-range capability making it vital for any amphibious ship to have a modicum of self-defence. Thus my first task on 2 April was to ask the staff of the Commander-in-Chief to ensure that the LSLs (which I knew had circular mountings on either bow) should have 40mm Bofors fitted. I telephoned the Fleet Warfare Officer, Commander Gordon-Lennox, who said that he had no idea where Bofors could be found but promised to see what he could do. He also made an interesting comment which I repeat, not to 'tease' the Commander but to highlight the difficulty in dragging a peacetime fleet to war. Gordon-Lennox told me that CinC Fleet had made the point already that we were to go to sea as equipped, 'For had not the Royal Navy always made the claim that it was ready to fight at all times'. I pointed out quickly that these were not Royal Navy ships but were in fact a slightly obscure form of Royal Fleet Auxiliary. He took my point and was as good as his word, but it took time.

My next concern was for mine counter-measures. If I was to take my Amphibious Task Group eight thousand miles to the Falklands I needed to know whether a sufficient force of mine-sweepers and mine-hunters were to accompany me. If not then should I simply have to accept the risk and was this really acceptable to CinC? Their speed of advance was similar to that of the LSLs but their sea keeping-capability was less and certainly their advance appearance in the landing area would destroy all hope of surprise. To achieve success a mine-clearing operation has to take several days.

I contacted the Fleet Mine Warfare Officer to be asked,

cheerfully, what it was I required and he would do his best to achieve it. I told him that since he was the expert he should tell me: he did, by suggesting that it was early days and perhaps I was taking the whole thing too seriously. 'Perhaps I am,' I said, but I thought he would agree that the moment I sailed my bluff might be called and it was prudent, therefore, to at least have thought through the problem before arriving in a minefield. Agreeing, he asked for time to think and rang back a few minutes later to state that there was apparently no intention to send mine counter-measure vessels but what did I think of taking some mine clearance divers. Since I knew nothing about clearance divers the question was passed back firmly to him. Within the hour Lieutenant-Commander Dutton of the Fleet Clearance Diving Team 1 (FCDT 1) appeared, rather reluctantly I thought at the time, with his Fleet Chief, FCPO Fellows. Brian Dutton made it clear that he did not believe that all this apparent turmoil would lead anywhere. He was at the end of a long and remarkable career and had obviously seen much of it before. He did not believe that the campaign would need his services. However, as the Fleet Chief left, he said, 'Leave it to me, Sir.' The next I knew was that FCDTs 1 and 3 were embarked and that, a little later, FCDT 2 had been formed from among the Saturation Diving Trials Team at HMS *Vernon* ready to sail in the *Stena Seaspread*. They were all to be invaluable in both mine clearance and bomb disposal.

A call was then made to Flag Officer Sea Training to see if he could send me a small team of damage control specialists (NBCD) to train up ships' companies on passage. I very much wanted to train any LSLs and merchant ships that might be with us in damage control in particular, but was concerned that an amphibious operation is an ideal target for chemical warfare. Nuclear did not bear thinking about and I doubted if the Argentinians would go that far, if indeed they had the ability, but it could never be ruled out. It was already evident that the use of merchant ships was likely: we had been practising with them on exercises.

There were a host of other supporting requirements and

information we needed. We wanted a photographic interpreter, patrol reports from earlier Royal Marines detachments in the Falklands, Flag Officer Sea Training's reports on Argentinian ships that had been through his hands; scrambling nets for merchant Ships Taken Up From Trade (STUFT) and I wanted 'gridded' maps and charts for Naval Gunfire Support (NGS).

I was told that the Royal Yacht was being brought to five days notice as a hospital ship and that HMS *Intrepid* could, if needed, be brought back into service in about ten to twelve days but there was absolutely no intention of going that far – much too expensive!

Having covered the essentials, I jotted down a few more queries: the first was what naval support would be needed on a merchant ship. I knew that Captain Tony Barratt, RNR, had prepared a paper on the staffing and equipment needs of Naval Parties in merchant ships that were taken up from trade and therefore labelled rather ungraciously 'STUFT'. In the recent Spring exercise in Norway he had reported to me that he had three young RNR lieutenants in various ships and asked what could he do with them. I had been concerned for some time by a view, held within the Royal Navy, that operating merchant ships created little problem. There were good procedures laid down that those ships who carried the NATO flag were allowed to be employed in convoys, as had always been traditionally done. These procedures were very different from those used between NATO warships and I wanted to operate them, and manoeuvre them in close quarters, like naval ships and for this they were ill-equipped and lacked experience. Tony Barratt agreed to look at the problem and make his report, but I had not yet seen it.

We also needed to provide small arms and defence for these merchant ships. We pressured the Fleet staff for small arms and, particularly, for 20mm Oerlikons, 7.62mm general purpose machine guns; even Bren guns and Lewis guns would do. These should be issued to every ship likely to join the Amphibious Task Group to provide them with a slightly better defence than they had at the moment. Again the Fleet Warfare Officer agreed to do his best. Also on my list of requirements were sandbags and flack-mats: we had used flack-mats during the Indonesian confrontation and if they did not have any real effect they certainly gave confidence to gun crews and that was important.

The bees in my bonnet had reduced their buzzing and I was pleased that the morning had not been wasted. As I waited for the helicopter, and then flew west, I went over the broader aspects of amphibious operations as I understood them and wondered if, as a result of such a mental review, I would still find myself concerned at the small size of my staff for anything more than set-piece NATO operations and what I should or could do about it. It was a process that was to be repeated in every spare moment over the next few weeks.

Admiral Ramsay, who was perhaps the most experienced British Admiral in amphibious operations, while clearly considering operations concerning divisions and armies, wrote a piece which is fundamental to most amphibious operations, even if they are of brigade level or smaller, whether an assault, raid or diversion. It read, 'A combined operation is but the opening under particular circumstances of a purely army battle. It is the function of the navy and the air to help the army establish a base or bases on the hostile coast, from which the military plan to gain the objective must be developed. It is upon the army plan for the fulfilment of its object that the combined plan must depend ... Once the army have decided how they wish to fight the land battle, it is necessary to examine how the troops can be put ashore to give effect to the army plan. In general it is the responsibility of the navy to land the army as they require, but as the plan develops, naval considerations will rise which must be discussed and agreed upon.' Admiral of the Fleet Lord Fisher had a little earlier put it more succinctly and typically: 'The British Army should be a projectile to be fired by the Navy'!

British experience showed that the execution of an agreed combined-joint army/navy-amphibious (take your choice) operation should be in the hands of the navy. American practice in the Pacific was built largely on the ideas developed by men such as Rear Admiral Lord Louis Mountbatten who was for a time in charge of British Combined Operations. The Americans' experience of massive amphibious assaults on Pacific islands confirmed the command arrangements which were finally written down in a NATO publication entitled *Allied Tactical Publication (ATP) 8*. The British had until recently had their own Joint Tactical Publication (JTP) series but these had lapsed and their bible on this type of amphibious operation was now *ATP 8*. Differences in description are largely semantic but 'amphibious' had come to mean a joint army/navy operation launched solely by seaborne forces. Admiral Ramsay's *Operation Overlord* was therefore technically not an amphibious operation but a very complex combined operation. The Falklands Campaign was clearly to be a combined operation with all three services contributing what they best could. Within the campaign there would be an amphibious operation and because of the geography of the Islands there was never likely to be a 'purely army battle'.

The reason why it was agreed that the execution of an amphibious operation should be in naval hands becomes reasonably obvious when one considers that the ships must not only reach but also off-load their precious cargoes at the correct point of disembarkation safely. Protection for these stages can only be provided by the navy, or, if close to shore bases, an airforce. To achieve this one must assume that the naval operation is under good control and has a reasonable hope of success. If it is not, then obviously a landing is at too great a risk and must be abandoned. This is a naval decision. The landing force, who may or may not be opposed on the beaches, will also need to decide on the risk of their success if the naval decision is that the operation can continue as far as they, the navy, are concerned. The landing force may also need time to match up with their equipment, organize in unfamiliar territory; only when the landing force commander is happy to take full responsibility for his own forces and no longer be supported by sea is it fair to expect him to go it alone. The relationship between the Amphibious Task Group Commander (CATF) and his Landing Force Commander (CLF) has to be extremely good if misunderstandings and confusion are to be avoided.

The practice had developed, therefore, that planning an amphibious operation would be carried out jointly with co-equal authority to either Service. This developed further to ensure that both the landing force commander and naval commander were of equal rank and in the same ship. There had been a number of unfortunate incidents, mainly where the naval commander was senior to the landing force commander and had chosen to rush off chasing enemy ships (a job he very probably understood better and enjoyed more!), while cheerfully taking 'his soldier' with him to see some action. The troops meanwhile were landed, if not leaderless, at least without their appointed leader. It was neither popular nor wise!

Because the execution of an amphibious operation remains a naval responsibility, assets such as the Special Boat Section (SBS) (Royal Marines trained in beach reconnaissance), the support helicopters and the landing craft are all under the CATF's operational control (OPCON) until the CLF is ready to be cast off when some or all of them could be transferred to his operational control.

As the Royal Navy's capability for amphibious operations reduced, it tended to be treated by naval officers with a somewhat cavalier degree of disdain. It was seen in some quarters as not really of naval interest and so involvement would probably be bad for promotion and should be avoided. It was a subject better left to Royal Marines who were given the task, after the Second World War, of maintaining some of the techniques and who, after all, depended on its continuing existence for the survival of their Corps. Let them make the arguments. And, it appeared to me, after several years in the Ministry of Defence, that they did, with or without naval help, quite well, as they and some ships were still there now they were needed. This was fortunate for me as I was enormously enjoying my job and peacetime involvement.

To some extent I suppose I was harking back to my schooldays at Marlborough when I was a Cadet Under-Officer in charge of 'Battle Platoon' which was enormous fun. We alone were allowed to fire blank cartridges while the rest had crackers or rattles! I was amused also to find many of the war cries had not changed out of all recognition. 'Tone, shape, shine, shadow' was still understood, along with several others. I felt at home with these Green Berets. They were not unlike the Fleet Air Arm characters I had lived with but who had disappeared with the fixed-wing carriers. I was determined to try and help but not yet totally sure of my role and whether my staff was adequate.

It was not that I was concerned at the calibre of my staff, but its size and, in certain particular cases, the experience available worried me. It was only a matter of months since they had been extricated from the staff of FOF 3 where some of them had been integrated and where they filled a more limited niche with other officers having additional expertise that I now needed. If FOF 3 was to lead the force then we should, at least, understand each other's problems, but I would have to look elsewhere for these essential experts that he could not spare.

My staff had already written a paper for the previous Admiral arguing the case, for instance, for a Staff Warfare Officer (SWO) to improve our ability to control any warships we may be given as escorts. It had not gone far in the prevailing climate of cuts but when the alarm was raised I managed to grab, from my Admiral's staff, Lieutenant-Commander Mike Goodman who I knew of old and who was to be a tower of strength as my Staff Warfare Officer; but he was alone for most of the time and the organization was to rely heavily (as planned but never practised) on *Fearless*'s two Principal Warfare Officers (PWOs). One of these, though, was also the Communications Officer and was to spend most of his time sorting out that massive task (plus those of two embarked headquarters) and the other was the Gunnery Officer who was to have enough to do bringing his ship up to fighting form and then getting on with the battles: problems that had not been highlighted during peacetime pre-planned exercises.

We had already begun to identify what might or might not be important at the various stages of escalation. The fjords and inner leads of north Norway provided an unusual setting for naval operations and they had their own specific requirements.

In April, 1982, it was not lost on me, nor my staff, that the topographical and meteorological conditions of the NATO's northern flank bore some similarities to those in the Falkland archipelago. Our training had not been in vain, far from it.

My staff was headed by Commander Mike Dickens, a navigating officer mainly involved in the detailed planning and execution of an amphibious assault. Under him was a Lieutenant-Commander, United States Navy, who as a planning officer was responsible for longer-term work and with liaison between us and our Striking Fleet Atlantic counterparts. It was obvious that he would not be allowed to come on the trip but when I tried to find another Lieutenant-Commander with amphibious experience there were none from which to make a choice.

Communications were covered by a Special Duties Branch Lieutenant (Lieutenant Chris Beard) assisted by a Radio Supervisor. They had experience of strategic communications and Main Communications Office management, but Chris was not a tactical signaller nor did he have the broader experience of electronic warfare that I required. I hoped that Mike Goodman would fill that gap. Theoretically the signals officer of HMS *Fearless* would cover this aspect but I was already concerned that this might not be practical. The climate of a navy reeling under further cuts, on top of an existing shortage of manpower, did not make the search for a properly balanced staff easy while it was lurching to war.

The only other naval officer with an operational background was Lieutenant-Commander Tim Stanning and, although fairly new to the staff, his career had included commanding a front-line 'Commando' helicopter squadron. He had a good knowledge of the tactical requirements of an amphibious operation and was to be invaluable as my Staff Aviation Officer (SAVO).

Military aspects of my staff were covered by Major David Minords, a Royal Marine trained in both landing craft and helicopter operations. His role as G1 was liaison between us and Brigade headquarters and in doing so would interpret the military aspects for the naval members of my staff. To assist him he had Major Guy Yeoman, with command experience in the

Royal Corps of Transport's Landing Craft Logistics (LCLs). Guy's essential duty as G2 was the loading and offloading of the ships and, under normal circumstances, controlling all landing craft movements. Major Tony Todd RCT (also with command experience of LCLs) was due to relieve Guy but I managed, thankfully, to keep both officers.

My Staff Officer (Amphibious Warfare), Dickens, left me shortly after the outset for compassionate reasons. Mike had had the courage to see me early on with a family problem which made him feel that he would not be able to support me fully in the manner he would have wished. We both therefore shopped around for his predecessor only to find that he was in hospital following a motor accident in Italy. I arranged for Mike to go to Northwood where I expected he would be needed to represent the amphibious aspects and act as my Liaison Officer there. If we did not go to war then he would provide valuable continuity with NATO until our return.

The Commander, or Executive Officer, of HMS *Fearless* (Commander John Kelly) was due to be relieved at that time but we decided to reappoint Commander George Pearson (Kelly's replacement and a navigating officer) direct to me. On the understanding that we would have a month or so before we got to the area of operations this would, we all felt, give George the chance to gain some experience. It was, though, far from satisfactory and extremely hard on George.

Finally I had a junior Lieutenant, Peter Crabtree, as my secretary, a Petty Officer (Writer), a Leading Writer, and a WRNS typist. We did not normally take either the writer or secretary with us on exercises and I had given little thought as to how they could contribute on operations. I decided to take Peter and the Leading Writer but leave the others to assist Mike Dickens. The final members were the driver, my leading steward and two 'baby' stewards who joined the ship's teams, and Radio Supervisor Taverner who helped Chris Beard with frequency allocation.

My peacetime staff, therefore, consisted of eight officers and eight ratings and was designed to plan, and then conduct, a small unopposed amphibious operation: it was not constituted to conduct surface, sub-surface, mine or air operations nor deal with intelligence or command and control communications. Nor did we have a Royal Fleet Auxiliary or Merchant Navy Officer to advise on ships taken up from trade.

When I was appointed COMAW I found it difficult to give my staff any direction since my office was near Portsmouth with the Admiral and most of them were in Plymouth with the Marines. It had also struck me that as my day-to-day job was more involved with the 3rd Commando Brigade and MGRM, Commando Forces, than with FOF3, here was an added reason to move to Devon. There was now much less of a link between the Admiral's staff and mine despite my continuing to hold the subsidiary title of FOF 3's Chief of Staff, Amphibious Warfare.

On moving my Headquarters to the Royal Marines Barracks, Stonehouse, we were made very welcome by Jeremy Moore and Julian Thompson, who found us splendid quarters in No 6 House from where I was able to both keep a much closer eye on my people and liaise better with Julian. It was then up to me to drive back to Fort Southwick (where I retained an office) at least once a week to report to the Admiral and attend briefings.

Now, on again to 2 April and a growing feeling of unease that our bluff was about to be called. This was coupled with an underlying fear that there was probably no one on CTF's staff who really understood the amphibious problem which looked, as the minutes ticked on, ever more likely to involve an opposed assault.

With these thoughts churning through my mind I arrived at Stonehouse that Friday and met Julian for a brief comparison and exchange of views. As neither of us had any real idea of what was to be asked of us our concerns were similar. Julian gave me a quick 'sitrep' on the developments so far and how he saw the thing moving from there and I briefed him on what I had achieved and what ships I saw being available. He, not surprisingly, was by no means yet in a position to provide the 'Army plan' or let me know 'how they wished to fight', which, as Admiral Ramsay wrote, was a pre-requisite of naval plans.

Julian and I were waiting to see how the command and control system would develop and we didn't have to wait long. At 1355 I was appointed Commander of the Amphibious Task Unit. By 1600 I had been given Operational Control (OPCON) of HMSs *Fearless*, *Hermes*, *Invincible*, *Alacrity*, *Antelope*, and the RFAs *Pearleaf*, *Olmeda*, *Resource*, *Stromness* and the five LSLs.

The South Atlantic Task Force was designated TF 317 with Admiral Sir John Fieldhouse (CinC Fleet) the Task Force Commander, or CTF 317. Rear-Admiral Sandy Woodward, as FOF 1 and flying his flag in HMS *Antrim*, was placed in command of all *Operation Corporate* (the chosen title for the campaign as a whole) forces at sea as Commander Task Group 317.8; in addition he was Commander of the *Springtrain* Task Unit CTU 317.8. I, due to fly my Broad Pennant in HMS *Fearless*, was nominated as Commander of the Amphibious Task Unit – CTU 317.8.3; Julian Thompson, another Task Unit Commander (the Landing Force) was nominated CTU 317.8.4. The submarines were to remain a separate Task Group, under the Command of Flag Officer Submarines (Vice-Admiral Peter Herbert) at Northwood. The nomination of commanders *vis-à-vis* the various Groups and Units was now clear but it was to change as we progressed. Naval Staff Organizations are normally drawn in the shape of a pyramid, Force being superior to a Group which in turn is Superior to a Unit, and then an Element, and so on.

It was manifest that the Commander-in-Chief wanted us to sail early and we would not therefore be able to go through the logical sequence for an amphibious assault. First should come the Initiating Directive, followed by the Landing Force Commander's Landing Priority Table drawn up to reflect what he is to achieve during and immediately after the initial landings. From this document the 'load and stow plans' for the shipping can be compiled. It is essential that ships (unless roll-on, roll-off and used as such) be loaded in reverse order and that equipment is spread across the fleet in a logical fashion so that enemy damage does not remove, at a stroke, any particular facility: all loading should be carefully tabulated and known. On this

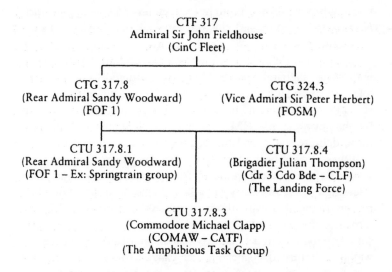

CTF 317
Admiral Sir John Fieldhouse
(CinC Fleet)

CTG 317.8
(Rear Admiral Sandy Woodward)
(FOF 1)

CTG 324.3
(Vice Admiral Sir Peter Herbert)
(FOSM)

CTU 317.8.1
(Rear Admiral Sandy Woodward)
(FOF 1 – Ex: Springtrain group)

CTU 317.8.4
(Brigadier Julian Thompson)
(Cdr 3 Cdo Bde – CLF)
(The Landing Force)

CTU 317.8.3
(Commodore Michael Clapp)
(COMAW – CATF)
(The Amphibious Task Group)

occasion we had no Initiating Directive and no aim other than to sail for the South Atlantic and so we possessed no Landing Priority Table. The one clear message was that we had to get to sea quickly and be seen to be at sea quickly.

It was also clear, however, that merchant ships would be required and that the 3rd Commando Brigade, Royal Marines, would be enhanced by further army forces. Headquarters Commando Forces Royal Marines therefore asked for two extra ships to be taken up from trade to carry 1,000 men each.

To my relief Tony Barratt's report arrived that morning and without ado I sent a copy to the Commander-in-Chief's staff where it formed the basis for all the Naval Parties in civilian ships. The only 'extra' they introduced was a doubling of the numbers and an up-grading of the Officer Commanding's rank. In simple terms this meant that there was more experience in these ships than I could have hoped for without, I believe, over-emphasizing the naval role.

Once news reached London that the Islands had in fact been invaded, any thought of deterrence, whether covert or overt became history. When brought to readiness *Hermes* and *Invincible* were tasked to embark the maximum of Sea Harrier and anti-submarine warfare (ASW) Sea King aircraft commensurate with air operations. Before lunch that first day, and after consultation with Major General Moore, *Hermes* was ordered to plan for her 'old' role as an LPH. She was now to embark a commando at full strength of 800 plus men, 'with Sea Harrier enhancement,' but by that evening MGRM's military requirements had taken a more definite shape and this requirement was cancelled.

It was already becoming clear that ships taken up from trade would be the prime method of transporting troops south thus releasing *Hermes* from any such duty. Regardless of that decision my staff, together with those of Julian's Commando Brigade, remained in no doubt that *Hermes*, in the LPH role, would somehow be required to launch any initial assault and while she was now 'returned' to her Harrier Carrier rôle she did embark 120 Royal Marines of A Company 40 Commando and 9 Sea Kings Mk 4 of 846 Squadron (Lt Cdr S.C. Thornewill) to keep this option open. These men and their aircraft were in addition to her 'normal' complement of twelve Sea Harriers from 800 Squadron and nine ASW Sea Kings Mk 5 from 826 Squadron. *Invincible* embarked eleven Mk 5 Sea Kings of 820 Squadron and eight Sea Harriers of 801 Squadron. Both ships were very full.

Of the Brigade's three Commandos, 40 Commando was ending a weapon training period near Liverpool, 42 Commando was on early Easter leave after the normal winter deployment in Norway and 45 Commando was just about to go on leave from their base at Arbroath (on the east coast of Scotland), while one of their companies was staging through Hong Kong having completed jungle training in Brunei. A substantial amount of heavy kit was still at sea *en route* home from north Norway at the end of the annual arctic training period.

In addition to the three Commandos a number of dedicated specialist units exist within the Commando Brigade that give it a greater measure of self-contained flexibility and independence when compared with an army infantry brigade. 29 Commando Light Regiment, Royal Artillery had returned to the Citadel,

Plymouth, from Norway with their 105mm light howitzers; 148 Battery Forward Observation Unit, Royal Artillery, (part of 29 Regiment, Royal Artillery) for Naval Gunfire Support and supplying forward observers was stationed at Royal Marines, Poole; unique to the Royal Marines, the Commando Logistic Regiment was back in its barracks from Norway cleaning equipment and re-stocking the Brigade's combat supplies. All members of this Regiment are united by their green beret although they come from many services to form five squadrons: headquarters, medical, transport, ordnance and workshop. The Royal Marines-manned Air Defence Troop with their Blowpipe anti-aircraft missiles had been stood-to and stood down; the Mountain and Arctic Warfare Cadre was in Plymouth after their own arduous arctic training period, as was the First Raiding Squadron Royal Marines with their mix of rubber and rigid-inflatable fast raiding craft. The Royal Marines Special Boat Squadron was back at Poole (but always at instant notice to move for national tasks or, under my command, for NATO ones); the Brigade Air Squadron of Scouts and Gazelles were now home in Yeovilton. The medium support helicopters (Wessex Mk 5 and Sea King Mk 4 of 845 (Lt Cdr R.J. Warden) and 846 Naval Air Squadrons respectively) were also safely back at HMS *Heron*, Yeovilton. The Brigade did not possess its own light tanks, light reconnaissance vehicles, organic area air-defence or heavy artillery.

Julian and I had moved our immediate staffs from Stonehouse to General Moore's Commando Forces headquarters about a mile away in Hamoaze House, Mount Wise. This was to be a time- and administration-saving arrangement as it was to the General's staff that all the major orders had been sent for dissemination and it was easier to arrange that all Landing Force requests to MOD or CinC Fleet were passed through their H.Q. It was much easier for us all to turn up at the same place.

What was surprising was that Derek Reffell, the Fleet Amphibious Authority, appeared not to be involved even in this early planning stage which was supposed by doctrine to be led by the Amphibious Task Force Commander – me. In the longer term the lead by MGRM had its advantages since the General and his staff would remain behind long after Julian and I had sailed. Their task would continue once it had been decided to send 5 Brigade as well. It was the first sign, however, that command and control might not follow standard procedures.

The first two questions that we needed to discuss urgently were, where are the Falklands and what is our task? Out of these two questions would fall supplementary points such as size and composition of the landing force and its mix and type of weapons and vehicles and the size and composition of the fleet: for how long should we plan to be away? Was there to be any shore support?

Most of us knew where the Falklands were of course. The Royal Navy and Royal Marines had maintained some form of presence there since the first British settlers, but few knew much more than that.

Were there beaches, were there airfields, was there food, water and fuel, was the climate arctic or sub-arctic, was there a hard surface road network and so on? To help answer some of these questions and to get people at least 'thinking Falkland' Major Ewen Southby-Tailyour was called in by Julian on 2 June to brief us all from his large collection of slides, charts and sketches. He was then commanding the Royal Marines' Landing Craft Branch at Poole and had commanded Naval Party 8901 (the Falklands Garrison) three years earlier during which time he sailed around the coastline surveying the beaches from a professional (and yachtman's) point of view. Initially it had not been Julian's intention to take him south but Ewen asked if he could come and so, in the Brigadier's words, 'It became apparent very quickly that he would be useful'. There were, though, others with sound knowledge of the area and there were 'kelpers' (as the Islanders call themselves) in the United Kingdom who were keen to offer assistance.

In addition to the shortcomings that I have listed there was no Joint Theatre Plan, nor, apparently, any other plan in existence for the re-occupation of the Falkland Islands. While there were some similarities between loading for the Arctic there were obvious and very marked differences for which we had never planned. There would be no 'host nation' and we would therefore have to offload (possibly during the opposed landing always considered so unlikely by the Government), protect ourselves and deploy forward using our own assets and fuel. This may seem obvious when faced with the likelihood of an opposed landing but it had not recently been practised. Planning therefore would need to be evolutionary. We based ours on the Joint Theatre Plan for mounting the UK-Netherlands Amphibious Task Group. Although it was the Commodore's duty to provide the Brigade with the Loading Plan, the 'loading and stowing' of the shipping, as I have mentioned before, depended on the Landing Force Commander's Landing Priority Table; this document depended on an Initiating Directive from London or Northwood and that we did not have – nor would we.

In practice, and because of the timings imposed upon us by the Government, we loaded the ships as stores appeared at the docksides, thus it was not until Ascension, some time later, that we really knew what we had with us and in which ships. The fact that we loaded in a hurry created problems. While we had a fair idea of what had been loaded and into which ship, we were never certain of the order and not therefore able to have confidence in an unloading plan. In an attempt to tabulate what we had and where, the Commando Logistic Regiment placed a representative on board each 'stores ship' for the express purpose of listing their contents. This was fine until various practicalities obstructed their work: they could not get at the stores due to the manner in which they had been loaded and, even when they could, they were prevented from signalling their findings by the 'minimize' on signals traffic.

The first priority at Hamoaze House was to establish the composition of the landing force (which was being added to the whole time) and from that produce staff tables for every unit, ship-by-ship. With so many 'moveable constants', a very loose directive and only three days over a weekend this was a complicated business, which made it even more remarkable that nothing serious was left behind or forgotten, although to hide the fact that there were problems would be wrong.

During those first few days the Brigadier asked for and was given 'T' (Rapier) Battery, Royal Artillery, equipped with twelve missile launchers. He also asked for, and was given, two troops of the Blues and Royals with their armoured reconnaissance vehicles, a total of four Scimitar and four Scorpion light tanks. The Brigade was augmented further by the 3rd Battalion the Parachute Regiment: thus the identification of shipping was the greatest threat to our speedy departure with the shopping list for ships altering each time the need for a new unit was identified and then added to the Brigade's Order of Battle.

Another unit that came on strength and for which space had to be found was 22 SAS: unannounced, the Commanding Officer (Lieutenant-Colonel Mike Rose) visited Julian Thompson in Plymouth over the weekend to ask whether or not they were wanted. Julian had had some of their members under his command in Northern Ireland and leapt at the opportunity. Later he was to write, 'Whether in typical SAS fashion they would have appealed to higher authority behind my back had I turned down their offer I can not say. My guess is that they would.'

We wanted the Commanding Officers of the SBS and the SAS to travel in my Flagship for they would be needed by the amphibious planners, but this met with an initial and polite refusal from Major Jonathan Thomson, Royal Marines (Commanding Officer of the SBS) who felt, quite understandably, that his place was with his Operations Officer (Captain Colin Howard) in HMS *Hermes*. Special Forces, particularly the SBS, and Advance Force Operations are commanded by (and respond to the needs of) the Commander of the Amphibious Task Group (me, in this case) in consultation, naturally, with his military counterpart, although there are a number of purely 'naval' tasks for which COMAW alone has responsibility when he would not need to consult the Landing Force. Once both COs were embarked in *Fearless* I think they realized (we certainly did) that they were in the correct ship.

46

That first day also brought orders for the embarkation of 350 men of 45 Commando in the RFA *Stromness* (two companies were to fly ahead to Ascension) which was to sail, fully stored, by 3 April; in fact she sailed on the 4th. An added complication with using *Stromness* was that at the moment she was in Portsmouth being emptied of stores and stripped of all military equipment, equipment that included communications, NBCD, and RAS fittings. All this had to be replaced, plus the men's accommodation as well as 11,000 aluminium panels for a temporary airstrip. She had taken six weeks to de-store, she now put it all back (plus much more) in just four days.

While the removal of the Argentinian invasion troops and their follow-up forces was being negotiated at an international level we continued to plan: not so much for war, *per se*, but to get south as quickly as possible. We were, though, conscious that success in amphibious warfare depends on planning for action while still in the 'home base', with the success of an operation depending on decisions and actions taken long before any ship is loaded with its first pallet, vehicle, aircraft or man. It is also a standard procedure in amphibious operations that even in peacetime all ships are loaded in the correct order 'for war'.

By speaking to the General's staff in Plymouth and the Admiral's staff at Northwood we pieced together various snippets of information that gave us hope that the situation in the South Atlantic could be solved by diplomacy. We were not, though, sanguine enough to allow our planning to be influenced by that possibility. On the other hand, to add emphasis and strength to the diplomatic negotiations, it was vital that we sail early, and be seen to sail with all the military publicity that could be mustered: we understood that. It was also suggested that a strong and unequivocal message be transmitted to the Junta indicating that we were serious in re-taking the island no matter what the cost. As always throughout the Falkland story the Foreign Office appeared to us to be worried lest we be seen by the Argentinians to be provocative. If we had had a little less of that attitude down the years we might not have been in the position we were at the beginning of April 1982.

It was hoped, too, that a strong, quick initial reaction might be enough, if not to reverse, then at least to halt the Argentinians in their nefarious tasks. In fact they continued to pour men into the Islands in the belief, presumably, that we would see the futility of engaging such a powerful force, in situ, so far from our own bases. Rightly, that only made us more determined to get on and plan for a landing against an unknown enemy across unknown ground supported by a tenuous supply route over an unpredictable time scale and all this eight thousand miles from home without the correct ships and with no major port in between. But then it can be argued (and certainly has been) that that is precisely what amphibious warfare is all about and why it can be so effective when no other method (military, political or diplomatic) presents itself.

Although the Brigade had often deployed with all three Commandos, plus their supporting arms for war in one cohesive block, as it were, (Borneo, Malaya, Cyprus, Suez, et al) modern training deployments now relied upon a variety of methods of travel combining RAF Support Command, the LSLs and the LPDs and between 1960 and 1976 the Commando Carriers HMSs *Bulwark*, *Albion* and *Hermes*. On a number of occasions the Brigade Air Squadron with its light helicopters had deployed to north Norway under its own steam and the embryo independent Brigade Landing Craft Squadron had been experimenting with a similar method of deployment through the inner leads; but this was the first time in recent years that the complete Commando Brigade (and an enhanced one at that) would deploy by sea with its full War Maintenance Reserve.

While Standard Operating Procedures, along with personal experiences, were available there was clearly much we had never contemplated and certainly much we had never exercised in recent years. For instance, the Brigadier and I and our staffs had never planned or exercised together during my time as Commodore. While my staff, in conjunction with that of the Joint Services Staff College, Latimer, ran the occasional amphibious planning course, this had not been attended by myself or some members of my staff, nor had it been attended by all of those in

Julian's staff who became involved in such planning. It had not been a pre-requisite for joining either staff. We had always known that we did not possess enough shipping and now we were about to identify the exact shortfall, but whatever merchant ships were requisitioned they had to have flight-decks of some sort and of that the Brigadier and I were adamant. We were not to be wholly satisfied.

Central to Julian's and my thoughts was the command structure which placed us directly under Sandy Woodward along with his *Springtrain* forces. We wondered how it would work out in practice but for the moment were reasonably content. It was a command structure based on rank rather than role, and if that is really what the Commander-in-Chief wanted then we would of course do our best to make it work. It was not in strict accordance with the American-dominated ATP 8 which requires the Commander Amphibious Task Force (CATF – me) to answer direct to an Admiral in overall command of all forces at sea, who, in this case, would be the Commander-in-Chief ashore at Northwood. The other relevant requirement is that the Commander Landing Force (CLF), although equal in rank and status, answers to CATF who is responsible for the conduct of all amphibious operations until the Amphibious Objective Area is secure and the land forces are ashore and self-sufficient. As I have mentioned, ATP 8 was both the NATO and national doctrine for the lack of any agreed national JTP. It was the procedure that FOF 3 and myself practised on all NATO operational exercises as well as in the command exercises held in North America. The latter were not attended by any members of the MGRM or 3rd Commando Staffs. We did find that the Americans with their very large amphibious and US Marine Corps forces had a greater obsession for rigid compliance with doctrine than we needed. Nevertheless their command approach had been proven many times and should not therefore be discarded lightly.

Ever since the Second World War NATO navies had been able to meet at sea and instantly go into action knowing exactly what tactics and procedures the command may require. This was achieved through a series of Allied Tactical Publications held by all NATO and many allied or Dominion navies. It could not cover all requirements but it certainly covered most and allowed Commanding Officers and staffs to concentrate only on changes to standing procedures which could be promulgated either for that immediate action or locally. As a system it worked exceptionally well and meant that everyone who wished to take an interest or were involved in the operation could follow the thoughts of their commander and the progress of the operation without excessive use of communications. I understand that such systems did not exist between NATO armies who would probably not expect to operate together at Unit level.

By 3 April the STUFT shopping list was being updated continually with the cruise liner SS *Canberra* (I discussed her requisitioning in more detail in the Prologue) already well into the pipeline. She had been joined by, among other tankers and stores ships, the *British Esk*, *British Tay* and *British Tamar*; the North Sea ferry *Norsea* was chosen and then discarded in favour of *Elk* (Captain J.P. Morton MN). In all STUFT ships it is necessary to embark the small 'Naval Party' which Tony Barratt had studied for me earlier that year. Their task is to run the military communications nets, advise the masters of naval operations and tactics as well as how to replenish at sea. As the Senior Naval Officer (SNO) in *Canberra* CTF had appointed Captain Christopher Burne (known since his days with the Britannia pack as 'Beagle') and while his was to be an inspired choice Julian Thompson felt uneasy at a naval officer being, *de facto*, the senior officer embarked in what was in some senses a troopship, particularly as that force was headed by three very independent and strong-willed Commanding Officers – two Royal Marines and one Parachute Regiment.

Indeed I had raised an eyebrow at a four-ringed captain being appointed to *Canberra* as his duties were not expected to be that onerous and mainly concerning naval tasks. As it also made sense to appoint a Deputy Brigade Commander for such a complicated and possibly open-ended undertaking, Colonel

Tom Seccombe (Royal Marines), a forceful and stylish personality with immense commando experience, was chosen by Julian. Regardless of whether or not The Beagle was 'senior' to the three commanding officers it made sense for Tom to travel in a separate ship from the Brigade Commander so he, too, was appointed to *Canberra*, the ideal foil for the eccentric Beagle.

The availability of civilian ships was not my only concern. It was clear to me that, if at all possible, HMS *Intrepid* should be brought out of her deep refit for a number of reasons: her presence would double the number of landing craft available to myself and the Brigadier and she could carry three medium support helicopters (although only operate two at a time). Lastly (and I hoped, least) she would be the reserve command ship if disaster was to befall *Fearless*. She had to come with us and I made this point strongly to the staff then, and again at our only Northwood meeting on 4 April when I received a very dusty answer indicating that she would probably not be available.

The pressure to sail as soon as possible was being kept up as indicated in a signal received by CinC Fleet from the Ministry of Defence ordering all ships not yet at sea to sail as soon as they were ready. Although we recognized the need for such action Amphibious Operations are a very specialized form of warfare and, as Winston Churchill once observed, 'have to fit together like a jewelled bracelet'. Quite so! They are very complicated and have to be planned and conducted with meticulous care but, through no fault of our own, we were having to jump fences before we were fully prepared.

As a direct result of this haste, the need for a midway halt for re-stowing and rehearsing was recognized and so both Ascension Island and St Helena were offered up. Since nobody on Julian's staff nor mine knew either of the islands we were undecided over which would be the more suitable. Several days after we sailed it became clear that although Ascension Island had only one suitable beach (and that capable of accepting just one LCU at a time) it did have an airfield capable of operating the largest aircraft. Although of very limited use for amphibious rehearsals, it was the only choice.

On the 3rd I received a signal from CTF ordering me to sail my Task Unit south once we had gathered together off the Eddystone Rock. I replied that I intended the rendezvous to be at midnight 6/7 April and would proceed at a stately 12-knot passage south (the average speed of the LSLs). This would allow time for various ships (*Canberra, Elk* – sailing on the 9th: *Stromness, Resource* – sailing on the 7th) to catch up by the time we reached Ascension. We would need the sea-time to shake down our drills which included Nuclear, Biological, Chemical and Damage Control (NBCD) training, flying, deck-landings (especially at night) and the ground-attack rôle for the Fleet Air Arm's Sea Harriers. I gave orders to this effect, stating additionally that a training guide was about to be issued and that ships were to conserve fuel and expend a minimal amount of ammunition *en route* to the half-way halt. After that things would probably be different.

On the 4th Julian gathered the growing number of his commanding officers in Hamoaze House at 1000 for their first major, joint briefing. At the same time the relevant officers and 'movers' on both staffs held the all-important Mounting Meeting just forty-eight hours after our standing start. Staff tables had been prepared and were already being dovetailed into the available shipping.

That we could hold a Mounting Meeting so soon was a remarkable achievement. We were, though, aware that the real problem would start after we sailed when we would have to plan how to unscramble the loading priorities forced upon us by the haste in leaving British shores. Impressive though it might have seemed to the politicians, the diplomats, the public and, hopefully, the Argentinians, it was definitely not the way we wanted to begin an operation and would eventually slow us down and delay any landing date. In practice the speedy deployment did not have the desired effect and, if anything, forced the Argentinians to hasten, and increase, their defences in the Falklands, but that is, admittedly, hindsight.

Julian's meeting was more of a general intelligence and information briefing than an 'orders' group. It was opened by

Ewen Tailyour with a lengthy 'ground' paragraph in which he highlighted the military problems of moving and fighting across the Falklands' moors and bogs and the naval problems of selecting suitable beaches. He produced a small map on which he had hastily scribbled notes alongside a number of landing sites, including an inlet called San Carlos – it meant nothing to any of us then. Later he was to expand and continue this service until just short of victory. His knowledge was biased neither towards the ground forces nor the naval forces but was purely amphibious in nature and was to be helpful to both CTGs embarked in HMS *Fearless*. Equally useful was a briefing by Lieutenant Bob Veal, Royal Navy, who had recently returned from leading a climbing expedition on South Georgia. He did much the same for those Islands as Ewen had done for 'his', Bob in particular, mentioned an Argentine C-130 flying up and down the coastline which indicated to him that 'they' had probably landed in a number of places by parachute, which got one or two people thinking.

After a number of specialists had presented their views, and suggestions, Julian concluded by saying how he felt the immediate future would run and gave orders for training priorities once embarked and on passage south. Without any more specific aim at that stage than to sail quickly it was not possible for either of us to say more; the real value of this meeting was to get as many as possible together for the first time for there were one or two new faces (mainly from the Parachute Regiment, the SAS and the Rapier Battery). It was important that we all knew each other as members of the same team. Unfortunately, I was not able to do the same for my own Commanding Officers who were scattered and, in some cases, already at sea.

Immediately after the briefing Jeremy Moore, Julian Thompson, Ewen Tailyour and I embarked in a Lynx helicopter for a flight to Northwood via Yeovilton for fuel. At HMS *Heron* I had a long talk with the Flag Officer Naval Air Command (Ted Anson – the CO of my first operational Buccaneer squadron when I had been his senior observer) and Captain David Williams during which I discussed the possibility of taking more helicopters in the RFA *Engadine*. With two helicopter squadrons (one Wessex and one Sea King) we could support one or at the most two Commando Groups on an exercise but for an enhanced Brigade at war with a seaborne logistic tail their numbers would be woefully inadequate. The Admiral was reluctant to support my suggestion as the ship was considered unseaworthy for such an undertaking and could be a liability rolling in the South Atlantic. We had, of course, no idea that we would operate in the sheltered waters of San Carlos where she was to become, rather late in the campaign, extremely valuable. As far as numbers were concerned Ted reminded me that he had always thought me greedy but would do his best; in fact, he did better than I could, at the time, have hoped.

The aim of the visit to Northwood was to discuss with Admiral Fieldhouse and his senior staff the amphibious aspects of our deployment as we then saw them. The flight had been straight-forward until an abortive attempt to land in the Northwood car park where there were no parking spaces left! We were 'unexpected' and so found a convenient field nearby where we were met by a Land Rover and taken swiftly to the 'hole' and Fleet's underground headquarters. I was taken, initially, to see the Chief of Staff, David Halifax, for what I always considered to be one of the more critical meetings.

Captain Jeremy Reed, the Assistant Chief of Staff (Warfare), (responsible for the tactical aspects of the Task Force) said that he knew little about amphibious operations and that anything I could tell him would be helpful, so, with the Chief of Staff's concurrence, I was asked to signal Northwood our, that is Julian and my, thoughts as they developed. In doing this we were all aware that the political background might change and that we should be prepared for any eventuality: a full-scale landing, small-scale raids or poising at sea for months. The best people to advise on these options were, they believed, myself in conjunc-tion with the Landing Force Commander. So began a series of signals largely drafted by Jeremy Larken who was expected to act as my Chief of Staff as well as Command HMS *Fearless*. The aim obviously was to obtain an agreed policy or strategy, but between the three of us we largely failed. If we had had a longer term 'command' plan (Julian and I were to develop our own) agreed with Northwood I do not believe that there would have been the muddle over our tasks that was to occur after the landings. Central to this non-existent strategy, or Concept of Operations, would have been an understanding, well in advance of their arrival, of the use of the second brigade. In consequence, the tragedy to the LSLs at Fitzroy might not have occurred.

At CTF's briefing shortly afterwards, Ewen repeated for the Admirals a potted version of his earlier 'ground and sea' brief. After this Julian and I aired our worries, concerns and wishes.

We emphasized the need for extra ships to transport the landing force and its equipment, including the 4,500 tons War Maintenance Reserve of ammunition, food and combat supplies – *Fearless* and the five LSLs being far from adequate – and was given assurance that the STUFT shipping bill was being afforded the utmost priority. We continued to argue for ships able to operate helicopters, particularly mentioning HMS *Intrepid*. CTF said that we should do the utmost to avoid an opposed landing and that when we did land it had to be conducted under the umbrella of air superiority. We, of course, agreed that to ensure that the best possible conditions would apply for a landing a sea and air battle would need to be won. We were promised all this as well as intelligence-gathering operations and demoralizing raids prior to any D-Day.

Admiral Fieldhouse did most of the talking but agreed with much of what we said and concluded by stating that he would seek clearance to impose a *cordon sanitaire* around the islands as the first step, but privately to Julian and Ewen in the corridor outside he turned and said, 'This is going to be a sad and bloody business – I only wish I could offer you more ships.' Doubtless this was honest, but it was not good for Julian's morale. CTF, though, was certain that the whole operation was, in essence, to be amphibious and that was good to hear. As for Concepts of Operations, a strategy or even the vital Initiating Directive, there was no mention, but then he, too, was waiting for them.

ATP8 is the amphibious bible for this type of operation and

contains a large number of definitions designed to refine and clarify thought in order to avoid confusion. Like all these publications it is regularly reviewed and argued over. The definition of an Amphibious Operation was basically one that was conducted to establish a landing force on a hostile shore in order either to prosecute further combat operations, or to capture a site for an advanced naval or air base, or, simply, to deny the use of an area to the enemy.

The first objective, particularly, seemed to fit in well with the way the operation was developing but none of these tasks were we yet ordered to do. So for what reasons were we to load and plan other than to be seen to be doing so by the enemy?

We were, though, satisfied that our four biggest concerns – shipping, intelligence, an unopposed landing (by which we did NOT mean an administrative landing) and air superiority – were being addressed. However, there were a number of aspects that were not satisfactory: we needed HMS *Intrepid* and her landing craft; we needed as many medium support helicopters as possible; we needed depth charges for use in enclosed waters; we needed some form of airborne or submarine-borne early warning and we needed to conduct operations (which included the well-tried command structure) in accordance with the British interpretation of ATP-8. The first two of these we were not promised, indeed we were given little hope that they would even be considered, and as far as the chain of command was concerned this was not mentioned. Before serious planning could take place we had to know for what we were planning and where the Amphibious Objective Area would be. Without this guide our task was, literally, without limits.

The presence at the meeting of my immediate superior, Rear-Admiral Derek Reffell (with his experience as COMAW and of an LPH command) gave us hope that he would be put in charge. An important aspect connected with Derek was the size and spread of expertise within his staff and, of course, I was part of it. If they were to be closely involved, in the Atlantic or at Northwood, so much the better. We presumed that the command signal of 2 April was probably only a temporary measure.

We returned to Plymouth in pensive mood, not quite sure what we had achieved, but quite clear what we had not achieved.

One aspect that had been discussed was the early deployment of the SBS and the SAS. Some wanted them to 'make a bang in the South Atlantic' as soon as possible (nobody said how they would get there nor what that expression actually meant), but neither Julian nor I were impressed by this philosophy. In reality these Special Forces would deploy to Ascension to await the arrival of the RFA *Fort Austin* with two further detachments of the Royal Marines' SBS earmarked for embarkation in the nuclear submarines *Spartan* and *Splendid*. A detachment of SBS was to sail in HMS *Conqueror* from the United Kingdom on 5 April.

Back at Stonehouse I addressed a number of points (many of which I had raised at Fort Southwick on the first day) in a series of 'sweeping up' and 'emphasizing' signals: a special communications back-up system plus SBS/SAS link direct to *Fearless*; details of all merchant ships' capabilities; point defence facilities for the RFAs and STUFT; NBCD teams to carry out short work-ups at sea and a request for more NBCD clothing and equipment for the civilian crews (which included respirators and once-only survival suits); sandbags to provide protection for ships' key points and, finally guidance on the camouflaging of ships, the painting out of pennant numbers and the availability of smoke canisters to use as a measure of air defence. At Northwood we had even discussed the old-fashioned favourite of ships' companies under close air attack, barrage balloons. I also believe that we discussed the possibility of taking with us one of the Royal Air Force's mobile radars which I think they still held. I am told, however, that this was not recorded and is therefore officially hindsight! We certainly didn't receive it.

That evening I briefed my team and sent them off to Portsmouth and HMS *Fearless* under Captain Jeremy Larken's command; she was due to sail on the morrow – 6 April. We, Julian and I plus a small number of Staff, remained behind in Plymouth with the intention of meeting up with *Fearless* somewhere in the middle of Lyme Bay. When we did, on the evening of the 6th *Fearless* was just entering a frontal system with heavy rain and rising seas. It was certainly outside flying limits for Sea Kings landing on an LPD. It was a disconcerting start but there was no doubting the determination of the aircrew to get us south so that they could get some action.

Both of us were happy to have grabbed a couple of hours of peace with our families. Sarah arranged for our children, Lucy (5), Sophie (4) and James (2) to go to a friend while we sat quietly under a holm-oak tree in the garden nursing our thoughts.

Jeremy Larken was an excellent choice as my Flag Captain and I was pleased to have him with me. I had begun to know him well that spring in northern Norway and liked his lively approach. He enjoyed doing things off his own back and he had drive, enthusiasm, stamina and ample courage, and was to give me excellent support throughout.

We arrived on board *Fearless* to find many were taking a little time to find their sea-legs in the boisterous weather. This allowed us at 'command-level' to collect our thoughts now that we had severed all physical contact with the United Kingdom and gave me breathing space to reflect: we were committed; we had the formation 'going'; we knew we were heading south but we knew not quite where, nor what to do. The weather was blowing up and I was in command of what I regarded as an 'excellent little force' with two carriers, one assault ship, one luxury liner, a number of troop ships and with an augmented Royal Marines Commando Brigade embarked. I was still not clear how I was to be allowed to use *Hermes* and *Invincible* and whether or not they were expected to operate in the commando-ship rôle. As there was no suggestion that they would be sent to join Sandy I initiated a flying programme (subject to weather) to practise my Amphibious Task Unit (as it still was) in defence from air attacks. This seemed to me to be the top priority while the carriers were under my command. We also had the NBCD teams with us and they had to be fitted into the training packages.

All in all we were at the start of a settling-down period with commanding officers told to think hard about how they were going to operate in war, in inshore waters. As far as the two staffs were concerned we began a series of 'Appreciations of the Situation' only to realize that to be successful you have to have a situation to appreciate which we did not, then, have. These appreciations follow a formal and logical sequence and are invaluable as an aid to clearing one's mind so that a distinct objective and means of achievement are defined. They are particularly useful at times under stress when clear and calm thought is difficult. I also hoped that they would help to bring the two staffs together, who, although they had now been co-located at RMB Stonehouse, did not in fact spend much time in each other's company thinking through problems. From these appreciations Jeremy Larken was able to draft signals back to Northwood expressing Julian's and my staff's broader thinking in the hope of achieving a clear long-term concept of operations. Deducing the threat was part of our problem for we were painfully short of information on the enemy and without an overall strategy or even an aim we were a little handicapped. Nevertheless, these were concerns and not complaints for we knew things would become clearer; in the meantime we had much of a practical nature to get on with such as listing the manifests of the shipping, studying the Islands in general and carrying out the hundred and one items of training and re-learning so necessary to an amphibious force at sea.

Before I left the United Kingdom I had discussed the STUFT requirements with CTF's staff. The ships had, obviously, to be seaworthy enough for an unknown length of time in the southern ocean away from any form of formal support and while this may appear obvious, when the *QE2* sailed she was found to be far from mechanically sound and clean, forcing her to anchor off the Nab Tower overnight to sort out defects in two of her three boilers. The ships had to be able to replenish fuel at sea which, in the case of *Canberra*, was vital as her endurance was limited to twenty-seven days at $18\frac{1}{2}$ knots. The designing and fitting of *Canberra*'s flight-decks provided the Southampton shipbuilders, Vosper Thornycroft, with a wide scope for imagination and ingenuity. Prior to the liner's arrival home from her world tour they prefabricated two flight decks and were still fitting these when she sailed for Ascension Island. Extra water tanks, and production capacity, was a problem that faced many ships, including our own LSLs; solved (in *Norland* for instance) by the loading of water bowsers in the car decks of ferries and the fitting of reverse-osmosis systems in other ships. Problems of communications and control facilities were more easily solved, by and large by 'carry-on' packs.

It was understood, even then, that some merchant ships might take part in amphibious operations (if they were to occur) and not just be employed ferrying men and stores south. Concern over the number of men in *Canberra* was certainly aired but put to one side on the assumption that for the initial phase of the assault we would have the services of *Hermes*. Her use as commando ship would prevent the need to bring too many civilian troopships close inshore (and within aircraft range) until a beachhead had been secured.

Another consideration was the employment of civilian seamen. The National Union of Seamen, the General Council of British Shipping, the managers of P & O and the MOD (Navy) met on 6 April to determine the position of civilian crews. With the offer of substantial bonuses for union members, all but a few elected to stay with their ships and under the normal discipline of their masters until 'active service' was declared, at which point they would become subject to the Naval Discipline Act. The bonus was agreed at 150% which compared well with the extra one pound per day paid to members of the armed forces during *Operation Corporate* – but then we do have the X factor! No foreigners were to be employed (except those members of Royal Navy and Royal Fleet Auxiliary ships' companies) resulting in 400 Asians being landed to HMS *Collingwood* from SS *Canberra*. When, on 10 April, the cruise ship *SS Uganda* was taken up from trade as a hospital ship compensation was sought (and received) to keep her 200 or so Asians aboard.

The two carriers and RFA *Olmeda* had sailed from Portsmouth during the morning of 5 April and were joined from

Plymouth by the two Type 21 frigates HMS *Alacrity* and HMS *Antelope*. Off the south-west coast last-minute stores were embarked by helicopter from Culdrose and Yeovilton. Things were to be delayed slightly by *Invincible* whose starboard, inner, astern fluid coupling required replacing with a spare flown out as she passed Land's End. It was eventually fitted at sea during which time she was limited to 15 knots while *Hermes* forged on to Ascension Island.

With the sailing of *Stromness* (Captain Barrie Dickinson RFA) on 8 April, carrying the bulk of 45 Commando, and *Canberra* (the next day) with 3 Para, 40 Commando, and 42 Commando – less M company already ahead at Ascension Island and about to embark in RFA *Tidespring* on the 7th for South Georgia – and *Elk* (9 April) carrying much of the forces' ammunition the Commando Brigade was at sea in eleven very assorted ships, scattered across a wide part of the ocean, seven days after the warning order.

We had sailed with little idea of what lay ahead and even for what we should plan. We had, too, sailed in a rather unmilitary posture for reasons which I have explained and which, although well understood, gave both Julian and me misgivings. Even on the return from the annual three months' training periods in north Norway the Brigade, tired, dirty and straight from the strenuous final field exercise in the mountains and fjords, would still embark in the homeward-bound shipping in the order it would be needed if diverted to a real war while *en route* for Plymouth. It was always a matter of pride that we did this, as well as being a matter of expediency and totally in accordance with the flexibility of amphibious warfare.

On 7 April and in consultation with Julian I sent the promised signal giving my orders for training while on passage. Fitness training was to be high on the list for all ranks, NBCD and weapon-handling likewise. I explained that a full intelligence study would start immediately. It was necessary for flying practice to begin as soon as possible but the lack of wind in the south-western approaches reported by the two carriers prevented this. *Hermes* asked permission to head south to look for wind in the Bay of Biscay or the Gibraltar training area, which I gave, informing Northwood of my decision. I told them not to go too far ahead as I wanted some air-strike and air-direction practice but shortly after this they were ordered by CTF to proceed direct to Ascension by 17 April. As this required an average speed of advance of 14 knots it allowed little time for flying and was to be the last time that they were to be under my command.

Initially my carrier and amphibious force, at sea, consisted of the following:

HMS *Fearless*
  COMAW and staff
  HQ 3 Cdo Bde and Signals Sqn
  Two Troops The Blues and Royals
HMS *Hermes*
  One company 40 Commando
HMS *Invincible*
HMSs *Alacrity* and *Antelope*
RFAs *Sirs Geraint, Galahad, Percivale* and *Lancelot*
  The Commando Logistic Regiment, the Raiding Troop
RFAs *Pearleaf* and *Olmeda*
RFA *Resource*
RFA *Stromness*
  350 men of 45 Cdo (Two companies flew ahead to Ascension)
SS *Canberra*
  40 Commando (less one company in *Hermes*), 42 Commando
  (less one company earmarked for South Georgia) and 3 Para.
MV *Elk*

Spread across the shipping, together with many even smaller organizations such as Explosive and Ordnance and Demolition (EOD) teams and postal detachments from the Royal Engineers, were:

29 Cdo Light Regt RA (+)
59 Indep Cdo Sqn RE (+)
845 and 846 Naval Air Squadrons (+)

3 Cdo Bde Air Sqn (+)
T Bty Air Def RA
SBS
D and G Sqns 22 SAS
M and AW Cadre RM
3 Cdo Bde AD Tp (+)

Meanwhile, although not involved at this stage with the amphibious force, Sandy had sailed his *Springtrain* ships from Gibraltar on the 2nd with the aim of being off Ascension by 10 April: he had with him ten assorted destroyers, frigates and RFAs and would meet, as warned by CTF, 'a strong surface group ex-UK on your way south'. On 4 April he was ordered to reduce speed to conserve fuel and to arrive now at Ascension by early evening of the 12th. Further changes were to take place which did affect the amphibious group. On 6 April Sandy was told to send ahead the RFA *Tidespring* with the destroyer *Antrim* and the frigate *Plymouth* to follow the next day. They were to be required for operations on South Georgia. Other movements took place: those with an amphibious purpose included RFA *Fort Austin* (having sailed from Gibraltar on 29 March) waiting off Ascension for three days while men from the SBS and SAS, together with assorted stores, were flown from the United Kingdom. She sailed on the 9th to replenish *Endurance* (as had been planned since before the invasion) and then, with the ice-patrol ship and the others from *Springtrain*, she was to stand-by for South Georgia.

On 9 April the Commander-in-Chief issued the new command and control directive to come into effect at midday on the 10th.

The three of us at sea were now nominated as equal Task Group Commanders with Sandy taking all the carriers and *Springtrain* ships into one group leaving me (as Commander Amphibious Task Group from now onwards) with whatever amphibious ships were with us or about to join. This would be added to and reduced by various destroyers and frigates throughout the war. Julian's command (as Commander Landing

Force, or CLF) stayed the same but was elevated to the status of a Task Group. The latest line-up, therefore, looked like this:

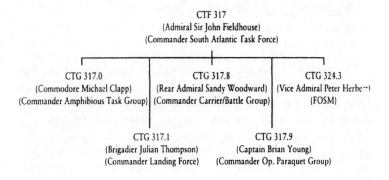

CTF 317
(Admiral Sir John Fieldhouse)
(Commander South Atlantic Task Force)

CTG 317.0
(Commodore Michael Clapp)
(Commander Amphibious Task Group)

CTG 317.8
(Rear Admiral Sandy Woodward)
(Commander Carrier/Battle Group)

CTG 324.3
(Vice Admiral Peter Herbert)
(FOSM)

CTG 317.1
(Brigadier Julian Thompson)
(Commander Landing Force)

CTG 317.9
(Captain Brian Young)
(Commander Op. Paraquet Group)

A fifth Task Group Commander (CTG 317.9) was appointed, Captain Brian Young, the Commanding Officer of HMS *Antrim*, who would lead *Operation Paraquet* into South Georgia. His group consisted of *Antrim*, *Plymouth*, *Endurance* and *Tidespring*. It was a tidier arrangement and took into account the operational differences between the groups as well as the geographic problems that Sandy would have should he go south early. He would not wish, I presumed, to be involved with other task groups not in his area. This organization was to remain essentially the same throughout the campaign.

In order to help clarify matters we were told by Northwood that CTG 317.8 was the 'senior CTG' purely to co-ordinate assets 'when necessary' but *not* to command. Thus, in effect, Woodward was to be '*primus inter pares*' on the spot but with us all having equal access to Northwood. This seemed a little strange to us since it is obvious that the Senior Officer would have such a task but it was, at least, clear. Both Julian and I felt that we would do our best to make any task organization work and we noted with mild disappointment that we were obviously considered too junior to make comments or observations on it.

In addition to sailing the Task Force as quickly as possible, and in particular the very public departure of the landing force element from the United Kingdom, the other priority was to sail the Battle Group ships as far south equally as quickly.

This was part of a complicated set of ship movements involving all the groups of the fleet. The carriers, the *Springtrain* group, the South Georgia group, the LSL group and the Amphibious Group, plus other small groups of ships, had left, or were leaving the UK to join as they became ready. On the 11th I ordered *Fearless* to detach at best speed ahead of her group (leaving HMS *Antelope* to bring on the LSLs) in order to get Julian and myself to Ascension in time for a planned meeting with CTF: by doing so the ship missed her own important rendezvous with the tanker *Olmeda*. This was to have an unfortunate and irritating knock-on consequence at the beginning of the re-stow.

During those few hectic days after leaving British waters Julian and I, together with our staffs and without any Initiating Directive, began brainstorming a number of landing options with a view to picking and choosing later. The political and diplomatic niceties were not our concern at that stage, planning being conducted on the assumption that we would be ordered to land (somehow, somewhere) when conditions were favourable. On that premise we needed to begin with the widest possible look at all the options of time and place so that, when (not if) the order came, we could pull the most suitable solution from the filing cabinet and look at it in closer detail. To achieve this we had to know more about the opposition, the country and its beaches and sea approaches to those beaches. Could they be defended against air, surface, sub-surface and Exocet attack? Were they suitable for slow transports and logistic ships? What about helicopter landing sites and their suitability for movement off them and what about the problems associated with living (and fighting) in the field while at the same time surviving under the prevailing weather conditions; what was the risk of sea or land mines, etc, etc, etc?

We had to know so much before we could consider a re-stow of the logistic ships to match the operational priorities for a landing: yet we did not know whether that landing was to be by air or by sea, or both, nor whether it was to be a political statement, military assault or unopposed manoeuvre prior to intensive land operations. There was a remarkable range of imponderables and unknowns.

The answers to some of these questions would come from intelligence acquisition, some from local knowledge, some from our leaders in Northwood and Whitehall and some from within our own Task Force.

I have mentioned the AOA – the Amphibious Objective Area. Basically it is a geographical area selected for the purpose of command and control and within which are located the objectives to be secured by the Amphibious Task Force. Obviously it must be of sufficient size to ensure accomplishment of the Amphibious Task Force's mission and it must provide adequate space for the conduct of the necessary sea, air and land operations.

The broad choice of an AOA can only be considered once an aim is established. It is then normally spelt out in an Initiating Directive which, in this case, was still notably absent. Choosing the AOA is one of the crucial first steps in the strategic planning of an amphibious operation: the exact choice of beaches, landing sites and stores areas etc. within the AOA, while largely tactical considerations, comes later but their rough identification is also vital to the choice of the area.

These concepts and many other factors have been carefully defined in the amphibious bible, ATP8, which distils years of practical experience. It was most helpful in confirming to a worried peacetime operator that the assault and initial unloading periods are primarily tactical and had to provide a quick response to the Landing Force Commander's requirements ashore. This phase, at least, could be reasonably carefully preplanned.

The general unloading period which follows the initial landing, it explained, is primarily logistic and is therefore almost always reactive to the demands of the Landing Force and to the efforts of the enemy. It was clear that this phase could not be carefully preplanned and it gave me much concern as to how we should plan to cope with it.

ATP8 was also clear that air superiority in the AOA was a prerequisite but, in acknowledging that complete destruction of an enemy air force is rarely achieved, it supported our view that all elements of the Amphibious Task Force must be provided with continuing air defence throughout the operation. Sandy, in the Carrier Group, would also need to contribute to the choice of AOA if air defence was to be properly planned.

Despite not knowing for what we were embarked, we were helped by two useful signals. The first was an 'Appreciation of the Situation' from Northwood on 8 April which followed the announcement the day before of the establishment of the exclusion zone CTF had said he would seek. The second and most useful of the two was received on 10 April and was described as the Outline Plan for the Establishment of Sea Control. Although these signals allowed our amphibious planning to continue in our own style, various parameters were laid down along with a number of key planning criteria and facts that would have to be solved before a landing could take place. I believe that this was the first time that we were formally given an aim, a vague one but nevertheless something on which we could base our planning. We were to: *Plan to land on the Falklands with a view to repossessing them.*

Jeremy Moore had joined Admiral Fieldhouse's team on 9 April noticeable by a change in emphasis in signals from Fleet Headquarters. Jeremy brought substantial experience and knowledge to bear on the planning team then being formed.

We began to be certain that, despite Sandy's interpretation of his orders to beat the Argentinians by blockade, all exchange of ideas then in being were, without doubt, the prelude to an amphibious landing. The Carrier Battle Group's ultimate task was to create the correct conditions for those landings.

By studying the problems faced by an occupying enemy we felt that we should gain valuable 'lessons learned' and so, to that end, Julian asked Ewen Tailyour to produce an estimate of how many men the islands could sustain and for how long. By the same figures we could also assess the enemy's living, hygiene, water and food conditions and so judge how severe his problems of morale and fighting efficiency would be if the blockade worked. While we were certainly expecting our own resupply problems over a logistic route of 8,000 miles, we felt that we should be able to seriously damage the Argentine links of just a few hundred miles. That we were to fail to halt a regular and, at times, intense C-130 pipe-line was not then in our calculations.

On Easter Saturday we were delighted to hear that *Intrepid* would follow, her presence being particularly valuable in the event that we would not be able to use *Hermes* as much as we would have liked in the LPH role. In this respect our fears were to be well-founded. We also received a reply from MOD UK (Navy) to a signal I had sent expressing a concern represented by some LSL Masters over the Chinese in, particularly, the LSL *Sir Lancelot*: 'There is no reason to doubt the integrity of the Chinese crews.'

Earlier on Easter Day (11 April) we received a signal from the Task Force Commander. It almost stopped Julian and me attending the church service where I marvelled at the padre's calm determination to continue despite the clattering and bangs from the ship's company galley next door which was working overtime with all the additional troops to feed. The signal read much as follows:

1. Overall task force directive still in course of production in MOD but understand tasks are likely to be listed in following priority order:

a. Enforce Falkland Island exclusion zone.
b. Establish sea and air superiority in Falkland Island exclusion zone as soon as possible.
c. Repossess South Georgia.
d. Repossess Falkland Islands.

2. Priority and urgency attached to b. will heavily influence d. which may now be later than planned heretofore. Hence

rethink is underway and assessments of practicable loiter policy
for amphibious group in hand.

3. Tasks b. and c. are viewed in similar time scale, as current
   intelligence indicates clear advantage in landing South Georgia
   earliest and cover for c. can be obtained from priority task b.
   forces operating on Argentine supply routes.

The thought of poising in the South Atlantic was fine for those in
London but not such a pleasing prospect for military
commanders south of Ascension. Poising may be a good political
pressure-inducing aspect of amphibious warfare, but it can take
its toll of fitness and motivation, not to say machinery and
equipment efficiency.

What we did not know then, but were about to be told by
CTF in Ascension, was that shortly after he had sent the above
signal he had received his Operational Directive from the Chiefs
of Staff. He was to tell us that there was apparently still a high
degree of caution and scepticism in the Ministry of Defence. In
particular the Army Staff remained unconvinced of the necessity
and likely success of an amphibious operation. He told us that he
had therefore been told that he might be required to repossess
the Falkland Islands but only when sea control was firmly
established and South Georgia recaptured. He would have to
wait for further instructions and so would we.

CTF knew that he had to plan to repossess the Falklands, even
if he, himself, had not yet been told to do so. The ambiguous
wording of the Directive made it difficult (possibly on purpose)
for him to argue successfully, at that stage, for troop reinforcements to assist in that repossession.

Easter Day was spent planning the re-stow requirements
(which were comprehensive) and improving the Amphibious
Group's counter-surveillance capability by such simple expedi-
ents as not ditching gash, imposing HF silence and introducing a
minimum use of other radio transmissions. Now that we were
getting south there was a need to sharpen everyone up on these
points. We heard from Captain Bob McQueen on Ascension:
the Amphibious re-stow would be hampered by the lack of a

69

suitable beach with only the north end of Clarence Bay being a possibility. The problems with all beaches, he said, were their steep gradients (usually a point in favour), the soft sand, heavy surf and breeding turtles.

By 2300 on Easter Day, 11 April, I had spent many hours with Julian looking at the possibilities of landing his Brigade in strength across a string of small beaches along the northern coastline of North Camp, East Falkland; possibly tying in with a small landing on the eastern sea-board of Salvador Waters. We wanted to have as many options as possible to present to CTF when we met him at Ascension, and this was just one of them. Ewen had produced a number of possible landing sites in this area but in the same breath warned us of the weather problems for each individual beach and, in particular, the percentage times that an onshore swell would make landing difficult if not impossible. These 'no-landing days' along the north-east coast were not numerous but certainly verged on the unacceptable for such a complicated operation and one which, once started, could not be allowed to stop. Apart from anything else the area was open to the sea flank and that meant submarine and Exocet threats.

Just before we reached Ascension Island the secure voice speech system (DSSS) was made ready in *Fearless* and reported by me to FOF 1 with a request that he should let me know the times when it would be suitable to have a discussion so that liaison at CTG level could begin. I also signalled that it would be a good idea if we could get our thoughts together on the meeting with the CTF but I never received a reply to either signal.

Among my other concerns at this time were measures of self-protection against magnetic or acoustic mines for the RFAs and merchant ships that would be supporting us inshore if it came to a landing. These fears were to be borne out by reports on 15 and 17 April from HMS *Spartan* that there had been considerable mine-laying activity off Port William and while this may have been a deception plan the Argentinians were known to possess a total of 200 ground mines and 80 buoyant mines. Mine-laying by submarine, Canberra or Hercules aircraft was, therefore a perfectly feasible military activity on their part, indeed I would have been very surprised, almost suspicious, had they not been doing so. CTF's staff took up my concern (expressed since 2 April) and studied the possibility of establishing a degaussing range off Ascension Island. The degaussing vessel, RMAS *Lodestone*, was considered necessary to run the range and to wipe ships, but by 20 April it had been decided, reluctantly, that the ship's poor sea-keeping qualities and the lack of a suitable area at Ascension ruled her out. However, FCDT I were able to join at Ascension on 13 April and were kept busy inspecting ships' underwater fittings until they embarked in RFA *Sir Tristram* on 21 April.

On 13 April CTF signalled the good news that four trawlers were being taken up from trade as minesweepers and, excellent news, that the *Atlantic Conveyor* was being studied as a 'fly on/fly off' aircraft ferry. More positive news was also received: the Carrier Battle Group would be required to sail south ahead of the Amphibious Group. This did not surprise me and was welcome. The sooner sea control could be established the better.

We were one day away from Ascension when Sandy landed on board *Fearless* during the forenoon of 16 April. I met him on the flight deck and we went straight to my cabin. There had been no warning of this visit, just a radio call saying that two helicopters were on their way and out he stepped with a few members of his staff. Julian and I had cleared our minds for CTF's arrival at Ascension the following day and were more than happy to have a chance to discuss with Sandy both the agenda and the options, as we saw them, that we both should propose to the Northwood team.

We were not, however, prepared for what was to take place. Although he was the senior, we had not expected Sandy to want to take the lead at this meeting in such a forceful and tactless way. We believed that we were the best people to discuss amphibious problems and expected him to want to hear our views. Instead he gave us a number of instructions which we considered to be complete red herrings. Unfortunately, since he was the senior, we would be obliged to waste our staff's time exploring them. Basically he had three ideas. The first was to use Carcass Island or possibly somewhere in the Byron Sound area such as Dunbar Island as a 'stone frigate' or stores dump from whence the Brigade would move out towards Stanley. Clearly he had no idea of the amount of equipment that would have to be landed, only to be moved forward once again over a very considerable distance.

We wanted to avoid landing on West Falkland in any form other than by raiding parties, diversionary operations, direct action tasks or intelligence-gathering patrols, most of which could be initiated without the enemy being aware of their existence. Anything more would waste time and energy, causing delays and an unnecessary thinning down of what few assets that we did have available for the main goal – Stanley. West Falkland was well within the radius of action of the Argentinian A4 aircraft.

The next idea was to construct an airstrip in the level and hard-bottomed valley that leads eastwards from Stevelly Bay in West Falkland. Ewen had always said it could, with not a little engineering work, take Hercules aircraft. The Admiral wanted to operate Phantom Air Defence Fighters during the opening stages of any assault but would not accept that the 3rd Commando Brigade (who would have other things on its mind anyway) did not have the plant, equipment, men or time. Stevelly Bay 'airfield' was again well within range of Argentinian mainland-based aircraft and would have taken months to prepare even if we had carried the right equipment, which we did not. It would have taken a great deal of defending during its construction (probably all the Rapier we possessed) and would have prevented further serious land operations.

Finally, Sandy instructed us to consider another and even more alarming idea he had. He said he was considering a 'feint' lasting two or three days using *Fearless*, *Fort Austin* and *Resource* as well as some LSLs. This required me to disembark some of my staff (and some of Julian's) to a destroyer, while *Fearless*'s group, acting as decoys, would close the Argentine coast in order to draw the Argentinian Air Force so that we could initiate an air battle. At the same time the two staffs would be closer to the Falklands coast in the destroyer 'making amphibious noises over the radio' simulating an assault. This raised two obvious concerns: one was the safety of *Fearless* herself – we only had one ship capable of commanding a landing – and the other was that both my and Julian's Task Group would be left leaderless.

All this was seen on board *Fearless* as an unnecessary attempt to dominate and it acutely embarrassed the naval members of my staff, while infuriating the Royal Marines and, more particularly, the Army members who were new to the Royal Navy and its quirks. Trust was broken and it would take a long time to repair.

Finally, we were told that the impending meeting would be informal and we were not to prepare set-piece briefs on any matter but be prepared to discuss his ideas and any CTF raised. We were to produce a shopping list which, in my case included over two thousand rounds of 4.5 Mk 6 (Variable Time (VT) and direct action (DA) fuses); at least two thousand rounds of 4.5 Mk 8; an ice-breaker if South Georgia was to be used by us and mine sweepers and hunters.

Just before we arrived at Ascension for Admiral Fieldhouse's *Hermes* meeting on 17 April it might be helpful to take stock of the British military position.

We had *Fearless* approaching Ascension Island along with *Hermes* and her retinue. In advance there were two SSNs in the Maritime Exclusion Zone with a third approaching South Georgia; the *Antrim* group of *Glamorgan*, *Plymouth* and *Arrow* were three days from South Georgia; the *Brilliant* group had sailed and was already well over one thousand miles south-south-west of Ascension Island; the LSLs, escorted by *Antelope*, were a few days north of Ascension steaming south at their best speed and the main landing force was off Ascension, apart from those members of the SBS, SAS and M Coy, 42 Commando, who had gone on ahead towards South Georgia. While we had no Initiating Directive, the military aim and my tasks had begun to clarify and be tabulated; the South Georgia operation just needed the final word and the plans for establishing the Total Exclusion Zone (TEZ) were well advanced. The 18th had been chosen as the first day we could land the SBS on the Islands by submarine, a landmark in itself and a decision we could make in isolation of any directive. Discussions covering an amphibious assault and subsequent repossession had started with outline plans being drawn up and filed while intelligence collection was now under way.

Without much firm direction from home, but with some ill-conceived ideas from our co-CTG, we in the amphibious flagship were getting on with it. We badly wanted to meet our Task Force Commander, the CinC Fleet.

CHAPTER TWO

PLANNING AND TRAINING

> It is good for us to studie in the time of peace how
> to defend ourselves in the time of warres and
> troubles; as generally we provide in harvest for to
> live in winter.
>
> William Bourne d. 1583
> The Arte of Shooteing in Great Ordnance 1578

ASCENSION ISLAND IS the tip of a seamount at the northern end of the Mid-Atlantic Ridge, rising from the sea bed to 2818 feet above sea level. Barren and rocky, with little vegetation, it lies close to the divide between the doldrums and the south-east trades. The highest peak, Green Mountain, is aptly named for it is on its higher slopes that the only plants are found in any profusion. This elongated cone is the extinct remains of a comparatively young volcano and there are traces of another thirty-nine smaller eruptions. The whole island covers no more than thirty-four square miles with about 1,100 inhabitants centred around Georgetown, off which we were to anchor. The Island is richer in fauna than flora, at least at the lower levels, although a number of animals had been introduced artificially for obvious reasons. Rabbits, wild goats and partridges formed a staple diet in earlier days. The Green Turtle lands between December and May to lay its eggs and there are large sooty-tern breeding colonies.

The Island is a British Dependency with no indigenous population. Its greatest asset is the 10,000 foot runway operated by Pan American Airways and from the earliest days of *Operation Corporate* it was clear that this would become an overworked facility. Already advance parties of men and stores had begun to swamp the meagre accommodation which is why the British Forces Support Unit was one of the first temporary organizations to be formed (on 6 April), under the command of the redoubtable Captain Bob McQueen, Royal Navy. He was to become ruthless in returning men he considered unnecessary, mostly from the Royal Air Force. Without Ascension Island there would have been no *Operation Corporate* and without Bob it is likely that the Island would have ground to a standstill under the weight of superfluous administrators. While they might have been helpful there simply was not enough room for everyone that the various commands at home thought should be involved. If well-intentioned, his enthusiasm for keeping numbers down in his command could, too, be counter-productive to the overall aim. For instance he sent back an ordnance specialist team asked for by Julian to identify and sort out the different 'army' and 'marine' stores arriving on the island. As a result stores were sent onwards to the wrong ships causing minor but significant chaos until Julian despatched some of his own specialists, men who had other tasks to perform within the brigade.

The far more important meeting with the Task Force Commander was scheduled for the morrow which Sandy had assured me would be an unstructured chat for which I was not to prepare anything other than notes on his South Atlantic Argentine Coast Adventure and West Falklands ideas. Julian, Jeremy Larken and I and a small number of our staffs flew across to the *Hermes*. Sandy welcomed us but as he showed us in he asked Julian to sit with him using the phrase, 'as you are my soldier'. While obviously a politeness, this must have confirmed in Julian's mind his suspicions of a change of command structure as he turned to me and said, 'Don't leave me, Mike. I am your soldier and you're my sailor. Stick with me.' We then sat together for the rest of the meeting and shared our thoughts. I have included this apparently trivial conversation since it shows the importance of the relationship and trust that has to be built up between the Landing Force and the Amphibious Task Force Commanders and which must be seen to exist by the forces under their command. It is more difficult for staff officers to squabble if they see their bosses working well together and this will filter down to the lowest ranks, inevitably with enormous benefits.

In the wardroom for the 'Fleet Brief', CTF, flanked by his air and land deputies, and attended by Captain Jeremy Reed and other staff officers, sat along the outboard side of the large room from where he began by explaining that the country was wholly behind us, as was by far the largest portion of world opinion. With that reassurance firmly established he tabulated his overall plan under five headings which I noted at the time as being:

'1. Set up an exclusion zone as soon as possible. There are two SSNs on station and *Conqueror* will be there in three days.
2=. To establish sea and air control as soon as possible. 29th April.
2=. To repossess South Georgia as soon as possible.
4. Plan to land with a view to repossessing (the Falklands).'

I took the fourth aim to mean that it had to be East Falkland and it had to be as close to Stanley as we could possibly get but that we might have to sit tight for a long time while the politicians deliberated. The place we chose would have to be outside easy range of their guns and counter-attacks. Our view was that we would have to stand back and dig in. We would need to look for a secure area where this could be achieved.

A final task was to get as far south as swiftly as possible with a significant group: I sidelined this note heavily as it was the one that worried me most. It was also the reason why I was to accept reluctantly that the LSLs (in particular) should go on ahead when the time came to move.

This swift move south with a significant force indicated to me that CTF was thinking of deterrence: an amphibious group in the South Atlantic early (reported by an Argentine aircraft or submarine) might make the enemy think that a landing would take place sooner than expected. What neither CTF, Julian nor I realized at that moment was just how poorly the ships had been loaded and what time would be needed to unscramble that problem.

Admiral Fieldhouse saw the window for landing between 7 and 21 May but made the point that, in his opinion, we did not yet have enough land forces. Another brigade, he added, was really outside the time-scale for an initial landing and therefore the 2nd Battalion the Parachute Regiment would be embarking in SS *Norland* (Captain Don Ellerby) and that, he said, was the best he could do. He announced that *Intrepid* was being brought forward as quickly as possible for operations but would not be with us for some weeks. Added snippets included the United States attitude which he described as being 'awkward'. We should therefore, he suggested, be careful when transmitting while US intelligence satellites passed overhead and certainly not when a Soviet one was. Chile's attitude was 'cooling' as the result of the cancellation of RFA *Tidepool*'s sale to them and would continue to cool until 'they see the Argentines losing'. Meanwhile, the Peruvians wanted an excuse to have a go at Chile; the split army/civilian Bolivian government was believed to be supplying the Argentines with aircraft while Brazil and the Uruguayans were sitting on their fences.

His staff were sure that the Bolivians had given C-130s to the Argentines and there was no sign of any extension to the Stanley runway (we knew that this would not have been possible in such a short time). The suggestion was made that the SAS might be used to stop any such extension and, in that context, CTF mentioned the possible use of Vulcan bombers.

CTF went on to outline the command structure and reassured us that while there had been efforts back at home to replace the commanders at sea, he had managed to resist attempts by other senior officers and the politicians to get their own men in place. The basis he used was that we were the three in command of the ships and forces at the time. Julian and I were relieved at this and were grateful we had a CTF who appeared to be backing us.

Many of the points raised by CTF had been aired in the MOD's Amphibious Operations Appreciation that had been ordered by the Chiefs of Staff on 8 April, sent to us around Easter and which CTF now wished to dissect. Among many other points the Appreciation made was its opinion that the Task Force should be able to establish sea control and a reasonable degree of air superiority over the Islands.

It acknowledged that the Landing Force might not in itself necessarily achieve the political aim, which, we now learned, was to re-establish the presence of British armed forces on the Falkland Islands and provide the means to effect military pressure on the Argentine force to surrender. The paper also commented that operations subsequent to a landing may have to be confined to attacks on selected Argentine positions and possibly to special force operations. Clearly a direct assault on the main Argentine positions could not be conducted without risk to civilians. This ambiguity was to influence our planning in later days.

However, the paper also made the assumptions we hoped would eventually prevail. No landings would take place until an effective sea and air exclusion zone had been established around the Falklands with the aim of landing a force ashore in the Falklands with a view to repossessing the Islands. This was interesting, even at this early stage, although it was to take on greater significance once we were ashore for we were never to be told to continue with the second part of the appreciation, that of actually taking possession of the Islands. Privately, Julian and I were to plan for operations beyond the beaches.

We were led to believe that this limited aim was the result of a reluctance by the Army and Royal Air Force members of the Chiefs of Staff committee to commit themselves to a battle they did not believe could be won convincingly. Also unknown to us in *Fearless* until this time was the fact that CTF considered the Chiefs' of Staff aim as an unrealistic compromise and that his aim (our aim) should include the instruction to break out of the confines of a beachhead as soon as we, on the ground, thought fit.

In the Amphibious Task Group we were now aware that the Amphibious Operations Appreciation did not go beyond establishing a beachhead from which we could (on orders) move towards the wider goal of total repossession. However, we believed we should plan to do so, as that, after all, is what CTF wanted us to do. To do so, Julian, on whom the initial and scene-setting military operations would depend, realized that while his own enlarged Brigade could affect a successful landing and foothold, it was probably not large enough to advance the whole way to Stanley with the certainty of swift success. But we were certainly not planning that he should sit on the beach once ashore and secure.

Neither did we intend planning for an opposed assault. That is not our way of doing things and is not usually the more successful unless massive overkill (including civilians) is intended or acceptable. Politically and militarily this was significant because it would be a very strong diplomatic bargaining point; a landing without bloodshed followed by a firm base on the Islands. It would be a strong lever against the Junta with British troops on the Falklands but with no lives lost. From our point of view it was better to plan to beat the enemy from a firm position ashore with full available logistic support rather than straight from the sea with all the problems attendant upon such an approach to battle. Military nooses are more easy to draw tight from positions of strength on land than from a few miles offshore, although, paradoxically, a strong force offshore can be a very large arrow in the diplomatic quiver with its flexible response and ability to change its objectives without an enemy knowing or being able to react in time.

As early as 11 April Admiral Fieldhouse had, he told us, been suggesting to the MOD that an extra Brigade would be necessary for any assault against Stanley. This requirement was borne out by the assessments of enemy strengths on 14 April by which time the number of Argentinians on the Islands had increased to 7,000 men and was believed to be on its way to upwards of 10,000. On that day, therefore, at a meeting between CinC Fleet and CinC United Kingdom Land Forces it was agreed that an extra brigade should be stood-by on the understanding that MOD would eventually give its approval. 5 Infantry Brigade was the chosen formation and the *QE2* the chosen form of transport. In fact she had been studied as a possible candidate as early as 5 April. She could be ready to sail on 3 May.

Julian's Commando Brigade consisted of about 4,600 men which was clearly not enough. CTF had already concluded that the numbers were too low just for a landing so the 'War Cabinet' was asked to approve the deployment of the 2nd Battalion the Parachute Regiment together with various additional supporting arms. This was agreed on 16 April and, while it was accepted that this was only a start the allocation of a totally new Brigade (already asked for by Jeremy Moore on the 11th) was not postponed. In fact (and without reference to Ministers) that Brigade was ordered to begin training by CinC UK Land Forces (not a member of the Chiefs of Staff Committee) and prepare for embarkation – sometime.

At this stage the talk was still to 'land with a view to repossessing the Islands'. Thus there was, perhaps, a natural inclination to delay any further troop mobilization in the hope that the political pressure, backed up by the swift and determined sailing of the Amphibious Task Force in a remarkable blaze of officially orchestrated publicity, would be enough. It was also understandable that further aggressive declarations of increased troop allocations might be thought to signal to the Argentinians and, perhaps more importantly, to the United Nations, that Britain was set on war and not negotiation. The uncomfortable feeling that filtered down to us at sea was that neither the Army nor the Royal Air Force were in favour of greater involvement as they believed that any conflict would be unwinnable and did not accept the Royal Navy's convictions. It was also even rumoured that they saw the operation as a put-up job to enhance amphibious warfare.

Not only does it appear that there was not much support for reinforcing the Landing Force beyond this second Parachute Battalion but it now seemed to us that there was further disagreement over the tasks for the force and thus, probably, its composition. On 12 April it had been reported to us that any planning criteria should be based on the following assumptions:

> The operations would last six months. The duration of the land battle should be not more than 30 days but logistics would be required for an occupation force of up to six months. Strengths of units, weapons and logistic support within the NATO area should be restored to declared levels as soon as possible.

We were also told that no orders would be given for a break-out from the beachhead until after the arrival of a second brigade for which CTF was arguing strongly but which, as we now know, was the subject of much procrastination. This suggested that no move from a beachhead would be ordered, other than patrolling and raiding, until that second brigade (if it was to materialize) was in situ: certainly the expression *'Plan to land on the Falkland Islands with a view to repossession'* indicated this. And if it didn't turn up ... ?

As we listened aboard HMS *Hermes* the North Sea ferry MV *Norland* was being requisitioned in Hull with a party from the Royal Navy and 2 Para on their way to join her. She would be fitted with landing spots for two Sea Kings and equipment for replenishing at sea, and would sail at midday on 26 April with 840 paratroopers embarked. The next day the *Europic Ferry* (Captain C.J. Clark) was also to be taken up from trade to carry the Battalion's heavy equipment and vehicles. She would sail on the 28th.

Julian and I were given little opportunity to speak, but when we did so we reiterated our need for *Intrepid* and more helicopters, all along stressing the necessity of air superiority, but I was left with the firm impression that these requests were politically unacceptable and that we were, perhaps, not senior enough in the chain to make such fundamental requests nor for those requests to warrant much attention. This was the country's most serious military 'international' crisis for many years and a critical part of it was about to be prosecuted by two rather junior officers, a fact that probably rankled with some back home. We had the feeling that we would just be told to get on with it with the tools that only they felt were necessary.

I could not help noticing that my Admiral, Derek Reffell, was not present, as he would, hopefully, have lent weight to my needs. His absence also suggested that he would not be in the command chain. I was to learn after the victory that he had in fact been refused access to Northwood where he had tried to offer his amphibious experience as he could see that things were not moving along the lines of normal practice and had wanted to lend Julian and me his support.

We argued our case for staying at Ascension Island to complete training and re-stowing stating all the while that we were anxious not to sail until the enhanced Commando Brigade was together. We were not keen to embark for the uncertainties of the southern ocean until ready in all respects for war.

For some this appears to have been seen as pussyfooting, but to us, who would have to carry out the operation, these preparations were vital. As though to emphasize our perceived position in the command chain, I found it extremely difficult to have an interview with CTF. I did finally manage it in the presence of Jeremy Reed (the Fleet Warfare Officer) when I asked for clarification of the command structure. CTF assured me that I was not and would not be operating under Sandy and that we would be totally separate when the amphibious phase came. Sandy would be required to support the Amphibious Task Force and react to its needs: all would be carried out in accordance with ATP8 and that was good enough for me.

Landing with our numerical inferiority would only be feasible if we were loaded correctly, chose the beaches carefully based on good intelligence and possessed air superiority. Any 'advance to combat' against a forecast, even at that time, of over 10,000 troops would require a firm logistic base ashore and a doubling (at the very least) of our own numbers. Three to one is the accepted norm for an attacking force but Julian's men, as they then stood, would be outnumbered by the same ratio. With a second brigade we would be closer to matching the required numbers if not actually having the advantage. Number-matching, though, can lead to false pictures for so many men are not combat troops and we suspected, in this case, that those who were were largely conscripts of doubtful quality. This should not be seen as over-optimism on our part but I knew that Julian's enlarged Commando Brigade contained 'the best'. Although outnumbered (but with the support they hoped they would have 'on call' by the time they were ready to move out of the beachhead) they should, in his own words, 'Hack it!' and hack it all the way to Stanley if required.

But we still had the present to contend with and as far as Julian and I were concerned we were at Ascension Island for six reasons, all of which we put to our CTF:

1. For training and field firing coupled with the testing of weapons and procedures including Forward Air Controlling and Naval Gunfire Support (FAC and NGS).
2. To allow time for the air battle to be won and the naval blockade to take effect.
3. To await the arrival of the remainder of the Commando Brigade in the ships that had to be resurrected from deep refit or from civilian trade.
4. To allow time for the collection of intelligence.
5. With nowhere else to go *en route* we had to wait until conditions were right for us to go direct to an assault. We could not poise in the South Atlantic with winter approaching. This was, of course, a function of the third point above.
6. For re-stowing from a 'northern flank stow' into an assault posture to fit the conditions facing us, still largely unknown, and the understandable result of our equally understandable dash from mainland Britain.

As far as the future beyond Ascension was concerned we favoured a careful and measured approach to the Amphibious Objective Area; we did not want to poise at sea; we did not want to assault straight into Stanley; we liked San Carlos and we also liked the Cow Bay/Volunteer Bay option as a possible alternative; we wanted to use *Hermes* in the LPH role; we needed intelligence as soon as possible but were prepared to wait for it and we had to sail straight to the beaches with no loitering at sea in the Austral autumn's bad weather. We would have liked the time and the place for rehearsals and in this respect argued, without success, that our two staffs should plan and conduct the South Georgia landings. Jeremy Moore told us firmly that CTF had decided that this would be 'done separately' and that we were to 'keep out and shut up!'

Forgetting the South Georgia plan, there was no doubt in my mind as CATF nor Julian's as CLF that we had to practise a number of skills at the highest level and not just at 'manoeuvre unit' level. We needed to rehearse the full landing procedure in the dark, in the correct formations and with the strengths, timings and distances as close to the real thing as possible. Julian and I knew that this would be difficult for a number of reasons: we did not know yet, and were probably not likely to know until after we had sailed, the exact place we would land for that was a function of intelligence and the eventual availability of *Hermes* as an LPH. Rehearsals should also take place as close to the actual time of the main landing as possible. Although South Georgia might have appeared suitable to the warriors at home for such practical drills, there were a number of significant reasons why it was a 'non-starter', the main one probably being that the final objective was 'up weather' to the west by some eight hundred miles and in the depths of the South Atlantic this has to be a vital consideration when operating very 'weather-sensitive' ships such as LSLs.

When we sailed from Ascension it had to be straight into battle. Therefore from our point of view it was best that we stayed as long as possible at Ascension to extract the maximum value from the facilities available ... and they were very limited indeed. That is not to say that we could have done without the Island as our 'launch pad' for it was to be a major 'war winner', but as an amphibious training and rehearsal area it had distinct short-comings: the wrong climate; no suitable beaches; no suitable landing sites. But there was nowhere else.

All the while the 'aim' of the future operation was still under intense discussion. It was not to be until well after the end of the war that we realized fully just how the aim of the landings had been arrived at, but that will come shortly. While we knew at the time that there was considerable indecision the full saga was, probably fortuitously, kept from us, for we had enough doubts ourselves about what was actually required of us without knowing the full extent of the political and military confusion back home.

By the day of the *Hermes* briefings 5 Infantry Brigade had been alerted by CinC UK Land Forces but not yet confirmed by the MOD nor, of course, ordered south. Our own CTF told us that he would continue pressing for their inclusion but that the initial landings would, by necessity of timings, be conducted without them. The Chiefs of Staff, he said, were happy that five battalions could seize and hold a beachhead, unopposed, and that was all that was required – at that moment.

This decision not to send the second brigade seemed to ignore the time gap that could exist between gaining the foothold and advancing on Stanley. Would we, having proved successful, have to wait for the second brigade to embark and steam for at least three weeks before joining us? Were they to help in the attack on Stanley in which case would we have to wait for them or were they to be a garrison allowing us to advance as soon as we were ready, possibly before their arrival?

When the choice of a second brigade was announced we learned that it was to be an *ad hoc* reconstruction of 5 Infantry Brigade, two of whose three battalions were (or were about to be) under Julian's command. These would now be replaced by the 2nd Battalion the Scots and 1st Battalion the Welsh Guards. We had expected the second brigade to be well trained, fully formed and co-ordinated with battalions and headquarters that had worked together for a considerable time on near-operational duties in BAOR. As it was to be, the team that joined us had not worked together apart from a hastily conceived exercise in the Welsh Mountains where command and control had not been the strong points; an added deficiency being the lack of its own logistic regiment. None of this was the fault of 5 Infantry Brigade as the Ministry of Defence were responsible for the allocation of 'force multipliers'.

Knowing, in 1994, how the decision to approve 5 Brigade's involvement was agreed allowed Julian Thompson to write:

'This (was) interesting because the indecision and prevarication on the part of CGS and CAS was to have an effect on 5th Infantry Brigade's logistic support and appeared to sow doubts in some peoples' minds on its role (on arrival). The 3rd Commando Brigade Logistic Regiment was established and equipped to support a Brigade of around 3,000+, and having supported a Brigade of around 5,000+ for the first ten days found itself having to service a light division of 8,000+ ... there was plenty of time before 5th Infantry Brigade sailed to have made up the deficiencies in their logistic support.'

Further factors emerged from this exploratory briefing with Admiral Fieldhouse. Sandy was to sail his Carrier Battle Group the next day with the aim of establishing the Maritime Exclusion Zone as early as 29 April. (The reason for the swift sailing of the Carrier Battle Group was understood but unfortunately it occurred without consultation with all those who had an interest and so the ships took with them much special military equipment that needed many longer and longer Sea King helicopter sorties to recover to the Island from the ships as they steamed south. A prime example of a single-service requirement taking precedence in a joint operation. A wait of two hours or so would have made the trans-shipment, mostly of SAS equipment, easy. Army tempers would have been eased. Was history repeating itself so soon?

Timings were a vital consideration. The gathering of intelligence was estimated to need at least fifteen days starting from 16 May. One assessment had the carriers being able to operate at intensive rates for six weeks and with the assumption that the land operations would last three weeks (an accurate prognosis as it was to turn out), this all suggested that the first date for a landing would be 23 May. If that was to be the case there might be time for HMS *Intrepid* and 2 Para in *Norland* to join us for a modicum of Ascension Island training before the Amphibious Task Group sailed for the journey south. Apart from the usefulness of remaining at Ascension Island for the reasons already stated, this latest estimate would allow Sandy's group to fight any sea and air battle without the added complication of having to defend a loitering force of merchant ships and comparatively slow and unwieldy amphibians.

It was also announced by CTF that South Georgia would not be used for poising or rehearsing, a decision that came as no great surprise to myself and Julian: it was not yet in our hands anyway. The decision that did concern us, though, was that neither HMS *Hermes* nor *Invincible* could be used in the assault role even for the first and vital wave of helicopter-borne marines, taking, for example, high ground or relevant objectives inland to keep any enemy at arm's length while the main landings proceeded. This would have been a normal and tactically sensible way to start any such affair: bad news that initiated a major tactical re-think.

Good news came with the statement by CTF that the three CTGs were now to plan their respective parts in the battle, thus further emphasizing our separate and equal commands: Sandy the maritime and air exclusion zones and support of any landings, and Julian and myself the amphibious operations: *per mare* and then *per terram*. I was asked personally by CTF to forward three landing options direct to him for approval, the implication being that he would not amend them and would accept my timings. This made it clear that we, in *Fearless*, would have the final say in the landing plans. In this the division of responsibilities was sharply defined although, naturally, no decisions could or would be taken in isolation of Sandy with his ships and aircraft, for his and their operating parameters were significant factors in our amphibious decision-making. During the discussions on the 17th the various choices for landing sites were aired for the first time face to face, we now having to alter our plans quickly to reflect that it would probably have to be an 'all landing craft' operation without *Hermes*. A 'North Camp option' was included, but eyes turned, frequently, to San Carlos:

the Cow Bay/Volunteer Bay area remained a strong contender depending on Argentine troop and artillery dispositions and whether or not the Junta would be prepared to concede victory after a token, face-saving battle.

There was further good news in that Sandy's three ideas, floated during his visit, were never discussed.

As San Carlos was surrounded on all sides by high ground above suitable beaches and a sheltered anchorage beyond Exocet threat it occupied more and more of my thoughts. I was, however, certainly very conscious that it was a long way from Stanley, but it also seemed somewhere close to the maximum radius of action of an A4 aircraft with a heavy payload.

Before he flew home the Commander-in-Chief dined with his senior commanders. I found it an uneasy affair, for I sat with men who seemed to think the whole thing was going to be terribly easy, while Julian's comments about 'big hands on little maps, that's the way to kill the chaps' rang in my ears. There was, for me, rather too much bonhomie and too little hard thinking and attentive listening to the comparatively junior officers on whom they would be relying for success.

During the evening Jeremy Larken left two of our latest 'appreciations' with Jeremy Reed and in return was promised 'similar appreciations' from the Maritime Tactical School. It would be interesting to see if we were on the same lines.

The CTF and his staff flew home and we were left to get on with planning but, and it was a significant but, no plan to secure a beachhead could be drawn up without knowing whether or not we would be required to advance on Stanley with or without the 'still-mythical' second brigade. It was disappointing that the CTF had not had time to visit my flagship *Fearless* and see the major changes we had made. In particular, the creation of our joint planning room. If he had done so, I like to believe that he would have been much reassured. Neither Julian nor I felt that we had had a totally fair hearing in *Hermes*.

In the mail I received a rather sad letter from Mike Dickens saying that he had attended Northwood but had been told he was not required and had therefore been sent back to our offices at the Royal Marine Barracks Stonehouse. The rest of the letter was full of future proposals for NATO exercises which he was monitoring.

Other problems emerged, as warned by Jeremy Moore. On 20 April General Haig telegraphed the British Government to say that in his view, 'It is imperative that you maintain military pressure. I see no other way of bringing the Argentines to a position satisfactory to you.' The knock-on effect to us in Ascension Island was that we were ordered on 22 April to sail immediately as a further demonstration of resolve. All training and re-stowing was to stop and we were to head southwards immediately to satisfy this latest diplomatic and ministerial idea, but this was clearly odd. We had met the initial 'political resolve' with outstanding success and we had met it on the strict understanding that we would not move further than Ascension until we had unscrambled the politically-induced chaos of loading, and certainly not until we, and the Carrier Battle Group, were ready in all respects for an amphibious assault.

I signalled Northwood explaining that any premature sailing would cause confusion, even disorder, and leave us worse off than if we had not stopped at all. However, I was obliged to halt all training and bring my Amphibious Task Group to four hours' notice to sail and eight hours' notice for full power. I also explained that it would take twenty-six hours from the time of any order to sail to ensure all essential stores were back on board, and that assumed no Mexeflote, landing craft nor helicopter breakdowns. I emphasized to London the specific penalties we would face if we sailed:

1. The restow would be only one-third complete and our assault capability would be worse than before because the restow would be even further out of balance.
2. The first line ammo would be wrongly sited.
3. The armament modification programme on Brigade Air Squadron aircraft would be only half completed.
4. The 105mm guns would not be calibrated and thus their efficiency would be impaired.

5. The CVRT (light tanks) would not be bore-sighted.
6. The Bofors would not be fitted in the LSLs.
7. The Mexeflotes would have to be left behind or sideslung on the LSLs as the only solution in the time available. This last choice would be unacceptable on seamanship grounds.
8. Essential assault drills for RM, Para and Blues and Royals and training in procedures in unfamiliar shipping (STUFT), craft and aircraft had only just started.
9. Vital small arms shooting was not yet accomplished and it was unlikely that conditions would allow satisfactory completion of this at sea.
10. We still awaited augmentees, Blowpipe and machine guns.
11. *Stromness* awaited 250 lbs of stores.
12. Luboil – 13000 gallons engine oil was needed to top up LSLs and *Stromness*; the average daily consumption was 400 gallons. Total holdings were 27000 gallons unevenly distributed. *Antelope* required 315 gallons OM33 and 259 litres OX38.

The signal ended with an estimate that at least five more days were needed to complete our tasks at Ascension Island. We waited anxiously for a reply and by 1400 were relieved to be told that the pressure to sail was off.

Although we did not sail early a by-product of the initial urgency to do so was the cancelling of the Rapier firing, for which gunnery instructors had been flown out. The consequences of this were to be felt during the first few days at San Carlos, as were the lack of the planned Naval Gunfire Support and Forward Air Control training.

The subjects of aircraft and anti-airfield operations were raised at a meeting on 23 April with the possibility of Vulcan bomber raids against Stanley being discussed. It had been considered earlier that the runway might have been lengthened to operate Mirages and Super Etendards but that was eventually dismissed as unlikely. Certainly Ewen Tailyour, when asked if this was possible, believed that it would be highly improbable in so short a time. Either way the thought of neutralizing Stanley Airport was an attractive one and one that could be attempted well in advance of the arrival of the Task Force.

Also that day a paper (the contents of which were later passed on to me) was considered by Ministers on the Strategic Options open to them. These ranged, as we might have expected, across the spectrum, focusing the Ministry staffs' collective minds on the requirement for a land battle to be part of the initial aim. As a direct result it was agreed that our aim was now to be more than that of just planning a landing to establish a British presence ashore because it would not achieve the aim of repossessing the Islands and it would lead to a military stalemate which would be the worst military outcome. A broader aim would allow us to plan the landings with a view to moving out swiftly if conditions were right. This was a significant change. It was what Julian and I were planning anyway and so we were much encouraged. The paper was then expanded to include the widest possible range of choices open to us starting with that of direct action on the Argentine mainland and moving down the scale. It was to be updated throughout the war, but we could no longer follow their thinking once we had sailed from Ascension.

On 23 April the Prime Minister visited Northwood for the first time, where, among numerous topics, Rules of Engagement were discussed. At that time there were a variety of 'Rules' in force relevant to individual ships or groups depending on their position: most insisted on the 'maintenance of the status quo', the 'avoidance' of provocation and a preparation to 'meet force with force' if necessary. Attacks on men and shipping were now allowed for those involved in *Operation Paraquet*, while the Carrier Battle Group on its way (but still north of 35°S) had no change from earlier instructions. Authority was being sought to deal urgently with the shadowing Argentine Boeing 707. The nuclear submarines had already been authorized to sink enemy shipping within the TEZ and only submarines outside it, but clearly these all needed constant review.

Changes in the Rules of Engagement were frequently asked for but with few satisfactory results. While these did not yet affect us fully at anchor off Ascension Island we were aware of the difficulties; so was CTF who sent a signal apologizing for the prevarication. It went much as this:

> I am very conscious that those of you who have been subject to rapid changes of orders or threat of such and suffered under inadequate ROE will be wondering how long this can go on. Mrs Thatcher was with us at Northwood yesterday and I am now confident that she well understands the impossibility of this situation continuing, and will put it right as soon as the politico-diplomatic position allows. UK must be seen to have made every attempt to secure peaceful solution, and only when all sensible avenues exhausted, and shown to be so, can the doves be satisfied and military initiative exercised.
>
> This coming week will I think be a watershed.

While all this was happening South Georgia was eventually retaken on the 25th, quite excellent news of course, bearing in mind the difficulties experienced at the outset of the operation with the insertion and recovery of the SAS and SBS; the SAS not helping by insisting, against experienced advice, on landing on a glacier. The expected weakening of Argentinian resolve, though, turned into a greater determination to defend the Falklands themselves, and that was bad news. My elation was tempered by the loss of a number of my precious Wessex 5 helicopters due to bad military planning. The conduct of the whole expedition (especially the use of my assets on an operation over which I had no control) emphasized to me that I should have been in command of what was a side-event. If we had gone down in greater numbers, it seemed to me at the time, the Argentines would have capitulated without us having to lose aircraft. Julian and I still felt that South Georgia was off the line of march and with our limited resources it made little military sense to risk assets for a political gain. That is of course a military view but I wondered how strongly it had been put. It was the first time (and not the last) that people were prepared, without consultation, to use my short-supply assets.

On 26 April I received the 'Outline Plan' for *Operation Sutton* (the actual landings on the Falklands) whose aim I was now told was: To land a force in the Falkland Islands with a view to repossessing the Islands.

Various tactical considerations were taken into account in this outline plan based on a firm assumption that any landing would be conducted on East Falkland. In the Options Paragraph San Carlos headed the list (we expected it to) followed by Port Salvador (not my second choice) then Port Stanley (only to be written out of the list later on), Goose Green, Egg Harbour and Port Sussex. The factors for and against each were résumés of all that we had passed back to Northwood and so came as no surprise.

Although only an outline plan, and advisory as far as we were concerned, the Execution Paragraph was of interest:

> A strong and sustainable British presence ashore will be achieved by landing 3 Cdo Bde RM augmented by two Parachute Battalion groups (about 5500 men) on or about the 16 May. The force will establish a bridgehead close enough to exert direct military and psychological pressure against the main Argentine force in the Port Stanley area. This may be enough to convince the Argentines that their own position is militarily untenable and that they can honourably agree to withdraw but the possibility that the enemy may advance for a decisive battle must be allowed for in selecting the position for the bridgehead.

The idea of exerting direct pressure against Argentine forces in the Port Stanley area certainly did not accord with our understanding that San Carlos would be a satisfactory spot. This raised the spectre of Berkeley Sound and the northern beaches which I had personally discounted because of the danger of swell and freedom for the enemy for air and submarine attack. Parts of the Command and Control Paragraph also bear repeating:

> 'Operational Command of TF 317 is retained by CINCFLEET. Operational Control of TF 317.8 is delegated to FOF 1 as the Commander Combined Task Force.'

It was this last puzzling phrase 'Commander Combined Task Force' that did not accord with the latest signal, nor with what I had been told personally by CTF who, by his title, had to be that man.

> 'Operational Control of the Amphibious Task Unit [now, quite suddenly we were a Task Unit again?] may be delegated to COMAW as Commander of the Amphibious Task Force (CATF). Comd 3 Cdo Bde is nominated as the Commander of the Landing Force (CLF). Subject to the overall authority of COMAW, responsibility for the conduct of operations ashore is vested in Comd 3 Cdo Bde. When the Landing Force is established ashore the Tactical Control of the Landing Force will be delegated to Comd 3 Cdo Bde RM as Commander Landing Force.'

While someone had clearly looked up ATP8 and had correctly expressed the relationship between CATF and CLF, this was still a little confusing. It implied that the task organization was to be changed back to the original one under which we sailed in which Julian and I were Task Units operating under Sandy as a Task Group Commander, but it was worrying. This was not what the CTF had told me at the meeting and nor did it accord with the present command structure where we three were co-equal CTGs. Other aspects such as the overall authority for the Amphibious Task Force followed normal procedures and obviously I would not wish to get involved in the conduct of operations ashore unless they involved my helicopter and landing craft assets or affected adversely any continuing off-load. Thankfully, it was an outline plan and not an order from the Task Force Commander.

On the 27th Sandy, the Commander of the Carrier Battle Group, received a simple directive from the CTF setting his immediate planning priority of preventing enemy operations in the TEZ. To execute this aim CTF told Sandy that the Government required him to:

1. Cut off the supply of the Garrison.
2. Discredit the Argentinian claim to sovereignty.
3. Provoke Argentine naval and air forces into action.

4. Provide effective local sea and air control for the main landing.

Sandy was also required, by Julian and me, to direct Advance Force Operations ashore and here we have the case of the Commander Carrier Battle Group acting on behalf of the Commander Amphibious Task Group who was acting in conjunction with the Commander Land Forces in the positioning of special forces. The SAS were given tasks principally involved in the long-term military operation by Julian, while the SBS were given tasks directly concerning potential amphibious operations by me. The SBS, therefore, were to cover such areas as San Carlos and the North Camp beaches while the SAS were to watch Stanley, Fox Bay, Port Howard and, particularly for me, the northern approaches to Falkland Sound.

CTF had instructed Julian and me to prepare just three candidates for the main landings and in this we were helped by Ewen Tailyour with his intimate knowledge of the beaches and sea approaches. His real value was to eliminate those areas that might have looked good on the charts but that he knew were not. While we studied likely areas, back in the United Kingdom plans were being made for the use of Vulcans to bomb Stanley Airport, Canberras to photograph likely enemy installations and Hercules to parachute special forces.

In practice the photo-reconnaissance flights could not take place, for there was, understandably, no permission from Chile to use its air bases for such operations. As for the Vulcan raids these had been ready from the 26th but delayed, equally understandably, while there was still a chance that the latest 'Haig Proposals' would be considered by the Junta. Such considerations did not materialize to the Government's satisfaction and so approval was given for the first attack during the night of 30 April/1 May, the same time that the Carrier Battle Group was due to arrive on the edge of the TEZ to begin enforcement.

Nor could the insertion by parachute of Special Forces take place as the in-flight refuelling equipment for the Hercules would not be ready until 8 May. Sandy, with our approval, made arrangements for the insertion of these forces by helicopter to take place from the night of 1/2 May onwards. Permission for 'direct action' (rather than intelligence gathering) would not come from the 'War Cabinet' until later, and then only for specific operations. Insertions of SBS patrols by conventional submarine (a well-practised and vital adjunct to amphibious operations) were not possible, for although we had asked for one from the beginning no such boat appeared until too late.

From the Amphibious Forces' point of view the lack of ground troops to reinforce Julian's Brigade after a landing and before a breakout was causing concern in some quarters. We felt able to cope with establishing a foothold or beachhead from which repossession could take place but that total repossession was unlikely to occur, with certainty, without an extra Brigade. We presumed that if they were to join us they would do so to act as garrison and be available as battle casualty replacements, if not actually to fight.

While these decisions and thoughts were being made and promulgated, we in HMS *Fearless* continued studying the various options for an Amphibious Objective Area that had been thrown up by the requirement to land 'with a view to repossession'. From an initial list of about nineteen AOAs that might have held suitable beaches we had whittled it down to our short list of three. We had not considered any landings on West Falkland nor had we considered further the possibility of landing anywhere on Lafonia. West Falkland had been dismissed because it would have meant a second landing across the Sound and we did not believe, anyway, that it would have put any real pressure on the Junta.

In the beginning, when we had assumed we would land using helicopters the North Camp beaches, in a line along the north coast east of Salvador and west of Macbride Head, had occupied our thoughts as a serious option and had met with early approval. However, since that long day in *Hermes* Julian had summoned Ewen to 'brainstorm' the San Carlos option. This was not for the first time but this time, in the knowledge that we would have no LPH to land the troops by helicopter, the study had to be conducted based on landing craft, and even a cursory glance indicated that San Carlos would be worth scrutiny in this regard.

Choosing an AOA anywhere demands the dovetailing of very many differing military, naval and amphibious requirements. Choosing an AOA in the Falklands demanded special attention.

From the naval point of view the anchorage had to have a difficult approach for, or be easily defended against, Exocet and submarine attack; the Argentine S209 submarine (German designed for the Baltic) made this last a significant threat. The land surrounding the anchorage needed to be low enough for ships' radars to detect distant aircraft or so high that approaching aircraft would have little time to identify and select a target. This, of course, had to be balanced against the ships' crews and radars being blind to these approaching aircraft which I expected to make a low-level approach and then to climb and use a dive-bombing profile. I also feared that the Argentines might have possessed a short-range, air-to-surface missile. In the event if they had stuck to using rockets and cannon they would probably have done more damage.

The air threat would have to be reduced by means other than anti-aircraft frigates. As a fixed-wing aviator I knew that a pilot needs at least three seconds of clear tracking time to aim a bomb accurately and so it was important to 'hide' the almost defence-less ships by putting some form of 'land' obstacle between them and an enemy aircraft. This led us to seek for as small an area as practicable in which to protect the amphibious ships while offering a degree of defence by Rapier. Our AOA had to be as far east as possible to reduce the 'time over target' of the AAF, to give our own Harriers longer in support and our men as short an approach to Stanley as possible.

As an ex-Buccaneer Squadron Commanding Officer I had carried out many practice sorties against shipping and knew well how a piece of high ground can put a pilot off his aim. It was no good lining the aircraft up for a superb attack only to find oneself flying into a hillside. So I was looking for a place where geography and small arms could play a sensible part in the defence of a merchant ship. Out at sea small arms are worthless by and large but in tight, land-locked waters they might be effective at putting a pilot off his aim if not at knocking him out of the sky. We had little choice and I did not relish being the target buoy.

With a limited number of ships under command (and most of these civilian or non-specialist) the AOA had to be taken by surprise with the minimum of loss *en route*. This argued for a night approach and thus for waters easy for STUFT (especially STUFT) and warships to navigate without using active navigation or defence systems detectable by an enemy. For instance, ships such as *Norland* had a very limited navigational fit indeed beyond the use of an 'active' radar, a magnetic compass still swung for the northern hemisphere and not even a pelorus for taking bearings from the bridge!

The AOA had to encompass a calm anchorage in order that the Roll-on/Roll off ships in particular could unload without hindrance from the weather or sea-state. Swell was a particular danger when loading or off-loading a landing craft or Mexeflote as the ship could pitch several feet. This meant water deep enough for the largest ships but shallow enough to prevent incursions by enemy submarines. Preferably, a good AOA for our purposes would not need many escorts for its defence. It had to have good holding ground and offer space for ships to manoeuvre. Mining had to be expected, and then largely ignored as we could do very little about it.

From the amphibious point of view the beaches within the AOA had to accept a brigade landing quickly into at least four different areas so that the commandos and battalions could swiftly achieve all-round and mutual defence for themselves and the anchorage as a whole; each beach needed to be within a short march to dominating ground which would have to be occupied against counter-attack; the beaches needed suitable gradients for landing craft and at least one beach needed to be co-located with a suitably large and flat space for a Beach Support Area. Dry landings were required to ensure that men were not put at risk of exposure or trench foot. This was especially important in the Falklands for a campaign starting in the austral autumn.

From the military viewpoint the beaches should have good infantry and tank exits; they ought to be out of direct enemy gunfire range and not obviously prone to immediate counter-attack. Any dominating ground had to be easily and quickly seizable. The surrounding area needed to be suitable for Rapier anti-aircraft missile sites and the routes from the beaches to Stanley (if we were to move out) had to be suitable for men on foot and light vehicles. The distance to Stanley should, if at all possible, be short and not dominated nor easily blocked or ambushed by the enemy.

There are several anchorages on West Falkland with most of these attributes but only one serious contender on East Falkland. Because it was such an obvious choice from the overall point of view it seemed likely that the enemy would also have discovered San Carlos and marked, mined and defended it. Other options were continually discussed and 'war-gamed', but their attractions tended to fade when compared with those of San Carlos. Certainly from my naval biased view there was really no alternative on East Falkland.

When choosing the AOA we had to start with a hard and clear look at the most obvious beaches within it and while this might be regarded as an impossible task in many seldom-visited areas of the world on this occasion we were in possession of what George Pearson, my Staff Officer Operations, described at the time as an 'embarrassment of riches of topographical information'. In asking Ewen Tailyour to accompany Julian and myself, at the expense of more formal advice from the Hydrographic Department, I fear we may have put one or two 'droggie' noses out of joint, but one look at what Ewen had had on offer on 2 April convinced us both that he, with his wide and almost encyclopaedic knowledge of the Islands, was better than any hydrographer who might have known everything about one or two specifically surveyed passes or anchorages, but not much else.

Shortly after leaving the United Kingdom Ewen had weeded

out all the unsuitable beaches and produced a shortish list of those worth looking at: from this we singled-out the most likely candidates: Cow and Volunteer Bays, Berkeley Sound, Salvador, North Camp, Egg Harbour, Darwin and various inlets off Choiseul Sound, and San Carlos. We had also looked at Carcass Island as a stone aircraft carrier and various tussac islands where we might have considered placing observation posts or forward operating bases for special forces; Kidney Island being just one.

San Carlos was within reasonable range, by helicopter, from Stanley, with no enemy bases *en route* apart from Darwin. It was, however, within direct striking range of Darwin and Goose Green, should we need to eliminate these enemy bases which we considered to be 'off the line of march' and which could, anyway, be contained by some other method rather than attack; San Carlos inlet was believed to be unoccupied; its topography would most suit Rapier; it was bordered by three suitable and separate beaches each beneath a possible unit objective; it could be readily protected against surface threats; it contained beaches suitable for the Beach Support Area and it possessed suitable flat patches for maintenance and Sea Harrier strips.

There were, of course, strong arguments against San Carlos which would take our ingenuity and forethought to counter if it was not to be confirmed by 'London'. For a start it was within range of un-refuelled Argentine aircraft; the approaches and entrance could be mined before and after a landing; it was possible that a submarine could lie in wait in advance of a landing or creep in undetected after one – a very major worry; there were few if any convenient areas where helicopters or Harriers could actually hide; it was a long way to yomp to Stanley if helicopters were not to be employed. Even then we knew that the shortage of helicopters would prevent their use for much more than 'ammunition forward and casualties back'.

Having chosen our AOA we would need to know that it was not actually occupied by the enemy nor mined, at sea or ashore.

Any opponent worth his salt would have put himself in our shoes and identified a similar place as our likely 'first foot' and would therefore prepare his defences accordingly, but another factor in our deliberations, and this is not hindsight, was the impression we had that the Argentinians expected us to do things the American way and land, if not straight into Stanley, then very close indeed. Luckily they appeared to be conducting their defence accordingly, as we were about to discover by courtesy of the SBS and SAS.

Having decided San Carlos would be our first but not the only choice Julian and I worked on the strategy we would adopt once his men were ashore and firm. Bearing in mind the distances by sea of some sixty miles from San Carlos to Teal and a hundred and sixty miles to Bluff Cove, we decided that movement towards Stanley would have to be mainly by sea along the north coast using Salvador Waters as an advance support base for resupply by landing craft and LSL. Any advance along the south coast was not only along the direction we believed the enemy thought we would take but, due to the longer distances involved be much slower by sea or would have to be conducted by helicopter.

It was already clear that after the initial assault the main workhorses would be the LPDs and LSLs. The latter were never fully equipped with morale-boosting equipment such as anti-flash, steel helmets or one-time survival suits as there simply were not enough. Much concern was raised over beaching the LSLs. Only Captain Purtcher-Wydenbruck of *Sir Lancelot* had ever carried out a beaching before and so all LSL Masters were briefed by him for this potentially hazardous manoeuvre.

Coupled with all this (and of the most immediate importance) the method by which we would land the bulk of the first waves had to be addressed. The 'loss' of *Hermes* and/or *Invincible* as helicopter carriers was a blow, but we had been given plenty of time to plan without them and with the arrival of *Intrepid* we did at least have an extra, albeit small, flight deck, plus her eight assorted landing craft. The one asset we could reliably plan on at this stage was the landing craft and we therefore decided to use these to get the troops ashore. This meant a night landing with the timing such that they would be 'firm' on the high ground in defensive positions by daylight. The effect was that we would

1. HMS *Fearless*, a Landing Platform Dock (LPD) or Assault Ship, in San Carlos Water. She is distinguishable from her sister ship HMS *Intrepid* only by the two black satellite communication aerials on either side of and half-way up her mainmast and the Commodore's Broad Pennant on her foremast. The ship is docked down and a LCU can be seen in the entrance to the dry dock at the stern. A Sea Harrier is refuelling on the flight deck, while a Sea King helicopter is operating over her bows. *(Captain John Morton, Merchant Navy)*

2. SS *Canberra* at Ascension practising troop disembarkation into a LCU alongside her lower 'gash' ports and with two Sea Kings on her flight decks. *(Lieutenant Ian Craik, Royal Navy)*

3. Wideawake Airfield at Ascension with eleven Victor Tankers on the dispersal pan preparing for the Vulcan bombing raid on Stanley airport on 1 May. *(Lieutenant Ian Craik, Royal Navy)*

4. MV *Europic Ferry* on 26 May in her 'battle' colours in San Carlos Water looking towards Sussex Mountains. Attempts were made to camouflage, but the 'day-glo' red was never fully hidden. *(Captain John Morton, Merchant Navy)*

5. MV *Atlantic Conveyor* weighing anchor at Ascension. Twelve Sea and Ground-Attack Harriers, one Wessex and one Chinook helicopter can be seen parked between rows of protective containers. *(Lieutenant Ian Craik, Royal Navy)*

6. RFA *Sir Lancelot* was the oldest of six Landing Ships Logistic (LSLs). Taken about 28 May, this photograph shows her stern ramp folded up for sea and her flight deck. Her two single 40mm Bofors are mounted on either bow just forward of the cranes. Alongside amidships is a life-raft and some Gemini dinghies being used by Clearance Divers and McGregor's volunteers who are working on bomb disposal and hull repair. *(Lieutenant Ian Craik, Royal Navy)*

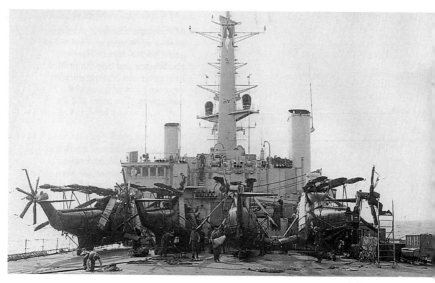

7. HMS *Fearless'* flight deck on the passage south with four Sea King Mk 4, by necessity, totally exposed to the elements and salt spray. *(Leading Photographer Toyer, Crown Copyright)*

8. MV *Elk* attempts an astern replenishment from RFA *Plumleaf* on passage to Ascension. This old and simple method was found difficult since the pipeline caught itself around *Elk's* underwater bow bulge. Subsequent replenishment was made alongside while underway. Eight 40mm Bofors mountings are sheltering under her fore-peak destined for the Landing Ships Logistic (LSLs). *(Captain John Morton, Merchant Navy)*

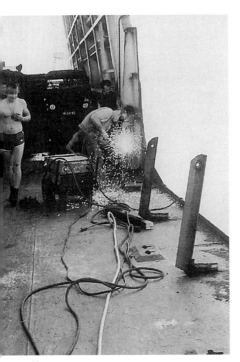

9. Drastic action on board MV *Elk*. Much of her 10ft high bulwarks are being cut away to create a flight deck. *(Captain John Morton, Merchant Navy)*

10. MV *Elk* at Ascension showing the hangar created out of her fore-peak, the bulwarks cut away on the port side and partially removed on the starboardside to allow the deck to be used by helicopters. Her roll-on roll-off ramp is lowered, but the 40mm Bofors has not yet been fitted on her upper fore-deck. *(Commander J. McGregor, Royal Navy)*

11. A Mexeflote pontoon at Ascension. These major workhorses were made up from sections to order and were powered by outboard motors, the crew remaining almost totally exposed to the elements and air attack.
(Lieutenant Ian Craik, Royal Navy)

12. The Russian intelligence gatherer (AGI) *Primorye* which took a close interest in the gathering amphibious task group at Ascension. *(Crown Copyright)*

13. The incredible cross-decking at sea on 19 May in the "Furious Fifties"! LCUs transporting men and equipment. HMS *Fearless* in the background docked down. Sea King helicopters continuing in their tasks. *(Crown Copyright)*

14. D-Day. 3 Para landing from LCVPs - somewhat after dawn. *(Crown Copyright)*

15. D-Day in San Carlos Water. The Argentinian aircrew making us welcome with bombs falling close to *Norland* and *Intrepid*. The two RFAs, *Fort Austin* and *Stromness*, are on either side of the photograph. *(Crown Copyright)*

16. A machine-gun position on board HMS *Fearless* made up from sandbags filled at Ascension while trying to avoid digging up Green Turtles' eggs. The gunner is searching a murky sky for enemy aircraft. *(Leading Photographer Toyer, Crown Copyright)*

17. Survivors from HMS *Antelope* on 23 May, dressed in their one-time survival suits and anti-flash, walking off a LCU within HMS *Fearless'* dry-dock and carrying all they possessed. *(Leading Photographer Toyer, Crown Copyright)*

18. HMS *Antelope's* last moments in San Carlos Water on 24 May. Business as usual, however, for the LCU, Wessex 5, Sea King 4, HMS *Intrepid*, a LSL, RFA *Resource* and MV *Norland*. *(Leading Photographer Toyer, Crown Copyright)*

19. Every morning I looked out towards Fannings Head to try and assess the chances of air attack by judging the cloud base. This photograph was taken on 1 June when 5 Bde arrived and shows *Intrepid* to the left of Fannings Head, warships, *Blue Rover* and the *Baltic Ferry* on the right. Air attack probable but the fog bank overland to the east (right) would give us major problems for several days. *(Lieutenant Ian Craik, Royal Navy)*

20. 2 June in San Carlos Water. MV *Baltic Ferry* with her stern door down being unloaded while refuelling from RFA *Blue Rover*. SS *Canberra* still disembarking troops of 5 Brigade and their equipment. The low cloud prevented air attacks but caused major problems ashore by severely restricting helicopter operations for several days. *(Lieutenant Ian Craik, Royal Navy)*

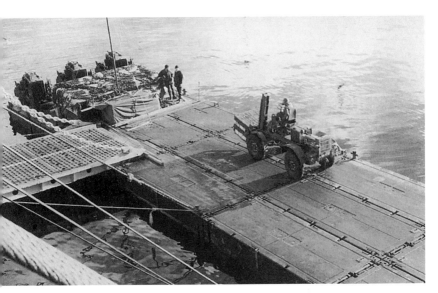

21. A Mexeflote secured astern of RFA *Sir Geraint* and MV *Elk* on 4 June. This allowed very rapid loading of *Sir Geraint* before her overnight passage to Teal Inlet to deliver the ammunition to 3rd Commando Brigade. Three outboard motors can be seen close to the 'shack', the crew's only shelter. *(Captain John Morton, Merchant Navy)*

22. Ammunition of most sorts piled 3 metres high, about 30 metres long and 18 metres wide in one of MV *Elk's* decks. The problems of selective unloading and subsequent re-securing for sea are easily seen. Unloading rates of 80 tons per hour were achieved by *Elk* but the landing rate onto the beaches was vastly slower. *(Captain John Morton, Merchant Navy)*

23. This sequence of four photographs was taken in San Carlos Water on 6 June. On seeing HMS *Exeter*'s missile launcher move, Captain Morton ran for his camera. In the top photograph *Exeter* has just fired one Sea Dart missile at an intruder. The second can be seen on the launcher just aft of the gun turret. In the second photograph *Exeter* has steamed ahead and just fired the second missile. The third shows the missile in flight, while the fourth shows the explosion and the smoke trail of the falling victim, a reconnaissance Lear Jet. *(Captain John Morton, Merchant Navy)*

24. HMS *Plymouth* on the morning of 8 June, hit by four bombs and on fire, but steaming back into San Carlos Water. Fannings Head on the right. *(Leading Photographer Toyer, Crown Copyright)*

25. One of the beaches at Fitzroy Settlement in Port Pleasant showing some trackway and the difficulty in landing equipment at high tide which reached to the foot of the cliff. *(Commander John McGregor, Royal Navy)*

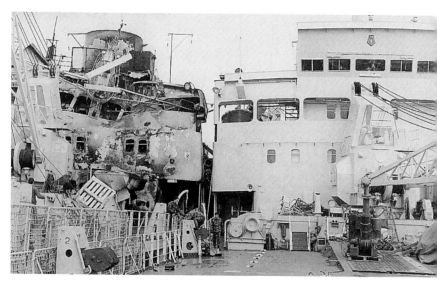

26. The damaged RFA *Sir Tristram* after the fire had burnt itself out, with her sister ship *Sir Geraint* alongside in Port Pleasant. The photograph shows how the aluminium bridge, crew's accommodation and flight deck had partially collapsed and in some places melted in the intense fire which, surprisingly, left her forward vehicle deck and lower mess deck almost untouched. *(Leading Photographer Toyer, Crown Copyright)*

27. Photographed on *Sir Tristram* on about 9 June. A scene enacted on several ships. The man on the right has his jet/spray nozzle in the spray position to enable him to get close to the point of fire by keeping cool behind the water cone while the man on the left pours on foam. This suggests the fire is still raging beyond the bank of steam or, perhaps, in the vehicle deck below.
(Commander John McGregor, Royal Navy)

28. Battle damage in *Sir Tristram*. Despite the lack of damage forward, the ship was, correctly, temporarily abandoned. Her position was known to the enemy. She was unable to move, without communications, working machinery or fire-fighting ability. Her Captain believed there was at least one unexploded bomb still on board but she was still heavily loaded with ammunition.
(Leading Photographer Toyer, Crown Copyright)

29. Two of the trawlers taken up from trade at anchor in San Carlos Water; LCVP on the left. *(Captain John Morton, Merchant Navy)*

30. MV *Monsunen*. The Falkland Island Company vessel commandeered by the Argentinians and later by the British and taken under command by Lieutenant Ian McClaren, Royal Navy. Here seen in Port William after the surrender, but still under the White Ensign. *(Lieutenant Ian Craik, Royal Navy)*

have to spend longer in the Exclusion Zone in daylight subject, particularly, to the Exocet threat, than I would have preferred.

The majority of support helicopters could only operate safely in daylight so we planned to launch them at dawn to lift guns, Rapier, ammunition and missiles from the bowels of the LSLs where they had been stored since sailing to protect them from salt water damage in transit. The aim was to have all defence weapons ashore and 'bedded in' by midday of D Day. After that, enemy reaction allowing, the general offload and stockpiling of stores ashore would progress using all available helicopters, landing craft and Mexeflotes. This move ashore would be as rapid as possible, and non-stop, with an estimated seven to eight days required to complete it. With a force of only two Commandos and host nation support, we were allowed six to seven days under NATO instructions and here we were with a force of about three times the size. True, we had more landing craft but we had fewer helicopters since already we had lost some. During this daylight off-load the helicopters would not be available for other tasks except emergencies.

Now back to the day-to-day work at Ascension. *Fearless* had been able to refuel at last and thus with the extra weight 'dock-down' and float out her LCUs. Various teams had flown out to assist in both military and naval training and through the exceptionally helpful offices of Pan Am's Manager, Mr Don Coffey, and Lieutenant-Colonel Bill Brydon, the USAF Station Commander, we were able to find suitable field-firing ranges and targets. There were, though, no areas for manoeuvres, no suitable beaches or landing zones: nor were there ever enough landing craft and helicopters to train and to assist with the re-stow.

However, all was not negative from the Landing Force's point of view and each unit or sub-unit received one helicopter training day, one day and one night working with landing craft and one day ashore to fire and test weapons. 2 Para were due to arrive twelve hours before we sailed, all together, allowing them time for just one daylight embarkation rehearsal into LCUs: not nearly enough as events on D Day were to prove, but this was no fault of theirs nor of their ships.

From my point of view we were at four hours' notice to sail for operations, but, as far as being required to sail for 'local' security reasons, this was assessed by the MOD as 'negligible'. There had been a submarine 'scare' when Sandy took his Carrier Battle Group south on the 18th, but nothing until the 25th. On this day the Argentine Government-owned merchant ship, *Rio de la Plata*, was spotted off the north-west coast by the British Administrator from his house. It turned out that she had been seen earlier off the north-west by *Canberra*. I despatched a Sea King to investigate followed by *Antelope* who escorted the merchant ship to the south west. Although unlikely, it was quite possible that she had launched some saboteurs but, more importantly, she would have assessed the size and structure of our Amphibious Group and if she had been listening to our radio transmissions would have been able to collect some important intelligence.

Suspicions were roused again that night (the 26th) when *Fearless* reported underwater noises in the anchorage. I sailed the Task Group at 2230 and tasked HMS *Antelope* to carry out a sonar sweep of the area before we returned. We knew that Argentina had taken possession of ten, four-man French-manufactured 'chariot' submarines in 1980 as well as two Italian CE2 FX60 two-man chariots. This could well have been the first opportunity to use them, although our assessment held that they would more probably wait until the conditions for their use (and the escape of their crews) was in their favour – among the Falklands and closer to 'home'. We were to reassess their *modus operandi* and the likelihood of their use once in San Carlos.

A second Argentine-owned merchant ship was watched by *Antelope*, but she headed south without stopping. A Russian 'spy ship' (the *Primorye*) now joined us, not unexpectedly, at the beginning of a lengthy and probably very boring stay that lasted until hostilities ceased.

One of my more pleasant duties were exchanges of dinner and drinks parties with the senior civilians ashore and masters and captains of merchant ships and RFAs. The Administrator, Bernard Pauncefoot, was quite excited at the thought that he could become a target and so any relaxing through social arrangements was worth while to build confidence in the British forces and me.

After the first 'incident' the ships had weighed and proceeded to sea to remain fully darkened and in sectors. Initially I was surprised that all my ships were still afloat at daybreak but the near misses certainly sharpened up the civilians and, indeed, one or two of the RFAs and warships. It was excellent training for what was to come and a means of drawing the group together so that by the time we reached San Carlos all the Commanding Officers and Masters knew me and I knew them. We obtained a level of trust which would otherwise not have been achievable until, perhaps, too late. My merchant ships were now already operating like warships.

The 'scares' I have mentioned, and the actions taken to counter them, played havoc with training and re-stowing, but on the 27th, and after consulting Julian, I was able to signal Northwood: 'After disrupted start and several distractions *Fearless*, *Canberra*, *Elk*, LSLs gaining much benefit from work-up. Estimate essential work-up package complete by 30 April.'

CTF's reply indicated that we should be ready to sail on the 29th to meet the Government's continuing demand that we leave early from Ascension Island. As this would mean that both *Intrepid* and *Norland* would miss all amphibious and shore training, I felt obliged to point out that for the sake of a few hours this was a bad idea. The Admiral agreed, but in doing so suggested that the LSLs sail on the 29th. This was to be the 'significant force' and their slow passage time required them to get south before the rest of us anyway.

To add to my worry and confusion I learnt that the politicians might now be deciding not to capture Stanley but just put the flag back on the Islands – somewhere, anywhere. The Government seemed quite happy to avoid what they believed could be a suicidal mission by simply re-establishing a presence, and that meant we could land far from the Falklands' capital; fine for them but 'they' would not have to face an air force closer to its home bases. It was Julian and myself who then said, 'No, we must be on the same side of Falkland Sound as Stanley.' There seemed to be no strategy behind our orders at all. Indeed, even Jeremy Moore on his visits to us could not help hiding his concern. We got the impression from him that Julian and I would do better to keep quiet and simply do our best.

Apparently there were still senior officers in the MOD who did not consider that a case had yet been made for the provision of extra forces either to break out of the beachhead or, subsequently, to repossess the Islands. This was a weak response to the Royal Navy's and the Royal Marines' request for sufficient enhancements for repossession and not just raising the flag; one way or another we needed confirmation.

Luckily, more positive views did exist at this level: Admiral Fieldhouse was invited to request, formally, for three further battalions, plus appropriate supporting arms, to meet what they both believed had to be the sole aim of the expedition: swift repossession.

On the 28th we heard from Northwood that CTF had attended the Chiefs of Staff meeting to present this case in person. He was reported as being unequivocal in his arguments and began by stating that, in his view, his task was to repossess the Islands and not merely to land 'with a view to doing so'. That being so, he needed the extra men to face an estimated 7,000 to 10,000 Argentinians. Neither the purpose nor sense of his argument could be denied. This was a campaign that might not be won until and unless the right conditions prevailed – presumably a successful landing by the amphibious forces. Until that success was achieved the MOD remained unwilling to commit further ground troops that we now know were actually earmarked and under training.

In other words it seems to have been a case of let us wait and see if the Navy and Marines can succeed and if not, 'we told you so' and thus the decision to delay sending the second Brigade was the correct one. By the same token, if we were to be successful and the second brigade was then sent Julian's men ashore and my ships, close inshore, would have a considerable wait before being able or allowed to break out. This added to our argument that, second brigade or not, we would have to plan on taking Stanley by ourselves.

On my return to the United Kingdom I quizzed CTF on this particular period as I found it one of the most interesting in the campaign. It was, of course, a crucial and difficult time of balance between political and military needs and therefore this meeting may have been something of a watershed. However, at our level, the uncertainty which reached us by way of limited disclosure of information, and, at times, simply speculation and rumour, had an altogether undue effect on our morale. Once we knew what our Masters were thinking and what we had to do and with what, we felt much more at ease and were rather more able to give our staffs positive guidance. We would, from that moment on, be doing largely what we had been trained for.

CTF appeared to appreciate my interest and explained to me that after his meeting in the MOD he had felt that the Army Staff accepted that his case justified reinforcement by a second brigade but that the MOD as a whole had to take a wider view of the issue and in doing so the Army Staff had doubted that the situation would merit a military operation on the scale he was suggesting. On balance they believed the present level of troops was acceptable but were justifiably concerned about the extra shipping and logistic effort needed.

CTF believed the Air Staff understood his worries about the troop levels but had felt that just one more brigade would hardly be sufficient; presumably for an early assault. If the sea and air blockade was effective then the Commando Brigade might be able to cope on its own. They were also concerned at the air threat to the landing force and so, again very sensibly, felt the priority should be for aircraft rather than troops at the early stages and had recommended that the Argentine aircraft carrier be taken out as soon as possible.

The Naval Staff, not perhaps surprisingly as there must have been daily contact with Northwood, supported CTF in his view that total repossession should be the aim and to do so argued that CTF must be given sufficient forces. Their priority also seems to have been aircraft and, after South Georgia had been retaken, ships before troops. They also appear to have supported CTF's request for better Rules of Engagement, particularly to allow the sinking of the aircraft carrier.

However, CTF was to tell me, two of the three Chiefs of Staff were firm in their belief that just two options presented themselves, both based on the assumption that we would establish a secure beachhead: either we could advance quickly towards Stanley, but with little chance of success or we could simply hold the beachhead until further decisions were made, presumably diplomatic. Either way Stanley airport had to be destroyed and the decision for or against a second brigade would have to be taken; if the answer was 'yes' then a Divisional Headquarters would need to be identified as would the transport. All this would take time while we sat it out in San Carlos or in a state of stalemate in the hills overlooking Stanley. As we now know, the Brigade and Divisional HQ had, in fact, been stood-to, as had the *QE2* among others.

What was not in doubt in the collective minds of the Chiefs of Staff was that it was not their decision, they could only advise Ministers. Surprisingly, bearing in mind the individual comments, the advice was that, to avoid the chances of stalemate in the South Atlantic, a second brigade should be sent. It was a happy decision.

No wonder, in hindsight, that with the aims of *Operation Sutton* (the landings) changing almost weekly (whether formally or through informal signals and discussions) the individual commanders on the spot interpreted their tasks differently. It was not to be until 12 May in his Operation Order that Admiral Fieldhouse was able to confirm the clear aim: 'To repossess the Falkland Islands as quickly as possible.' Almost a month had passed since the vague 15th April directive and six weeks since we had been stood-to. Thus it was hardly surprising that throughout this lengthy time of intense planning and speculation, within the Task Force and at Northwood, different interpretations had grown up over the words 'Plan to land with a view to repossession'. CTF appeared to see this as a delaying tactic to the provision of the infantry reinforcement which he felt was so necessary to meet his aim of repossession. Julian and I took it to mean that, once landed, we were largely confined to consolidating a beachhead until the second brigade arrived, after which we were to break out and advance on Stanley using the 'new' troops mainly as reserves and as a rear-area garrison and to Sandy it meant bringing pressure on Argentina, through a landing well away from Stanley, which would force a diplomatic withdrawal. Never was a good modern secure conference system more needed. It would have been worth its weight in diamonds at this time. What may have been a blinding glimpse of the obvious to my CTF was certainly not to Julian or me.

Within the Royal Marines Headquarters itself there were doubts about the whole conduct of the planning and its aims, manifested in the note from the Chief of Staff which ran pretty well as follows (these, not by collaboration, since neither of us had access to him, mirrored Julian's and my thoughts):

1. I am becoming increasingly concerned about the landing of the Amphibious Task Group in the Falkland Islands and the subsequent reinforcement by 5 Inf Bde Gp with Harrier and helicopter assets. Recent discussions by the Chiefs of Staff in committee and proposals by CinC Fleet have all contributed to my concern.

2. The landing phase starts with the establishment of the TEZ on 30th April, and runs through a period of about 15 days to the preferred landing date. During this period the following must be achieved:

a. The TEZ must be effective and remain so throughout.
b. The threat of the Argentine aircraft carrier must be removed.
c. Air and sea superiority must be established and held over the islands and surrounding sea.
d. Port Stanley airfield must be neutralized (including air defence

weapons) and the Argentine air assets (both fixed wing and helicopter) stationed on the islands must be destroyed.

e. Accurate intelligence of beaches, terrain and enemy positions is essential.

f. Argentine logistic dumps must be harassed and their effectiveness reduced.

3. Once all the precautions have been achieved, a landing against light opposition is feasible. Without any one of them we are landing our forces into a dangerous situation, bearing in mind the relative strengths of the enemy and ourselves. This preparatory or softening-up period is probably the most important part of the whole landing phase. At the present time we have not prepared a coherent plan for this period.

As I emphasize many times (on purpose) there was never to be a coherent plan for the 'softening-up' phase nor for any phase subsequent to a landing: the Chief of Staff to the Commandant General, Royal Marines, hit the nail on he head and, it appears, was one of the few to emphasize this point before our arrival.

While some might view this memorandum as being pessimistic, it expressed no more than the worries that we in the Amphibious Task Group also held. It was a sensible summing up of the position by one who understood the problems of amphibious warfare and who knew also that on this occasion, when so many odds were against us, we had to get it right first time.

On the 29th Jeremy Moore flew out for the last time to brief and be briefed on our latest (and last) plans. Our two staffs presented three operation orders accompanied by views on which of the three options should be taken up and under what circumstances. We emphasized our preference for San Carlos, representing as it did the area with the least military and naval disadvantages, the two most significant of which were its closeness to the air threat and, consequently, its overland distance from Stanley.

Berkeley Sound was a good option (apart from the possibility of an onshore swell in the, reasonably rare, easterly winds) but if we were to take this option we would have to rely on the enemy not moving his heavy guns into range. The disadvantages of the Cow Bay/Volunteer Bay option was largely weather-based, although the 'going' under foot to Stanley was appalling and the inevitable bottle-neck at Green Patch would need to be negotiated. As this settlement was occupied by the enemy Julian was adamant that any landing should not force upon him an inevitable battle before he was close to his final objective – Stanley.

Aircraft, mines, Exocet and submarines were 'naval' concerns of these last two options. Privately (and additionally) Julian and I held a high regard for Salvador Waters and intended to keep it up our sleeves if the enemy prevented us using any of the others. Salvador's main disadvantage was the narrowness of its entrance which could be blocked by mines or a sunken ship (ours by mistake or theirs if they thought quick enough and in advance). Certainly, we were looking at the area as a staging point for his proposed advance across the north towards Stanley.

Ewen Tailyour, in a moment of subjectiveness in his advice, tried, by applying spurious military reasons, to steer us away from Volunteer Bay for it was the site of the only King Penguin colony on the Islands. We listened politely to what he had to say … and then left it on the list!

By the time of Jeremy Moore's second visit to Ascension, we had, in fact, gone firm on San Carlos, subject to confirmation by the SBS that the beaches were indeed as described by Ewen and that they were free of enemy and likely to remain so. San Carlos was not perfect but it came closer than anywhere else to meeting the naval, amphibious and military requirements tabulated earlier. The credit for this choice belongs, alone, to the amphibious and landing force staffs in HMS *Fearless*.

On 30 April three 'landmark' events occurred: Sandy's Carrier Battle Group reached the edge of the Exclusion Zone; the frigates *Argonaut* and *Ardent* arrived in the Ascension anchorage and were able to take some of the weight off my staff and the LSLs sailed south escorted by *Antelope*. This last satisfied the politicians as an 'invasion force' could be seen to have sailed for operations in the South Atlantic. With the pressure for the 'main' amphibious force to sail now lifted we were left with an estimated five more days of uninterrupted military and naval training.

I had been reluctant to let the LSLs go early but I feared for their ability in the southern seas with the embarked Mexeflotes and their own weak bow doors; at least they could plough on at a slow and safe speed. I had planned for them to sail on the 29th but with our 'water-carrier' due in that day it made sense to wait to fill tanks: they, and the RFA *Pearleaf*, sailed shortly after midnight on the 1 May unescorted until *Antelope* could catch up after a brief defect rectification.

For some of my staff and my Leading Steward May Day began alarmingly when I gave them a rendition of the Padstow May Day Song. I hoped my son would enjoy his third birthday. The rest of the day produced a mixed bag of good and poor news best described in the words of the time in my staff diary:

COMAW staff officers, SMEO, AWO (A) continue to visit STUFT and RFAs as they arrive Ascension. A major problem with STUFT is the provision of fuels and other consumables; STUFT not following any procedure, requesting from ships at Ascension and particularly *Fearless*. Press leaks lead to temporary press comms silence and adoption of a sliding scale of control. In preparation for conflict COMAW requested Fleet to supply more flak jackets and helmets for upper deck crews on board LSLs and *Fearless*. LSLs who had already left had been asked at Pre-Sail Conference if they had any problems now signalled that they are short of food! To enable a more balanced division of responsibilities the following organization instituted at Ascension. CTG 317.0 retains overall responsibility for the co-ordination of naval and amphibious operations and exercises. Also planning, issuing of directives, ordering night steaming sectors for ships not involved in the defence of the area and informing *Argonaut* of ships available for operations and exercises at sea. *Argonaut* will issue necessary instructions for the surface and sub-surface defence of the local area. Plan and issue the daily naval training

I spent some time ashore with the Group Captain at Wideawake Airfield, marvelling at the boldness of the RAF's attempts to help us out or, as some rather more unkindly said, to elbow their way in on the action. Nimrods had been operating from Wideawake since 7 April, providing surface and sub-surface surveillance and transport aircraft were already doing wonders. A bombing raid was now being planned on Stanley Airfield. To reach the target with one Vulcan needed about eighteen Victor tanker sorties but the in-flight refuelling equipment on the Vulcan had not been used for ten years and the aircrew were barely practised – the aircraft having sufficient range on its own for NATO purposes. That it reached the target area must have signalled a strong message to the Argentines that their mainland targets were also vulnerable and after the war I believe there was evidence to show that these raids had obliged the Argentinians to deploy their Mirage III air defence fighters around their northern bases and cities and, probably, give up short-term ideas of extending the Stanley runway to take their jets. Life was therefore made far easier for our Sea Harriers and ourselves in San Carlos as a result.

Damaging a runway with a conventional bomb is far less easy than one might imagine. Bombs fall in sticks and only one or possibly two have a chance of hitting the runway itself, since, to improve the odds, they must be dropped across the length of the runway to reduce line error and by a large number of aircraft if more than one crater is required. I was a little surprised, therefore, to see emanating from Sandy's force claims that Sea Harriers with fewer bombs could 'take out the airfield in one strike'. Perhaps, unknown to me, we had a runway penetrating bomb but I thought not.

From the start the volume of signal traffic had risen to astronomic proportions and the Whitehall communications centre, let alone *Fearless*'s grossly overworked main communications office, was struggling to cope. On my staff I limited releasing signals to myself and one other, while the brigade staff had to have a major re-think. They were used to operating along Army lines with each staff officer releasing his own signal. Julian was obliged to follow our methods and keep the length and classification of the signals down as much as possible. It was not easy and to ensure a signal got through it had to be of Priority precedence or higher.

Sandy was intent now on reaching one or two more milestones: he wanted to follow up the Vulcan raid with Sea Harrier attacks on Stanley and Goose Green airfields on 2 May; he wanted to hunt down and sink the conventional Argentine submarine believed to be operating twenty miles north of East Falklands and he wanted to ensure by threat or direct action that the aircraft carrier *Veintecinco de Mayo* and the Exocet-fitted cruiser *Belgrano* were immobilized. He needed to begin the insertion of Special Forces and he wanted to start an intensive period of naval gunfire against selected targets, mainly airfields and aircraft. Most of all he needed aggressive Rules of Engagement.

The destruction of the Argentine carrier was uppermost in Sandy's mind and to this end the submarine HMS *Splendid* was authorized to sink her within or without the Exclusion Zone. This fell within the 'Rules' for she (the carrier) could, of course, launch aircraft from outside the Exclusion Zone against targets well within it and the neutralizing of enemy air power was a precondition for a landing. Authority to destroy her was issued by Ministers on 30 April. The *Belgrano*, too, could stay outside the Exclusion Zone and engage targets inside it with her guns and Exocet outranging most of the armament possessed by the British: an interesting factor when one considers the events and the spurious arguments trotted out by left-wingers after the event.

It is true that Sandy had addressed the problems of collecting intelligence and establishing the air and sea blockade (including the destruction of Stanley airfield) and rendering the enemy carrier ineffective by shadowing her with nuclear submarines but, as the Royal Marines Chief of Staff was warning these things were vital and without them we would indeed be in danger. In the end not one of them was to be fully effective apart from the neutralizing of the Argentine navy (which Sandy was to achieve so effectively by sinking the *Belgrano*).

Sandy had, as we have seen, toyed with ideas to lure the Argentine forces out so that they could be engaged but that plan involved the use of *Fearless* as a sacrificial lamb inshore of the mainland. It was a good idea in theory but quite the wrong decoy.

In fact the Royal Marines Chief of Staff was probably unaware of an exchange of signals on the 30th between Northwood and the Carrier Battle Group which, in essence, authorized the beginning of hostilities within the Exclusion Zone and which culminated in Sandy telling his Commanding Officers that they now had a 'free hand to sink, burn, destroy or even capture anything Argentinian that moves inside the TEZ.' Using, incidentally, a much-loved phrase known to be first said by Admiral Vernon in 1739. As a rider to the decision to activate the Exclusion Zone Sandy was also given permission to attack the enemy aircraft carrier wherever she was: HMS *Splendid*'s search now carried even more meaning. The Argentines had rejected Haig's peace plan late on the 29th and on the 30th CTF spoke directly to Sandy telling him that he now had authority to enter and enforce the Exclusion Zone the following day with enhanced, almost unlimited, Rules of Engagement. Negotiations, other than for full capitulation by the Argentines, now no longer had a chance, as they were about to discover.

As we now know these events culminated in the sinking of the *Belgrano* on 2 May, followed on 4 May by the attack on HMS *Sheffield*. We all abhor needless loss of lives but this was now war and a war that had to be prosecuted as harshly as was necessary by both sides. Off Ascension Island there was the sudden realization that 'this was it'. Any turning back would now be difficult.

As we waited for 2 Para and HMS *Intrepid* the Royal Marines and 3 Para route-marched and shot while the amphibious ships and their escorts practised ASW duties, NBCD, main weapon and sensor checks and tests. Parachute trials were carried out with the Mk IV Sea King and the Blues and Royals tried firing their main armament across the open ramps of the LCUs as they approached the coast, probably, if we had told them, against the advice of the Director General Surface Ships at Bath and the Chief Naval Architect.

On board the *Canberra* a method of embarking troops into landing craft was successfully developed using spaces normally reserved for gash. Julian and I watched a night practice and felt we were getting on well in turning our mixed bag of shipping into a useful amphibious force. Earlier I had been taken around the ship by Beagle Burne and noted to my horror the vast cathedral-like engine rooms and the habit of steaming without watertight doors closed. This had to change.

MV *Elk* was turned into a rudimentary aircraft carrier through the violent application of an oxy-acetylene cutter to remove her bulwarks which were then tossed without ceremony into the sea. Commander John McGregor, *Fearless*'s Engineer Officer, had peremptorily asked me for permission. I gave it in the belief that he may have already acted and was relieved when the owners, the P & O Shipping Company, approved. *Elk* was also fitted with two 40mm Bofors to give her some defence and bring her more in line with the LSLs, while her high forepeak was made into a useful hangar.

Problems which exercised John McGregor's engineering team included water production for many of the merchant ships and others in need, the reverse osmosis plant in *Norland* being particularly badly engineered in the rush to get her down with us. It was soon found that the Royal Navy was inadequately provided with welders but luckily the Royal Engineers came to our aid.

Other problems the electricians and engineers solved were repairs to the tug *Salvageman*'s diesel cooling water pipes and re-wiring the *Irishman*'s burnt-out galley and making steam pipes for *Sir Geraint*'s evaporators.

The *Atlantic Conveyor* received helicopters and Harrier GR3s from the United Kingdom and we waited desperately for the arrival of the newly recommissioned *Intrepid*. As she had sailed with few stores, her original ship's company and no embarked military force or headquarters she would give us added flexibility in our re-stow and take some of the weight off my overloaded and hard-worked Flagship. Many of the men in *Fearless* slept on camp beds in strange places and such was the increased size of the embarked force that one junior-rates mess deck was occupied by not very junior staff officers. Even some of the passages and flats had had an extra 'deck' laid on top of food boxes. This was fine for those under five foot ten but not much fun for the rest of us who, invariably and painfully, forgot to duck.

All 'departments' throughout the group were occupied with duties beyond their normal calling. The *Fearless* padres for instance were quite suddenly required to act as censors of the vast amount of mail despatched daily. Some enthusiastic Royal Marine clerk had published the date and place of the landings in his Daily Routine Orders (distributed throughout the ship) forcing me to restrict the movement of men and mail ashore or to any other ship. Of course all that was also a waste of time, for when we sailed our own Secretary of State for Defence announced the fact to the waiting world, thus allowing even an uneducated Argentinian with a global chart to make an intelligent guess at our time of arrival off the 'Malvinas', if not exactly where.

The censorship had an unusual twist in that, in my concern at the way the operation was developing, I had written to my wife and enclosed a statement that she might wish to produce if it had all ended in catastrophe. Unknown to me my letter had missed the post and was swept up with the batch of mail that had to be censored. She received a letter which looked more like a piece of shredded wheat but at least she realized that I had found time to write. Certainly it was no use as a statement. The censors, who had only been asked to check that no indication of dates or places were included, clearly attacked my letter with relish, even though it did not include anything of operational significance.

I had already found at this stage that I had mentally and, I suppose, to some extent spiritually, taken on the attitudes of a monk. I had sailed with very little kit, partly because it was still packed from our recent move and there had been no time to search for it, and partly because I saw no purpose in taking more than the essentials and very few personal items. From that first signal in Fort Southwick my mind had turned on little else but the campaign and my family had had to take very much second place in my thoughts. It must have been an extremely difficult time for my wife, but I would never be able to forgive myself if I had lost one soul through my own carelessness.

While we had an internationally declared hospital ship, the *Uganda*, and three hydrographic survey ships earmarked as 'ambulances' with us, we needed to designate a Primary Casualty Receiving Ship (PCRS) and to place Surgical Support Teams (SSTs) in various ships. Julian had already expressed his concern on NATO exercises that we had no seaborne first aid capability for his troops and now this became a matter of high priority. I borrowed Surgeon Captain Ian Young from Sandy's staff as my Senior Medical Officer who then proceeded with various Staff Officers to survey a number of ships which we believed offered a reasonable capability. We needed ships with flight decks and looked at *Intrepid*, the LSLs and *Canberra* as a start. Although some of the other merchant ships were now capable of accepting helicopters, I did not wish them to stay in the front line. *Canberra*, with her team of nurses who had refused to be put ashore, and with her easy passageways, was an immediate option. The survey helped us understand the problem but I don't believe we really solved it. Ian Young summed it up all neatly in a signal on 30 April stating that all RN ships and most RFAs and STUFT now had a medical officer with full surgical support available in *Invincible* and *Hermes*. Three Surgical Support Teams were formed and allocated, one to *Hermes* and two to *Canberra* with the *Hermes* SST and one of *Canberra*'s ready to move ashore when required. *Canberra* was described as having 'hospital ship' facilities. We should perhaps have had helicopters with red crosses painted on them but there were too few for this luxury.

Two welcome visitors from CTF's staff were Captain Rob Woodard, Royal Navy, and Colonel Tim Donkin, Royal Marines. I was not sure of the real reason for their visit, but assumed Northwood were beginning to realize our concern. I vented some of my frustration on Rob, since I knew him well, on being, as I saw it, kept in the dark. The uncertainty was being most strongly felt by the Brigade staff but my own were not immune. We had been planning and training furiously but still had no indication that our plans were acceptable to CTF.

By 4 May my Task Group disposition was as follows:

Intrepid, *Norland* (with 2 Para embarked), *Europic Ferry* and *Atlantic Conveyor* were closing from the north with *Fearless*, *Argonaut*, *Ardent*, *Stromness*, *Tidepool*, *Canberra* and *Elk* at Ascension while *Antelope* was escorting *Pearleaf* and the five LSLs to the south. By the 5th my team had prepared a brief for all STUFT ships passing through the staging post relieving Bob McQueen of some of this work. The amphibious and military work-up was going as well as the facilities allowed with the following drills being practised by every commando or battalion:

1. Cross decking by helicopter.
2. Two-company groups in assault landing drills.
3. Simultaneous helicopter and landing craft deployment ashore.
4. Embarkation and disembarkation into and out of LCUs by night from *Canberra* and *Stromness* under way and at anchor.
5. Zeroing and firing of all personal, troop and support weapons.
6. The exercising of command and control of 1–5.
7. The proving of the Sea King Mark IV in the parachuting role.
8. The successful firing of SNEB from Gazelle helicopters.

The Brigadier and I and our staffs had still never exercised together but under the circumstances seemed to be doing well at the planning. Certainly as far as Julian and I were concerned we shared most meals and much of our time, either on board or on shore together, and I do not recall an argument or discussion that remained unresolved amicably. At staff level, not so surprisingly, this was not entirely the case. Specialist knowledge and the determination to have one's way when not understanding another's needs, as well as a reluctance to compromise politely, all came to the fore from time to time. We still had to be tested under live operational conditions.

And all the while we continued to check the anchorage with sonar sweeps and keep an eye on potentially hostile sea and air activity. It was a diversely busy time and Julian and I longed to get our groups together, polish off the ships' commandos' and battalions' training period and get southwards.

CHAPTER THREE

ADVANCE TO CONTACT

> The advantage of time and place in all martial
> actions is half a victory, which being lost is
> irrecoverable.
>
> Drake, April 13, 1588, to Queen Elizabeth

AT 0700 ON the morning of 7 May 2 Para had arrived in *Norland* and *Europic Ferry* to be plunged immediately into their one rehearsal with LCUs under Guy Yeoman's supervision. Julian and I made a quick visit ashore to say thank you to the Administrator and Bob McQueen.

I also made a hurried visit to *Norland* to welcome her to the group. While clearly an attractive asset providing good accommodation, it quickly became obvious that her stern ramp was intended for shore Ro-Ro terminals and was too high to make it possible to transfer stores direct to landing craft or Mexeflotes. She did, however, have a side opening which helped as the mass of cargo on her lower vehicle deck could just be shifted onto a landing craft by this exit, but it would be slow. In addition her communication fit would impose severe limitations. Commander Chris Esplin-Jones certainly had a challenge but he would rise to it magnificently.

At 2200 that day the bulk of the Amphibious Task Group weighed and sailed under cover of a tropical night with ships darkened for the South Atlantic while Bob McQueen ashore on Ascension Island continued to transmit on his radio circuits as though we were still at anchor, even to the point of simulating my ships' replies. The Administrator asked his St Helena workforce, many of whom were ham radio operators, not to discuss our movements on their radios. To hide our departure further our initial course took us due west and so out of sight of the Russian AGI loitering off the east coast of the island. It was aggravating in the extreme, therefore, to hear our sailing announced by our own Secretary of State for Defence over the BBC's World Service! Not even the Russians could apparently believe their ears as the AGI was reported to have been seen circling the island several times before heading back to its eastern position where reception was clearly better with Moscow.

The five LSLs (*Sirs Lancelot, Tristram, Galahad, Percivale* and *Geraint*) accompanied by the RFA *Pearleaf* and the water carrier *Fort Toronto* had sailed early on 1 May. HMS *Antelope* (Commander Nick Tobin) caught up with them later that day with orders to take this group via the great circle route towards the TEZ. On the 2nd I had ordered a change and told Nick Tobin to take his charges to a position 1545 miles south by west of Ascension and about 2040 miles west of Buenos Aires where I wanted them to poise, safe from Argentine aircraft. When ordered, (expected to be about 10 May) they were to join us to the south-west. Things changed very slightly as *Antelope* was to hand over her duties to *Antrim* then heading north accompanying RFA *Tidespring* carrying prisoners of war from South Georgia. CTF believed, rightly, that the large DLG and her Sea Slug missile system was a more useful escort than the Type 21 frigate with one gun.

Canberra, Tidepool and *Elk* had been sailed under *Argonaut*'s command on 6 May with *Ardent* in company. Northwood had wanted this group to sail direct towards the LSL's rendezvous point, but, as Kit Layman (Captain of *Argonaut*) unarguably, pointed out by signal, 'Whole war depends on survival of (COMAW's) main body,' which has, he continued, 'a complete lack of air defence assets'. He suggested that as the enemy were likely to 'make extraordinary efforts to attack undefended Task Group,' he should be routed much further east. He was right, of course, and the rendezvous position was moved 300 miles further away from South America.

The final unit of the Amphibious Task Group, HMS *Intrepid*, sailed from Ascension on the morning of 8 May. Her very late arrival was welcome but meant that I believe throughout the campaign her Commanding Officer, Peter Dingemans, was at a disadvantage since he had not been party to all the thinking and planning that had taken place. He had more practical experience of amphibious warfare than myself or Jeremy Larken and it is probable that this would have been useful. He joined up with us the next day and we were now all of one company apart from the five LSLs which we would catch up. The sixth, *Sir Bedivere*, having been released from army duties and loaded with the balance of 3 Commando Brigade's War Maintenance Reserves of ammunition was due to arrive off Georgetown on the 9th. She would also have on board 11 Field Squadron Royal Engineers, FCDT 3 and an RAF 'bomb disposal team', and was to sail on the 14th with an estimated time of arrival in the Exclusion Zone of 23 May.

Two days after Rob Woodard had returned to Northwood, David Halifax, the Chief of Staff to CTF, telephoned me at sea to say, 'I understand you feel we have a communications problem'. I explained that I was concerned that at this late stage we had still not received confirmation of where and when to land or any idea of a strategy after landing. He replied that we were 'as one' which was encouraging to know. In fairness, David Halifax was undoubtedly more concerned with Sandy's problems in the South Atlantic which were more immediate and he probably understood them better. Jeremy Moore had been appointed the CTF's Deputy Land Force Commander and through him Julian had access to Northwood. David probably thought this was enough and there was no need to provide me with a similar line of contact. I was aware that my own Staff Officer had been ejected from Northwood and since I had heard nothing from Derek Reffell had to assume that he was involved elsewhere, possibly on NATO duties. I repeated my message that, although the Navy could react quickly, it clearly took the Military much longer. I also told him of my concern that my staff were fully occupied with the demands of my ships and that we needed all the time we could get to make the final detailed plans. An early decision was essential.

With our departure we had, effectively, and at last, joined the war proper. The day after sailing *Argonaut* detected a shadowing Argentine Boeing 707 with no doubt at all that it was a military aircraft employed on military business probably as the result of listening to the BBC. Approaching from the direction of Argentina with its radar searching with a wide sweep, it switched to a narrow sweep when it had found us, before turning back to the south-west, mission accomplished. Non-combatant civilian airliners do not behave like that nor did its electronic 'signature' suggest that it was our customary Russian 'Bear'. On 6 May Northwood had pleaded strongly with Ministers for our Rules of Engagement to allow for the destruction of this nuisance, but by the 9th we still had not had a response. Their fear was that without positive visual identification there could be no question of engaging this aircraft, unseen, with surface-to-air missiles. We did, though, impress that by its very operating characteristics it had to be hostile, and we wanted it 'splashed'.

Not to be put off by another weak but understandable response to a real threat to the security of the venture, I asked Captain Mike Layard, the Senior Naval Officer of *Atlantic Conveyor*, to devise a way of keeping one of his Harriers at high alert between the containers lashed to the upper deck. It was a risky scheme which would have needed a certain amount of luck to recover from a sortie, but we planned it anyway and asked Ascension to provide a refuelling tanker if we should actually launch so the Sea Harrier could recover to Ascension. There was of course nothing new in this. Courageous Hurricane pilots did the same thing from merchant ships in the Atlantic and Russian convoys of the last World War and theirs was very much a one-way/once-only flight.

Our plan was accepted on the 10th and the ROE were

changed to allow us to shoot down any aircraft that came within forty miles, provided it could be identified as hostile by either visual identification or, significantly, by its 'flight plan and pattern of behaviour'. Our chance came, and went, on the 15th when, with a Boeing directly overhead during the afternoon, the weather was too bad at sea level to launch vertically (and certainly to recover vertically) the one Sea Harrier not wrapped up in a 'dry suit' for the journey south. Lieutenant Commander Tim Gedge, its pilot, had to be disappointed along with the rest of us.

Atlantic Conveyor was a remarkable vessel. A huge container ship with a roll-on capability through her stern doors, she was packed with valuable equipment of all descriptions: tented accommodation for a Brigade, runway making equipment, six hundred cluster bombs, gallons of kerosene, and an immense amount of NAAFI stores and victuals for the Task Force, most of which would be needed as soon as the Landing Force was well established; some of it we might well wish to use before.

Perhaps the most encouraging part of the passage down was watching three Russian Bear D reconnaissance planes making what was now a fairly regular visit. This time, however, they must have been as surprised as we were proud. They turned back and made several photographic passes as they watched *Atlantic Conveyor* being refuelled underway beside *Tidepool*. What they probably did not notice, but the Kremlin undoubtedly would when they saw the photos, was that *Atlantic Conveyor* was the guide, with the almost as huge *Tidepool* keeping station on her. It was a first-class piece of seamanship and an excellent example of how the merchant ships and crews had adapted to our needs.

Before he had left Ascension Island Sandy signalled me to the effect that 'he was off to fight the war and we should follow as best we could when we were ready'. We were now ready and on our way but he seemed to continue to believe that his blockade would be effective and that all the Commando Brigade would have to do was to turn up in time to monitor the removal of a hungry and defeated army.

This was, of course, to be a nonsense for the blockade was never to be tight enough to stop the nightly run of C-130 aircraft into Stanley. As we shall see, if the Argentines had not surrendered when they did the Commando Brigade's guns as Julian was to write, 'would have been in range of the airport and would have stopped the flights for good'. We were to discover that the Argentine army, as a whole, was never close to starving, indeed, most of the Commando Brigade ate their rations for the last few days of the war, due to our lack of helicopters. The enemy soldiers ate better than ours throughout the land war.

Once we had sailed it was necessary to review our plans so far with, in the language of the day, 'nothing ruled out and nothing yet ruled firmly in'. The loss of HMS *Sheffield* (within the defence perimeter of The Carrier Battle Group) was the first practical indication that promises of air superiority over the fleet, let alone over the AOA, were unlikely to be fulfilled.

This unpalatable, but not unexpected, fact substantially affected our thoughts of adopting a 'seaborne' logistic support policy. It was now clear that we should plan to get everything ashore as quickly as possible after the landings and move the empty ships out of range to the east. This was a fundamental change to our strategy. Certainly until just short of D-Day we were being told that any threat would be countered but our own assessments never produced such an optimistic prognosis. A more honest view from the beginning would have been better, particularly as we now know that in private (and to Ministers) CTF held the same view as ourselves. It was to mean a lot of fundamental re-thinking at a time when we should only be sorting out the final details.

The choice of the Amphibious Objective Area (the requirements for which were discussed in detail in Chapter Two) was now my most important planning task. There was not to be a second choice of AOA, for, once committed, there could be no turning to another area if we failed first time; it was to be a one shot landing. With the amphibious fleet of just a few years back we might have been able to pick and choose almost up to H Hour for such is the remarkable flexibility of a truly amphibious fleet, but now no longer. Before Jeremy Moore returned to England for the final time on 29 April he left Julian and me with a message from CTF: Admiral Fieldhouse wished us to choose the place and the date that we, not he, thought best. Because we insisted on waiting for *Intrepid* and *Norland* with 2 Para we were able to narrow the date to between 18 and 25 May. Jointly in HMS *Fearless* on 10 May we took the decision, openly and finally, that San Carlos was to be our Amphibious Objective Area. We kept CTF and Sandy informed of our deciding processes.

Having at last made our choice our minds turned, temporarily, to other supporting factors for an amphibious assault: deception plans, advance force operations, survival, hospital ship positioning, air-sea rescue and all the many threats that might prevent me from launching the 3rd Commando Brigade ashore as required, 'At the right place, at the right time, in the right order and without significant loss'. Having said that, the worry that exercised me most in those days was what to do if we were to lose a major amphibious ship and its precious 'cargo'. The problem was complex and so inundated with variables that it was easier to conclude that the fog of war would be at its thickest, making instant decision-making the only correct action. Although thinking the problem through at irregular intervals was useful, I only issued simple guidelines to cover the eventuality.

We fully understood that with so many eggs in so few baskets the loss of just one major ship would spell disaster and while we were acutely aware that the loss, at sea in deep water, of, say, *Canberra* would bring the whole enterprise to a halt we were accepting that risk and believed (in the absence of anything to indicate otherwise) that CTF was too. We had mentioned our concern to Jeremy Moore at Ascension when all agreed that there was not much we could do about it. We presumed that this was reported back to Northwood.

Deception plans had to be carried out by ships from Sandy's Task Group as only his escorts, not mine, were in a position to deceive. However, as with all the 'amphibious decisions' over the 'where and when' of the landing, these, too, were conducted to plans drawn up by Julian and myself. The aim was to help the Argentinians in their almost certain assumption that we would land, USMC style, directly into or very close to Stanley in a once only *coup de main* (or even a *coup de grâce*!). To this end we arranged for spurious radio circuits to be activated and allowed various artefacts of amphibious impedimenta to 'drift' inshore indicating reconnaissance landings to the south of Stanley Common. HMS *Glamorgan* was tasked with this *Operation Tornado* designed to draw enemy forces to cover these beaches. This was a most useful exercise in deceit that I hoped helped to keep significant forces well away from the west of East Falkland.

On receipt of the first Draft Appreciation the commanding officers of the SBS and SAS had been able to outline their *modus operandi* for gaining the all-important data on the enemy and our proposed landing sites. Parachuting into East Falkland had been considered possible as early as 12 April providing the Americans could offer the use of their long-range transport aircraft and they, in turn, depended on up-to-the-moment weather reports from a radio ham on the Islands: reports that never reached me. Sadly, this method of insertion did not take place.

The transport used to insert the Special Forces patrols were submarines, helicopters and fast raiding craft and, later, a conventional submarine, the first patrols being put ashore at the beginning of May. In overall terms the SAS would report on the enemy in and around Stanley, Darwin and the road between and to achieve this Mike Rose (the SAS Commanding Officer) stated in his first look at their impending work: 'It may be possible, given the necessary assets for patrols to live in the built up area of Port Stanley. It may be possible for them to be supported by friendly civilians.'

In the meanwhile the SBS would concentrate on likely beaching sites on both main islands. However, before the first insertion Julian and I re-confirmed that meetings with civilians were forbidden except in emergencies.

For the Special Forces there were other considerations. If caught the SAS had no reason to be ashore other than hostile whereas any Royal Marine (SBS) caught could claim to have been a member of one of the original two Naval Parties. Initially it was planned that all SAS ranks would carry identification giving them the same supposed status as the SBS. Knowing that the Argentines held the 'Order of Battle' of the Naval Parties, plus their names, we might not have got away with this ruse. Another consideration concerned communications: the SBS had no experience of working their burst transmission sets from the Islands despite having proposed just such a proving exercise in 1981. (It was refused with the excuse that the results from such an exercise would never be relevant!)

The SAS had less need to be cautious because they had hand-held satellite communication sets and were able to speak direct to *Fearless* and the UK. In contrast, one transmission from the SBS overlooking the San Carlos area (for instance) could have blown the whole thing so these men would walk for miles in order to make their morse code reports to a base station. The SBS, correctly, could take no chances and in many cases would wait until after they had been returned on board before delivering their information.

Intelligence 'targets' that Julian and I set included the morale of the enemy, their command structure, types and numbers of weapons (particularly defence, anti-air and anti-sea systems) sites of enemy concentration and their ability to move troops (in bulk) by helicopter across country or around the coast. Mine-fields (on land and sea), communications centres and so on were further targets.

We suggested that various targets for sabotage should be identified with a view to neutralizing them 'as required' or when suitable; these included air defence installations, forward stock-piles of arms and ammunition, all military HQs (including Government House), storage depots including fuel dumps, plant machinery, plus parked aircraft and berthed or anchored shipping. One plan, which could have been easily achieved and which was given some consideration, was the poisoning (or even destruction) of the Stanley water supply. This would have caused the greatest hardship to the enemy but of course to the civilians as well; for this latter reason alone it was, obviously, shelved.

For some never-explained reason we did not start off with a quiet, conventional submarine for special forces' work but eventually (on 18 April) HMS *Onyx* was earmarked. Sailing on 26 April she was due to arrive in San Carlos on 31 May. It was a great pity that she had not been despatched in time to reach us before D Day for the four nuclear boats in the South Atlantic were not ideal for SBS insertions in shallow water, and anyway were largely employed elsewhere blockading the Argentine Navy and carrying out a different form of intelligence gathering and monitoring.

From the very beginning, and contrary to some reports about their total independence the SAS were directed by Julian, but with my concurrence when involved with amphibious work. Indeed the Commanding Officer of the SAS stated in his initial prognosis: 'It is most important that both the offensive and intelligence gathering operations of the SAS remain under the operational control of the Commander 3 Commando Brigade and that apart from *Operation Paraquet* no elements of the Squadron are detached to under command other Task Forces in support of other operations.' There was one exception: in order to release an SBS patrol for beach reconnaissance I asked for the SAS to watch Falkland Sound from the area of Jersey Point for I was particularly worried about enemy ship movements and any possible mining in that area.

Eight four-man patrols of the SAS were inserted by Sea Kings from HMS *Hermes* over the first three nights of May, landing in the Stanley area as well as Bluff Cove and Darwin in accordance with Rose's initial instructions. They also landed at Port Howard and Fox Bay, while the SBS began their beach recce tasks across almost the whole archipelago.

For all SBS insertions their Commanding Officer worked very closely with me. Neither of us had inserted men operationally on this scale before and the responsibility weighed heavily on us. This was quite right, but the proof of his, and his men's ability, was that they lost not a single man, while at the same time they collected the information without which the landings could not have proceeded.

Gathering intelligence was one thing but collating it and acting upon it were quite another. There was no qualified intelligence cell nor officer to support me or my staff. It was not until very late into the operation that I became aware of an Army Intelligence cell embarked in HMS *Intrepid*, and I certainly was not privy to the results of their work, which still seems odd. On 2 April an officer had been sought who would take on the additional responsibilities of Staff Intelligence Officer (SIO). Lieutenant-Commander Chris Meatyard was MCD (Mine Counter Measures Diver) trained but it soon became apparent that either intelligence or diving would take up his time, but not both at the same time. Despite acquiring Lieutenant-Commander Dobinson to take over Chris's intelligence duties and the further acquisition of an RAF Officer, Flight Lieutenant White (of whom more below, and who was to be killed in an air accident over the North Sea shortly after the war), my organization never matched that of 3 Commando Brigade. The lack of a dedicated intelligence cell was a serious omission but one that was filled by a mixture of both *Fearless*'s own and visiting officers on loan.

An example of the excellent background advice that would be provided by Flight Lieutenant White was the daily air threat reduction assessments with which he presented an insight of enemy numbers available, modes of attack, rates of attrition and the knock-on effects of this to the Argentinians – and of course therefore, to us. With hindsight all this information appears, perhaps, immaterial but at the same time it was to be a major factor in maintaining morale and a determination to stick it out in San Carlos, an area which I considered best for our survival but which some were to see as a trap which would 'certainly lead to heavy casualties and disaster'. They were wrong.

Most sources of raw intelligence data (other than those from our special forces on the ground) were fed direct to CTF and not to us in *Fearless*. Thus much of the information that we did receive had already been collated and evaluated. Because of delays inherent in any communications system its tactical value was often reduced. Even so, much of the information was to be quite remarkable for the insight it gave. The need to protect sources of information is accepted as paramount. While it could be argued that Julian and I would have preferred the raw data to be fed to us direct this would inevitably have required a bigger staff to cope with it, filter it and collate it. It is a very fine balance. By and large we were happy with the system that existed, although the delays in the receipt of information gained from within our own force did irritate. Some of this had to be sent back 8,000 miles before it could be released to us. There must be a quicker system.

Essential for amphibious operations is the ability to seek and destroy mines, for by its very nature this form of warfare is able to inflict the greatest disasters in shallow waters from these pests. While I was pretty certain that Falkland Sound and San Carlos Waters were not mined, it would have been nice to have had this hunch confirmed.

On 10 May Sandy detached HMS *Alacrity* under the command of Commander Chris Craig to make a pass up the length of Falkland Sound. This was a brave move by the Type 21 frigate but I was then and remain now, unconvinced that one pass by a small ship indicates the absence of mines. Apart from the safe transit of this waterway it was nearly a night of mixed blessings for the Fleet. *Alacrity* engaged and sank the 830 ton Argentine supply vessel *Isla de los Estados* off the Swan Islands but was herself to be targeted by the submarine *San Luis* when in company with *Arrow* off the north coast of East Falkland the following morning. The single, wire-guided SST-4 torpedo is believed to have hit *Arrow*'s torpedo decoy, which, of course, is why we tow them astern!

The particular submarine threat I mentioned above was to be short-lived for the *San Luis* returned to her mainland base on the 11th having surfaced only once in the previous month and having had no contact with the British fleet apart from this brief and unsuccessful encounter. Thankfully for us she was away just when she would have been needed most by the Argentinians – but we did not know it then.

On 12 May, at long last, we received CTF's Operation Order containing his new aim which was to now, 'Repossess the Falkland Islands as quickly as possible'. The Op Order also confirmed that San Carlos had been accepted as the Landing Force's destination, which was just as well as Julian had already distributed his forty-seven page written orders that same morning and planned to give his verbal Brigade Orders based on them the next day. The one aspect not yet firm was the date. That was also being left to Julian and me to decide (it would then be confirmed from London depending on the up-to-the-moment political situation), although our choice was now narrowed further to between the night of 19/20 May and the night of 24/25. Whichever day was chosen there was still much work to be done.

To Julian's and my surprise the Operation Order appeared to us to be a rather hurriedly put together signal that (even if I had been landing just one commando under NATO conditions) called for a very tight landing schedule. I said so to Northwood but was simply told that they knew that and I was to do the best I could.

The operation was to be conducted in six phases:

Phase 1. Blockade of the TEZ. [Already happening]
   2. SF recce and direct action tasks. [Already happening]
   3. Amphibious Landing including mine-sweeping operations. [We possessed no mine-sweepers, as CTF knew]
   4. Land operations before the arrival of 5 Brigade.
   5. CLFFI to join HMS *Fearless* and 5 Bde to land.
   6. Repossession of the whole islands. [But were we to wait for the second brigade before breaking out? Was 5 Brigade to be used as reserves or in the front line, etc?]

Some limits were set:

   1. Phase 3 not to be carried out until sea and air superiority achieved or this phase to be carried out by night.

2. Casualties to civilians to be avoided but some damage to civilian property acceptable.

Timing guidelines were issued: the Amphibious Task Group was not to enter the Exclusion Zone before 18 May with D-Day not before the 20th. CLFFI – Commander Land Forces Falkland Islands, as General Jeremy Moore had now been appointed – would arrive in the TEZ about 28 May with 5 Infantry Brigade about 1 June. However, there was still no Concept of Operations for the post-landing period nor, in the same context, any indication whether 5 Brigade was to remain in San Carlos or whether they were to take part in active operations – a decision, either way, that would affect our actions on landing. While we could understand that the initial landing of the troops could be made at night this would not be possible for the off-load. The signal was therefore something of a muddle which did not encourage the Army and Royal Marine members of the landing force staff to have much more faith in the Royal Navy. My staff continued to take the brunt of this ill-ease.

Later that day Julian received a signal from CLFFI in the form of a directive:

1. You are to secure a bridgehead on East Falkland, into which reinforcements can be landed, in which an airstrip can be established, and from which operations to repossess the Falkland Islands can be developed.

2. You are to push forward from the bridgehead area, so far as the maintenance of its security allows, to gain information and to forward the ultimate objective of repossession.

3. You will retain operational control of all forces landed in the Falklands until I establish my headquarters in the area. It is my intention to do this, aboard *Fearless*, as early as practicable after the landing. I expect this to be approximately on D+7.

4. It is my intention to land 5 Inf Bde into the bridgehead and to develop operations for the complete repossession of the Falkland Islands.

But, as I noted at the time, Jeremy Moore was instructing my

Landing Force Commander and not me and yet it was my responsibility to secure a bridgehead – or, I felt more correctly, a beachhead. Once again we seemed to be turning the drill book upside down and, while I was quite prepared to do my utmost to make the operation a success, this sort of confusion only makes for difficulties, particularly between the staffs, and it was all very late in the day for good, safe planning to be achieved.

Julian and I felt that this directive, while helpful, was too vague, omitting as it did any reference to a strategy for a subsequent land battle, for the initial landings needed to be planned and conducted with some future concept of operations in mind. Paragraph 3 should not have been stated as an order to Julian since all landing craft and helicopters, who would probably be ashore, should remain under my operational control until after the amphibious operation. Nor was there (apart from a loose reference at Paragraph 4) any definitive talk of 5 Brigade and its tasks. Were we to wait for them? Were they to look after Fox Bay and Port Howard, Darwin and Goose Green or were they to advance with the commandos or form a garrison at San Carlos – or what? What was clear was that Julian should not move his Brigade from San Carlos until after the arrival of Jeremy Moore, although we were drawing up plans for any such move.

There were, therefore, one or two refinements we needed to suggest, and I did so in what I deliberately intended to be a discreet signal high-lighting; our belief that repossession of the Falklands would be, in a sense, a continuing amphibious task; our doubt that the amphibious offload phase would be completed inside a week during which time we should not necessarily engage the enemy but consolidate the beachhead and build a Harrier pad before patrolling, probing and recceing the northern routes towards Stanley. We also felt it important to conduct demoralizing and intelligence-gathering raids on Darwin and selected targets on West Falkland. In the event we were to be far too busy to do much raiding and quite correctly Fox Bay and Port Howard were to be contained by night bombardments allowing the main military force to head for the main prize. In addition we did not plan to land all the Brigade stores but to keep significant stocks afloat (and way to the east) with the idea of bringing them forward as the Brigade advanced along the north.

My signal also showed that Julian and I were thinking, from the beginning, that we wanted to advance as soon as we were ready and able and that we did not want to get involved with a southern flank. Although we knew Port Salvador to be exposed, with care and ingenuity it would allow penetration by landing and raiding craft beaching close to Mount Kent and the hills near Stanley. Guns and heavy stores could be transported without wasting the few helicopters.

The CTF agreed with Julian's and my outline thoughts and signalled a partially helpful reply which roughly read:

> During phase 6 (the) concept is to continue operations as outlined (by you) for Phase 4. Intend enemy reserves at Darwin/Goose Green be destroyed as soon as possible to allow freedom of manoeuvre and if opportunity offers for you to achieve this during Phase 4 I will welcome that. However, we must still aim to close with the main enemy at Port Stanley. Static defensive positions there will be destroyed piecemeal making maximum use of artillery, NGS, close air support and ops at up to sub-unit level, particularly at night to exploit superior training of our troops. 5 Inf Bde will reinforce these ops once they are ashore. Enemy on West Falkland, if not destroyed, will be isolated by naval blockade. I suspect they will surrender once Port Stanley has fallen.

Thankfully, we were on much the same lines. However, I saw that the option of destroying Darwin/Goose Green was less essential. We had no intention of using the long southern route and we could hold the high ground overlooking them. An attack would involve a major helicopter-borne operation which to my mind we did not want to consider at all until fully ready and probably, therefore, not until the Division had landed. Darwin and Goose Green had not of course yet been reinforced. This is not hindsight; we both thought this at the time. Nevertheless we noted the requirement. On other matters Julian's view (expanded in a later chapter) was that this Op Order had not been written by anyone with a knowledge of land fighting, for a 'soldier' knows that static defensive positions are seldom, if ever, destroyed by artillery or naval gunfire. Here, at last, was a real hint on how 5 Brigade was to be used – but only a hint.

Sandy now had confirmation that our choice of San Carlos had been accepted by 'London' and was in a position to discuss timings and support. He reminded us that to meet a D Day on the night of the 19/20 May the decision to proceed towards the AOA would need to be made by the evening of 18 May, at which time the Amphibious Task Group would have to start its transit of the Exclusion Zone. He reminded us, too, that local weather would be a deciding factor and that an unopposed assault would need overcast weather for the approach – factors which, naturally, had always been uppermost in our minds.

A second signal exercised his worries over air superiority – and, heaven knows, we had them as well! He believed that we were not giving 'sufficient recognition' to the air defence of the AOA to which I replied that, although we continued to express concern over this aspect, our worries had always been met with promises that no landing would take place until the air threat had been eliminated. He was worried (were we not?) that while he was fog-bound far to the east we would be defenceless apart from Rapier. He therefore urged us to get Rapier ashore at the earliest stage, a deployment that, from 2 April onwards, had been given the utmost consideration by the two staffs in *Fearless*.

To some extent we saw Sandy's signals as yardarm-clearing exercises. We had discussed these matters at great length between ourselves and had tried to brief him. We were only too well aware of the need to activate our air-defence weapons as soon as possible. He, of course, had until now been preoccupied with his earlier duties and needed to understand our problems. He was also the senior CTG and as such no doubt felt he had an overall responsibility for us. I did not, though, share Sandy's trust in Rapier as I knew it was a point and not area air defence system and that we had been issued with the 'daylight only' version. Ever since Julian and I had worked out for ourselves that air superiority was unlikely to feature over the beachhead we planned to rely heavily on defensive procedures.

What was missing in the equation was any concept of Argentine Air Force operations. Did they use a dive-bombing attack or simply stick to rockets and front machine guns? Would they come in mass waves in order to saturate our defences, as I thought most probable, or would they come in dribs and drabs?

I did not expect them to use a low-level delivery without high drag bombs (bombs with retarding parachutes or tail fins) as this was potentially very dangerous for the aircraft. If the bomb exploded there was unlikely to be sufficient distance between the explosion and the aircraft for safety, and the pilot could easily kill himself. The low-level approach was, however, much safer against heavy guns and missiles which needed radar control as the radar was liable to bounce off the sea and create inaccuracies at low level. It was also an extremely accurate method of delivery. We had practised it many times and, even with concrete or inert bombs, I knew enormous damage could be achieved by a half-ton lump hitting a ship at about 400 knots, but San Carlos Water was surrounded by land and they would therefore have less to fear from guns and missiles than, I hoped, small arms.

A dive attack, if correctly executed, allows for adequate separation between aircraft and explosion for safety without losing too much accuracy. By introducing vertical as well as lateral movement I felt it would be potentially the more dangerous for us. Our machine gunners would have a more difficult task in tracking and shooting down the aircraft, and so I considered it possibly the wisest choice for the Argentine aircrew.

I appreciated that at some 400 miles from base few of the aircrew would have enjoyed flying a single-engined aircraft over the sea and even less returning to base if it was damaged. Most aircrew fly because they enjoy the excitement and, possibly, the glamour of handling high performance aircraft, and few join with a killer instinct. This, like pushing a bayonet into another man, has to be trained and I doubted if the Argentines' aircrew were of this calibre as I understood most of their flying had been overland against largely unarmed dissidents. Maybe they trained against shipping but there were few naval threats to practise against in the southern hemisphere. We would, of course, need that battle-winner, luck, but I have always felt that luck can be generated by careful planning and it was to this end that we had been working flat out since I sighted that signal in Fort Southwick.

Apart from the closeness of the Argentine Air Force, the main reason why I did not, totally, like San Carlos was the range at which our own Harriers would have to operate; this had been discussed at length with Sandy who believed he could just support us at that distance.

As far as the air defence of San Carlos was to be concerned Flight Lieutenant White and I spent a considerable time together, after some difficulty, it has to be said, for White was not used to talking to senior officers especially one with rather more Buccaneer experience than he! Although, as a Fleet Air Arm Observer, I was happy to do my own sums, I was, throughout the war, determined to get the staff to do the work so I could double-check my own calculations. White 'flew' himself in his imagination from the mainland airfields, let himself down through cloud and chose his identification points to make his approach to San Carlos and other planned anchorages. We agreed that it would be a little like flighting duck and tried to discover the significant aspects which would determine the anchorage positions for the initial phases of the landings. I placed *Canberra* inside what I believed would be a tight turn (for an aircraft) close to the entrance to San Carlos, thereby hoping to catch the enemy aircrew by surprise. If damaged, and providing she sank upright, we knew that in that position her upper decks would be clear of the water. This did not bear thinking about, nor was it discussed with any of the *Canberra* officers, although I would be surprised if they had not done their own sums.

While there is a possibility that, with luck, we might have detected enemy aircraft by radio intercept (their radio discipline was to be quite good) the chances of doing so in sufficient time would be unlikely. This was to mean that without airborne early warning radar we were unlikely to be able to catch them before they had made their attacks; attrition would have to be conducted after they had done some damage, but at least some might not return. As Seacat was the only ship-borne surface-to-air missile that might have had some capability in enclosed waters I planned that *Fearless* and *Intrepid* would be stationed at each end of San Carlos Water and the amphibious force. *Fearless*, having the staff embarked and possessing the only satellite communication system I placed at the slightly safer southern end. This also allowed the SATCOM dish to 'see' the satellite over Fannings Head. Having placed what I called the 'citadels' at either end and realizing that the 4.5″ gun frigates would be useless in that role because of land clutter and lack of warning time for their radars, we would have to rely on all manner of small arms, Very pistols, chaff decoys and rockets, if only to make the pilots believe that they were under heavier fire than they were. I was only sad that the brown, smoke-puff was no longer in naval service, along with barrage balloons and smoke.

The question of air-superiority is a contentious one. It is a positive phrase for a very subjective situation. We could never hope to have the air superiority the Allied Air Forces achieved in the first few days of *Operation Overlord* and so we had to be prepared for a considerable air threat if they chose to punch hard and suddenly. This, after all, is the main advantage of aircraft. When made that promise by CTF in Northwood I realized that it was more for political/public relations than as a statement of fact. During the approach to the AOA I was equally clear that if the AAF was not attacking Sandy's ships, it was because they were either too far away or that they were saving themselves for us.

The way was now open for the three CTGs 'on the spot' to discuss the final events leading up to the landings. What intelligence we did have, then, of enemy dispositions indicated a sizeable detachment of aircraft based precisely nineteen miles from the entrance to Falkland Sound at Pebble Island. Julian discussed it with me and invited Mike Rose to begin his planning for this task as early as 7 May, the day we sailed from Ascension.

It was then discussed with Sandy and the raid was set up. Although it was a form of amphibious advance force operation and was to use helicopter assets of mine, now deployed forward with Sandy, I took no further part in the discussions, leaving it to Julian and Mike Rose.

The eight-man recce for the Pebble Island Raid (as it became known) was inserted by Sea King into the eastern coastline of Port Purvis at midnight on 12/13 May. They lay up during the next day and crossed to Pebble Island by boat at 0400 on the 14th. By 1700 that day they were able to confirm that the two 'crossed' Pebble Island grass 'runways' were the base for a number of aircraft. The main raid was 'on'.

At 2030 that evening HMS *Hermes* and *Broadsword* had detached from the Carrier Battle Group to a position seventy-two miles from the SAS's landing site. D Squadron was launched in three Sea Kings at 0225 on the 15th from this spot to land on the south-eastern coast of Pebble Island (Phillips Cove) at 0350 where they were met by the recce party.

Meanwhile HMS *Glamorgan* had detached from the Carrier Battle Group at 2030 on the 14th to take up station for a diversionary fire plan onto First Mountain (overlooking the Pebble Island settlement) at H Hour. Between 0350 and 0610 D Squadron received their brief and moved to a lying up position overlooking the objective twenty minutes before H Hour at 0630.

During the course of the next forty-five minutes the SAS destroyed more aircraft than had been destroyed by more conventional means over the previous fourteen days. When the raid was completed it was an immense relief to know that a significant number of Pucara, in particular, had been among those destroyed.

Four Sea Kings were despatched to collect the recce and assault teams who were safely back on board at 1045 allowing the carrier and her escorts to return to the fold by 1230 on the 15th at the end of a classic operation that cost the enemy dearly: to be precise six Pucara, four Mentor, one Skyvan, one ton of 20mm ammunition and rockets, about one thousand gallons of fuel, all adding to a severe loss of confidence and morale. It was a brilliant little action and I hoped to find an opportunity to complete a similar one against their helicopters which I regarded as possibly an even more dangerous threat as they allowed for an Argentine counter-attack, perhaps directly on to the beachhead and shipping in San Carlos. If they achieved this early in the campaign then it could prove fatal to our plans.

A second direct action, Special Force Operation, was planned, but I was not privy to it. Once again one of my valuable Sea King Mark IVs was lost and I suspect that an anti-submarine Sea King with its better navigation system would have been more usefully employed.

However politically exciting and militarily useful these raids were (I remembered the uncleared use of my Wessex in South Georgia) I wondered seriously just how many troop-lift aircraft I would have lost by D Day. Command of the support helicopters was not clear despite telephone calls to Northwood. I hoped Sandy would not see them as his assets as they are normally allocated to the CATF at the start of an amphibious operation and this had not formally occurred. The two squadrons were housed throughout the task force in penny packets. 846 Squadron had five Sea Kings in *Hermes* for night advanced force operations, with nine more spread between *Fearless, Intrepid, Elk* and *Canberra*. The few Wessex 5 of 845 Squadron were stored below decks in *Intrepid* and on *Tidepool, Tidespring, Resource* and *Atlantic Conveyor*. Two had been lost in South Georgia and some remained at Ascension. In all at this stage we had about fourteen Sea Kings and five Wessex operational which was less than we could normally expect on an exercise.

On 13 May, with our destination (but not timings) confirmed by Northwood, Julian gave his orders for the amphibious landing of the 3rd Commando Brigade and I sent a signal to all ships under my command:

As we close our objective I wish you to pay careful attention to the following:

a. Visual lookouts. A forgotten but vital art especially in inshore waters. They must become more reliable than electronic gadgets.

Nurse them and ensure their reports are published on board correctly and quickly.

b. STUFT. Don't expect warships or RFAs to notice things first. Don't by shy, lives depend on every piece of information.

c. Communications. Cut non-essential traffic …

d. Time Zone …

e. Morale. Keep me informed of any problems, in particular if you believe I can help. Other problems are up to you. I cannot control threats and so we must attempt to reduce their effectiveness. Once in our objective area life should become simple and predictable.

On 14 May the following was written in the staff diary: 'SNOs and Masters of STUFT now showing increasing concern on degree of usage of STUFT in TEZ/AOA. COMAW trying to assuage.' All along, the merchant ships had been under the understanding that they would not be involved in 'the fighting war', while it was obvious to Julian and me that they would be essential and I was trying to get London to come clean about their use.

At about this late stage Sandy asked us to seriously consider Low Bay in Lafonia as a beachhead option. In his view it offered 'clear arcs of fire for anti-aircraft systems and good, large, well-protected anchorage'. But around the edge of this otherwise ideal spot there was not one beach across which troops and vehicles could be landed. If they could have landed they would then have to pass through the geographical and military bottleneck of Goose Green, whether they wanted to or not. I much preferred San Carlos for the defence of my Task Group, but avoided argument by simply sending a signal with Julian's agreement that the Landing Force Commander did not like it. It could have been a major last-minute spanner in our works if we had been ordered to use it and would, I believe, have spelt disaster.

The contents of Julian's 'O' Group did not come as a surprise to the participants, for, signal or no signal from CTF, he had issued the forty-seven page long Brigade Operation Order a few days earlier. In effect this document was a set of advance confirmatory notes to what would be given at the 'verbal' Orders Group. I would hold my equivalent, the Pre-Landing Conference, once the Helicopter Assault Landing Tables, the Surface Assault Schedules and the final planning signal – OPGEN Mike – had been sent, none of which could be detailed and confirmed until Julian had, after agreement with us, finally decided the order in which, and by which, we would put his units ashore, consolidate, defend and supply them, the whole planning process being cyclical between the two staffs.

After the preliminary paragraphs detailing topography, friendly and enemy forces, Julian stood to give his mission. In the time-honoured manner this was short, direct, clear, unambiguous, given by him personally and repeated. The 3rd Commando Brigade was to conduct a silent night landing in the San Carlos Area supported and escorted by ships of the Royal Navy, Royal Fleet Auxiliary and Merchant Navy. By dawn the Brigade would hold the high ground above San Carlos Settlement, the disused Ajax Bay mutton factory and Port San Carlos Settlement. As soon as possible after first light one Light Gun Battery would land to be followed by the Rapier Battery and then the remaining guns.

George Pearson, my Senior Staff Officer, gave a short naval brief. In another life he would have made an excellent Scottish minister and, when he suggested our approach to San Carlos might be their longest day, there were looks of distinct concern among some of the soldiers.

We were now committed to a three-wave landing that required 40 and 45 Commandos to beach simultaneously before moving to high ground: 40 Commando to Pony's Valley Bay (Blue Beach) two hundred yards or so north-west of San Carlos and beneath Verde Mountain and 45 Commando to Ajax Bay (Red Beach) and thence to Campito Hill. In the second wave 3 Para would take Port San Carlos via the beach to the west (Green Beach) and then move on to Settlement Rocks and 2 Para would pass through the beach south of San Carlos settlement secured by 40 Commando before turning southwards to seize Sussex Mountain. To make matters easy all the beaches matched the

Commando or Battalion Regimental colours. The third wave required helicopters to begin the lift ashore of the supporting arms at first light. 42 Commando (whose regimental colour is white) would remain on board the Great White Whale, *Canberra*, as Brigade reserves. The Logistic Regiment would stay afloat initially to land supplies from the shipping. They were warned, though, that a move ashore would be imminent and that when required it would need to be conducted with as much speed as our limited assets would allow.

The two troops of the Blues and Royals would land one each with 40 Commando and 3 Para. Numerous other tasks were given and confirmed in the written orders: combat engineer support, medical, priority of work in the Brigade defence position, and on the OP screen. My own Staff Officer Operations gave the outline for Naval Gunfire Support, the helicopter and landing craft plans and the composition and movements of the supporting warships, RFAs and STUFT. Timings (but not yet the date of the day itself) would all be confirmed in the highly detailed OPGEN Mike signal that we could now complete and distribute. This was the name given for the general operational signal covering all the details of an operational assault. It is laid out in a standard order to avoid confusion. To the newcomer this is a complicated document so we issued blank copies for those not familiar with the format. (For instance, confusingly, H Hour is when the landing craft first 'hit the beach' while L Hour is when the first helicopter lands on its objective.)

The unconfirmed timings (which were to be altered yet again anyway) had been the result of compromise, as, indeed, was the order of landing and the entire amphibious operation. Up-to-the-minute information was to reach us shortly before D Day, forcing even more last-minute changes. Although Julian's overriding concern had been to land safely (and that meant without the loss of men at sea or during the final approaches) he had told me the time by when he wanted his men in their positions and between the two of us we had worked back from that. Ideally, of course, he had preferred to land as soon after sunset as possible to give his men the maximum amount of darkness to approach and secure their objectives on the beaches and their co-located heights. I, of course, wanted to approach the AOA under cover of the same amount of darkness which suggested a landing at or just before dawn. Some days before, in the nature of amphibious operations, we had agreed an acceptable compromise, although this was not yet promulgated, for we still needed London's final word of command and confirmation of the landing day.

To emphasize the reality of the situation *Operation Corporate* had at last been accorded the status of Active Service effective from midnight on 14/15 May. Among other legal niceties the press were now under military discipline (about time too, I remember thinking at the time!) and given the rank of army captain. This status affected the civilian crews rather more seriously.

Fortunately most of the Masters were RNR, but many of their crews were not. Julian and I had found the press a major problem from the start which we could well have done without. This was to have unfortunate results. Basically there were too many of them and we found them too demanding at a time when we had vital things to do. We could not take the risk of them coming on board *Fearless* where the planning was taking place. We could not afford valuable helicopter time to show them what we were doing and to educate them by visiting ships, etc. Once we got to San Carlos they all went ashore in the hope of finding action, which was a relief to me. We had also had fairly strict instructions on what to tell them, which I found too constrictive. It would have been better if we had had one or two trustworthy men in whom we could confide and the quality of reporting would have been much improved. As it was, they had to seek their stories from any source, and they did. Julian had been very concerned at Ascension that one member of the press had, for instance, attempted to stir up rivalries between the Para and his Marines. He had been adamant that there should be no cap badge politics in his Brigade.

On 15 May I held my Pre-Landing Conference in HMS *Fearless* for the captains of all ships, (war, auxiliary and merchant) plus their navigators, PWOs and, where appropriate,

SNOs. At this meeting my staff promulgated my instructions for the groupings and approach route to San Carlos, which would be amplified in OPGEN Mike. In outline the Amphibious Task Group would head due west into the Total Exclusion Zone and then turn south-west for the entrance to North Falkland Sound. Before entering the Sound we would split into three sub-groups for anchorages and fire positions where appropriate. These would range from south-west round to north-west of Chancho Point at the southern entrance to San Carlos Waters. No ships would enter San Carlos Waters until the beaches and high ground were in our hands. All landing craft would launch in Falkland Sound. That was the broad plan.

The first group into the Sound would be the escorts *Antrim* and *Ardent* whose task was to give us early warning of any enemy operations that might be in the area; *Ardent* would also be needed for Naval Gunfire Support onto Goose Green. Next would come *Fearless* followed by *Intrepid* one mile astern, escorted by *Yarmouth*. The LPDs had to get in as early as possible for they needed time to ballast down, flood their docks and launch their heavy-lift landing craft. The second group, with the main troop lift escorted by *Plymouth* in the lead, would consist of *Canberra*, *Norland* and *Stromness* followed by *Fort Austin* and finally *Brilliant*. The third group with immediate stores, Rapier and guns, escorted by *Broadsword* and *Argonaut* would be the five LSLs and *Europic Ferry*. They would not be needed until after daylight when their loads would be landed straight onto the beaches from the San Carlos anchorage. I would have liked a Type 42 Destroyer as well with her Sea Dart but Sandy was absolutely fair, had to safeguard the carriers and knew more about 42/22 'combos' than I did; he believed that as I had *Antrim* with me with her Seaslug, heavier gun and greater close-in air defence capability and two Sea-Wolf-fitted Type 22 frigates I was as well catered for as I could reasonably expect. He needed the Type 42s with their longer ranged Sea Dart missiles to defend the carriers.

Further orders included action on air attack, submarine attack and the instruction that all anchor cables were to be prepared to be broken and buoyed with every ship at immediate notice to sail. While Masters were given the authority to slip and manoeuvre during attacks (if they felt safer) they were not to get in the way of the escorts who would never anchor. LSLs, if hit badly, were to run aground. *Fort Austin*'s ASW helicopters would be on continual anti-submarine duties in the Sound under the direction of *Argonaut*; they would initially check out San Carlos, as would a Lynx fitted with a magnetic anomaly detector.

I ordered all escorts to keep to the sides of San Carlos and used the expression 'a duck shoot' to impress upon captains that I expected the aircraft to fly in relatively predictable paths. I expected them to use a low-level approach, but then to pull up and make a shallow dive attack. That being so, I believed that all fire would be directed upwards and towards the middle of the water making it relatively safe for the men ashore and afloat. I called this the 'Clapptrap' and it was set up to achieve the maximum attrition rate with our extremely limited capability. In fact, when the aircraft did not approach us in shallow dives but chose to attack at sea level with standard bombs and no retard fins or parachutes, I formed the opinion that the pilots were thinking of their own skins first and found enormous relief and comfort.

Broadsword, whose Captain, Bill Canning, was senior to me on the Captain's list, would be in overall command of all the escorts within the Amphibious Task Group. Due partly to the primitive nature of the LPD's operations room it was normal practice for warfare duties to be farmed out to the escorts with us acting as a monitor. It was not totally satisfactory as we lost direct control which I felt was important in such a tight and unusual situation.

On the 16th we received information from an SBS patrol that there was now an enemy position occupying Fannings Head overlooking the entrance to Falkland Sound. It was possible, too, that this was not just to observe and report but to induce a delay to any British landings, should we choose such an area. I did not know then, although it was not difficult to guess, that this OP possessed some anti-armour weapons. A small anti-tank weapon could play havoc not just with 'soft-skinned' landing craft but (as

Lieutenant Mills had showed them in South Georgia) with warships and their weapon systems. I dubbed this enemy detachment 'The Fannings Head Mob' and invited my staff to think of some effective way to prevent them from reporting or firing. This they did, taking advice from the Brigade staff.

While the Fannings Head Mob were not likely to alter our overall plans significantly (we decided to enter the Sound via the western entrance where the water was deep and the current, we hoped, ran strong, making mining difficult, instead of to the east of Sunk Rock). Further news from the SBS did cause some changes. Although concerned about Fannings Head I was more worried by reports that the enemy strategic reserve, thought to be at Fitzroy, was in fact deployed north of Darwin and within easy striking distance of Sussex Mountain, 2 Para's objective. If the enemy were given just a few hours warning they could be on the hill first, particularly if they had sufficient helicopters.

With only enough landing craft to land two commandos/ battalions at any one time and with the need, now, to get 2 Para onto their objective as early as possible, and certainly before any other activity had put the Argentinians on notice of a landing, we decided to put the paras ashore in the first wave and 45 Commando into Ajax Bay in the second. With a ten-minute advance on 40 Commando landing in Pony's Valley Bay this would now give 2 Para a clear run to Sussex Mountain and help avoid any mix up should there be enemy between the two San Carlos Settlement beaches if the two units landed simultaneously. Given a modicum of luck, they would be able to advance on Sussex Mountain a little earlier and unhindered.

This of course meant that the two sides of the 'loch' would not be taken simultaneously and that any enemy on the west bank would have an hour or so to engage both units on the opposite side, but we reckoned that Sussex Mountain and Verde Mountain were of more importance and certainly did not believe that there was much chance of a substantial enemy force being on Wreck Point with no escape route. It did, though, add emphasis to the necessity of having a frigate with its 4.5 inch turret accompanying the landing craft. On the 18th I chose HMS

Plymouth for this task, for whom Ewen then produced a written navigational guide to the kelp and local problems in San Carlos Water.

While all this was being deliberated we received news from CTF that the Britannia Royal Naval College annual Argentine Prize 'May not be awarded this year'. Quite so!

The South Atlantic Task Force came together, nearly in its entirety, for the first time during 18 May and even for a naval officer it was an impressive sight. It was not quite complete, for *Invincible* and her escorts were already in the Total Exclusion Zone nearer the Falklands.

At lunchtime, I flew across to see Sandy in order to confirm that we were both content with what was about to happen. Julian had declined the invitation for no more ulterior motive than that he really had nothing to contribute and, indeed, it was not his business. Julian had made his plans in concert with my staff; it was now up to me, with Sandy's support and help, to 'make them so'.

The meeting was helpful. I had taken in my hip pocket copious detailed notes of my plans and was ready to answer any questions he may have. In fact he asked no questions, merely saying that it was now his role to support us and from his tiny sea cabin he showed me his Operations Room. This brought home to me the fact that he was living in very cramped quarters, whereas I, with no similar sea cabin, was living in considerably more style and comfort with my dining room at hand for briefings and planning. I had space to hold discussions and think whereas he was obliged to work under very much more restricted conditions and I did not envy him.

Sandy was sympathetic to my needs, agreeing with me that the AAF was obviously now saving itself for an all-out attack against my force at a time appropriate to them. He was, though, adamant that the carriers, at least until a forward operating base could be established ashore, needed the utmost protection: if we were to lose them before the landings then there would be no landings. I was in total agreement and returned to *Fearless*.

I was relieved, and briefed Julian accordingly, that Sandy had not given any impression that he saw himself in charge of the entire operation but that he was now clearly keen to see that we were successful and would do all he could to help. He would of course continue, as the Senior Officer, to exercise control over the allocation of naval assets, reacting to any request I may make. We seemed to be on track together.

The thought of taking *Canberra* with three major units embarked into Falkland Sound had always filled me with horror, and I had said so; but what else could I do? This had been put to CTF, Jeremy Moore and Sandy at Ascension but as nothing further was ever said I assumed that CTF was accepting the risk. They all knew, too, that there could be no serious transfer between ships possible after we sailed. We had, after all, passed through the area known as the Roaring Forties and were now entering the Furious Fifties.

And yet the evening of the 18th produced the largest change to our plans. During those last days before D Day we conducted a large number of pre-H Hour, cross-decking, fine-tuning moves designed to reflect the final landing order. All was set. Orders had been issued, men (if not equipment) were now in the correct ships as far as had been possible, complicated timings for loading into landing craft had been promulgated and practised with great care (but only once in some cases) at Ascension Island. Now all waited for the final word to 'Go'! Instead, that evening we received an invitation to move two of the units out of the luxury liner.

I had always made it quite clear that the bulk of the men would have to land from the ships in which they sailed, the silence from Northwood allowing us to believe that this was acceptable. Now, the only way to cross-deck was by landing craft, an unlikely event in the South Atlantic at the onset of winter about 300 miles from the nearest land – and that hostile.

The invitation to redistribute the men was unambiguous so that night we sat down with our staffs to find a solution. As each marine or paratrooper carried between seventy and one hundred pounds weight the helicopter lift for well over one thousand such laden men was huge – and unacceptable. We could have steamed to South Georgia or even to an out-of-the-way spot on West Falkland but neither of these were practicable: South Georgia was 'down weather', albeit only four days, and any cross-decking in Falkland Waters would need combat air patrol Harriers and escorts that would, inevitably, have compromised our plans. Any delay to the landings (now assumed to be the 21st) while we waited for suitable weather was equally unacceptable for two reasons: the men were hyped-up and cooped-up and could quickly go 'off the boil' under such conditions while the enemy could, at last (and in time) 'twig' that the San Carlos option was a good one from our point of view, and manoeuvre accordingly.

But the order when it came was not such a surprise to me (although unwelcome) as it may have been to Julian, though he didn't show it. Having stated that I was always worried at the use of *Canberra*, my concern now was that we were taking troops from a ship they knew well and from which they had all practised their assault procedures and were putting them into ships already grossly overloaded – and that certainly was a risk. *Canberra* had been designed to allow hordes of untrained, blue-rinsed Americans to escape with some safety from a fire; as she was not overloaded with three major units the troops would have had a better chance of escape from her than they would from the ships into which we were about to cram them. *Canberra* had enough life rafts for all her passengers; neither *Intrepid* nor *Fearless* could boast the same at 'overload plus'. On the other hand it could be argued that both the LPDs were designed to take on about 5000 tons of water as ballast, making the chances of sinking due to mines or torpedoes less probable than with any other warship or merchant ship in the Task Force; this was a notion we did not want to put to the test. The LPDs were also (but only marginally) better defended. In support of the LPD argument *Canberra*, with her great cathedral-like engine rooms, would sink like a stone if damaged underwater.

We considered a jack-stay transfer which, while possible, would have taken too long, and there would have been difficulty over the men's kit and weapons. What we did decide was that despite her overloaded state HMS *Fearless* would take in 40 Commando and HMS *Intrepid* 3 Para. A serious consideration was our position if for any reason the transfers had to be aborted in midstream. We could have units split across the fleet and that really would mess up D Day. 40 Commando was in the first assault wave using *Fearless*'s landing craft anyway and 2 Para would still have to be collected from *Norland* as planned. 40 Commando would at least be spared the slow business of embarking for an assault from *Canberra* through her inadequate side doors and 3 Para should not find the alien business of loading into landing craft too difficult (even without training) from a ship designed to launch an assault, which their present home was very definitely not designed to do! The practicalities of the cross-decking problem, though, were not solved. We turned in (praying for miracles) to make a final decision in the morning.

Very sadly there was one major catastrophe. A Sea King launched from *Hermes* with about seventeen men of the SAS on board crashed shortly after take-off, killing everyone. I was not to see Mike Rose look so stunned again but the war had begun and we had to get on with all the other tasks submerging us.

We delayed making any further decision on cross-decking until dawn on the 19th when, by sheer chance, Julian and I looked over the side and unbelievingly, were able to say to each other, 'It's on!' I could tell Northwood that the sea was quiet enough to use landing craft and that we would go ahead as best we could. I was loath to use helicopters as they were already employed in, to my mind, more important cross-decking than that of major units at such a stage of the operation. Paradoxically, there was always to be argument over my perceived over-use of helicopters but fortunately my own Fleet Air Arm experience and that of my squadron Commanding Officers told me that the more you use an aircraft the better it works. Up to a point I agreed!

At the same time that day, before dawn on the 19th, Jeremy Larken had called Ewen from his bunk. During the night the wind had dropped leaving a very long, six-foot, benign swell running and no sea. Jeremy sought a landing-craft officer's advice. Ewen was, then, the most experienced landing craft officer embarked in the fleet and so they conferred at the after end of the flight deck and down in the dock. LPDs had launched LCUs in heavier seas but always close to 'outside' engineering support if, say, it had been impossible to raise the dock gate again or pump out the ballast tanks. The prognosis on this day was that superficial damage would occur to the craft and the wooden-clad dock walls but, under the circumstances, these had to be acceptable risks. The order was given and probably the most remarkable mid-ocean, cross-decking exercise in history took place: just one man fell in (he was rescued wet but unharmed) and there was only minor structural damage. Nobody but the Almighty can take credit for this and I privately thanked him.

I had originally planned to issue the Helicopter Employment and Landing Table (HEALT), Surface Assault Schedule (SAS) and Operational Plan for the landings (OPGEN Mike) that day but this unexpected game of 'pass the parcel' had introduced amendments which needed to be incorporated before these vital, complicated and lengthy documents could be delivered 'by hand' throughout the Task Force.

With all diplomatic avenues exhausted, the 'war cabinet' gave approval on the morning of the 18th for the landings to proceed subject to final confirmation on the 20th. Consequently, at 1145, the Chief of the Defence Staff informed the Commander-in-Chief Fleet that he was authorized to execute *Operation Sutton* – subject to that final confirmation. For my part, by the end of the 19th all was ready for CTF's executive signal and so I informed him that as we were about to enter the Exclusion Zone we were ready to receive the command to 'Go!' I assured Admiral Fieldhouse that the Amphibious Task Group was now 'In all respects ready for war' and that the Task Force was complete.

On the 18th everybody knew this (including the Argentines), for yet another security breach occurred when the BBC announced that the two groups had joined forces and were now in a position to 're-invade', information that could only have been cleared by the MOD.

I seethed with anger (as did all in the Amphibious Task Group) for I was well aware that the operation was dangerous enough without having our only real key to success – surprise – jeopardized.

In anticipation of the final command I decided finally (with Julian) that H Hour would be 0230 local (0630 GMT) on the morning of 21 May and so made another signal to Northwood, copying it to Sandy in *Hermes*.

As a result, CTF asked to speak to me direct on the secure DSSS radio circuit before making his final decision and discussing it with the Prime Minister. The conversation was brief but encouraging:-

'Are you ready to go?'

'Yes, sir!'

The rest was an excellent conversation with the Admiral very calm and supportive and me trying to match his cool by sounding as cheerful as I could, especially as I was able to tell him personally that the cross-decking had gone miraculously well, for which he was extremely grateful. He then asked me, searchingly, about the state of the Landing Forces' morale and that of my own people, particularly the civilians. I explained that all morale was, in my view, remarkably high and that neither Julian nor I wished to delay. The weather for the morrow looked to be ideal with low cloud and we should not miss the chance. He asked me if I had spoken to Sandy and I confirmed that we had had a useful meeting at the end of which we both understood each other's problems better. CTF seemed content with that and told me that he would now seek the final confirmation. With that given, he would send a signal releasing us for the assault. He wished Julian and me, and our respective forces well.

'You are,' he ended, 'very much in my thoughts and prayers.'

As far as I was concerned this fitted in nicely with our standard procedures and I went off to debrief Julian. The signal releasing me duly came. I then sent Sandy the traditional request of all

Junior Officers to their Seniors at sea for permission to proceed in accordance with previous orders. This was duly approved. In his report of proceedings, Sandy stated that he in fact made the decision and ordered us to sail, but I never received a signal in that vein. I would at the time have been surprised if I had as it is very clearly laid down in amphibious practice that it is a decision that can only be made jointly by the Landing Force Commander with his Amphibious Task Force Commander. These were, of course, Julian and myself, and we were working to a Commander-in-Chief as our Task Force Commander who gave no indication that he had given the Carrier Battle Group Commander authority over us. It is unfortunate that, from small misunderstandings like this, major niggling and festering mistrust can arise. For this reason alone it is important to stick to agreed procedures as much as possible.

Relations with one's co-Task Group Commanders are always difficult as each has different priorities, needs and problems. (One Commander's bad weather is another's good and so on.) As far as my relations were concerned I was determined to keep the Argentinians as my enemy and that on no account was I going to get into any battle with Julian or Sandy, and certainly not with my Task Force Commander. Because of the requirement to be co-located and of co-equal rank, relationships with Julian were, I still consider, very good. Relationships with Sandy who was both senior and operating at a considerable distance from me were bound to be more difficult, particularly since the secure voice satellite system (DSSS) was so infuriatingly erratic. His voice sounded like a Dalek and it was extremely difficult to hold an easy and relaxed conversation.

Now finally committed, Sandy had the difficult decision to make over how he would support and protect us. Obviously, I needed protection up-threat but at the distance that the carriers were from San Carlos this was unlikely to be achieved for any length of time by Sea Harriers, and so I looked for a Type 42 with its long-range Sea Dart missile system. I knew little about the Type 22/Type 42 combinations, or 'combos' as they became called. In view of the importance of the carriers this was perhaps expecting too much and a compromise which pleased neither of us because of the risks involved. Once we had a forward operating base (FOB) well established for the Harriers, and with the troops dispersed and the majority of stores ashore, the situation should improve markedly we hoped.

In addition to a 'western' defence I wanted the Sea Harriers available up-threat at about fifty miles from the AOA. In the event, for the landings themselves, we had two Type 22s (for point defence) and a Seaslug fitted destroyer (for limited area air-defence) while the carriers remained in the eastern quarter of the Exclusion Zone accompanied by all the Type 42s. If nothing else this was to ensure that while the enemy aircraft might not be engaged head-on during their approach they would, with our pilots' skill and good air direction from my frigates, be caught as they returned having done their dirty work. Not ideal, indeed far from ideal, but this was the best we could do. After the landings I wanted three CAP (Combat Air Patrol) positions, one directly up-threat, one to cover the entrance to San Carlos and one over the north of Lafonia to catch them if they came up the Sound from the south. My aim was to make the AAF pilots' task difficult by having Sussex Mountain at one end and giving them a dog-leg round Chancho Point/Fannings Head at the other. However, three CAPs needed at least six aircraft on station, a further six on deck-alert and a further six in transit. As this did not take any account of the Carrier Battle Group's own defence I knew that it was to be an impossibly high bill for them to meet. Harriers of course do not hover while looking up-threat, they have to patrol in, say, a figure of eight and so for substantial periods would not be looking in the direction of the threat – another consideration we all had to ponder.

In practice my experience suggested to me that the chances of head on attacks by our own aircraft would be slim and that the Harriers would have to rely on a stern chase and their Sidewinder missiles. I knew all along that my ships would probably have to take the first attacks and that the anti-air warfare control ship would have to tip off the Harriers. It is unfortunate that there was not sufficient time to talk to the

Harrier Squadrons' Commanding Officers when I had met Sandy. I would have been able to learn more from them about their capabilities and so discuss our air-defence problems in detail. At our meeting Sandy had made it quite clear that he did not expect to be able to get more than, say, two aircraft overhead as combat air patrol at any one time. If we were to perceive a definite pattern in the Argentine operations (which is what happened to begin with) he would put it up to four. We were to achieve that later with the commissioning of our Harrier pad near Port San Carlos. The importance of Rapier and our own self-defence against air attacks as well as the early establishment of a forward operating base for the Harriers was obvious.

Having been blessed with perfect weather when we needed it most, for the cross-decking on the 20th, within the Exclusion Zone we were further blessed with the miracle of perfect conditions for our approach. This time the weather was unpleasant but not excessively rough, with very low cloud which would not be good for conventional air attack and poor but acceptable visibility at sea level which would be good for visual inter-ship communications and control without using radar or radio except in very limited circumstances.

On that day I asked the Commanding Officers of *Broadsword*, *Antrim* and *Argonaut* (who were to be the individual warfare controllers) and *Intrepid* to come on board and discuss my signal ordering the formation for the daylight approach and for the defence of the AOA: respectively, Bill Canning for overall coordination, Brian Young as the anti-air warfare controller and Kit Layman as the anti-submarine warfare controller. I had never operated with a Type 22 and so needed advice on that ship, her systems and capabilities. I would like to have asked the captains of the other ships such as *Yarmouth*, *Plymouth*, *Brilliant* and *Ardent* but felt that I should have some captains still in their ships as we were very definitely on the edge of the 'attack area'. This was a useful, quiet meeting at which I was particularly pleased with the overall commitment and quiet determination of these officers. We made a small adjustment to the use and positioning of the two Type 22s with their Sea Wolf point defence missile systems, but otherwise they were happy with the screen that my Staff Warfare Officer, Mike Goodman, had proposed.

One threat raised by Peter Dingemans from *Intrepid* was that of mines, but as we knew very little indeed about the enemy's mining capability I told him that we were accepting the threat and I left it at that, although, as an ex-Captain Mine Counter-Measures, it was not wholly unreasonable that he was unhappy. He had arrived late on the scene, though, and so had not been fully in the picture and of our way of thinking towards such threats. On the 'need to know' basis he may have not known that for some time we had had the SBS and SAS watching the obvious areas and had received no reports of mine-laying activities. In our favour we assessed that Argentina would keep a large percentage of its 200 or so ground mines and eighty buoyant mines back for their mainland coastal threats and would therefore have very few to deploy in the more obvious places such as the approaches to Stanley and the co-located beaches. We deduced that with few obvious ground troops in the area they did not think that San Carlos was an obvious place for us to choose and so would not waste mines on it.

It was during this meeting that CTF's single code-word (Palpas) to proceed with *Operation Sutton* was received. As it was not unexpected it caused no 'butterflies', indeed a certain amount of relief that we had, at long last, been 'cleared for action'. Brian Young kept things in proportion by seeking out a case of claret from the wardroom before he returned to his ship and once the bottles were stowed all was ready!

We had been poising at 51° 20' S, 54° 00' W and at 0900 on D-1 headed through the Exclusion Zone in daylight with the aim (once we received the final 'Go') of transiting the last 100 miles to the anchorage in darkness. *Invincible* escorted us very close astern at this stage giving us Sea Dart coverage, CAP support if needed, morale support, a surface attack capability using her Harriers and an additional anti-submarine capability using her ASW helicopters to augment those carried by *Fort Austin*. It was a moment that deserved a memorable signal but no one on

Fearless's bridge was able to drop their concentration and create one. I sent a signal to her Harrier Squadron, 801, quoting their motto, '*On les aura*'. I had commanded the Squadron and previously been the Senior Observer and while I knew none of the young Harrier pilots I assumed they were very much like the professional aircrew that I had grown up with – at least I hoped they were! Eventually she had to break off and take up her station on the edge of the Exclusion Zone north-east of Stanley and about 130 miles from San Carlos.

From now on I kept my ships in a very tight formation with clear instructions to the escorts on what to do if a submarine attack was perceived – they would stay between us and the threat while we either scurried back towards Sandy or dog-legged. The enemy only possessed conventional submarines which (when submerged) could not catch us if we were going away. Of their surface fleet we knew little except that it had yet to venture forth but we did know that with air-to-air refuelling we were now well within range of aircraft and Exocet.

We entered the Total Exclusion Zone on a defensive, long-legged zig-zag with short zig-zags superimposed. We had received CTF's daily résumé of the news summary that morning that had told us, and confirmed to the World, that we were on our way. The summary taken from the published news of the day read:

1. PM says (Argentine) response 'unsatisfactory'. Details to be published before parliamentary debate on Falklands today.
2. Tension mounting as UN Sec Gen appeals to both sides to make effort to obtain peaceful settlement.
3. Argentine Foreign Minister has made bitter personal attack on Mrs Thatcher, accusing her of intransigence and a lack of understanding.
4. New MOD broadcasts, aimed at Falkland Garrison began last night with news, music and gossip plus warning that invasion imminent. Invasion theme echoed in all this morning's UK press reports. *Express* claims special forces already ashore to start disruptive action when main force lands.

My Amphibious Group (including its escorts) of about nineteen ships was now complete. The RFAs *Tidepool* and *Pearleaf*, the merchant ships *Fort Toronto* and *Atlantic Conveyor*, which were not strictly mine anyway, were despatched, together with *Elk* who would be called in later, to the Carrier Battle Group. I wanted with me only those ships vital to the Commander Land Forces in the initial stages; to risk others would be foolish until secure ashore and with a working air defence system. *Elk* in particular might cause the same devastation as a small nuclear bomb if she was to be hit while in the anchorage. On meeting the Carrier Battle Group, *Atlantic Conveyor* had flown across her Harriers but kept her Chinook and Wessex helicopters until called in direct to the AOA. Much as we would be desperate for troop-lift helicopters there was, at that stage, no room for them anywhere else. There was also a shortage of pilots. And we had been led to believe that the Chinooks were to be kept back for 5 Brigade.

My support helicopter force had been moved around once again and now that three Sea Kings had been lost 846 Squadron was reduced to eleven aircraft: four each in *Fearless* and *Intrepid*, two on *Canberra* and one on *Norland*. Three operational Wessex remained with the group in *Resource* and *Antrim*.

The Amphibious Objective Area anti-air warfare control was to be under the command of HMS *Antrim*. It had been my decision at my captain's meeting to declare the AOA (as is quite normal) a no-fly zone for British fixed-wing aircraft up to 3,500 feet but this left plenty of scope for the Sea Harriers above the zone. Unknown to us, Admiral Fieldhouse had commented to the Prime Minister on 16 May that, 'While a massed air attack by day was likely to be the main threat to the landings ... the difficulties in countering it should not be overstated.'

I was not sanguine, nor did I believe that we ever overstated our concern. (Indeed we probably had not pushed our case strongly enough in the early stages when being promised immunity from the air threat.) I believed that now it had come to the point, *Antrim* and the air-defence ships she controlled, plus the Harriers and Rapier would be busy, hard pressed but, I trusted, successful.

The submarine threat was to be co-ordinated by Kit Layman in HMS *Argonaut* with the surface threat the responsibility of HMS *Broadsword* (who was also area defence co-ordinator). My main anti-submarine force was *Fort Austin* with four ASW Wessex embarked and so, at great risk to herself, I was to keep her in the AOA until D+4. I also had a Lynx fitted with a Magnetic Anomaly Detection device to seek out and map any such irregularities on the sea bed across the entrance to both the Sound and San Carlos Waters. Additionally, I was grateful for *Plymouth* and *Yarmouth* with their single, triple-barrelled anti-submarine mortars which would be useful in shallow waters.

We dreamed up all sorts of ideas such as making a controlled minefield by stringing depth charges between Chancho Point and Fannings Head but we ran out of people and time and I feared that if this scheme was not properly organized we would lose one of our own ships in the entrance. I remained intrigued that we were not threatened by submarines; why the one stationed off Macbride Head never came round to the Sound puzzled me, but also gave me the impression (like their aircraft were to do on occasions) that some individuals were not that keen to kick us out, or at least risk their lives doing so.

I once read an assessment that during the Second World War the majority of shipping was sunk by a minority of determined submarine captains and, while the others took their toll, they were less likely to press their attacks home. With only four submarines I reckoned that the Argentine submarine commanding officers were most likely to be in the latter category and I very much hoped they would prefer discretion to valour.

Kit Layman's anti-submarine policy was encapsulated in his signal of the 19th to the supporting ASW ships. They were exhorted to 'hound any contact to death by deterrence (including the dropping of depth charges at random) and then, if failing to sink them, the submarines were to be excluded from the area by harassment, fear and exhaustion. Nothing was to be spared in bringing about their destruction: only the utmost aggression was acceptable'. Kit would, too, have been aware of Sandy's assessment of the enemy's submarine operations aired in a signal he had sent on the 16th in which he suggested that 'conceivably' three Argentine submarines were on station. Sandy demanded that all 'Keep our little ears to the ground, our movements sinuous and our local friendly helicopter busy'. He ended with the comment that submariners tended to be dull and boring people who found it difficult to get out of their ruts and hoped that Argentine submariners were the same and would, therefore, not stray from their patrolling areas. He, of course, was a submariner!

The surface threat was being monitored (among other duties) by our three SSNs ranging in search across the South Atlantic but they could not be everywhere and so we were to keep a continual and wary eye in that direction. We only knew of two small patrol craft in the Islands, but, of course, were well aware of the 'fleet' still within territorial waters. In practice the line-up of the two navies (if theirs was to 'escape' into deeper waters) was not that unequal: we had two carriers, they had one; our Sea Harriers had a very short radius of action in comparison to their A4s; we had ten escorts (five fitted with Exocet) and they had nine (eight fitted for Exocet but not necessarily carrying them) and, the greatest discrepancy, we had four nuclear and one diesel submarine on patrol (or about to arrive) while they had, possibly three operational conventional boats. Initially therefore some attrition of the Argentine Navy and Air Force was vital and to this end Sandy had tried to provoke the enemy into battle, but, as the result of sinking the *Belgrano* he could only engage their aircraft. Indeed, before, and certainly after, the landings it was we who were to lose aircraft and ships at an unacceptable rate.

We suffered one slight 'scare' with reports that a British-built, Exocet-fitted Type 42 (plus an unidentified number of escorts) was at sea to the east of Puerto Belgrano. HMS *Spartan* was sent to investigate but found only a fleet of Japanese fishing vessels which (hardly surprising, considering the size of fishing ships in these waters) were producing similar radar echoes to those expected of the warships.

As far as mines were concerned we continued to dismiss the possibility so far from Stanley. I decided that only if and when a ship was stopped by one would I deploy a helicopter towing a noise-making machine or the AMS Mk 1. This was not bravado nor foolhardiness but a function of time, and the fact that we would not have any proper mine-sweepers anyway until well after the latest possible date for the initial landings. We knew of the minefield guarding the entrance to Port William.

By 1 May the intelligence picture had indicated sixty-seven assorted aircraft on the mainland (and in the aircraft carrier) available to the Argentinians (assuming 60% availability) including four Canberras, twenty Skyhawk A4Bs and twelve A4Cs, nine Mirage 3s and twenty-two Mirage 5s (the Daggers). Additionally they had approximately fifty-two Pucara and, dispersed throughout the islands, an assortment of other aircraft and helicopters believed to include four T34C Mentors, four MB 339A Aeromacchis, two Skyvans, four Chinooks and 'some' Hueys.

We were certain that the ground troops numbered now about 12,000 (including nine infantry battalions), armed with AAA guns, Tigercar, Blowpipe and Roland anti-aircraft weapons plus supporting radar warning and guidance radars, mostly the AN/TPS 43 and AN/TPS 44 systems. Many of the men were conscripts and so of an unknown but possibly poor quality in the far-from-ideal living and fighting conditions they would be facing, but, as we all know, fanaticism can produce surprising results.

During our approach to the Islands I stood for a short while on *Fearless*'s port bridge wing and watched my mixed force of amphibians, merchant vessels and warships as it forged its way westwards waiting for the expected air attack that never came. Desperately going through my mind for the millionth time were thoughts of what might occur, whether or not I had taken all the correct steps, whether or not I had the right balance of forces, whether or not my assessment of the problem was the right one. Like everyone else in the force I had never been involved in this type of confrontation before although unlike most I had served in

Korea as a midshipman. My Snottie's nurse, Lieutenant Commander A. M. Power, wrote on my report that I had acquired considerable wartime experience which would be of great value later. It was to be thirty years before I could use it.

I pondered, too, what the Falkland Islanders thought of it all. I had the feeling that this was a 'just' war. It was certainly the first conflict in which I had taken part where I and my men were risking our lives for British subjects. Every other campaign had been for the protection of some other race. If our luck of the previous two days was anything to go by then the Almighty was undoubtedly on our side (and probably a Kelper!). The conviction that I had felt with Sarah beneath the holm-oak tree in the garden at home was greatly strengthened.

At that point I must have slipped into a form of involuntary daydream because I next saw a stream of people dressed in Elizabethan clothes drifting across my imagination. I had no idea who they were (although I was certain that Drake was among them) but they gave encouragement by saying, 'It's always like this before the action and there is nothing to fear from the Don.' (I felt they should have realized that the most numerical race in Argentina were the Italians with 40% – but let it pass!)

My forebears have lived in Devon for centuries and were much involved with the sea. I wondered afterwards if any of them had been playing games with my imagination. I came-to to find Surgeon-Captain Ian Young at my shoulder quietly asking me if I was all right. I was very touched. Sea command is lonely at the best of times but this command was stretching the point. I was genuinely grateful and thanked him and felt a lot better.

I do not like to believe in premonitions as I am of the opinion that bad ones can lead to a form of defeatism but this, and an incident on Easter Sunday when I was convinced my father, a regular soldier, was sitting alongside me at the church service just to 'see that I was OK' (he died in 1965), I found rather intriguing and comforting. These two tiny incidents were probably explained by the deep tiredness and worry that prevailed but, conversely, they both boosted me immensely.

As I have mentioned, I sailed with very few belongings and

among the most precious were a collage from my five-year-old daughter and a postcard showing a single elm tree from my sister-in-law with the note, more than somewhat perceptively, that she hoped it would lend me some of its strength. Seemingly glued to a very small area of the ship, I tried to escape whenever I could for fresh air and calm. One of my delights was to see Major Mike Morgan, the CO of 148 Battery, sitting in his deckchair. He invariably had an enormous and encouraging grin for me.

So far so good for 'this' leader, but what of the man commanding the Argentine forces in the Falklands? We knew the military régime's reputation on the mainland and we had even met one of those responsible for a number of international atrocities when Captain Alfredo Astiz was captured without a fight at Grytviken. Lots of bark but no fight there, as is so often the case with bullies. The 'GOC Malvinas' might be a different matter, although we suspected not despite the following unflattering report I received during our long journey south, compiled, I believe, by Julian's intelligence team. The fact that the photograph attached to the report was of another general was overlooked on the 'tarred-with-the-same-brush' principle!

'General Benjamino Menendez was appointed as Military Governor of the Malvinas after the invasion: the Malvinas is the Argentinian name for the Falklands.

'He has an infamous reputation as being responsible for the death of many political prisoners at the La Peria concentration camp. Many were brutally interrogated, tortured and 'transferred' – the official name for being executed. At the time Menendez was in command of the 3rd Army Corps in Cordoba province.

'In spite of Argentinian assurances that the civil rights of the Islanders will be upheld Menendez had already instituted the following measures:
a. 180 days' imprisonment for action that may 'disrupt normal co-existence, order and public tranquillity'.
b. 60 days for "disrespect" and "irreverent behaviour" towards Argentinian national symbols.

c. 15 days for leaving home without permission. Those who require help must show a white flag.

d. Spanish to be taught to all inhabitants and Libre will be the official currency.

e. Driving on the right hand side of the road.

Assessment

'It is clear that Menendez is a brutal personality with very little concern for human rights. He shows a degree of understanding of Psy Ops by making the Islanders show a white flag for assistance. Apart from the colour being easily recognizable it is the accepted notification of surrender.

'Menendez is a military man with presumably some experience of combat against guerillas and/or terrorists. He is likely to consider the lives and property of the Islanders as dispensable even if the situation is hopeless and is assessed as the type of person who might not hesitate to carry out a "scorched earth" policy.'

It struck us that the sooner we got on with 'Repossessing the Islands' the better.

CHAPTER FOUR

ASSAULT

It is warm work, and this day may be the last to any
of us at any moment – but, mark you, I would not
be elsewhere for thousands.

> Nelson in the *Elephant*, April 2, 1801,
> to Lieut.-Colonel the Hon. William Stewart,
> commanding the troops embarked.

ALL TIMINGS FOR the landings and subsequent operations
are given in GMT for that was the time zone we kept in order to
keep us in line with Northwood. This worked well for Sandy's
and my naval forces. In my case it was extremely helpful to get
up four hours earlier than nature intended as we could have
breakfast, the morning brief and be well on our way before
dawn. The morning would see us busily setting about the rest of
the day while the afternoons were spent waiting for or under air
attack. For the landing force, who were closer to nature, it
created some difficulties.

To make an H Hour of 0630 (GMT) i.e. 0230 Local Time
from the loitering position of 51°20' S; 54°00' W, 140 miles east
of Cape Pembroke, relied on a departure time of 0900Z on D-1
and passive navigation at a speed of advance of 12 ½ knots. As it
was important to mask the eventual destination until the last
moment the route through the Exclusion Zone was designed to
take the Amphibious Task Group to a point fifty miles north of

Macbride Head and from there to the Eddystone Rock off Cape Dolphin. This should also avoid the submarine we believed to be off Macbride Head. I also wanted to be well out of sight of any casual visual contact from aircraft milling around Stanley. There was always the possibility that one of my ships would inadvertently make smoke and I certainly did not want that seen. From there the final approach took us to the west of Tide Rock, as far from Fanning Head as possible – and then to the various anchorages and individual 'race-tracks' required to launch and defend the landing craft. The AOA was a very simple box based on a line running due south from Cape Dolphin for thirty miles and west for fifteen miles. It was quite adequate for me – I felt it would make an easy shape for the aircrew in particular to remember.

Any real deception landing would have taken rather more troops than we had, although one of the great advantages of Special Forces of the calibre of ours is that, with the modern automatic weapons at their disposal against an inexperienced and frightened enemy, they can give the appearance of being a larger force than they actually are: the Darwin garrison commander was to say later that he thought he was under attack by at least a battalion. We had long planned that a diversion would take place against this complex while the need to 'sort out' the Fannings Head Mob had been a recent addition to our plans. Added to this, I asked Sandy to carry out the main deception plan and he detached HMS *Glamorgan* on D-1 for the penultimate time in her role as *Operation Tornado*'s deceiver. This time I wanted her to close to the south east coast of East Falkland and bombard ten targets between Bertha's Beach and Port Harriet. Although I was to assume that this was carried out, I never received a confirmatory signal. However, Julian and I hoped that the Argentinians would see any attack or landing (even in San Carlos) merely as a diversion to the perceived main landings in the vicinity of Stanley; perhaps we were wasting our time as they were probably expecting a landing in the Stanley area anyway. On the other hand this might have reassured them: to our advantage.

During the 20th I felt sure my tight-knit force had remained undetected despite a number of 'activities', the BBC, our proximity to the Islands, and a sudden clearing of the weather an hour or two before dusk but, once again, it was the Almighty who should receive most of the credit. These 'activities' included a successful Harrier strike against fuel dumps at Fox Bay, although they failed to stop three Hercules flights into the Islands, one of which resupplied Fox Bay by parachute. The Harriers could not be everywhere and the enormous disadvantage to our air operations from the lack of airborne early warning was daily becoming more apparent. We had entered the Exclusion Zone with HMS *Invincible* close astern for the first few hours until she peeled off to port to take up her station towards its eastern edge; we felt rather more vulnerable then but the cloud base was low and visibility poor which was probably a better defence than anything concocted by man.

The Amphibious Task Group had detached at 1415 from the Carrier Battle Group to begin the run westward. At 2000, as planned, I sent *Antrim* and *Ardent* ahead an hour before we reached Point Oscar (a 'staging point' one hundred miles from the AOA) by which time we were already about half an hour late. *Ardent* steamed at high speed beneath Fannings Head (unnoticed, it seemed, despite a 30 knot wake and her Olympus gas turbines) for her gunline in Grantham Sound (which she reached at 0100 on the 21st) ready to support the diversionary raid by D Squadron SAS against Darwin, while *Antrim* prepared to fly off a thermal imaging recce of the Fannings Head Mob.

In preparation for dealing with the Fannings Head Mob we had flown a party from 148 Commando Forward Observation Battery, Royal Artillery from *Intrepid* to *Antrim* during the day where they met 3 SBS and Captain Rod Bell, Royal Marines, a Spanish linguist. *Antrim*'s Wessex would fly a thermal imaging recce with the OC of the 148 Battery party and OC the embarked SBS patrol to Fannings Head, return, brief the assault teams, load in two waves then land four miles to the east, and down-wind of, the enemy. The Argentine position would be approached by Bell armed only with a loud-hailer and twelve-volt battery to see if they would surrender without loss of life. Jonathan Thomson (the C.O. of the SBS) had concerned me a little by saying beforehand that his men would not aim to kill but to capture and while, with hindsight, Julian (to whom Jonathan had first mooted this idea) and I would have preferred a more aggressive stance Jonathan's plan was to 'test their mettle' to see if others would be amenable to this approach. It was therefore a sensible and humane approach to our first encounter. Only if they did not surrender would they be attacked by the SBS supported by *Antrim*'s guns.

The result, I'm afraid, showed that Admiral Jackie Fisher was still right: 'The essence of war is violence, and moderation in war is imbecility.'

For this operation we were also given the added bonus of thermal-imaging recces of Port San Carlos, San Carlos, Race Point, Middle Bay and Ajax Bay. The 'Mob' was easily identified on Fannings Head but thankfully no signs of enemy positions showed up elsewhere. The Wessex returned and after briefings the men were inserted as planned. While being observed, the 'Mob' appeared to engage *Antrim* who was by now in the entrance to the Sound causing the naval gunfire observer (Captain Hugh McManners) to bring down twenty rounds of V.T. fused air burst above their heads. Their next move was to pack up and start heading east. The prime objective of the mission had been achieved as the enemy were no longer in a position to engage the ships at that moment entering the Sound, but the secondary aim of capturing and interrogating was still outstanding.

Covered by the SBS, Rod Bell crept forward to tell the Argentinians over his loud hailer that they were surrounded and that it would be better for all if they gave themselves up. They didn't and seemed to the SBS to be approaching their positions 'with intent'. The order was given to engage the enemy with sixteen SBS GPMGs firing full tracer. Bell decided to stop this 'apparent massacre' and went forward a second time protected by two SBS marines but again with no apparent effect. By dawn a number had escaped, a number had been killed and four had been captured. Later four more were picked up wounded. The prisoners were too young and frightened to be of any intelligence value and simply complained that all their officers had fled.

The positive result of this short action was the silencing of any weapon against the Amphibious Task Group but the severe 'down-side' was to be the shooting down of two Gazelle helicopters by the fugitives later in the day, after which the survivors in the water were also targeted. Only one aircrewman out of the four survived and he was badly wounded. A number of points were learnt, the main one being that humanity in war (firing to frighten rather than to kill) has to be exercised judiciously. Going in with the intention of being 'kind' is not a safe policy, it assumes too much of the enemy. War is an aggressive business and has to be conducted as such – within few, but well defined, rules. Few, if any, of us had served in a 'real' war before and we took in the lesson. Fortunately it was a relatively cheap one.

On their way in the SBS patrol had detached a team to check out 3 Para's Green Beach as this had been impossible a few days earlier. Taking in Port San Carlos Settlement as well, they identified no enemy, a fact that led us to conclude later that those who had obviously been there had all been asleep and thus not expecting any invasion in their area.

Ajax Bay had been watched by the SBS since early May and the San Carlos observation patrol re-inserted during D-5. All pre-landing recces were reporting minimal activity, but there had been a period, rather too long for Julian's and my nerves, when we heard little or nothing from the men ashore. While they peered into the mist and fog neither they nor we could be certain that their nil reports gave a true picture.

Glamorgan was again busy on *Operation Tornado*, this time from the north-east of Macbride Head where she fired one hundred rounds (including starshell and chaff) over and on to the beaches of Berkeley Sound. At the same time her Wessex helicopter was flying spoof missions and her communications team operating deceptive radio circuits, thereby, we hoped, confirming the enemy command's view that at long last the invasion had begun, and roughly where they thought it would.

Back on board the *Fearless* all was going a little slower than hoped. We turned to the south west at midnight but, infuriatingly, did not realize for some time that we were behind schedule as *Fearless*'s navigator had been relying on one of Ewen Tailyour's small boat satellite navigation systems that did not take account of zig-zags! With his eye glued to the 'modern' device and not his 'dead reckoning' and navigation plot, our speed-made-good was not being assessed accurately by John Prime. He suddenly woke up to the problem and we increased revolutions. The weather had been thick for the approach but now as we closed the northern entrance to the Sound in our three separate columns, it cleared. A further small delay occurred as we flew off D Squadron SAS from the LPDs for their tasks at Darwin, a lack of suitable wind for the laden helicopters being the major cause.

We had been on strict radio and radar silence since entering the Exclusion Zone with even the pipes on the ship's broadcast banned. We now had as many men as possible above the waterline to avoid torpedo or mine damage, with those on the upper deck 'hidden' to avoid sniper fire. It must have been a ghostly (or even ghastly) sight to anyone ashore as nineteen 'warships' slid quietly and darkly through the northern entrance to Falkland Sound. Certainly no navigation lights gave the game away and not one candle power of light shone out from behind the blackout screens. Yet behind those screens five battalions of men, plus their support, were completing last-minute preparations: large breakfasts, blackening of faces, the umpteenth checking of magazines and bayonets.

Well before H Hour *Fearless*'s Amphibious Operations Room (the AOR) had been closed-up under the direction of my SOO and G1 – Commander George Pearson and Royal Marines Major, David Minords. One of the desks central to the AOR's business is the Supporting Arms Co-ordination Cell. Here sit representatives of various services and arms until they too move ashore with the Brigade staff leaving liaison officers for such continuing naval tasks as gunfire support, special forces operations and the offload. The support helicopters and landing craft are also run from this room as are many of the communications and intelligence networks. Central to the mechanics of the offload I had my two Royal Corps of Transport majors under the direction of the G1.

The AOR is one of a complex of planning rooms immediately below the bridge which include the Intelligence Room, the Main Communications office and the Ship's Operations Room. The Ship's Operations Room was antiquated and really only capable of operating the ship and no longer for taking command of an Amphibious Group.

But here a word of explanation: the whole amphibious force, ships, aircraft, landing force and landing craft, etc, are technically called the Amphibious Task Group, while the expression Amphibious Group is used to mean the ships only. I was therefore not only the Amphibious Task Group Commander but also the Amphibious Group Commander.

The Amphibious Operations Room was designed to command the overall Amphibious Task Group from conception in the 'home-base' to change of operational command from the Commander Amphibious Task Force (CATF) to the Commander of Landing Force (CLF) when in CLF's opinion, as ATP-8 has it:

1. The Force beachhead has been secured.
2. Significant tactical and supporting forces have been established ashore to ensure the continuous landing of troops and material required for subsequent operations.
3. Command, communications and supporting arms co-ordinating facilities have been established ashore.
4. CLF has stated that he is ready to assume full responsibility for subsequent operations.

CATF then becomes the Commander Amphibious Group (CAG) only and is free to leave the area and perhaps plan and execute another amphibious landing with a different Landing Force Commander, whereupon he would once again become a

CATF as well as continuing as an Amphibious Group Commander. Not yet, nor for some days after Julian's move ashore, would the change of operational command (CHOP) occur. The British interpretation of ATP-8 allows the Brigade Commander to move ashore as soon as possible to command the land battle, while remaining under the authority of the Commodore until the 'CHOP' can take place. American land force commanders, I understand, tend to stay on board until the 'CHOP', thus, I suspect, leaving them liable to be remarkably unaware of the situation with their command ashore for those vital first days. Julian, I guessed, might wish to be off as soon as the beaches were secure, and I would support that. I raise this fundamental point now as it is relevant to our relationship at this delicate time and it is certainly arguable as to which view is best overall. Remember, neither Julian nor I, nor our staffs, had ever executed an assault together before or even practised a dummy one.

In the meantime I ordered *Yarmouth* ahead into the Sound at 0215 to take up her anti-submarine patrol station across the northern entrance between North West Islands and Poke Point. She was in position by the time we passed Jersey Point at 0258, exactly seventeen minutes late because of the navigational misunderstanding. *Yarmouth* was then moved further south to stop anything getting at us from that direction. Meanwhile *Antrim* was at her allotted station off Cat Island as *Plymouth* moved into position at the junction of San Carlos River and San Carlos Water, while the last ship in, *Brilliant*, took up her position under the West Falkland cliffs of Many Branch Harbour. *Argonaut*'s duty was to 'stopper the bottle' between Fannings Head and Jersey Point. I had decided to have *Fort Austin* with her ASW helicopters anchor close inshore between Chancho Point and Cat Island while the 'troop ships' anchored along a north-south line further offshore, the whole force of 'troop ships' being within one mile or so of the shoreline.

Fearless and *Intrepid* came to their pre-ordained anchorages at 0345 and 0337 respectively. The troop ships then followed to anchor inshore of the LPDs on the route the landing craft would need to take. We had stopped for the first time since Ascension, just a few minutes late as the anchor cables ran into fifteen fathoms of water sounding as though they should be heard in Buenos Aires. All around us now was the quiet and peaceful backdrop of black undulating hills against a slightly less dark and starlit sky. It was cool and far too clear, adding perhaps to the slight dread of the occasion, but so far so good and with our main task lying immediately ahead I concentrated my mind on stage-managing the landings and supporting Julian with any last-minute requests or change of plan due to enemy action or mechanical breakdown.

I had been so relieved that we had so far been without air attack and without losing anybody that I felt nothing could really go wrong with this phase, and so, thinking that the following day was probably going to be the longest of my life, I lay on my bunk and listened to the intercom as Jeremy Larken and the teams carried out their instructions. I knew it all by heart and so could follow it happily while dozing quietly but, as we approached the anchorage, I re-joined Julian in the AOR. Despite various defence cuts that had trimmed our staffs to the point where they were only capable of commanding an 'administrative landing', the AOR, now in action for the first time in its real role, seemed to be working smoothly.

I was not leaving the last-minute worrying to Julian – far from it – but during our approach I had stayed alert with every nerve jangling as I listened to the various radio circuits and tried to detect the slightest change in a voice that might have indicated an alarm such as an air attack or the break-out of the Argentine surface fleet. As far as I knew we were further towards the mainland than any British surface group had then ventured in daylight and while our nuclear submarines were patrolling to the west it was not possible for them to cover every enemy ship. So concerned were we that they might have made a run for it that for days afterwards we were to continue searching West Falkland looking for their Exocet-fitted Type 42s, in particular.

More delays dogged the landings. *Fearless* had a problem with her ballast pumps and was temporarily unable to sink low enough to float out the LCUs, and, as these were vital for the first wave with 40 Commando, it was a frustrating wait. I knew Jeremy and his team well enough to know that all that was possible was being done to get things moving and if I was anxious my heart went out to Julian and his troops who would suffer the most from any delay to H Hour. I had purposefully chosen a launch position outside San Carlos waters to provide last minute uncertainty to an enemy of our final destination and to avoid any involvement of the ships with the possibility of fighting on the beaches. *Plymouth* would be available for local and instant naval gunfire support from within the final anchorage.

With no radio circuits active (except the VHF, and then only for emergencies) I went briefly to the bridge wing and watched as the landing craft eventually floated out from *Fearless*'s dock to orbit off her bows. A similar scene had been enacted by *Intrepid* within eleven minutes of dropping her anchor, her LCUs now steaming towards *Norland* and 2 Para. It seemed impossible that we had not been spotted: nineteen ships, 268 4.5 inch shells on to enemy positions accompanied by helicopters over the settlements earlier should have woken someone. In fact, back in Stanley, Brigadier-General Menendez had been alerted, but only by reports of HMS *Glamorgan*'s activities off Berkeley Sound, which was precisely why she was carrying out that operation.

The flotilla of sixteen landing craft slowly sorted itself out, hampered by an understandable delay with 2 Para's disembarkation from *Norland* as the men and ship had had only one, day-time, practice weeks before. To moor the LCUs it was necessary to move some of the ship's lifeboats, a problem that had not arisen in the controlled conditions off Ascension Island. Our wait would be all the more anxious, for by the time Ewen Tailyour had shepherded together his charges and crossed the Line of Departure (between Chancho Point and Fannings Head) he would have lost most of the time we had managed to make up. Although the landing was being conducted under 'silent routines' a short VHF radio conversation took place. The final LCU to load from *Norland* had difficulties and at some stage a parachute soldier had fallen between the craft and the ferry, crushing his pelvis. Should we send the fully-embarked 40 Commando on ahead to retrieve something of the H Hour timings or should we wait even longer (until the whole of 2 Para was ready) to avoid a muddle on the beaches with units landing in the wrong order and in two halves?

Julian spoke with his deputy, Colonel Tom Seccombe, riding in the lead LCU, and Tom spoke to Ewen. Julian wanted the landing craft, containing about eighty-five percent of the first-wave troops, to set off immediately and allow the last LCU to finish loading correctly before making its own way to Blue Beach. Both Malcolm Hunt of 40 Commando and 'H' Jones of 2 Para concurred, although they had little choice but to obey their Brigadier!

Eventually the lead craft crossed the Line of Departure sixty-five minutes late and with full throttle steamed direct down the centre of the 'loch' towards 40 Commando's orbiting position.

The navigational plan for the approach, out of sight of the landing ships, had been designed at a speed of six knots to make an H Hour of 0630. This in turn would have given the troops time to reach their defensive positions before dawn and the expected ground and air counter-attacks. Ewen had planned a circuitous route skirting the western edge of the kelp (where, he hoped, mines could not have been laid) to a position off Ajax Bay where he would leave 40 Commando circling while he piloted 2 Para to their Blue Beach Two in Bonner's Bay. Ten minutes later 40 Commando would land across Blue Beach One at Pony's Valley Bay to the north of the settlement.

Precisely forty-five minutes after the designated H Hour the first troops of 2 Para were ashore and on their way in the darkness; ten minutes later 40 Commando secured San Carlos Settlement and began their way up to their reverse-slope defensive positions to the east and north.

We waited, cut off from news of the landings until the first craft re-rounded Chancho Point to make for *Intrepid* and 3 Para. There were sighs of relief for the craft were obviously empty of troops and, to mis-coin the phrase of the time, we had counted them all out round Chancho Point and we now counted them all back. The last group of landing craft peeled off to make for *Stromness* and 45 Commando. All had gone well so far and not as late, perhaps, as we feared it could have been, but there was now yet another delay, this time with the loading of 3 Para from *Intrepid* and 45 Commando from *Stromness*. Two very frustrated Commanding Officers (Hew Pike and Andrew Whitehead respectively) champed at their bits while dawn broke over the anchorage, cold, calm and very clear indeed. This second wave was landed in broad daylight at Green and Red beaches.

The only opposition to the ground troops – and it was hardly that – occurred when 3 Para's leading sections engaged with mortars a party of about forty enemy fleeing into the hills east of Port San Carlos. This party was made up of the remnants of the Fannings Head Mob meeting up with their compatriots sleeping in the settlement. On seeing a battalion supported by armoured vehicles land at Green Beach they retreated towards Cerro Montevideo. It was these men who were later to shoot down two Brigade Air Squadron Lynx helicopters.

With dawn we waited the 'massive air assault' promised by the Argentines against the lightly armed RFAs and civilian ships. Increasing daylight saw the beginning of the helicopter lift. Our two support squadrons had been reduced even further than I could have imagined from the normal NATO exercise level we had been used to. 846 Squadron had sailed with fourteen Sea King 4s and were now down to eleven but four of these were fitted with night vision aids making them awkward to fly in daylight. 845 Squadron had six Wessex 5 aircraft locked in *Atlantic Conveyor*, two had been lost in South Georgia and several were scattered around the force or left behind on Ascension for general duties. This allowed them only four at San Carlos out of a total strength of sixteen. All in all, therefore, we had about one half to two-thirds the normal lift capacity for our first live day.

The key to the repossession of the Falklands depended on troops ashore in strength and well supported before any counterattack by land or air had time to materialize. All else would be invaluable but it was this first move that had to be successful. As the day progressed the realization that the enemy had made (and was making) two fundamental mistakes became clear. I was not surprised that they had let us land unopposed as we had planned to achieve this, but I was astonished that when they did attack they engaged the wrong targets. This was obviously fortuitous, if not for the recipients of those attacks, then at least for the success of the operation as a whole. We had, of course, planned to land where the enemy was not but we had also expected that the troop and supply ships would be the prime targets of the inevitable air assault – not the escorts. To give the enemy some due, he had a land mass the size of Wales to defend and about fifteen thousand miles of coastline to cover against a landing, but the tasking of their air attacks was professionally disappointing.

Meanwhile *Canberra* had anchored at 0417 one and a half miles south-south-west of Fannings Head and at 0930 the final column of ships, the LSLs and *Europic Ferry*, entered North Falkland Sound.

By midday (Greenwich Time) – breakfast time (local) – all ground objectives having been secured, the air attacks began in earnest.

Not too surprisingly, some of the enemy pilots were hesitant during those first hours, for, as I had hoped, the mass of tracer and visible armament thrown into the sky surprised them, and it was, too, their first taste of battle. Inside San Carlos Water I had planned that a pilot would have less than thirty seconds to assess the situation, choose his target, place his aircraft at the right height, speed and dive angle, avoid his wingman, make the right switches and steady his aircraft for at least three seconds to aim his weapon, release it and then make his escape without collision. It did not matter whether he approached from the north or over Sussex Mountain. While I have little doubt that this felt like a lifetime to many of the pilots as they faced the tracer and Very pistols, it also seemed like a lifetime to us! It was on this argument that I chose a ceiling of 3,500 feet for my AOA as although 4.5 inch gunfire and Sea Cat could probably reach higher, not much else would and I wanted the Sea Harriers to feel free to fly overhead if they wished. Out in the Falkland Sound the pickings were obviously much easier and of course our ships were seen well before those in San Carlos.

Another interesting argument had gone through my head but I was to keep quiet about it on board and in my later discussions with Sandy as I felt unable to try and sell it to the merchant ship and RFA Captains who would undoubtedly see things differently. This was that, given the brief period of time in which the Argentine aircrew had to make up their minds, it was better to offer them a large number of targets than only a few. They would be more likely to spread their bombs at random across the shipping and hopefully most ships would survive. Giving them only a few targets would almost certainly mean that they would be able to concentrate their fire, saturate the target and most likely sink it. This, because of our loading plan, would be the worst result. The decision was taken for me because the loading plan necessitated most of my ships coming in on the first day, but it was an argument that was to return later, particularly when the enemy airmen showed that their aim and fusing were none too good.

Antrim had been first into direct action with her bombardment of Fannings Head, but she also carried two flight controllers. She therefore controlled the Sea Harriers on CAP duty based in holding patterns west of Grantham Sound and north of Pebble Island. D Day's first friendly aircraft sortie was launched at 1035 and the second ten minutes later. Sandy's plan was to have at least one CAP on station throughout and two pairs airborne whenever an attack was inbound. Time-on-target was about thirty minutes, with this being seriously reduced during low-level, high-speed chases, so, in the absence of early warning, it was not going to be easy.

The submarines in the area did not see, or hear everything and sometimes misunderstood. They clearly could not be expected to tell the difference between aircraft involved in administration or repositioning flights. High-flying aircraft could sometimes be detected by my own ships' radar but most of the approaches appeared to be at lower level. Air attacks were therefore to be often unannounced. Nevertheless, the submarines were to be of immense value and their contribution highly regarded.

The first enemy aircraft to appear did so at low level round the coastline. An Aeromacchi MB 339 flying from Port Stanley on an early morning recce rounded Fannings Head to meet what the pilot was to describe as 'The whole British fleet at anchor,' but Lieutenant Crippa also met GPMG fire and Blowpipe missiles from *Canberra*, a Seacat from *Intrepid* and 4.5 inch shells from *Plymouth*. He departed to make his report but not before unleashing eight 5-inch rockets and a burst of 30mm cannon at *Argonaut*, causing casualties. Crippa's report tied in with the radio report from a Goose Green-based Pucara pilot transmitted before he foolishly overflew the SAS and their Stinger ground-to-air hand held missiles. Much to Mike Rose's consternation, the seventeen-year-old Bofors aimer on the bridge wing of *Fearless* had asked whether he should open fire, only to be told that that was precisely what he was there to do, but by then it was too late. Transition to a 'war mentality' can be slow!

Second into action at 1123 was *Ardent*, where, from a position 22,000 yards from her target of Goose Green airstrip her Mark VIII 4.5 inch gun destroyed one Pucara and caused confusion (together with the SAS) among the enemy. Despite later intense air attacks *Ardent* was to give further fire support to the SAS as they disengaged. She had been chosen as she possessed the only gun capable of hitting at such a range and if I had had more frigates I would have sent another to keep her company. She was a sitting duck to air attack, I knew it and so did her Commanding Officer. However, her task was essential to the containment of Goose Green and prevention of counter-attack at that critical time, and she carried it out successfully, acting as an unplanned but vital decoy at the same time.

At 1145 the enemy's ability to launch a land-forces counterat-tack was reduced further by an attack on the Mount Kent helicopter park where RAF GR3s destroyed one Puma and one Chinook; a second Puma was damaged. A second GR 3 sortie was launched from *Hermes* but only one aircraft was serviceable after take off. On being told that there were no targets for him, the pilot (Flight-Lieutenant Glover) sought out Port Howard and was shot down on his second pass while taking photographs of troop positions. Injured, he was captured and repatriated at the end of the war. This sparked a signal from CinC Fleet reminding us that this was the first carrier-borne RAF strike for a generation but the action had reminded the younger aircrew of what my generation already knew; that sorties of one aircraft were not really on and that second passes over enemy positions were inviting disaster. Experience that was to be ignored or forgotten at least twice more during the ensuing days, with the predicted results.

I had often asked Sandy to target enemy helicopters, but he was to admit to me later that when he received my signal he did not understand the importance of this request. He was expecting to be asked to engage more 'offensive' targets. It seemed to take him some time to appreciate that without helicopters their ground forces would also have been paralysed.

By the end of the first day *Argonaut* and *Antrim* were both badly damaged by air attacks with Alan West's *Ardent* abandoned, at anchor and sinking by the stern. Kit Layman's *Argonaut* could float and fight but not manoeuvre while *Antrim* as Local Air Co-ordinator was now unable to operate her Seaslug systems and so was destined to act as an ASW and surface escort ship with the Carrier Battle Group. *Brilliant* had been hit by sixteen 30 mm cannon shells and had taken casualties. Her First Lieutenant (Lieutenant-Commander Lee Hulme), carrying out superb work as the fighter direction officer, was wounded but still at his console. *Broadsword* had also been hit by cannon shells down her port side causing casualties. Of all the frigates under my command only *Plymouth* and *Yarmouth* (the two oldest – *Plymouth* was actually celebrating her twenty-first birthday) escaped unscathed. Also unscathed, most mercifully, were the troopships.

The unexploded bombs came as a surprise and we were unprepared. In *Sir Tristram* Fleet Clearance Diving Team 1 (FCDT1) was called out at about 1400 to investigate a large

183

unexploded bomb in the *Antrim*. Fleet Chief Petty Officer Fellows with Leading Seaman Sewell and Able Seaman Pullen flew across to find a 1000lb British bomb with a severely damaged tail fuse which made it impossible to ascertain whether it was armed or not. Mr Fellows sought advice on *Antrim*'s DSSS facility from Northwood and, after a hole had been cut in the flight deck, hoisted out the bomb and lowered it over the side into the sea, keeping the bomb carefully in the same plane all the time. The air attacks continued meanwhile.

While this was happening the reports that both *Ardent* and *Argonaut* had unexploded bombs aboard were received, but nothing could be done until the ships were safely in San Carlos Water. Obviously too late in the case of *Ardent* where other bombs had exploded.

My job had been to land the landing force 'without significant loss' (although this phrase does not appear in any of our 'bibles') – and I had. Significant losses had been incurred by my ships, or by the landing force after disembarkation, unexpected perhaps but within my remit, as it were. My job, as always, was to defend and manage both the AOA in general and the offload of logistics in particular. Following the successful landing of the troops I puzzled why the AAF targeted the warships. As they had failed to stop the landings I assumed that they would now be briefed to prevent the supplies from getting ashore: I was not far wrong.

With all 'bayonets' ashore, apart from 42 Commando (two companies as reserve troops in *Canberra* and M Company still on South Georgia) the massive offload operation by LCVP, LCU, Mexeflote, Wessex and Sea King to the various beaches and landing zones could now begin. Initially these movements were on a 'stop-go' basis for every time Air Raid Warning Red was called across the 'guard frequency' and the ships' sirens were sounded, craft and helicopters would duck into some cove or re-entrant to avoid being targets and also to avoid being in our own arcs of fire.

For our helicopters the greatest single danger was to be hit by the mass of small arms fire pumped into the sky ahead of the enemy pilots as a barrage into which it was hoped they would fly.

For the landing craft cox'ns there was no quick manoeuvre they could take anyway and by the time they realized that a raid was on its way in and they had altered course to 'take cover' it was usually over. As confidence and boldness reasserted themselves after the first few tense hours of trying conditions they all (the helicopters and landing craft) went about their business without deviating. In fact they suffered from the dangers of 'friendly' or expended ordnance on surprisingly few occasions. One LCU lost a ten-man life-raft (positioned alongside the wheel-house) when it was knocked overboard by a Seacat missile! Nor were the ships' companies afloat and the troops ashore safe from 'own goals', although none are recorded except for one marine with a British bullet embedded in his puttee and a 40mm shell which landed on the deck above Jeremy Larken's cabin in *Fearless*. Troops on the slopes either side of San Carlos Water would fire horizontally (or even below) on to attacking aircraft with their shot falling among their opposite numbers on the far bank. The aircraft were not conforming precisely to my plan, but it was most certainly stimulating!

It was obvious that the Great White Whale herself was a prime target; they could hardly miss her presence, nor her significance, in the anchorage. As such, I was keen to get *Canberra* out and on her way to safety at sea, while Julian felt that same sentiment about his reserve troops moving ashore. These feelings were echoed by the Commanding Officer (Nick Vaux) and the Senior Naval Officer ('Beagle' Burne) on board. Soon into the after-noon the offloading of 42 began by LCU in to Green Beach One (one and a half miles west-north-west of Green Beach Two where 3 Para had landed) and from where they were to push on to take Cerro Montevideo. That completed, I ordered her to sail by midnight with the growing convoy of wounded ships and men.

During the day (and after the Captain, Dennis Scott-Masson, had sent his signal, 'Have delivered passengers as requested', *Canberra* took aboard the remaining ship's company from HMS *Ardent*, sixteen casualties from HM ships, plus two from the Brigade and three captured Argentinian wounded. She also carried three dead from the Gazelles to be buried at sea. I was glad that I had not ordered off the nursing staff in *Canberra* as I had intended at Ascension. They had insisted on staying on board and were now to give most welcome succour to the wounded. Nelson, who knew a thing or two about women afloat, wrote, 'They always will do as they please. Orders are not for them – at least I never knew one who obeyed'!

Although the sailing of *Canberra* was a sensible decision, having to do so before she was fully unladen caused problems that were to live with us for the duration of the war. She took with her 90,000 man-days of rations and the First Line stores for 40 and 42 Commandos and 3 Para. *Norland*, when she sailed, also took those for 2 Para. The knock-on effect was that the Brigade's Logistic Regiment had to start supplying food and stores immediately instead of after the first forty-eight or so hours. This was not a satisfactory start to the land campaign and, in ways, was a measure of the success of the air attacks against the store ships. They may not have been hit but their contents were still denied us. Neither *Canberra* nor *Norland* had left San Carlos for good.

It was becoming obvious to me and my staff, but I suspect less so to the Brigadier and his staff, that a well regulated disembarkation of their stores was not going to be possible. Julian had for some time decided that he would establish a Brigade Maintenance or Beach Support Area somewhere in the vicinity of San Carlos after the initial troops were consolidated ashore on, perhaps, D+2 or D+3. What was probably arguable was the amount of stores he actually wanted landed and the amount he wished to keep at sea 'on call'. I was certainly influenced by the thought that he might have to 'hole up' in San Carlos for some weeks if not months and that the equipment might, then, be better spread around the San Carlos shore than resting 'under water'. We had always discussed operations along the northern flank and this would mean a logistics depot based somewhere on the edge of Salvador Waters. But we had to react to the operational situation at the time and that indicated to me that the transports were about to be targeted and that they should be emptied as soon as possible and sent east.

I was right but luck of sorts continued to help as the Argentine bombs remained incorrectly fused for a few days until this mistake was announced by the BBC. The cosy off-load on to exposed north-eastern beaches would clearly have been a disaster and I was glad we had not chosen that for our first assault. I was none too keen to try now while the Argentine airmen still had some sting.

My most immediate problem for the second day was going to be air defence of the logistic ships and for this I hoped that all twelve Rapier sites would be fully operational and zeroed in – if that is the right expression for a missile system. Some had put great faith in the Rapier and, perhaps, had hoped that it would be the answer to our expected problems from shortly after H Hour onwards but such was not the case. While I had had to plan the anchorage on that basis I had always looked at its defence by Rapier with a somewhat cynical eye: especially when, in conversation with the Rapier Battery commander, I discovered that the planned disposition of his sites had been made by computer into which had been fed the need to cover the ground troops and not the anchorage itself. Fortunately San Carlos Water was reasonably narrow and we could expect some coverage from Rapier over my ships, but it is essentially a point and not area defence system.

I was not alone in my cynicism. Indeed by the end of D Day we proved what we already knew and that was that the security of the offload had to depend on early warning, good air direction, determination and accuracy from ships' guns and missile crews. Many of the captains had had their air defence views hardened by their exertions throughout 'day one' and continued to argue their case, now from positions of experience.

It was no surprise, therefore, that after the captains of the two Type 22 frigates (both damaged) had discussed their tactics that evening Bill Canning of *Broadsword* sent me (as his immediate commander on the spot) an unequivocal signal which he copied to Sandy. He believed that 'Air defence must be extended further west so that raid survivors rather than total effort reach the Sound. This could be achieved by bringing carriers closer or resurrecting Type 22/42 combination west of Falklands. It might at least result in Argentine air effort being divided.' Bill Canning went on to remind the addressees that a serious but predicted problem with the Type 22 frigate was the inability of its Sea Wolf radars to 'see' efficiently over land, and without Sea Wolf the ship's capabilities were limited.

While agreeing (I knew little of Type 22 or 42 operations) I could only manage the air-defence of the AOA with what Sandy, whose reply was predictable, gave me: 'Carrier group cannot risk half our long-term air-defence force by coming much further forward than 56° 30' W.' They had come as far west as 56° 06' W during the day which had not been far enough for us. Sandy, though, did agree to a '22/42 combo' to the north-west of the Islands and so HMS *Coventry* with her Sea Dart missiles was despatched in place of the planned Seaslug Guided Missile Destroyer *Glamorgan* who had, herself, been due to replace the damaged destroyer *Antrim*. Mike Goodman, my main warfare adviser worried about 'the combo'. He preferred, as I did, not to experiment at this critical stage and to have the escorts in the anchorage. I did not know at that time that the combination had already been tried.

Julian and I were concerned about the use of West Falklands settlement airfields and discussed with Ewen whether or not they were suitable for resupply by C-130; he thought not. Nevertheless, I sent *Brilliant* that night to insert an SBS team into King George Bay by boat and helicopter to check; all the while she could continue to repair her damaged Sea Wolf system. She was back in the 'safety' of San Carlos Waters at dawn, having put men into Roy Cove by boat but having failed to do the same by helicopter at Chartres and Dunnose Head after lights were observed ashore.

Argentine defensive plans were interesting. From 1 May they had expected an amphibious landing in the vicinity of Stanley, believing that the first Vulcan strike and follow-up action by the Sea Harriers was the prelude to our landing. To this end they had mined the beaches they they had themselves used on 2 April and laid an offshore minefield in the Cape Pembroke sea area. (We discovered that the mines had been laid on a sloping sea-bed causing many to drift with the current into deeper water. By the time we arrived the minefield was not at all solid.) Anti-personnel and anti-tank mines were eventually laid to defend various smaller garrisons across the Islands but the main defences had been reserved for Stanley.

For two or three days before our arrival Menendez will have received reports of possible landings along the coast south of Stanley and in Berkeley Sound, but it was not until the SAS diversionary raid at Darwin that he must have felt that his worst fears were about to be realized. It had been a long wait. The morale of his men taking a hammering with each debilitating air and gunfire attack, the slowly worsening weather and the uncompromising attitude of the people he had come to 'liberate'. It might be assumed that when our assault did come he probably felt a relief – of sorts.

The Berkeley Sound shelling and spurious radio circuits had been the first intimation of a landing, but Menendez had heard all this before. It was not until the Darwin garrison reported being under attack from a British 'battalion' that he knew that this might now be the immediate prelude to the 'real thing', even if it was not yet where he expected it to be. Shortly after these reports (at 0500) he had received the news from his Fannings Head lookout that they, too, were now under attack. At this stage Menendez alerted the Junta's South Atlantic Area Headquarters at Comodoro Rivadavia which instantly (but already well after daylight) ordered the despatch of the first flight of Daggers from Rio Grande at 1225 in two waves of four. We were aware of these taking off and went to Air Raid Warning Yellow at 1300 and 'Red' fifteen minutes later. *Antrim* and *Broadsword* in the Sound were to be their targets. The Harriers had not had enough warning to intercept these aircraft and only managed a stern chase but with the distance from their home-base increasing they had to return to the carriers 'empty-handed'. One Mirage had been 'splashed' by *Broadsword*'s Sea Wolf.

Two quiet hours then followed without interruption, except by Pucaras flying what we assumed were armed reconnaissance flights from Goose Green, one of which was shot down by a Harrier on CAP.

Shortly after 1545 four Skyhawk A4Bs approached the AOA (as we had again been warned) with one only making an attack; two turned back and one jettisoned its load against the unfortunate Argentine ship *Rio Carcarana*, still beached off Port King as the result of an earlier attack by Harriers. *Ardent* was attacked so low by the remaining A4 that her 992 radar was bent 20° out of line, although it continued to operate efficiently. This aircraft escaped but of the next flight of four only two managed it back to the mainland. Two were shot down by Harriers and the other two returned to the mainland having decided not to attack.

A concentrated period of mainland-based air attacks then took place, starting at about 1700. With warning we were able to pick up the incoming raids over one hundred miles to the west. *Argonaut* and *Brilliant* detected what were identified as Super Etendards and gave the appropriate warning. The one thing that was unlikely in San Carlos (which was one of the factors in our deliberations) was an Exocet attack. Nevertheless these aircraft were not welcome, for their ability to lead other aircraft through low cloud could indicate further raids. The Harrier CAP was vectored towards the radar contacts where four Daggers were sighted. One was shot down at 1730 close to Chartres with a Sidewinder, while the remaining three pushed on towards the AOA. Unseen, due to the CAP concentrating on this first wave, five Skyhawks now entered Falkland Sound from the north to attack *Argonaut* under Fannings Head. The three Daggers were close behind diving to sea level from the Many Branch Harbour re-entrant.

These were the first waves of a fifteen-minute 'blitz' by the AAF involving at least twelve more aircraft covering Falkland Sound and to a lesser extent San Carlos Waters, which was to leave all but two of my escorts damaged. Three of the Daggers were shot down by CAP at 1752. At 1755 two flights of three Argentine Navy Skyhawk A4's entered the Sound from the south where they came up with *Ardent* three miles south-west of North West Islands. She was returning to the fold after her successful Darwin shoot. Her duties now were to split up any attack approaching from the south but in fact was to have all attacks from that direction directed against her alone. Two out of nine 500 pound bombs from the first three Skyhawks hit and exploded aft in the flight deck area, while a third lay unexploded in the after machinery room. All the frigate's weapon systems were now out of action leaving her to rely on hand-held machine guns and the 20 mm. The second wave of enemy aircraft also hit her aft, causing extensive flooding and serious fires. Now sinking by the stern and with the fires and flooding uncontrollable, *Ardent*'s gallant captain had no alternative but to ask *Yarmouth* to take off his crew. Many managed to scramble across without getting wet, Commander Alan West being the last to leave.

Of this last wave all fell prey to the CAP, which must have been devastating to the air force squadrons on the mainland. I was elated but expected further attacks up to nightfall. There were, however, none. The success had been the safe landing of the 'bayonets', the departure of *Canberra*, *Europic Ferry*, *Norland*, accompanied by HMS *Antrim*, and the destruction of at least fourteen assorted aircraft and helicopters, mainland- and island-based. With these losses must have gone a large number of their senior aircrew, as I cannot believe that a squadron would have sent junior pilots on its first attack ever. This would not have been good for the morale of the aircrew left. It pleased me enormously and, based on my assumption that only five percent of pilots are brave, I felt that subsequent attacks might not be pressed home with such fervour, as indeed some on D Day were not. I was convinced at the time, and we now know, that no clear aim had been given to the attacking pilots, except (with very limited time) to engage the first target they saw. Tomorrow could, however, be very different and I was far from certain just how much more punishment we could safely take.

My greatest pleasure, and one shared by my escort captains, was that Julian Thompson could send a sitrep that ended,

'Brigade ashore and going firm.' It had, after all the worrying, started really quite well.

As night fell Jeremy Larken and John Prime, his navigator, came down from the bridge in high spirits, rather like two small boys who had been watching a good western. I, however, was completely drained. I had spent most of the day dashing between the ship's Ops Room and the AOR and had received reports that *Canberra* had been hit on no less than six occasions. On one of these she was 'definitely, positively, on fire', but it was actually the smoke from a ship's fires beyond. I had been worried, too, that undamaged ships would get caught up in rescue attempts at the expense of fighting and felt moved to send a straightforward signal exhorting the warships to keep on engaging the enemy and worry about survivors later.

I was more than a little dazed by our 'corporate' efforts that day, the culmination of so many imponderables coming together and with nothing found wanting. I was also trying to clear my mind to decide whether or not we had actually been successful. In truth, I was thrilled with what we had achieved and yet, obviously, desperately sad for those who had not made it to nightfall to share this success, and that included those who had been killed in various incidents leading up to D Day.

Julian returned aboard that evening after visiting his men and in a gesture that I recognized as 'typically Thompson', he stood to attention in front of me and made a little speech. He had watched from ashore and been 'overwhelmed' by our efforts to fight and was so encouraged by it that there was no way he was going to let us down. With our mutual desire to do our best for each other now firmly cemented, my morale could hardly have been higher. I was extremely grateful but lost for words to reply as graciously. I rather feebly stumbled off to the comfort of my cabin.

That night I sat down with my senior staff in an attempt to write a report, but it had been a hectic day with no precise knowledge of how many air attacks we had received, we could not be accurate. Conversely, Sandy, doing roughly the same thing in his Carrier Battle Group, had a much clearer idea as he could stand back, listen to the HF air defence circuit and count as it were, and listen to his pilots being debriefed. To us in the 'Clapptrap' survival and the action had been all-important and not bureaucratic record-keeping.

From Ewen's descriptions, the Logistic Regiment had long identified the derelict mutton processing factory at Ajax Bay as the best place for a Brigade Maintenance Area and this was now earmarked, additionally, as the site for the Brigade Medical Officer's 'Red and Green Life Machine' – under the command, and largely due to the initiative of Surgeon Lieutenant-Commander Rick Jolly who commandeered the Surgical Support Teams and forced us to abandon the original idea of using ships. It turned out to be a good decision but I was alarmed to see this very large man with huge boots standing to attention in my cabin without taking his cap off as naval officers traditionally do. He continued to wear his green beret as if he was a Royal Marine. He was too frightening a vision to refuse!

My staff and I were now moving into areas that we had never practised and had found difficult to imagine. The three exercises in which I had taken part had involved only one commando, sometimes two squadrons of helicopters and the minimum amount of stores for landing. Here we were with the equivalent of five commandos, considerable supporting arms (light tanks and Rapier for instance) and yet with a reduced number of helicopters, already depleted by earlier operations in South Georgia and South America and only a few more landing craft.

I was now faced with the normal procedures of offloading but under far from normal (peacetime/admin landing) conditions. It was to be a very steep learning curve and would become fairly shambolic at times. We had in very limited circumstances and on rare occasions practised procedures whereby the Brigade asked for commodities and I delivered them from whichever ship they happened to be in. Now, when the Brigade asked for something it was probably spread across three different ships and none of these, or only one, might be in San Carlos – the rest being possibly two days away at sea – and it soon became apparent that it was not often at the front of the pile and so easily found.

From now on the Commanding Officer of the Commando Logistic Regiment would tell my staff each day what ships he needed to unload in the anchorage and I, in turn, would then tell Sandy shepherding our logistic ships out at sea. But not always did we get the ships in for which I asked, for various reasons.

We were entering the unplanned general unloading period of an amphibious operation. I was also tasking escorts for night operations out of San Carlos, partly in order to give them a chance to fight back at the enemy: the insertion of SBS patrols and the use of their guns in NGS was just what was needed. Initially I planned to remain at anchor at night in San Carlos in order to rest the merchant ships and to avoid any risk of collision while the frigates were packed off in different directions. Each evening, too, I would sit down with John Prime (*Fearless*'s navigation officer) and approve his ideas of the anchorage positions for those ships due in from sea on the morrow.

I had wanted *Intrepid* out of San Carlos Waters to reduce the chance of losing or damaging an LPD, but the arguments for keeping her in could not be contested. Mike Rose pleaded with me to keep her as his men had cached most of their 'funny' gear on board and did not want it landed anywhere: she also provided a second two-spot flight deck, plus fuel and maintenance facilities for landing craft as well as helicopters. She was fitted with Seacat and had a duplicate amphibious operations room (but no SATCOM). At a very early stage I had invited her to modify her offices to match our own in *Fearless* so that if we were hit we could move across and find everything very much as we knew it. I also asked her staff to come across on a daily basis to be briefed. Everything that could be was, therefore, duplicated; they could, if necessary, take over at the drop of – a bomb!

Having landed the bayonets, I worried mainly now about five things: getting Julian and his men back if I was to lose all their kit and therefore be unable to sustain them; sustaining them if and when they moved forward; what to do if the anchorage came under counter-attack; chemical warfare and the odd rogue submarine or destroyer. Now that the troop ships had been despatched I had to plan into which ships I would load the

Brigade if we had had to conduct a withdrawal under attack (I was never allowed by the Royal Marines to call it a retreat!). I did not plan to leave Julian but if there had been a massed air attack and all my ships had been damaged or destroyed I worried whether the Brigade was 'balanced' enough to sustain itself against a determined land attack at the same time: I feared they were probably not. We had not had sufficient time to discuss how we would recognize such a critical point and in view of the somewhat chaotic conditions that probably always occur at this stage, the decision may well be a subjective rather than an objective one. This is not the best way to reach the correct opinion but possibly the only way. It is also a strong argument why amphibious operations are naval operations and thus why the Commodore must retain control until the Brigadier is ready, and able, to go it alone. One cannot move without the other at this early stage. 3 Commando Brigade understood this, but as we will see, this is precisely what 5 (Army) Brigade found (but ignored) when they tried moving without the other. They suffered the consequences and we got caught trying to help them.

An amphibious operation, beyond all other considerations, has to be a balanced operation and I did not feel too balanced at the end of D Day – relieved that it had gone as well as it had, but definitely off-balance.

I had not expected the submarine, if it existed in our area, to show during daylight with all the ships and helicopters milling about but I certainly expected him to creep in once darkness fell. I had also been uncertain about surface ships and had had *Brilliant*'s Lynx search to the south of the Sound.

Lastly, I was sad not to have been able to say goodbye to the captain of *Ardent* and his crew for they and *Antelope* had been the two frigates with me that winter in north Norway: I considered them to be the only two escorts specifically worked-up for amphibious operations.

Perhaps the real actions of the day are best summed up in the words of my staff war diary which, if I remember, read:

'After a clear night the day broke fine with perfect flying weather. This continued until after dark. H Hour was delayed as a result of minor navigational problems and an under-estimation of the time it would take to disembark fully equipped Paras by boat. This had been done once only at Ascension and then only briefly. Advance Forces had detected the presence of the enemy on Fannings Head by thermal imagery, *Antrim* provided excellent NGS and the Argentinian force is thought to have been reduced but chose not to surrender as quickly as expected. All other landings successful with no opposition. Priority was given to disembarking guns and Rapier. Some ammunition and beach support gear also landed during the course of the subsequent persistent air attacks.

'Initial air attacks appeared poorly planned and were not pressed home. They were concentrated on the ships in the San Carlos Water anchorage. Later the escorts became the prime targets and attacks in the open water of the Sound were pressed home, mostly at low level. Count was lost of the number of attacks. However, at least 35 attacks were made on the Task Group. It was thought that between TG 317.0 (the Amphibious Task Group) and Sea Harrier CAP, under *Antrim*'s control, playing a magnificent part, about 15 were downed. GR3 had at first light taken out a Chinook and Puma while the SAS claim a Pucara. Without *Antrim*'s direction the damage to shipping would have been far greater since some eight enemy aircraft can be claimed by CAP.

'*Antrim* continued to cope despite damage including an unexploded bomb. *Argonaut* was covering the northern sea approach, primarily for ASW and was badly hit. Two UXBs remain to be removed. Royal Engineers EOD team were embarked during the evening and one of the bombs was rendered safe. She was towed by *Plymouth* to San Carlos Inlet where she will be anchored in a position to use her Seacat and communications. *Ardent* suffered several attacks and was abandoned in a sinking but anchored position. She had earlier provided first class NGS to help cover a Special Forces withdrawal near Port Darwin. *Broadsword* took one aircraft but suffered splinter damage and lost her Lynx; she continued as surface warfare co-ordinator and anti-submarine warfare co-ordinator throughout. *Brilliant* also took one aircraft but suffered more and only had one Seawolf serviceable. *Plymouth* and *Yarmouth* were fortunate and appear unscathed. All Amphibious Ships virtually untouched.

'Rapier after its long sea journey is thought to need time to settle down and since the pm air attacks concentrated on escorts it was not properly tested.

'Lesson – constant CAP under tight control essential to provide ships defence and sufficient attrition.'

Meanwhile, to the east, Sandy was becoming impatient with the lack of success of Rapier, particularly as he appears to have decided that as soon as the missile points were operational he could remove all the escorts from the AOA except those required for naval gunfire support and anti-submarine work, a decision with which I was not happy. My views on the efficacy and coverage of Rapier had not altered.

However, two summings-up of that first day put things into a perspective I understand: the first was CinC Fleet's signal which read:

'At the end of the hardest day's fighting we have known for many years you should all feel well satisfied that you have achieved the aim of establishing the beachhead. Our casualties are of course tragic, but in the circumstance are much less than might have been. The Argentine losses have been severe and you have established a moral ascendency. Well done. Keep your guards up.'

The second is a quote from an experienced and distinguished frigate captain who was there on that day (his ship was rocketed and by the day's end still had two unexploded bombs lodged aboard): Kit Layman later wrote:

'If the history of the Royal Navy is a good guide, ships are there to be used and therefore *risked*.

'The Royal Navy has never minded losing a few ships in the knowledge that warfare is a risk-taking business. Hitler, Mussolini and Anaya [Commander, Argentinian Navy] hated losing ships and withdrew them (in extreme cases scuttled them) rather than have them sunk.

'The amphibious assessment was that the job could be done. It was done and the losses were acceptable.'

Kit Layman was absolutely correct. I hoped Brian Young of *Antrim* enjoyed some of the claret he had borrowed from our store.

CHAPTER FIVE

THE GAME'S ON

Their force is wonderful great and strong; and yet
we pluck their feathers little by little.

Drake

D+1 WAS A slightly different day, described from memory as:

'A quiet day of consolidation in the AOA. The *Ardent* survivors
were transferred to the *Canberra* (last night) and departed the
AOA in company with *Antrim, Europic Ferry* and *Norland.*
Argonaut towed into anchorage by *Plymouth* and then further into
San Carlos Water by the LCUs to enable her to commence
repairs/dispose of her second UXB in a less vulnerable position.
Brilliant applied first aid and it was decided to sail her pm to *Stena
Seaspread* for repairs. *Coventry/Broadsword* combo worked to
westward but had little luck as most Argentine air activity
appeared to end near Weddell Island. One or two A4s made half-
hearted bombing runs towards twilight. The weather (cloud base
low) is thought to have given them an excuse for going home.
Overnight *Antelope* joined to replace *Ardent.*'

After the first day virtually nothing was done now 'according to
plan' and we entered a phase of considerable '*ad hocary*'! One
part of my staff, principally led by George Pearson, was looking

at naval warfare problems and deciding which ships should enter and leave the anchorage while juggling permutations of loads, quantities and whether or not they could transfer stores out at sea. The overall aim was to fulfil as many of the Land Forces' logistic requests as we could. They were also looking at the use of the escorts in the evenings and so a routine developed whereby captains and warfare officers would attend my morning brief on board HMS *Fearless* before the air attacks began after daybreak. These briefs would include orders for night-time NGS and insertion or extraction of the Special Forces patrols, hopefully, giving them the day to plan. All the while we had to organize the communications frequencies in order to avoid confusion and conflict. As always I ordered a close look-out to be kept for enemy ships such as a Type 42 destroyer acting as radar picket and hiding (with its Exocets) among the western islands.

Another part of the staff, the more military side, was tasking the LCUs (and to some extent the helicopters) and fulfilling logistic requests. David Minords took the lead in this in addition to his liaison duties with Headquarters 3rd Commando Brigade ashore. His job was to ascertain what the Commando Brigade had in mind and what their basic concept of operations might be. I was anxious that we kept up with the Brigade's thinking rather than merely reacted to their requests. This was not easy.

I had been a little surprised with the speed with which Julian moved ashore. He and all his staff went without really discussing their departure with me. I was aware that Julian had effectively two watches of tactical staff officers. This would provide what I would describe as a main and an alternative command post which was obviously a prudent concept and one that I had followed in trying to set up *Intrepid*. I believed that the Supporting Arms Co-ordination Centre in the AOR on board *Fearless* provided the facilities for one of these watches while the other was setting itself up ashore. I was not clear whether his logistics, intelligence and other cells could be spread evenly between two headquarters, and thought that he would probably wish to spend much of his time in daylight rushing around to see how his Commanding Officers were getting on and assessing their potential against counter-attack, etc. I hoped then that he would return on board for the evening brief and be available for discussions with me and my staff. My theory was that he would still be able to command his men ashore from on board, provided the communications were adequate. Hopefully, the day would come when he felt that he was sufficiently established ashore to allow him to move permanently with his staff but I did not expect this to happen before the amphibious operation was over. In the event, partly I suspect because he quite reasonably did not wish to risk losing part of his staff to enemy air attack, he decided to take everyone ashore leaving his deputy, Colonel Tom Seccombe, and Major David Baldwin to act as his Liaison Officers. Although I had met Tom Seccombe in the *Canberra*, I scarcely knew him or he me. He could not therefore be expected to read my mind in the same way that Julian could after our weeks together on the way south. It was another example of the lack of previous exercising at Brigade staff level and the fact that we had been so involved in making sure that the initial landings went correctly that we did not have time to look closely at how Julian and I would personally operate together as the rest of the amphibious phase continued. I missed my informal chats with Julian very much and, despite the efforts of the Liaison Officers, found it very difficult, with all the immediate problems that my ships provided, to stand back and look ahead in order to provide him with the long-term support that I knew he would need.

I needed to be sure that the liaison was working well, particularly for air defence and naval gunfire support. I wanted to anticipate the wishes of those ashore so that our support would be instant, but we spent much time guessing their requirements; nor were we helped in this by the one, secure-voice VHF circuit being continually tied up by the logisticians allowing Julian and me very little chance to communicate. I was delighted when he managed to come on board for a chat but he too was extremely busy and it was not easy for him to do so. He couldn't come during air attacks as I was pre-occupied and raiding craft rides at night were not popular as the craft were so often required for inserting Special Forces patrols.

I had for some time regretted not bringing with me a WASP helicopter dedicated to the use of myself and my staff. This we sometimes did on exercises because there was plenty of space for one. As this campaign developed, it was clear that the Brigade would need more space and I therefore decided against taking a WASP and insisted that Staff Officers took pot-luck with Sea Kings and Wessex helicopters as they moved around the force. This made life extremely difficult for them and awkward for me throughout the campaign.

During my few exercises, it had always been me that had had the time to dress up in my 'you can't see me' camouflage battledress complete with boots, puttees and all, and wander off ashore and get in the Landing Force's way – but then we had never practised such a complicated off-load and were never under air attack or needed to co-ordinate our air defence since it was a host nation responsibility.

After the departures on the night of D Day I was left with the two LPDs, five LSLs, *Fort Austin* the two Type 22s *Brilliant* and *Broadsword*, the elderly Leander *Argonaut* and the two even older Rothesay Class frigates *Plymouth* and *Yarmouth*. I had lost *Ardent*, sunk, and *Antrim* had been sent east for repairs. *Brilliant* could not operate her Sea Wolf (but remained invaluable as an air-defence control ship) and *Argonaut* who could float and fight but not move. Once we realized that *Argonaut* could work her operations room she took over the air defence duties from *Brilliant*. Sandy agreed to send the Type 22/42 combination so *Coventry* with her Sea Dart and *Broadsword* with her Sea Wolf missile systems were by dawn patrolling north of Sedge Island. They were physically outside my AOA and therefore strictly not under my operational control. Between them these two could not only control CAP but engage enemy aircraft, close-in as well as at a distance. I now also had the newly arrived *Antelope*, which was most welcome as I had come to respect her Commanding Officer, Nick Tobin, who was desperate to get in on the action.

On this day we were relieved that the AAF did not try too hard to penetrate our defences and apart from one or two radar detections in the afternoon (believed afterwards to be Mirages escorting Hercules), we remained reasonably unmolested until just before dusk. With the CAP having a long transit from the carriers they had no time to chase further west. In fact the Argentine pilots turned safely away once they realized that they had been spotted. This strengthened my view that a large proportion of the enemy pilots were unwilling to press home their attacks. The low cloud base may have had some influence, on this occasion, but I expect that the unexpected pilot-losses the day before was the major factor. These losses must have had them licking their wounds while they reviewed their attack profiles.

As a result of radars detected by ships, we suspected that there may be enemy radar sites to the west of us on, perhaps, Weddell Island and Byron Heights. These would have been well positioned to guide incoming enemy aircraft and warn them of approaching Sea Harriers; I tasked the SBS who were to spend fruitless hours looking for them. It was a cautious but prudent decision even if we found neither radar nor enemy troop concentrations. It added greatly to our intelligence picture and allowed us to relax a little about West Falkland.

We did, though, receive two unannounced attacks at 2000 when a pair of Daggers, followed very swiftly by three A4s, flew into San Carlos Waters. They hit nothing and nor were they hit by the ships or Rapier, still settling down after its long sea voyage.

At dusk on D+1, at Sandy's request, I sent *Coventry* back to the Carrier Battle Group with our thanks and brought *Broadsword* into the night-time peace of the AOA.

On the logistics front I asked Sandy to arrange for *Canberra* to transfer her Brigade stores to *Norland* who would then return under cover of darkness, but this turned out to be impossible in the time scale we were operating. Most of these items never reached the Commando Brigade.

When *Argonaut* had been brought into the sheltered waters of San Carlos her unexploded bombs were investigated. One was lodged beneath a boiler and could not be removed without jarring or re-orientating the bomb. The naval divers did not have the same bomb disposal equipment as the Royal Engineers and called the Engineers over to try and render the bomb safe *in situ*. This they managed and *Argonaut*'s ship's company then removed the bomb. The other bomb remained lodged in a flooded Seacat magazine and would have to wait.

Fifty-nine Harrier Combat Air Patrols were launched during that day, including a successful strike against one of the two small patrol vessels, *Rio Iguazu*, in Choiseul Sound when she was caught steaming towards Goose Green with two 105 mm guns embarked. She beached herself at Button Bay with at least one dead on board. The guns (her cargo) later made their way to their destination by helicopter in time for one of them (the second had been damaged by the Harriers) to take part in the defence of Darwin against 2 Para. Finally they were captured and used to our advantage.

Further Harrier activity included a four-aircraft attack against Goose Green, but this time no Pucara were spotted so their targets were shifted to enemy defensive positions. At 2030 a flight of Harriers returning from a photo-recce of Weddell Island airstrip (nothing seen) asked permission to attack the Falkland Island Company's coaster *Monsunen*. I'm glad they asked first for I refused their request for two reasons. I was worried that the 'kelper' crew might still be aboard and thought, too, that if we could capture the vessel intact she would be very useful in helping to solve our re-supply problems. She may also have had information on minefields.

It looked as though the coaster was on her way from West Falkland for she was heading south-east off the southern entrance to Eagle Passage. If we could capture her she might reveal intelligence about military installations at her departure point, which I assumed was Fox Bay, or her destination, which could have been Goose Green. This was an ideal task for the SBS and precisely one of the roles for which they train and another good reason why they were under my command.

Our plans laid, *Brilliant* and *Yarmouth*, an hour and a half after the Harriers' request, were invited to embark a section of SBS and execute the intercept, although there was a delay loading the Marines. At 0400 a Lynx helicopter reported that she had found a small vessel in Lively Sound and, on investigating, had been engaged by small arms fire. Orders to heave-to were ignored so *Yarmouth* illuminated the quarry with starshell and fired HE ahead of her. *Monsunen* was then beached on the west coast of the Sound while her crew escaped across the rocks. The SBS assault was called off as it was thought her 'cargo' might include a military force of some strength who could have stayed behind in ambush, so we left her there for recovery later. Ewen's advice was that the kelp she rested in was very thick and likely to cushion her from serious damage in the meantime.

Brilliant continued seaward to join the Carrier Battle Group in order to have her Sea Wolf repaired, while *Yarmouth* returned to the AOA by dawn with the SBS. Although we did not have the coaster under command, at least she had been immobilized, and that was a start.

I remained conscious that one of our main priorities against the enemy had to be the destruction of his helicopter lift capability and that if we could destroy that and the few small ships still available for moving troops I would be doing Julian and myself a great service. I once again asked Sandy to task his GR3s accordingly.

The night was also a busy one for *Plymouth*. She returned to Roy Cove to collect the SBS team dropped there the night before and this time successfully inserted a new team by helicopter into Dunnose Head to watch that airstrip and to check if there was an elusive radar site in the area. I remained suspicious by the ship reports and wanted clarification. Overnight, too, *Antelope* escorted *Stromness* and *Norland* back to the AOA with their urgently needed stores but a delay to their departure time from the Carrier Battle Group meant that they were still well north of Falkland Sound at dawn. I was not happy and waited with fingers firmly crossed for their unmolested arrival.

Meanwhile, back to the massive task of unloading the Brigade's stores and the tasking of helicopters and landing craft. Because of the relative shortage of these assets and somewhat uncertain loading plans, my two RCT Majors were spending most of the daylight hours and some of the night hours visiting the stores ships as well as having actually to carry out the tasking. This was a heavy burden on them which they performed, to my mind, exceptionally well and very diligently. It was, however, difficult for me to find out what their problems were so that I could try to look ahead and help them as every second seemed to introduce yet another problem. The lives of my other Staff Officers were not all that dissimilar.

An added and unexpected drain on our helicopters was the necessity to supply the Rapiers with one Sea King on permanent call for the delivery of stores and petrol for their generators. This annoyed both Julian and myself for we did not think we were 'getting our money's-worth' from these weapons anyway. Instead they were draining our already tiny airforce.

We were all conscious that the Brigade had its stores spread across fifteen ships and that these could not all be off-loaded in the anchorage together. On the first full day, therefore, we initiated the concept that some of those ships that had been partly offloaded by day would sail at night for the protection of the Carrier Battle Group where they would attempt to switch loads if the outgoing ship only had a few tons left and the incoming one had room. Of course we continued offloading other ships by night; on the basis that as there were no enemy OPs overlooking the anchorage itself we could use dim lights. Fine in theory, but the landing craft and Mexeflote crews needed a modicum of rest, their craft needed fuel and maintenance and it was only then (night-time) that we could swop over the shipping from sea anyway.

At about this time an Observation Post was suspected on Mount Rosalie and, while this only covered the entrance to San Carlos and not the anchorage itself, they could certainly listen to our VHF circuits. Our circuit discipline was not very good and was at times so full of idle gossip that I was asked to go to the AOR and listen in. It improved but with men of different training and backgrounds it was never to my mind satisfactory. Sadly, perhaps, the worst discipline was on the HF voice anti-air warfare circuit which was taped and followed by many Falkland

Islanders, and must have been easy for the Argentinians to listen into. Several Falkland Islanders have described to me how they very quickly deciphered our short-term positional codes and were able to follow more than just the air war. Not very good!

With the allocation and tasking of Special Forces to be slotted in, often with no notice and demanding precedence for helicopters and landing and raiding craft, there was ample scope for 'not pleasing all of the people all of the time'. The main call on the landing craft and helicopters should have been the unloading of the shipping but added tasks such as the sudden requirement for three LCUs to tow in the crippled *Argonaut*, while essential, did not help the planning, nor the timings, nor tempers!

Joint operations will always bring their surprises. An irate staff officer reported to me that the paras had individually buried our very expensive lifejackets loaned to them for their LCU journey under the peat at the top of their beach! All I could picture were hundreds of dogs burying their bones or, I wondered, were they ensuring their safe survival if a counter-attack developed!

A routine was developing in my task group, by natural selection rather than by any force of design. My staff were beginning to develop a kind of watch-keeping system, but for me this was not possible. While I was used to listening to the command intercom for 24 hours each day on exercises, these seldom lasted more than ten days and this one had now been going on for six weeks at least and was likely to continue. I tried to take as much of the strain as I could from them yet remained conscious that nobody was going to thank me for making a bad decision because I was over-tired. Pacing was vital as we had no idea when it would end. I encouraged the staff to try and relax but it was not easy for them.

An added corollary to this was the fact that I refused to use precious Sea Kings to get me about and therefore did not manage to visit my ships as much as I should or would have liked to have done; on the other hand, warships are self-contained units with excellent inter-ship communications at all times of the day. As CATF, though, I needed the captains (and, particularly the civilian masters) to know me and to have confidence in me even if they could not see me. While I would have liked to have been leading, in person, from the front as it were, I was forced to command via the radio: not what I would prefer but the best I could do under the circumstances. (which is why I gave lunches for the captains and masters of my Amphibious Task Group, and its escorts, and why I visited all ships companies in Ascension.)

D+2 (Sunday, 23 May) saw significant successes and set-backs. Among the good news was the destruction (out of a total of twelve enemy aircraft destroyed) of two Pumas and an Augusta helicopter gunship supplying Port Howard with ammunition. The luckless *Rio Carcarana* was once more attacked. So far she had been hit by Sea Harriers, once by *Ardent*'s Lynx firing Sea Skua for the first time in action, and once by Argentine aircraft. She had also been targeted by *Argonaut*'s Lynx but the Sea Skuas failed to engage. This time she was hit by *Antelope*'s Lynx (again using Sea Skua) requiring me to send a signal forbidding any further waste of ammunition. If the Argentines wanted to do so again that was their business! At least our aircrew were getting excellent live firing practice should they be needed to operate against the Argentine fleet.

What set-backs we suffered during this phase of the operation were largely the result of repeated air-attacks on the AOA from a mixture of aircraft, the most significant being four Skyhawks that had flown, unseen, via a route that brought them east of Darwin, then back across 2 Para's position (who reported them at 1635) and above *Antelope*'s Lynx (which they fired at but missed), on then to Fannings Head where they turned, splitting into two pairs to attack the San Carlos shipping from two different directions. *Antelope* was hit manoeuvring within San Carlos Waters. Between her small arms and a Sea Wolf from *Broadsword*, one Skyhawk crashed into the water. It had probably been helped in its final death throes by hitting *Antelope*'s mast. The Type 21 was hit by two bombs and although neither exploded one crew member was killed as they came in. I had actually been a little concerned about *Antelope*'s position as she had been pushed further out from the coastline and further north, possibly by the next ship down the anchorage swinging a little high up, and so was less protected by the surrounding hills than I would have liked. Nevertheless she was wounded but operational and came to her anchor off Ajax Bay while asking for a bomb disposal team as soon as possible.

The same Royal Engineer team who had been so successful in the early stabilization of *Argonaut*'s unwelcome visitors were sent across but this time the well-tried de-arming technique failed and the team decided to use a small defusing charge. This fired correctly but the bomb itself exploded moments after the team began moving towards it. Staff Sergeant Prescott was killed and his Warrant Officer so badly injured that he was later to have his arm amputated: a great loss of two remarkable men, early in the campaign.

With fires breaking out and the crew already mustered on the fo'cs'le and quarterdeck Jeremy Larken summoned a pair of LCUs to see what assistance they could offer but already the landing craft had broken off from their offloading duties and were on their way. Despite being ordered to stand clear the two cox'ns took their craft alongside with hoses. Thirty minutes after the explosion and with the complete midships section alight, Nick Tobin had no choice but to give the order to abandon ship. The LCUs were still alongside and not a further man was lost, but we were a second Type 21 down. Two minutes after her captain left (again the last to do so) a series of explosions started and the next morning, after one final blast (which was probably the second bomb cooking-off) *Antelope* sank with her bows and stern pointing to the sky in the middle of the loch, a dreadful reminder to us all of the destructiveness of air attacks.

That evening I gave Nick my bunk and a whisky and when she finally broke up and sank at 1200 I took him quietly up on deck and we shed a tear together. I felt desperately sorry for him as he had tried very hard to join us, yet this catastrophe occurred on his first day. He asked me if I would address his ship's company, but I said, 'No, there is no need'. He was not to know that the previous evening I had gone below to the tank deck and had spent about an hour with his men without them knowing who I was. They were a superbly motivated and gallant crew; the final sight of them disembarking for the trip home with their chins high was a stirring sight and a reminder to me of just how good a properly led and disciplined ship can be. I felt very proud of *Antelope*, Nick and his ship's company.

An additional feeling, however, was, 'Here we are packing off some excellent men from the two Type 21 frigates and yet we are short-staffed and with some ships undermanned.' Judging by their morale not one man would have refused if I had asked them to stay to help out, but, I was told, the rules for survivors in this modern age are the rules – and bureaucratic ones at that!

Antelope had been preparing to take an SBS patrol that night (the 23rd) on to Weddell Island to watch the airstrip, and a 3 Para patrol onto Great Island (East of Fox Bay) to watch for shipping, but these now had to be postponed.

In *Argonaut* discussions continued over their second bomb. *Fearless*'s engineers made a patch to cover a hole in the ship's side so pumping could begin. While on board Chris Meatyard with his clearance divers heard the explosion on *Antelope* and feared the worst. He assumed that RN personnel, less used to such activities and without the correct tools, would have to render bombs safe on their own. That night Chris had the unpleasant task of entering the flooded magazine with an *Argonaut* diver and removing the remains of a member of the magazine's crew. He also had to remove *Argonaut*'s temporary patch so that the more permanent one made by John McGregor's team could be fitted.

All these bomb disposal operations were interrupted by me deciding to order FCDT1 together with some 55000lbs of stores out of *Sir Tristram* who was nearly empty so she could sail clear of the anchorage that evening. FCDT1 were to base themselves in *Intrepid*.

At the end of the day Captain Bill Canning in *Broadsword* made another signal, this time to FOF1 and copying it to me, in which he continued to discuss the employment of the 22/42 combo. He estimated that during the last half of the afternoon he had been attacked by an estimated ten enemy aircraft and 'recognized that (his) attempt at objective thought is inevitably coloured by the unhappy experience to date of feeling a bit cornered'. Bill believed that, among other disadvantages, his position *vis-à-vis* the AOA gave him 'little or no warning, a poor Electronic Signal Measure [ESM] environment, no air defence ship and a weapon system that was limited to its secondary role or only an emergency mode of operation.'

He strongly believed that we should vary the tactics by taking the fight to the enemy as often as possible and suggested moving the 'combo' further north but, preferably, to the west of the Islands as an early warning. He asked, once again, for the Harriers to be allowed a much greater 'time on target'. His final plea concerned Rapier. 'There seems little co-ordination yet with Rapier batteries. Are we in their way?'

The aircraft were not brought significantly nearer but Sandy did agree to release *Coventry* again to join the Type 22. The effectiveness of this frigate/destroyer combination was, or should have been, four-fold:

1. Early warning for the AOA, at least from one direction.
2. Guidance and direction of Sea Harriers assuming they had the time overhead to be so directed.
3. Provision of the destroyer's Sea Dart for long-range targets.
4. Provision of the frigate's Sea Wolf close-in protection.

The problem with Rapier was simple: the ships were not in their way. Despite the efforts of their crews, the missile systems were just taking time to recover from the journey and the joint co-ordination with naval forces had only recently been planned and never practised before. It would not be until D+4 that eleven out of the twelve Rapier firing points would be operational. They and any joint procedures were casualties of the changes in direction we received at Ascension.

Towards evening *Yarmouth* was attacked by at least four Daggers but she emerged from the splashes still unscathed. Many more flights were reported to have taken off than reached us although we remained at a high state of alert throughout daylight, slowing the offload. The good news (or perhaps the less bad news) was that the enemy still seemed to be targeting the warships and escorts and that their bombs were clearly fused for a dive attack. If the pilots had stuck to the designed delivery methods for their British-built ordnance and not chosen the much safer low-level delivery methods they would have brought our efforts to a halt – particularly if they had used high-drag bombs suitable for the attack profiles they were adopting. By the time they realized their mistake and re-armed their bombs (they were told by the BBC World Service, always, I was assured, keen to provide balanced reporting of their problems that day – the 23rd) the Brigade's stores were moving ashore and we were, as it were, on our way.

That night (23rd/24th) I was at last able to send the empty LSL, *Sir Tristram* out of the anchorage. A certain routine was also developing with the ships' movements already for *Broadsword* continued on to a rendezvous with *Coventry* for the combo operation the next day while Plymouth handed over her outgoing charges and returned with the incoming *Resource* and the newly arrived LSL *Sir Bedivere*.

Earlier, during D+1, *Coventry* had detected air activity over West Falkland reinforcing the view that the airstrips at Dunnose Head, Roy Cove, Weddell Island and Chartres were being used to break the blockade into West Falkland. I had asked for a GR3 strike on the 23rd on to Dunnose Head but at first light altered the target to Pebble Island which, through reports from my ships of radar transmissions from the area, I believed was still being used. This alteration was not approved by Sandy as it was received too late to change the sortie's mission without confirmed intelligence. The result was that the strike went in an hour late against an empty Dunnose airstrip. An hour or so later a strike was finally sent in to Pebble Island but the enemy had left and the GR3s once again wasted valuable ordnance against aircraft already destroyed by the SAS.

D+3, Monday, 24 May, was not a good day and was to get worse before it got better. It had started with *Antelope* blowing up and sinking. I now had two ships sunk, twelve ships at anchor (three with unexploded bombs in them – *Argonaut, Sir Galahad* and *Sir Lancelot*). Five escorts were patrolling either inside San Carlos Waters or to the north of the Sound just out of my operational area. *Argonaut* had been towed in closer to protection by three LCUs during an air raid.

Support helicopter operations were causing concern. Partly it was because we had so few and partly because they were spread around the force, and so it was decided to try and consolidate as many as we could ashore. 846 Squadron moved ashore seven Sea Kings while 845 Sqn. took the Wessex from *Resource* and *Tidepool*. 846 was well dispersed on either side of San Carlos Water which, while safer, added to its problems.

From the staff diary, as I recall:

'Offloading and setting up of the Brigade Forward Operating Base north of San Carlos (off Bonners Bay) settlement continued. This will be ready to accept AVCAT on the 25th. It is now thought that positioning of 22/42 combo needs re-considering as most raids have begun to close San Carlos from the south. *Plymouth*, *Sir Percivale* and *Norland* departed the AOA at 2200Z. *Plymouth* then brought in *Tidepool* and *Sir Bedivere* and conducted a RAS (L) with *Broadsword*. Overnight *Arrow* and *Yarmouth* carried out Special Forces insertions.'

Sir Bedivere had brought with her FCDT 3 led by Lieutenant Bernie Bruen and Chief Petty Officer Trotter. They had their first taste of action when a bomb struck *Sir Bedivere*'s crane rigging before hitting the forecastle and plunging into the sea without exploding.

Early in the afternoon both *Sir Galahad* and *Sir Lancelot* reported unexploded bombs and Lieutenant Bruen's first job was visiting the ships after dark when the risk of air attack was the least.

That night brought other scares with *Fort Austin* reporting tapping on her hull. Other ships near her also made similar reports. While at anchor all ships were running *Operation Awkward* routines that required them to drop one-pound scare charges over the side at random intervals to deter divers. If this was not working we had a problem and divers from FCDT 1 and

3 were sent across to search. I sailed the remaining ships. Water along the hull washes off divers at about four knots and a limpet mine is removed by just a few more knots. Nothing was found and I felt, though, that we should try and anchor at night if we could. It was less tiring for the Captains and it was certainly less disruptive to our work.

Meanwhile, Julian began plans for a raid on Darwin, not because he felt it was tactically an important target but because he was anxious to forge ahead with his instructions to assert moral domination over the enemy. An 'inexpensive' morale-damaging raid was the best military choice for that rather than a full-scale battle. With his departure for the shore and the subsequent loss of any close liaison I was not aware of Julian's 'future intentions' and while his Deputy, Tom Seccombe, and Major David Baldwin would attend briefings ashore they seldom came back with requests for advice, nor, significantly, requests for action.

In *Fearless* we had a growing feeling of unease that some of the Brigade Staff were taking the line that now the troops and the headquarters were ashore there was no need to inform the Navy of their plans. All the Navy had to do was carry out their demands for stores, support, etc, and we weren't doing that to their entire satisfaction. In short, we felt they were not thinking along joint warfare lines but on self-centred single Service ones. If true, this lacked imagination and probably stemmed from a shortage of joint training as well as the feeling that had grown up with the Royal Marines that their future may not lie with a Navy who would not support them with adequate shipping, feelings encouraged by any slightly tactless move by Senior or Junior Naval Officers. This was irritating, for I was still in control of the amphibious aspects of the operation and Julian knew that, even if his Staff had forgotten. I was not interested in the detail of how they went about their business (I had neither the training, experience nor the Staff to run a land battle) but I had to be part of the planning and strategic thought processes until the termination of the amphibious phase. Even situation reports were being sent for action to all their Units but only to me for information. Sandy and CTF were not always included. I was obliged to ask Julian to improve this aspect as we all needed to know what he was up to and what he was planning.

In my private notes for the day I made reference to Special Forces tasking. I was concerned at the breakdown of liaison between the Brigade staff and ourselves:

'Special Forces are still being tasked by me. We must avoid muddle and therefore the Brigadier's latest signal should have been staffed by both staffs. Should be OK as it doesn't vary much from previously agreed position but from my position the Brigadier is not yet on his own (if he was I would not still be here as a target!). His signals must be carefully put to CTF 317 (the Commander in Chief, Fleet) if they affect any Special Force – me – LCUs – support helicopters – ships – Sea Harriers – GR3s and not just put to 317.1 (Moore in *QE 2*) who can't take charge.'

This highlighted an anomaly (and serious gap) in the military chain of command, paradoxically just as we, the Amphibious Group and Landing Force, needed the clearest possible direction, guidance and understanding of orders. Before flying out to Ascension Island to join the *QE2* on 20 May (D-1) Major-General Jeremy Moore assumed command of the Landing Force leaving Lieutenant-General Richard Trant as the Land Deputy to CinC Fleet back at Northwood. The snag was that, once embarked in the luxury liner, my new military 'opposite number', and (now) Julian's operational commander, lost contact with the force to which he had just been appointed – and at the most crucial period of all. Julian and I decided to carry on as before, but I suspect the confusion may not have helped at staff level. Nor, I believe, did General Trant's staff understand my overall role in the affair.

Northwood was now sending operational tasking signals to Jeremy Moore at sea with copies to Julian, but Julian could receive no instructions, nor confirmation, from Jeremy. It was an unsatisfactory state of affairs, particulary since I was still in command and should have been part of the chain. Reasonably, Julian believed that he should continue with his previous directive sent by Jeremy on 12 May which included the order to 'push forward from the beachhead area so far as the maintenance of its security allows, to gain information, to establish moral and physical domination of the enemy.' From our point of view there was no question of land battles nor of an advance in strength against Stanley until both Brigades were ready, but on the 23rd Julian received a signal from Northwood: 'Now that 3 Commando Brigade is established ashore the earliest opportunity must be taken to invest Port Stanley from positions on high ground to the west which dominate it.' Quite so, but, first, they were not properly established and next, what of Jeremy's wishes and future plans? Nothing from Northwood seemed to agree with them. This latest signal did, however, indicate that 5 Brigade was coming down in support and not necessarily to take part in any full-scale pitched battles. Did we now wait until Jeremy was on the spot to confirm or deny this new move or did we ignore his original orders and do as we were now being told direct from Northwood?

On the 24th I joined Julian for lunch in the gorse of San Carlos to discuss the future and found that we were both still very much thinking along the same lines and that as far as our own relationship (by far the most important of them all) was concerned we were still on one net. During that meeting Julian and I discussed the numbers of ships in San Carlos Waters and agreed that with commodities spread across so many there was little more we could do to balance the offload of specific items against the safety of the ships. We both wanted everything possible ashore, but Julian, understandably, wanted it ashore in the correct order and the correct proportions. We had petrol in one ship, diesel in another, food in a third, ammunition in a fourth and so on. Personal gear spread across the fleet was also a serious problem. We felt we could only reduce the number of ships at anchor once the units ashore had at least a reasonable amount of equipment to make them feel partially equipped and able to sustain operations.

The decision as to whether to stay and raid from the security of San Carlos (as ordered by Jeremy) or to move out and 'invest

Stanley' (as ordered by Northwood) exercised us considerably. One suggested that the army Brigade was coming to garrison and the second option suggested that it was coming to fight. We hoped that it was coming to do both.

Neither Julian nor I had ever considered a southern flank approach, believing, first, that that was the line of advance expected of us by Menendez (at least he expected an amphibious landing close to the south of Stanley) and, second, it was a lengthy and bad piece of flat coastline with few identifiable features for the passive navigation of slow RFA and merchant ships by day, let alone by night. I had written off this approach as being too far, too difficult and too dangerous to support by sea and not much better by helicopter.

Nor were we keen to conduct a second amphibious assault along the south coast while I was happy to consider doing so along the north if only to gain moral ascendency. We also ruled out targets on West Falkland for 'moral ascendency' purposes as they would have required us to head in the wrong direction, and would mean less Harrier coverage and greater AAF disruption. Julian's phrase 'off the line of march' fitted the bill.

The Darwin/Goose Green complex was the only, and nearest, choice that we knew of and one that could possibly be 'raided' without excessively disrupting the already tenuous offload. 2 Para was the closest unit to this objective and was given a formal warning order by Julian on the 23rd. I would supply helicopters to fly in guns and ammunition but would have to balance this requirement with the offload and first tentative move out towards our already chosen stepping stone of Port Salvador. One of my frigates could offer naval gunfire support and Sandy would be asked to provide close air support and CAP. A brief battalion raid against defences, missile batteries, airstrip, equipment, command posts and stores dumps should satisfy Jeremy's wishes and keep Northwood off our back.

Ewen suggested taking the Battalion to the southern end of Brenton Loch by landing and raiding craft, which would have been an imaginative approach by a Parachute Battalion, but after much discussion with the Commanding Officer, 'H' Jones, this was declared too risky from both the night navigation point of view as well as the military. Jones decided, in his words, to 'tab it'.

I agreed to supply four of my five night-vision-goggle-equipped Sea Kings during the night of the 24th/25th and have a frigate within range and on call. Jones's plan had D Company moving ahead to secure Camilla Creek and, when briefed and ready, they set off by foot at last light in deteriorating weather. Shortly after their departure the weather worsened considerably to the point where the only heli-borne insertion we could achieve was D Squadron, SAS, onto Mount Kent. (This had been given the first priority use of helicopters as it accorded exactly with our joint plan to move out along our own chosen axis.) The Goose Green option, simply to please the military and politicians in the United Kingdom not only seemed to us tactically unsound but also a waste of precious time, energy and supplies and took second place in our deliberations. Now, with no guns to support an attack and with Julian anxious to get moving along the northern flank he spoke to an angry 'H' Jones ordering him to bring back his men to Sussex Mountain: the raid was off. As this was the only night on which Julian and I were prepared to divert assets to anything other than the advance along the north coast we did not plan to resurrect this ill-conceived expedition.

While Julian summoned his team to reorganize, I and my team concentrated on tasking the helicopters and naval gunfire support ships, at the same time taking care to ensure that the general defence of the AOA and the unloading of the amphibious ships in particular continued unmolested. *Broadsword* and *Coventry* formed the 22/42 combo north of Pebble Island clear of any radar-confusing land mass; Bill Canning and Tony Morton had asked for an anti-aircraft Observation Post to be placed on Chancho Point which, coincidentally, we too had been considering. We actually placed it on the nearby Wreck Point.

All the expected raids that day occurred during the half hour between 1345 and 1415 and not only were they concentrated but they came from different directions; an added surprise being that the pilots had decided to go for the amphibious shipping and transports in San Carlos Waters. The only good thing was that their bombs remained incorrectly fused and their aim continued to be erratic since a half-ton lump of iron is almost as dangerous to a ship as a live bomb, as I had learned years before.

Five Skyhawks attacked from over Sussex Mountain aiming at the three LSLs, *Sir Tristram*, *Sir Bedivere* and *Sir Galahad*, all of which received hits by 1,000 lb bombs. At the same time five Mirage were detected by the 'combo' approaching the Jason Islands but these turned back before CAP could be vectored to intercept: the 'combo' had worked, if not by destroying aircraft then by putting them off. Twenty minutes later four Daggers flew north into San Carlos firing cannon at *Fearless* (who received two casualties among the 40/60 gun crews) and *Sir Galahad* – again. A second bomb hit *Sir Lancelot*. *Coventry* fired Sea Dart at the departing aircraft, and missed. Four more Daggers now approached the AOA from north of Pebble Island with *Broadsword* directing the northern CAP to intercept. This time there was success and three of the flight were shot down. A final attack came from the south up Falkland Sound with three Skyhawks turning into San Carlos Waters between Fannings Head and Chancho Point to attack heading south. All three were hit with one crashing into King George Bay on its way home. There were no hits on shipping.

Although we had suffered severely with a total of four ships hit (two twice) we were still operational. The enemy, on the other hand, had suffered again: out of a total of twenty-four aircraft thought to have taken off, eight had aborted after take off (this was particularly encouraging), four were known to have been 'splashed' and six damaged by gunfire. If we add those that were damaged at Stanley during the day and those claimed by the ground forces, we believed that somewhere between six and nine aircraft had been destroyed. My greatest concern was that the enemy were now targeting the landing ships and showing signs of interest over the land forces.

The latter had not escaped totally unscathed. 45 Commando received a bomb which exploded 30 yards from their Royal Engineers recce section; 42 were targeted at Green Beach Two by a Skyhawk. 2 Para claimed one Skyhawk shot down and another damaged, while 40 Commando also claimed one Skyhawk brought down by machine-gun fire. 3 Para received an air-burst bomb and engaged a Mirage that entered their area from the direction of Smylie Creek. Whether this change was deliberate or merely a continuation of the 'take any old target in sight' syndrome, I could not be sure.

The 'combo' had worked after a fashion, particularly with the effective directing of CAP for it had helped to split up the waves and turn back at least one. David Hart-Dyke in *Coventry* believed that 'land clutter' had still been too bad and argued, as had Bill Canning, that the two of them should be stationed among the western islands to achieve maximum effectiveness with their arcs of fire clear to the west towards the Argentinian approach. Sandy agreed that they should remain the next day and left it up to Bill to decide the patrol area. The view of Flight-Lieutenant White and my staff was that, with the raids now appearing to enter the AOA from the south, an even more fundamental repositioning of the 'combo' was in order. Unfortunately I could not ask for a second combo to the south as *Brilliant*, the only other Sea Wolf-fitted ship, was, I believed, still being repaired.

However, despite the interruptions and the bombs lodged on board various ships, the offload was less delayed than I feared: the greatest delay being suffered by the Brigade's War Maintenance Reserve in *Sir Galahad*, but we did have ashore the aluminium panels and the fuel handling equipment for the VSTOL strip from *Stromness*. *Norland* (having brought in 3 Para's vehicles, second-line ammunition and food) and *Sir Percivale* were also empty and ready to sail as soon as it was dark. All the loose stores were being unloaded direct into Ajax Bay in much greater profusion and perhaps speed than the Brigade logisticians would have liked but the alternative of not unloading every time as soon as it arrived could risk whole ship-loads being destroyed at one go.

The bombs in *Sir Lancelot* and *Sir Galahad* both needed removing and the ships needed to be repaired as quickly as possible for they would be required in the next stage, the support of the landing force, when they reached the enemy lines close to Stanley. I had to make an unpleasant decision and tell *Argonaut* that they would have to live with their bombs till these ships had been cleared as we had no further bomb disposal teams. *Sir Lancelot* was nearly empty but *Sir Galahad* had on board a considerable amount of ammunition. *Sir Lancelot*'s bomb was the more difficult of the two and while the crew were disembarked (the Chinese to *Stromness* and the officers between the two LPDs) Fleet Chief Petty Officer (Diver) Trotter earned his DSM working on the problem. *Sir Galahad*'s bomb was at last placed into a gemini (packed with Kelloggs Corn Flake boxes to cushion any shock) on the 26th to be lowered into deeper water that day. With the Chinese sailing in *Stromness* from the AOA on the 25th, two very relieved foreign crews found themselves with a day or two of enforced 'leave' away from San Carlos. Fears that they would not return (prompting contingency plans for the employment of junior ships officers from across the fleet) proved unfounded and both ships became operational again, *Sir Galahad* on 26 May but *Sir Lancelot* not until 7 June.

Once again John McGregor's engineering team of volunteer welders/cutters and spare hands was called in. They cut an exit route for the bombs and provided the necessary blocks and tackles and slings. *Sir Galahad*'s bomb, again a British 1,000lb bomb, had stopped in the battery shop and looked the easier to extract of the two. Even so McGregor had to ask for additional assistance from *Stena Seaspread* out at sea with Sandy.

This operation was also interrupted by the hurried removal of FCDT3 from *Sir Bedivere* so that the ship could also clear the anchorage on the evening of the 25th. They too went to *Intrepid* which was placing them all under one roof which was an uncomfortable risk. The experience so far had allowed the FCDTs to plan ahead, technical support teams being provided by both *Intrepid* and *Fearless*. We were much better prepared for any future contingency.

In all, Sandy's air groups flew fifty-six Harrier CAP missions in support of my AOA during the day. We could not have asked for more, particularly when I considered that these were in addition to a number of his own tasks, such as the bombing of Stanley runway where a Pucara and one helicopter had been damaged. Two GR3s had been at alert all day for 3 Commando Brigade but were not called for.

Part of the routine we had developed since we arrived in San Carlos was an evening personal chat with Sandy. My staff had been talking to his staff whenever necessary during the day to set up the ship movements, etc, and I tried to explain what I thought the Brigade was up to. From what I have already said, this was not easy since I was not fully in the picture myself. With Julian ashore, he was unable to use the DSSS system, however bad it might be, to speak to and brief Sandy himself. It was a good argument for the Landing Force Commander to remain on board *Fearless* for longer. This problem was to continually dog us throughout the war. Although the Land Forces could argue that the Navy really did not have a need to know in great detail what they were up to, we certainly needed to know in general terms what their future intentions were if we were going to be able to assist. It was essentially a naval war in which the Landing Force had a major, but arguably, not totally decisive role to play. They in their turn did not need to know the details of the naval engagements. A broader view and acceptance of others' needs would have been helpful, in short, a combined operations approach not simply a joint amphibious or single Service one.

While at Ascension we had asked for Spanish-speaking interpreters and some had arrived, only to be sent back as we feared for their relations still in South America. However, a Sub-Lieutenant Stollery in *Fearless* had passed his 'O' Level Spanish and we sat him down to listen to the Argentine aircraft frequencies. He learned 'air speak' very quickly and was most helpful, but it was interesting to watch the face of a young radar plot rating when, over the speaker, came the Sub-Lieutenant's voice with the news that the leader of the next strike had designated *Fearless* as his flight's destination. We waited and waited and waited for the bang and then happily gave up when it was obvious that they had turned back or found another target.

The anticipation slowly started to wear us down and we found it very difficult to concentrate on planning while the air attacks were about. Luckily, our 'Greenwich time' routine meant we had already done most of the planning by the time the attacks were expected. The realization that fear and even perhaps terror were not far away made us take all the more care in our decision-making and instructions. It would take a few more days to be properly battle-hardened, but even then we would still feel drained by the suspense. We felt more akin to submariners under a daily depth charge attack and I, for one, longed to be on the bridge and not confined to the offices below decks.

That night of 24/25 May I sent *Sir Percivale* and *Norland* out of the AOA. They were now empty apart from *Antelope*'s survivors in the North Sea ferry and while they sailed to comparative safety, we inserted the recce team from 3 Para into Great Island (delayed by *Antelope*'s loss). HMS *Yarmouth*'s insertion of an SBS team into Port Salvador to recce Teal Inlet and the eastern end of the waters was aborted when the ship's boats became unserviceable.

Norland now joined *Canberra* at sea and, as I no longer required them, they were both 'chopped' to Sandy's Opcon. He ordered them to South Georgia on the 25th to collect 5 Infantry Brigade from the *QE2* (not allowed into the war zone because of the emotion her name would cause if sunk) and to transfer home-going survivors.

With the morrow heralding Argentina's 'Navy Day', it seemed unlikely that they would forget to mark the occasion and any celebration had to include us! Sandy was determined not to be caught napping, nor, which might have been more likely, caught napping by an enemy-enforced naval battle while his hands were tied behind his back looking after so many RFAs and civilian ships so, while reviewing his procedures, he instigated *Operation Red Button*, designed to push all non-fighting ships well to the east in an instant allowing him to fight a sea battle unhindered.

Sandy had listened to my description of the dilemma over stores ships in San Carlos and advised that I empty the AOA of even more stores ships despite the inconvenience to the military ashore. I did not consider it appropriate to employ the argument that, while the Argentinian aircrew continued to attack the first target they saw, providing more targets might reduce the overall risk as it was vital to maintain the morale of the Merchant and RFA crews. However, we were not yet in a position to be too arbitrary as the variety of stores needed was still considerable, sometimes essential and spread between several ships. I did not in the end therefore sail as many as he wanted, although probably more than Julian found acceptable. As a result the Admiral sent a signal on these lines:

> Regret that from here the continued exposure of up to nine non-combatant ships of various kinds in Carlos Water while they are unloaded slowly in parallel, rather than the one or two that could be emptied in 24 hours flat and returned to safety appears to be nautical nonsense.
>
> I accept that it may, however, be military sense, despite the considerable risk to both ships and your assets in them, but require your confirmation by dusk tonight so that any strictly unnecessary ships can be sailed.

I sailed *Fort Austin* during the night of the 25/26th with her ASW helicopters. This was to leave me with just two elderly Type 12 frigates for anti-submarine work. It was a risk which I discussed, and agreed, with Sandy. We could have landed the helicopters, although that would have meant disembarking all their torpedoes and stores, but as we had deduced by then that the submarine threat had passed we could do without them and the administrative burden, but the absence of the ship with her copious quantities of a wide range of stores was a definite plus to the AAF. I also delayed the arrival of *Elk*. I was sorry to see Commodore Sam Dunlop leave as his presence in San Carlos had been a source of quiet strength to me, but his crew had watched bombs skipping over them causing slight damage, so the decision was easy. With her departure and that of *Stromness*, *Resource*, *Tidepool* and *Sir Bedivere* I was able to reduce the number of daytime targets offered to the Argentine Air Force but at least we could now off-load those within San Carlos Water more quickly.

While Sandy's signal was undoubtedly seen on board as more yardarm clearing, for he and I had already discussed the problem, he was undoubtedly trying to support and stiffen me. I was not sure I needed it, but nevertheless from his point of view I was in the thick of it and probably not able to think too clearly. While I was quite certain we were coping, I could understand his feeling of being 'left out of things' and wanting to influence the decision-making. Also he had to be much more concerned with a longer view of the war, in contrast to my immediate short-term position, and was worrying about how the Royal Navy could survive. He had time on his hands to think and he was my senior. For those who understand the Navy, or know Sandy, although he was not my boss, it was unlikely he would keep quiet!

As a direct result of the previous day's air attacks I changed the RFA ships' anchorage positions in the AOA; by coincidence no STUFT were with me at this time. Ships were now anchored tucked as close as possible under the eastern shore with *Intrepid* still at the northern end and *Fearless* as far south as we could sensibly put her. I now stationed *Yarmouth* even further south than my Flagship to meet, head-on, any aircraft from that direction. I kept the two frigates *Plymouth* and *Arrow* in what was becoming their 'usual position' just to the east of Chancho Point and south of Fannings Island; from where the main attacks seemed to be coming. Without permission to be further west Bill (*Broadsword*) and David (*Coventry*) had decided their 'combo' position should now be some ten miles north of Government Island.

On the morning of D+4 the raids started half-heartedly with four (possibly more) Skyhawks entering Falkland Sound from the west. They attacked no shipping but *Coventry* shot one down as it headed home.

The first raid actually into San Carlos appeared just before midday (local) and to begin with it seemed as though our plan was working with *Yarmouth* taking out one of this wave of four Skyhawks attacking from the south. The pilot ejected close overhead *Fearless* to be picked up, with a damaged knee, by an LCU under the command of Colour Sergeant Johnston (who had already distinguished himself alongside *Antelope* and who was to be killed in Choiseul Sound later). One more Skyhawk from this same wave was also 'splashed' by a 'combo' Sea Dart. Two other raids were aborted, but there were yet more raids on their way. One appears to have been warned by either the Pebble Island garrison or returning aircraft, of the existence of two British warships to the north-west of Falkland Sound and the aircraft altered course for the 'combo'. *Coventry* was sunk and *Broadsword* damaged, including the loss of her Lynx. This was only the second occasion that the Argentine bombs seemed to have been fused correctly for low level delivery. The second raid was the first against the Carrier Battle Group since 4 May. Sandy's ships were some eighty miles north east of Cape Pembroke with, among others in company, the *Atlantic Conveyor*. All CAP aircraft airborne were in defence of my amphibious group with no aircraft airborne in support of the Carrier Battle Group.

As the information being received was proving reasonably accurate and timely we felt that there should have been enough warning to launch CAP for head-on engagements before the enemy reached the AOA, but this was not happening due to lack of aircraft and distance from the carriers; nor, though, was it invariably infallible. Dingemans was moved to comment direct to me and Sandy that while we have no knowledge of aircraft availability it is for consideration that on receipt of early warning information we increase the numbers on CAP as a matter of course to meet them on their arrival. The information was correct both times today.

In fact this was Peter's second signal for it succeeded one reminding me that we had additional warning of the attacks through the interception of the radars on the Argentinian C-130 while these aircraft were believed to be refuelling the bombers. He suggested a CAP-Trap for the Hercules without which the fighter/bombers could not complete their missions.

For that night (25/26 May) I had earlier approved an observed shoot onto Argentine positions in the Fox Bay vicinity. HMS *Plymouth* conducted this with a party from 148 Battery, Royal Artillery, and although the party themselves suffered severe tribulations due to the weather, the kelp and, on their with-drawal, a propeller lost off the Sea Rider insertion craft, they made it back to their mother ship thanks to David Pentreath's determination to stay longer than he should have. When the wind turned offshore the observation team rigged a jury sail on their paddles and managed to pass their position and progress to *Plymouth* by taking bearings on the flashes from the frigate's guns: no harm done in the end and the frigate was back with its full 'complement' by dawn. The damage to the enemy however was significant with the action described by a Royal Artillery Officer as a 'classic 148, RN, SBS-(style) raid'. They were even overflown by the nightly C-130 heading for Stanley but had not the weapons to do anything about it except report its presence.

During that same night I ordered Jeremy Larken to carry out the SBS insertion into Salvador Waters that *Yarmouth* had failed to achieve and, having more luck, we were back, successfully, in San Carlos before dawn.

Ashore at San Carlos D+4 had proceeded with a re-arrange-ment of the Brigade's plans. Having scrapped any southern flank/Darwin notions Julian sat during the evening with his closest advisers in his Headquarters dug into the diddle-dee and gorse on the isthmus that joins Little Rincon with the mainland. Determined to get out and on once the extra helicopters arrived from the *Atlantic Conveyor* he was now ready for them; crews could be found and I had agreed to call her in on the 26th, but had not yet done so. Until then, as far as we were concerned, she and her vital cargo were safe under the Carrier Battle Group's umbrella. Julian would use the extra helicopters for the initial move forwards after which they would revert to 'force assets' mainly for the support and deployment of the new Brigade.

I had asked Sandy to launch the longer-ranged Chinooks from as far as possible in order to save time but he had refused, for reasons unknown to me. Then, at about 1800, news reached us that in addition to the loss of *Coventry* earlier in the day *Atlantic*

Conveyor had been hit by two Exocet and was on fire and abandoned. This was a devastating blow because we then heard the helicopters, four Chinook of 18 Squadron (RAF) and six Wessex 5 of 845 Naval Air Squadron, were mostly still embarked, only one Chinook escaping. Later I asked for the aircrew to be sent to me but again this was not approved.

The Brigadier needed time to consider the implications of this blow and as the team broke up one member declared that the Brigade would now have to 'bloody well walk to Stanley'. Julian ordered a full conference for the following day – the 26th.

In fact the Brigade was not aiming to walk to Stanley but to prepare the way forward for swift action to take place soon after the arrival of the second brigade. All thoughts of diversionary raids with no support were now totally dismissed, with whatever movement assets remaining being employed, in toto, along the northern flank. Success at Goose Green and Darwin might have helped to 'gain moral ascendency over the enemy' but as the dual settlements were off the line of march and with no sensible transport to get to them, they could be dealt with, in due course, by other less expensive and time- and energy-consuming methods. Indeed, with troops forward along the north and 'investing' the hills around Stanley, (as ordered by CTF himself) the enemy's Lafonia garrisons could be cut off and left to wither, or be dealt with as a subsidiary attack by the reserves due in shortly.

But Goose Green had not been forgotten in London nor by those senior officers who had declared on D Day, with uneducated haste, that 'Now we have landed we will move, and move swiftly'. From the news broadcast and Northwood reports it seemed that the country, too, appeared to be clamouring for action on land to appease the losses at sea. Just a few more naval losses without a positive land victory might seriously alter public – indeed World – opinion: everyone wanted action on shore. I have to say that public opinion was of little concern to me. With all the other communications on board we had considerable difficulty listening to the BBC World Service broadcasts. I and, I believe, Sandy and Julian were content to fight on and the quicker we did so the better our chances of success.

In support of Julian for the offload I still had the original fifteen assorted Sea Kings and Wessex that I had had on D Day. The one Chinook which had been airborne when *Atlantic Conveyor* had been hit was not yet available to me. Out of this total I had to give one Sea King to the Rapier battery; four more Sea Kings were not available during daylight hours as they were fitted with passive night goggle equipment (their crews and fitters needed rest after strenuous night sorties inserting NGSFOs and Special Forces patrols) and aircraft were on call for casualty evacuation. After these deductions we had ten aircraft which were barely enough to lift the guns and ammunition forward let alone take on any other task.

The only ship in my group to have a hangar was the *Elk* and it would have been stupid to keep her in San Carlos simply to provide all-weather shelter for helicopter maintenance. Without a ship like an LPH there was no second-line maintenance facility either at sea in San Carlos or ashore and all maintenance had to be completed in the open air in the dawn and dusk periods both to avoid using torches and to ensure that valuable daylight flying hours were not wasted. Added to this maintenance problem it was already clear that there were insufficient tasking cells spread throughout the brigade to ensure full use was made of the helicopters at all times. There was nothing we could do about either problem but Mike Cudmore, my Staff Air Engineer, worked flat out to ensure the maintainers had the correct spares as soon as possible.

As an example, it is not often appreciated how 'expensive' the Royal Artillery's guns can be in terms of helicopter hours. I asked Julian to tabulate a typical lift to illustrate the problem: 'To lift a battery of six 105 mm Light Guns with 480 rounds per gun and two half-ton vehicles (for battery charging) plus 'the gunners' requires eighty-two Sea King sorties. Just to lift 480 rounds forwards takes sixty Sea King sorties, 120 Wessex sorties or a 'mere' twenty Chinook sorties.'

If one then takes the flying distance from San Carlos to Mount

Kent (where Julian wanted the guns) as a fifty-mile, one-way trip (flown tactically) and allow for fuelling from one-spot ships in San Carlos it would take all available Sea Kings two days and would permit no other helicopter tasking whatsoever. We believed that this, despite our efforts, was never fully accepted by Northwood or Sandy; in the same sense that the terrible 'going' under foot for the infantry was not appreciated either. Few believed us when we said, as often as we had to, that the average speed of men (fit men carrying heavy loads) across this country was about one mile per hour.

Those aspects of Julian's original plan that had been completed before the Chinooks were lost included the insertion (during the night of the 24th) of an SAS recce party on to Mount Kent to prepare for 42 Commando's arrival and the SBS into Salvador Waters to carry out a recce there prior to the move of Brigade Headquarters to Teal Inlet. Those aspects that had not been completed (nor even started) included the move of 42 Commando and the guns by helicopter.

While tasking his staff to study the possibility of moving the logistic support along the north coast by helicopter at the same time that his men marched, Julian received a message in the cowshed that he was required to take a call from Northwood on the Ajax Bay satellite terminal. A Rigid Raiding Craft sped him across the loch.

CTF's personal orders to Julian were unambiguous and unequivocal; he was to re-activate the Goose Green raid and move out of San Carlos, a move that had never been part of our original orders from Jeremy but one for which we had planned nevertheless. In his words, 'More action was required all round.' Julian returned to the settlement cowshed, not surprisingly hurt and angry, and summoned his Commanding Officers. Jones was to keep to his original plan while one company of 40 Commando would replace 2 Para on Sussex Mountain. 45 Commando were to move across from Ajax Bay before dawn on the 27th and then 'yomp' to Douglas Settlement carrying all their support weapons, food and ammunition. 3 Para would 'tab' to Teal Inlet. I was asked to ensure that helicopters and a naval gunfire support frigate was available for 2 Para while Sandy was tasked to have GR3s on call for ground support. 42 Commando would remain in reserve but be ready to fly to Mount Kent once the other units were in place, helicopters released and the landing zone secure.

That morning I had been summoned to the DSSS to speak with David Halifax, CTF's Chief of Staff. He explained that a number of people were jumping up and down in Northwood thinking that we are being far too slow. I tried to explain the situation to him by saying, 'It is a bit like Scapa Flow. We haven't a great deal of air cover from the hills on either side; it is an open loch with peat bogs and we are dumping the poor old marines here, with their gear, as fast as we possibly can – day and night. We simply can go no faster. We allow at least a week during a Norwegian exercise for just two commandos with Ro-Ro terminals etc and a host nation to help. Here we have no more assets, real air attacks, and a brigade equivalent to at least five commandos, plus all the other bits and pieces and the full war maintenance reserve. I simply do not understand how you think I can do it any quicker. I have always said that I may need eight days or so and that depends on the enemy's air force and the weather.' He went on to ask why I thought the Argentinian air attacks had lessened and I could only suggest the possibility of poor weather and crosswinds at their bases. He seemed to agree.

With that David Halifax sounded happier for he had something to report back. He asked me if I would like him to phone Sarah and tell her I was OK. I was delighted with the first sign during this campaign that anyone in Northwood cared for my morale and thanked him.

If I had been given any inkling of what CTF was planning to say to Julian, I would have pointed out my duty as Commander Amphibious Task Force and being in overall charge of this part of the operation. I might also have added that we were specifically never told to do more than establish a foothold and that we had done with remarkable success. Any criticism of Julian in particular was unfair. Together we had done precisely what had been asked of us originally and even now were trying to dovetail two new and conflicting sets of instructions. On balance

I thought that we were doing 'quite well'. I had so far not lost one item of the Brigade's kit to the enemy action, even it if was not being landed as smoothly as the logisticians would have liked, and I had achieved this under fairly constant threat of air attack in less time than I had said.

On D+1 we had been asked to send a 'future intentions' signal which, in accordance with Jeremy Moore's last instruction, had us exploiting forward while still ensuring the security of the AOA which was vital to the land operation. Now Julian felt he was doing just that and even perhaps exceeding this remit by planning to send three commandos/battalions along the north with one remaining in reserve and one remaining to defend our backs from the west. Originally he intended to recce and carry out aggressive patrolling but he certainly had not intended to move all but one of his major units out of San Carlos until the arrival of 5 Infantry Brigade. However, this was not now how CTF saw the future as indicated by a signal on the 24th giving the Northwood assessment of the situation. Nor did the résumé of the enemy's ability accord with our empirical perceptions.

Northwood, it seems, believed that the enemy did not possess the will or the means to engage in serious ground operations, believing that all that was required was swift and strong action from us to bring about his defeat. Northwood assessed that the enemy's airpower against men on the ground did not amount to a significant threat provided (and this was interesting) Blowpipe was deployed and that helicopter activity was restricted as much as possible to night time. But, for fast jets to be effective against men on the ground they need direction – particularly when in a single-seat fighter – and this they did not have. Northwood had an unrealistic opinion of Blowpipe as well; 'they' did not understand the problems of night helicopter movements without PNGs of which we only possessed five sets; we had not accounted for as many of their available Pucara (a real danger to infantry in daylight) as Julian and I would have wished and we were sure that we had not yet accounted for enough of their shore-based Skyhawks to have seriously reduced that threat.

I personally believed that the idea that 'they' did not possess the will or the means to engage us on the ground was an arguably rash opinion. We had not yet come across their ground forces in any strength and had no idea whether they had, or had not, the means to advance. We were trying to destroy their helicopters but that was all. Our land forces were still outnumbered by men presumably well dug in and our forces would be off balance as they moved forward. All this helped me to believe that, now that the initial landings were over and consolidation was going well, the threat to the landing force was greater, but it was not insuperable.

If their aircrew were any guide to the rest of their armed forces there was certainly determination but there was an equally clear will among some of the pilots to survive and that helped Julian and me to deduce that, being mostly conscripts, they would be a patchy enemy, man for man, on the ground. It is of course possible that Northwood was receiving intelligence to which we were not privy and we had to take that into account when listening to advice or reading signals but fundamentally these problems arose through the surprising (to me) lack of communication and wish for a full understanding of each other's problems. Modern warfare and the Falklands War in particular can, and did, move very fast. Agreed principles, concepts of operation and procedures based on a thorough understanding of the needs of both the higher and lower command levels are more essential than ever before.

The verbal orders on the 26th forced Julian's and my hand. When I heard that he had received this 'kick in the arse' I decided to tell him that if it would help, I would now be happy to end the amphibious phase which was nearing completion rather sooner than I had hoped. Jeremy Moore was due to arrive with Sandy the next day and it might be helpful if I could be there with them both and brief Jeremy on his way into San Carlos.

I rushed ashore to tell him of my thoughts and found him ashen-faced and very bitter. I don't think he wanted to see any naval officer ever again! Nevertheless he agreed with my plan and I told him that I would go back to *Fearless* and send the signal which would give him operational control and not just the lower level tactical control of the helicopters and that my two Staff Aviation Officers would transfer to his command. I would leave Peter Dingemans in *Intrepid* in charge of the anchorage with instructions to continue the off-load using the landing craft as best he could. I also told him I would give him HMS *Arrow*, a Type 21 frigate, to provide naval gunfire support to 2 Para.

In summary: the beachhead had been secured; Julian had a good single secure line of satellite communication back to Northwood but none to Sandy. This system had been placed, with my agreement, at Ajax Bay near the Logistic Regiment Headquarters and the Field Ambulance. We felt that this would be a sensible place where it could wait until Jeremy Moore arrived as it could more easily be protected and that that was probably where Jeremy would wish to establish his headquarters if he could not do so in *Fearless*. It was certainly too heavy for Julian to carry forward, bearing in mind the shortage of helicopters.

As far as the amphibious phase was concerned, there was an estimated one more day of off-loading of his immediate requirements left so I think it is reasonable to say that the conditions laid down for this change of operational control which were discussed in Chapter Four were fairly met.

The most important thing now was for me to bring a fully-briefed Jeremy to San Carlos as quickly as possible and by doing that he would have time to think before landing and would not be met with the problem only on arrival at the beach.

Sandy, too, was making his appraisal, but he had a less complicated problem. He was firm that, as the Royal Navy had taken the battle to the enemy and suffered the consequences, it was now quite definitely the turn of the ground forces to go 'high risk'. This attitude may have formed the basis for a number of discussions he had with Northwood and were possibly the cause of the contradictory signals now being received by the amphibious forces. Sadly, he failed to understand what the landing force was up to and complained that: 'His' ships (they were actually mine!) had landed 5,000 tons of stores for about 5,000 men (equalling, he points out curiously, one ton per man); were they, he wondered, still waiting for their 'nutty'. His naval assessment signal that evening made the following points:

1. Transactions since last audit have been less than satisfactory. There are now several outstanding accounts to settle. The *Coventry* and the AOA experience has revealed some uncomfortable facts about our modern weapon systems. The *Atlantic Conveyor* experience has given us little comfort on the chaff front but not much else except a further feel for the Etendard's radius of action which still stands at approx 440 miles.

2. Main lessons learnt:
a. When in open seas stay outside 440 miles from Arg airbases in daylight/good flying weather.
b. Stay under Rapier cover if a. not achievable.
c. Etendard probably attacks first contact he sees and turns 180° immediately after release. Wouldn't you! SAM engagements in centre of main body thereafter unlikely to be valid except on 'blue' air or surface.

3. Future intentions. No change except to increase pressure on Port Stanley by land, sea and air.

Sandy clearly continued to retain a high opinion of Rapier, despite my evening briefings, and, with no strong evidence to the contrary, I believe that my assessment was the truer one. In contrast, he did not seem to hold any good opinion of the efforts of the Commando Brigade for his complaints continued: 'They've [the Commando Brigade] been here for five days and done fuck all.'

There were, too, differences of naval opinion over what the best action a destroyer or frigate should take when under air attack. Some captains believed that the best manoeuvre was to offer an end-on view to the incoming target as that was the smallest; others believed (and the Carrier Battle Group staff were among them) that presenting a broadside view to the enemy was better as the full range of weapons could be brought to bear. 'The broadside lobby' felt that if a bomb dropped on the beam and fell short it could skip over the hull but if dropped from ahead of the ship and skipped it might drop down on to the stern. Other considerations needed to be taken into account; a bows-on attack against a ship steaming fast made it less likely that the skipping bomb would fall quickly enough to hit the ship; many beam attacks were deflected by the mass of small arms that could be trained at the aircraft and many pilots, being inexperienced, hit the stern or missed astern. *Coventry*, though, was hit fair and square, broadside on with all three bombs detonating and with a mass of tracer in the sky. Theories, as so often, were less reliable than empirical observations.

My stock-taking sent to CTF in Northwood and copied to the other CTGs in the South Atlantic for the 26th was rather more calm, positive and detailed than Sandy's; I did not wish to dwell on the past for we were engaged in a war and had to move forward with clear plans, even if I did not agree with those plans now emanating from Northwood. They were, I felt, plans which conflicted with those from Julian's own 'immediate' commander, who I was about to support.

1. 3 Brigade is now very nearly self-sufficiently established in AOA and poised to embark phase IV. Anchorage very nearly clear (except crippled *Lancelot*, *Galahad* and *Argonaut*. Estimated duration 2–3 days).

2. Intend begin transition to phases IV and V by sailing *Fearless* pm 27th May to proceed east to RV with CLFFI (Moore) while appointing *Intrepid* SOPA AOA (Senior Officer Present Afloat in the AOA).

3. With effect from 272200Z:

a. *Fearless* will be ordered sail San Carlos to proceed to intercept *Antrim* with CLFFI and staff embarked.

... and so on detailing the fine print of the arrangements.

I sent a second signal tidying up one or two other factors and gave orders for ship movements in and out of the AOA during my absence on board *Fearless*: these included the extraction of 3 Para's four-man patrol on Great Island which had been keeping an eye for shipping as well as on the entrance to Fox Bay. They had had nothing to report, but at least this had given me confidence, and were needed back with their battalion.

The 26th had been a quiet day as far as air strikes were concerned due in large part, I suspected, to cross-winds at the departure airfields and to the low cloud over us; we, though warned of air activity in the vicinity of the AOA, still managed a full day of uninterrupted offloading, by the end of which *Europic Ferry* was empty, as was *Sir Geraint*.

We appreciated that having both Fleet Clearance Diving Teams in *Intrepid* was silly. FCDT3 went ashore to join the growing army of miscellaneous people at Ajax Bay. They were just in time to be settled in for the air raid on the following day. It was a fortunate move as they were to be of considerable help to the overcrowded medical teams later in the campaign.

By the 27th, therefore, my part in the delivery of 3 Commando Brigade to the beachhead and the establishment of a secure AOA was, in large measure over though *Operation Corporate* was to remain a joint maritime operation to the end.

The Transport Area (TA), which is what the AOA becomes when the amphibious phase is over, could do without myself and my Flagship for a few days, providing I briefed Peter Dingemans exactly what the Brigade needed for the move of 45 Commando and 3 Para along the north and 2 Para towards Darwin. What had been originally termed a 'raid' (an expression not familiar to the Parachute Regiment) designed to destroy, harass and demoralize was now to be a full-scale attack with the aim of staying in the captured territory.

During the night of the 26th/27th I sent HMS *Arrow* in to the Sound to cover the Para's advance southwards and ordered *Intrepid* to Salvador Waters to insert another SBS team while the unloading of *Sir Lancelot* in San Carlos was to continue the moment that her bomb was removed. My last act was to tell *Intrepid* that on our return she would be sent to sea for a well earned but brief rest and to wish her luck while I was away.

By 2200 on the 27th I was happy that all was in hand with 3 Commando Brigade, the defence of the TA and the offload and felt I was at last able to tell Jeremy Larken to 'drive like stink for

Antrim and Jeremy Moore'. I had my first full night's sleep for about three weeks and woke feeling very much better. I also hoped that those of my staff who had come with me were also able to recoup a little. I had time to discuss with Jeremy Larken and the staff how the previous week had gone and felt that there was little we could, or would need to, change after the forthcoming watershed. We had initially climbed a rickety ladder of learning but were now in a firmer position to offer a hand-up to the incoming team and while we had lost a pair of frigates we had not lost a landing ship. *Ardent* and *Antelope* had done what they were there to do: get between the enemy and the amphibious ships while the landing force consolidated and re-grouped ashore. Both had taken their share of enemy aircraft and both Commanding Officers and ships' companies had acquitted themselves well. We knew, too, that the next offloading would probably be longer because merchant ships only were being used, and although against a diminished air force, nevertheless against one that had, too, gained invaluable experience, so I commissioned a brief résumé of the AAF's current position under the heading:

'Argentine Air Tactics Against TG 317.0.

'Fixed Wing Ops.

'Argentine aircraft are attacking TG 317.0 flying Hi-Lo-Hi profiles ... in waves of 2 to 3 aircraft each wave, up to three waves per attack ... The Argentines do not appear to press home their attacks ... once engaged by air defence systems ... The weapons carried are up to 2 x 1,000lb bombs each aircraft and have been delivered in the skip bombing mode so far ... Undoubtedly the weapons being used and the delivery mode do not give enough time, on the majority of occasions, for the bombs to fuse correctly ... The Argentines now appear to be aware of this fault and will almost certainly attempt to rectify it by either increasing the arming time or altering weapon delivery profile ... With the use of retard devices they would be able to carry out shallow angle dive attacks or visual straight and level attacks at about 150 feet, releasing the weapons at about 0.75 miles from the target. Using the shallow angle dive attack method would involve a low and fast approach with a final pull-up to approx 1200 feet before diving onto the target. This manoeuvre would cause tracking problems for air defence systems up until the final dive stage when the aircraft would have to track the target for a limited period of time.

'An alternative method which (they) may consider is medium toss ...

'Helicopter Ops

'The majority of helo ops on the Islands are being used to resupply/equip troops ... The A109 would be used as local air defence for these ops or for attack on isolated targets on the ground, both hardened and soft ...

'Blockade Running

'The air blockade on the Falkland Islands is continually being broken by transport traffic. This is being done either at night or by the use of diversionary tactics. The C-130 blockade runner has on at least two occasions been observed with Mirage III as escorts or as a diversionary measure. There is a marked increase in the number of blockade runners being successful in their mission.

'Assessment

'Fixed Wing Ops. The tactics and weapons used by the Argentines must be reconsidered by them now. Targets can therefore expect a change of tactics in the near future ... The remaining Exocet missiles must be targeted against the carriers to deprive us of mobile air defence platforms ... The tactics which may be employed would be a large diversionary attack against TG 317.0 and the beachhead to engage the CAP and certain air defence ships while the ... Exocet would engage the carrier group.

'Helo Ops. Helo Ops will continue as long as the Argentines have ... helos on the Falkland Islands. These helos must be taken out either by air or ground forces.

'Blockade Runners. With the increase of blockade runners being successful the Falkland Islands are being supplied with vital equipment and food. It must therefore be possible for troop re-inforcement as well. (Build up in Comodoro Rivadavia of the 4th Airborne Infantry Brigade and 3 × C-130.) It must therefore be of increasing importance to terminate these flights either by airfield denial or by destroying the aircraft whilst *en route*.'

The 28th was a 'normal' day of work for the amphibious group. Brian Dutton of FCDT1 removed *Argonaut*'s remaining bomb while FCDT3 investigated three unexploded bombs which had welcomed them at Ajax Bay the afternoon before. In this they were helped by an RAF EOD team. In the evening FCDT3 then returned to *Sir Lancelot* and with much cutting and rigging managed to remove the final bomb the following morning before any further air attacks. All ships were now clear of these torments.

Ashore 45 Commando and 3 Para yomped their way forwards along the north coast and 2 Para began their advance on Darwin. In South Georgia the *QE 2* arrived and began to cross-deck 5 Infantry Brigade to the *Canberra*. My staff's log for the day reads:

'Overnight *Yarmouth* bombarded Port Howard. Unsuccessful insertion of D Squadron patrols onto Mount Kent due to poor visibility. Offload continued with BMA well established ashore. *Elk* arrived and sailed overnight and after recce and planning some two hours offload (of ammunition) achieved. Survey *Argonaut, Sir Galahad* and *Sir Lancelot* complete. *Argonaut* restoration progress-ing, *Sir Galahad* work progressing well. *Sir Lancelot's* FCDT anticipate removal of UXB overnight. Much air activity during the day but not directed against shipping due to poor visibility.'

In the Transport Area in San Carlos Waters they were particularly thankful for the lack of air strikes as *Elk* contained 2,000 tons of ammunition and if she had 'gone up' she would probably have taken a number of ships in the anchorage with her. Later on, and after discussions with the master and SNO, we brought her in and kept her for it was not time-effective to bring her in for just two hours. The balance was losing her to air attacks or losing her at sea to badly stowed ammunition shifting across the cargo decks. She, of all ships had to be properly secured for sea and that took time.

This extract from the log also gives a hint of the enormous activity that was taking place in San Carlos quite apart from the off-load and the defence of the ships. Chris Meatyard's diving and John McGregor's engineering team were flat out dealing with the unexploded bombs and repairing damage. Equally busy was Commander Mike Cudmore, my Air Engineer Officer, who had joined us at Ascension. He was to achieve marvels in supporting the two helicopter squadrons and later the much enhanced helicopter force. *Fearless*'s ship's officers appeared almost everywhere, assisting in some often small, but nevertheless important, operation. There was a magnificent atmosphere of determination and enterprise, enlivened by men like Mike Rose who, disdaining to wear anti-flash gear, wore an extraordinary hat with earflaps and earned himself the name of Genghis Khan.

Regardless of the operational reasons for doing so, many of my staff were unhappy with the moral principle of *Fearless* and, my staff, leaving San Carlos Water and the Transport Area for the 'deepfield', and I agreed with them. We felt a sense of guilt but under the worsening communications I was certain it was the most sensible action for me to take if our command and control was not to become a major problem.

CHAPTER SIX

NEW BOYS

The Army go so slow, that seamen think they
never mean to get forward, but I dare say they act
on a surer principle, although we seldom fail.

> Nelson in the *Agamemnon*, off Bastia,
> February 28, 1794

WE FELL IN with HMS *Antrim* well to the east of the Exclusion
Zone and I was delighted to meet General Moore again and have
the chance to brief him on what I thought was actually
happening ashore. Naturally, he had many questions. We also
collected Brigadier Tony Wilson of 5 Brigade and a mix of
officers from the two staffs.

Fearless then turned for the carrier group where General
Moore and I went on board *Hermes* and met Sandy who again
stressed his role as supporting and explained to us both the need
for urgency as the ships had now been at sea a considerable time
and he could not guarantee their serviceability for very much
longer. Jeremy, inevitably, had little to contribute and we moved
on to discussing what I could or should do now that the
amphibious operation, *per se*, was over and my job complete in
that regard. I put forward the idea of becoming a Naval Chief of
Staff to Commander Land Forces Falkland Islands (Jeremy
Moore) but this was turned down as I would have no executive
powers. It was clear that there was a continuing need to have an

inshore Naval Task Group Commander and since the same assets that I had used for the amphibious landing would now be needed to land 5 Brigade, it was obvious that my role would continue much as before. In fact it widened in scope in that I took authority for all naval operations west of a line cutting across East Falkland and not simply within the old amphibious operation area.

We even discussed a title since Jeremy had claimed the title 'CLFFI' and Sandy was already 'FOF1' which, though meaning Flag Officer First Flotilla, could easily be Flag Officer Falkland Islands. I suggested Commodore Falkland Islands or COMFI which amused me since the knowledge that I was returning to San Carlos made me feel just the opposite. I was having to struggle to believe our luck would last.

We then had a rather entertaining little session in Sandy's sea cabin which was minute. There was only room for Sandy and Jeremy to sit together on his bunk and for the photographer to stand sufficiently far back to take a video. I opted out and stood in the heads behind the cameraman, the redoubtable Bernard Hesketh who had walked ashore in Normandy on D-Day, while the BBC attempted to make an interview along the lines of Wellington meeting Nelson, but it was all rather stilted.

To clarify matters I produced the following summary under the heading: The Role of COMAW in Future Operations in the Falkland Islands.

1. COMAW (and staff) will act as the principal Naval Adviser to CTG 317.1 [Jeremy Moore] and in particular will act on behalf of CTG 317.8 [Sandy] in coordinating the naval support of land operations.

2. Specific areas of responsibility are seen to be:
a. The seaward defence of the TA from air, surface, sub-surface and sneak attack.
b. The coordination of movements into/out of the TA, negotiating with CTG 317.8 on shipping movements and the requirements for escorts to convoys.

c. Planning and conducting further amphibious operations as required by CTG 317.1.

d. The coordination of surveillance and the naval support of operations by Special Forces on West Falkland and the offshore islands. Such operations initially to be limited to ensuring that the enemy is not able to build up sufficient forces in the area to pose a significant threat to the operations of the main land forces and the follow-on shipping.

e. Liaison with CTG 317.8 for the provision of naval forces for NGS, Special Forces operations, TA defence and logistic support/replacement of warships involved in these operations.

f. The coordination of mine counter-measures and continuous assessment of the sea mining threat as it relates to land force operations and re-supply.

g. The long-term support of naval aircraft and landing craft in support of the land force operation.

This command concept was to exist until I handed the job over to my relief (after the war) who then became the Naval Chief of Staff to Commander British Forces Falkland Islands – CBFFI. I was undoubtedly still an independent CTG but I had stressed the problem of communications and had therefore taken on a co-ordinating responsibility as the jam in the sandwich between Jeremy and Sandy. Clearly it could only work if I was kept informed but I was the only person with secure voice communications to Sandy and, since Jeremy had decided that he would probably remain on board *Fearless* and not go ashore early in the campaign, I hoped to strike up a liaison with him and his staff. I expected that he would discuss his problems direct with Sandy on *Fearless*'s DSSS when he was aboard. Northwood appeared only too happy with my proposals as long as the three of us got on with the job.

At the change-over of military commands I had taken stock of my relationship with Julian to see if there were any lessons to be learned before I 'started again' with Jeremy Moore. Relationships with Julian had, I felt, been good, despite a worrying time at the latter end of Ascension and parts of the passage south when we were both pre-occupied with our own requirements. Part of the difficulty had arisen because Julian had been able to discuss his problems with Jeremy as CTF Land Deputy but I had no one who seemed prepared to take on a similar role for me. It meant that we were not always certain that we were talking with or to someone with the same voice or that our ideas were getting to the right people in Northwood. I hoped now that this type of problem would have been removed.

During our return to San Carlos I briefed the General and we settled down to a routine similar to that I had had with Julian in that we shared our briefings and meals together. What was immediately apparent was that his Staff Officers, being largely one rank higher than the Brigade Staff, were also that much more experienced. Furthermore, they had had plenty of sleep and were very fresh and uncluttered with ideas. I and my still very tired staff were enormously encouraged.

Jeremy was deeply concerned at the treatment Julian had received as he knew him well and held him in high regard. With Jeremy present, Julian would now be able to get on with the actual fighting, leaving Jeremy to handle Northwood and the politicians. Both were to play their parts exceptionally well.

At about midnight on the 28th/29th I received a signal in HMS *Fearless* from Julian which made me feel I should have stayed behind. It was difficult to work out whether it was good or bad news:

'Darwin settlement secured and Goose Green settlement sur-rounded . . . Fierce fighting ensued after capture of Darwin. With fierce spirit and determination 2 Para advanced to Goose Green and cut off settlement before last light. One Scout helicopter shot down. One enemy Pucara splashed . . . 45 Commando secured Douglas Settlement and 3 Para secured Teal Inlet before last light . . . Casualties . . . total killed 15 including CO, Adjt and 2 i/c A Coy 2 Para, total wounded 34, one officer missing . . . Future intentions . . . capture Goose Green . . . reinforce D Sqn 22 SAS on Mount Kent with one Cdo (-).'

A second signal was received the next night a few hours before we were due into San Carlos. This cleared up any apprehension and was stunningly good news except for the casualties Julian had suffered:

'Day dominated by culmination of 2 Para's magnificent action at Darwin/Goose Green and surrender of 1200 Argentinians . . . Day began with announcement through intermediaries (Manager Goose Green and Manager Port San Carlos) that Argentinian commanders wished to discuss safe conduct of 112 civilians in recreation hall. Negotiations quickly led to surrender agreement arranged by 2 i/c 2 Para who accepted surrender at short ceremony from Argentinian Air Force and Land Commanders . . . Civilian population overjoyed at relief of settlement. Some had been locked in recreation hall for thirty days . . . 2 Para consolidated position and checked captured enemy weapons and equipment including 3 x 105 mm howitzers and 3 x AAA guns . . . 45 Cdo and 3 Para firm in Douglas and Teal Inlet settlements respectively. Patrol and ops from each during day in response to reports of enemy OP patrols in Mount Simon and Evelyn Hill feature area . . . Insertion of 42 Cdo (-) on Mount Kent at 2230Z aborted close to LS because of bad weather . . . Future intentions, re-attempt 42 Cdo (-) insertion Mount Kent . . . 3 Para to clear Malo Hill feature. Search and destroy enemy observation points, secure battery fire base to east of Mount Kent for future operations . . . 45 to secure base for Forward BMA and Bde HQ . . . Paucity of helicopter assets for sustained resupply of units well forward of beachhead where latter especially prone to attack by Pucara and armed Huey gives cause for concern . . . Multiple Rubic Cube pattern of ship movement for regular offload already causing shortages (of) logistic natures. Future intentions and planned operations constantly being bedevilled by logistic tail wagging teeth.'

My staff diary for the 29th was much as follows:

Fearless 0001 R/V with *Antrim* outside TEZ to collect CLFFI and HQ Staff plus Brigadier Wilson (Cmdr 5 Inf Bde) and staff. Proceed to within TEZ to R/V *Hermes* at 1730. COMAW,

31. Argentinian prisoners of war queuing up to embark for their passage home on about 17 June. This is the Public Jetty that was previously cleared of Argentinian 'cards' by *Sir Bedivere's* Chinese crew. *(Commander John McGregor, Royal Navy)*

32. The Argentinian patrol craft PC 82 *Islas Malvinas* which sensibly remained in Stanley harbour. Her sister ship was attacked and abandoned in Choiseul Sound. Here under the command of Lieutenant Ian McClaren, Royal Navy. *(Lieutenant Ian Craik, Royal Navy)*

33. The Argentinian vessel *Yehuin*, captured in Port Stanley, here under command of Lieutenant Ian Craik, Royal Navy, ferrying to ships in Port William after the surrender. This vessel was used to lay the minefield at the entrance of Port William that was reported by HMS *Spartan*. *(Commander John McGregor, Royal Navy)*

34. The joint RFA/Welsh Guards memorial service on board *Sir Tristram* in Port Pleasant on 23 June for those lost in *Sir Galahad* and *Sir Tristram*. *(Leading Photographer Toyer, Crown Copyright)*

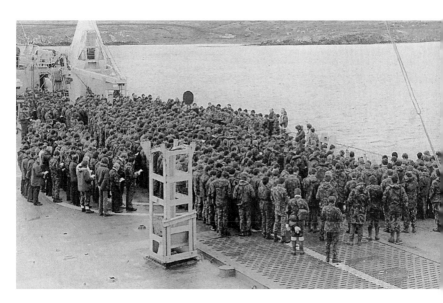

35. D-Day - 1. The co-author, Commodore Michael Clapp (right), Amphibious Task Group Commander, and Commander John Kelly, Executive Officer HMS *Fearless*, talking to men of 40 Commando on the night before the landing. *(Leading Photographer Toyer, Crown Copyright)*

36. Commander George Pearson, Staff Officer Amphibious Warfare SO(AW). *(Crown Copyright)*

37. Major David Minords, Royal Marines, GSO 1 (AW). *(Crown Copyright)*

38. Commander Mike Cudmore, Staff Air Engineer Officer (SAEO). *(Crown Copyright)*

39. Commander John McGregor, HMS *Fearless* and Staff Marine Engineer Officer (SMEO). *(Commander John McGregor)*

40. Lieutenant Commander Tim Yarker (left), Group Aviation Officer (GAVO), with Lieutenant Commander Bill Pollock, Senior Pilot 846 Squadron, who spent most of the war inserting and recovering Special Forces by night. Taken before the campaign in Norway when Yarker was commanding 846 Squadron. *(Crown Copyright)*

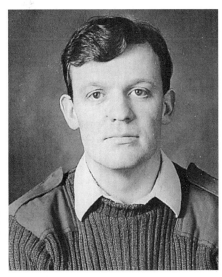

41. Lieutenant Commander Mike Goodman. Staff Warfare Officer SWO(D) with his wife after his investiture. *(Crown Copyright)*

42. Major Guy Yeoman, Royal Corps of Transport. GSO 2 (AW). *(Crown Copyright)*

43. Lieutenant Commander Chris Meatyard, Staff Mine-Countermeasures and Clearance Diving Officer (SMCDO), being welcomed home by his daughter Katie, aged 6. His wife, Christina, on the right and his mother, Edna, on the left. *(Mr RK Meatyard)*

44. Lieutenant Commander Tim Stanning, Staff Aviation Officer (SAVO) *(Crown Copyright)*

45. Major Tony Todd, Royal Corps of Transport. GSO 2 (Ops). *(Crown Copyright)*

46. Major Ewen Southby-Tailyour, Royal Marines, co-opted Landing Craft Commander and Falklands inshore expert, and co-author. *(Robin Adshead)*

47. Brigadier Julian Thompson, the Amphibious Landing Force Commander, (CTG 317.1 and later CTU 317.1.1)

48. Lieutenant Peter Crabtree, secretary SEC (AW).

49. Captain Bill Canning, Royal Navy, Commanding Officer HMS *Broadsword*, in overall charge of the Escorts.

50. Captain Jeremy Larken, Commanding Officer of HMS *Fearless*, in flack jacket, anti-flash and tin hat, congratulating Ordinary Seaman 'Ron' Moody, a 40mm Bofors aimer who, on 27 May, had shot at and shaken a Sky Hawk as it flew away. The aircraft was flown by Primer Teniente NM Velasco (who had led the strikes against HMSs *Argonaut* and *Coventry*) who was forced to bail out over West Falkland. *(Leading Photographer Toyer, Crown Copyright)*

51. Captain Brian Young, Royal Navy, Commanding Officer HMS *Antrim*, the Anti-Air Warfare Controller. *(Crown Copyright)*

52. Captain Kit Layman, Commanding Officer HMS *Argonaut*, the Anti-Submarine Warfare Controller. *(Crown Copyright)*

53. Captain Peter Dingemans (right), Commanding Officer of HMS *Intrepid*, and Commander Bryn Telfer, his Executive Officer, the strain of life in San Carlos Water showing on their faces. *(Crown Copyright)*

54. Captain David Pentreath (centre), Commanding Officer of HMS *Plymouth*, together with his First Lieutenant, Lieutenant Commander Iain Henderson, Lieutenant John Cook, Navigating Officer and Chief Communications Yeoman Tommy Doak on their return home. *(Crown Copyright)*

55. Commander Alan West, Commanding Officer of HMS *Ardent* (right), talking to Captain Mike Barrow, Commanding Officer of HMS *Glamorgan*, at a dinner on board HMS *Victory* to celebrate the triumph. Captain Barrow carried out the deception operations for the landings. *(Crown Copyright)*

56. Commander Tony Morton, Commanding Officer of HMS *Yarmouth*. *(Crown Copyright)*

57. Commander Nick Tobin, Commanding Officer of HMS *Antelope*. *(Hague Studios)*

58. Commodore Sam Dunlop, Master of RFA *Fort Austin*. *(Crown Copyright)*

59. Lieutenant Commander Simon Thornewill, Commanding Officer 846 Squadron, (Sea King Mk4s), standing in front of a crashed Pucara.

60. Lieutenant Commander Roger Warden, Commanding Officer 845 Squadron, (Wessex Mk5s), who had the unenviable task of commanding his Squadron from Ascension Island while most of his helicopters and personnel were spread throughout the South Atlantic. The Squadron grew to 26 aircraft.

61. Captain Barrie Dickinson, Master of RFA *Stromness*, celebrating the 'Southern Christmas' in traditional style with the youngest Royal Marine embarked. *(Crown Copyright)*

62. Captain Robin Green, Master of RFA *Sir Tristram*, and Captain Phil Roberts, Master of RFA *Sir Galahad*, at a television interview on their return. *(Crown Copyright)*

63. Captain Chris Purtcher-Wydenbruck, Master of RFA *Sir Lancelot*. *(Crown Copyright)*

64. Captain David Lawrence, Master of RFA *Sir Geraint*. *(Crown Copyright)*

65. *Sir Percivale's* Officers. Left to right: Keith Truscott, Alastair Bagg, Mike Hilton, Derek Harbord, Bob Campbell, Hohm Mursell, Peter Hill, Captain Tony Pitt (Master) and Alan Johnson. *(Captain Tony Pitt, RFA)*

66. The P&O team celebrating their safe return. From left to right: Captain Mike Bradford, Second Master of SS *Canberra*, Captain Dennis Scott-Masson, Master of SS *Canberra*, Lord Inchcape, Chairman of P&O, Captain J G Clark, Master of SS *Uganda*, (the Hospital ship and not part of the Amphibious Group) Captain D Ellerby, Master of MV *Norland*, and Captain J P Morton, Master of MV *Elk*. *(Crown Copyright)*

67. SS *Canberra's* Medical Team that gave her 'Hospital Ship Status' and who insisted on staying in the war zone. From left to right: Angela Devine, Nursing Sister, Jack Last, Dispenser, Dr. Peter Mayner, Surgeon, Rosie Elsdon, Senior Nursing Sister, and Assistant Surgeon Susie West. One can almost envy the wounded! *(Crown Copyright)*

68. Captain Chris J Clark, Master of MV *Europic Ferry*, owned by Townsend Thoresen. *(Crown Copyright)*

69. Captain Chris Burne, Senior Naval Officer SS *Canberra*. *(Crown Copyright)*

70. MV *Elk* at Ascension. From right to left: Constructor Commander Rod Puddock who supervised the dismantling of *Elk's* bulwarks, Captain John Morton, Master, Commander Andrew Ritchie, his Senior Naval Officer, and an Army Officer surveying their work. *(Crown Copyright)*

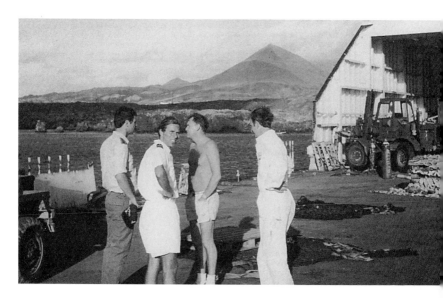

71. Chief Petty Officer Siddle was one of Commander McGregor's volunteers. With neither training nor experience in bomb disposal, he and his team spent two days cutting their way down to this 1,000 lb bomb in RFA *Sir Lancelot* over 28/29 May, while the threat of air attacks continued. When Lieutenant Bruen of FCDT 3 reached it he found it was fully armed and should have already exploded!.
(Commander John McGregor, Royal Navy)

MV *Norland's* Royal Naval Officers. From left to right: Lieutenant Commanders I Hughes and C Shorter, Commander Chris Esplin-Jones and Lieutenant Commander J Wingate.

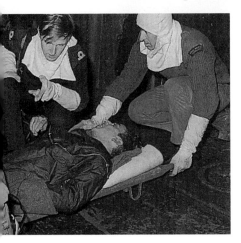

73. Sub-Lieutenant Stollery, left, the only Royal Naval Officer embarked with any knowledge of Spanish, attending Lieutenant Ricardo Lucero who hurt his knee when ejecting from his fatally damaged Skyhawk close to HMS *Fearless* on 25 May.
(Leading photographer Toyer)

74. On 2 June, 1982, at Ascension Island FCDT 1 relaxes.
    Back Row:-
      Ben Gunnell, Bill Bauckham, George Sharp, Lester Geofreys, Stan Bowles,
      Dave Barrett, FCPO Michael Fellows, Nigel Pullen, Billy Everden,
      Lieutenant Commander Brian Dutton (C.O.)
    Front Row:-
      Dave Southwell, Tony Groom, Nobby Noble, Ian Milne, Billy Smart,
      Wilky Wilkinson and Jan Sewell.

75. Major General Jeremy Moore, Commander Land Forces Falkland Islands (CTG
    317.1) and Rear Admiral Sandy Woodward, Commander Carrier Battle Group,
    (CTG 317.8) on board HMS *Hermes* on 29 May. *(Crown Copyright)*

MGRM and select staff crossed to *Hermes* to hold talks with CTG 317.8. On completion of meeting *Fearless* escorted by *Minerva* proceed to AOA. In AOA *Argonaut* UXB removed. AOA under sporadic air attack throughout the day. At 0400Z two unidentified aircraft dropped bombs that landed 10 miles east of San Carlos. Ashore day culminated in 2 Para action at Darwin/Goose Green and surrender 1200 Argentinians. Signal from COMAW noting that while there had been some bruising revelations by Press he was keen to continue Press lubrication and hence request Marisat ship R/V *Fearless* in TEZ to transfer copy.'

So we re-entered San Carlos Waters during the morning of 30 May to find that Julian had taken Goose Green, very obviously to the vast relief of the General who had, quite rightly, seen all the political aspects of the action due to his early involvement with Northwood and Mrs Thatcher. He knew what they wanted back at home and now they had it.

It was difficult for Jeremy for, despite my staff's and my briefings, he had to start thinking all over again – and along the lines of reality Falklands-style not Northwood-style. He also had to decide for himself what his role would really be. While Jeremy had been incommunicado Julian had received 'new' instructions from the Land Deputy in Northwood and until they (Jeremy and Julian) spoke together it was not clear to either whether these were compatible. Whatever Julian had started had to be continued and, if necessary, it was Jeremy who would have to alter his ideas. Luckily he had an open mind and the change-over was smooth.

Out at sea Sandy had also received reinforcements bringing him up to the highest total of ships he would have throughout the war. In San Carlos Water I had now to consider future operations which were no less demanding than the original landings and which, in some respects, were to be more difficult due to the continuing *ad hoc* nature of what was to come. To a point the original landings had been relatively easy because we had given them weeks of thought and planning.

I now had a Divisional Headquarters with two Brigades to

support and that Division only had logistic support for one brigade; we had only one extra Chinook and there were not enough helicopters for one brigade; we had no extra landing craft and the offload was incomplete; nobody had seen fit to send us the manifests of the ships that came south with 5 Brigade; but Jeremy's excellent Colonel Ian Baxter, his Colonel AQ, at least knew what they held if not where it was actually stowed, he having largely requested the equipment. Naval gunfire support would now be needed on the flank (although we did not yet know about the second flank); Special Forces operations would now be needed along both flanks; casualty evacuation would now be doubled and there now existed the possibility of twice the number of prisoners of war as both Brigades advanced along their individual axis. The Commando Brigade's move and the arrival of CLFFI did not mean the end of maritime operations, indeed it required the doubling of our efforts in respect of geography as well as support offered.

From now on I would be required to react to requests from the Divisional Headquarters and not those direct from either Brigade. I was also to act as the main point of contact between FOF 1 and CLFFI since I had 'secure voice' communication in both directions. I was still responsible for the maritime aspects (operational, logistic and routine) of any seaborne advance along the coasts of East Falkland or, if necessary, onto any part of West Falkland. I was also tasked with conducting harassing raids to the west and the deployment of Special Forces within my area which was west from a line running due south from Cape Dolphin.

Up to now Julian's and my theory had been that we could not afford to open up a second flank but with troops already part of the way along that route as a result of the attack on Darwin and Goose Green, Jeremy Moore probably had little choice but to continue. Now he had begun his move away from the beachhead and stores dumps Julian just wanted to get on and finish the job, but he knew that if 5 Infantry Brigade was to be used for Stanley he would have a wait on his hands while he shared the already meagre movement and support assets.

The AOA had officially been disbanded on the 27th on

completion of the amphibious phase. We now resurrected it officially as the Transport Area (TA) at midnight on the 31 May/1 June. San Carlos was also now the Force Maintenance Area (FMA) for all supporting operations up to the fall of Stanley, with the unloading of 5 Infantry Brigade (and the residue of 3 Commando Brigade's supplies) occurring as space in the anchorage (and ashore) became available. The risk of air strikes simply had to be accepted and so I was to keep the ships in San Carlos for longer periods than was acceptable to CTF (and Sandy) but often for shorter periods than the military would have preferred. There were to be, for instance, days when tankers remained at anchor in San Carlos and other ships carrying highly combustible material or explosives had to be put at risk as scares and air raids continued day and night. If those risks had not been taken we would probably have still been there weeks later – if we had survived.

Initially both Brigades would draw supplies from San Carlos, but this was to change. If he was to advance along the south Tony Wilson would want, quite naturally, to have his own stores depot along this axis. As a result we were to create two Forward Brigade Maintenance Areas (FBMAs); one at Teal Inlet for Julian Thompson's 3 Commando Brigade beginning on 2 June and another for Tony Wilson's 5 Infantry Brigade at Fitzroy on 7 June. The FBMAs would be supplied by ships loaded to each Brigade's wishes (including aviation fuel for helicopter parks), a major plus for their logisticians.

The first meeting of the new teams took place during 30 May in the San Carlos Settlement cowshed. This gathering was to become the subject of a rather awkward painting which hangs in the Royal Marines' Commando Forces Officers' Mess. I am shown wearing sea boots (which I never wore) and looking out to sea (my responsibilities were rather more towards the shore).

Jeremy Moore, thankfully, was pleased with the efforts made so far and, equally thankfully, did not intend to alter our concept of operations as far as the northern flank was concerned. Indeed he had little to offer us other than confirmation of the status quo. 2 Para would go firm at Goose Green and revert to 5 Infantry

Brigade's command, whence they had come. I had already given control of the SBS to 3rd Commando Brigade; with Jeremy's agreement I took back operational control of the helicopters from Julian and gave tactical control of some to the General to pass on to his brigades as he felt necessary; the landing craft would remain under my operational control while I would transfer tactical control to the Division and the Brigades when and as required. To this end I earmarked a small team of aviators to join the Divisional staff. I remained responsible for the administrative and logistic support of the helicopters and landing craft as I had Mike Cudmore and longer term maintenance facilities at sea.

Our daily briefings would continue much in the same vein as before Julian moved ashore, except that the morning ones would be more navy orientated as we had been up all night and could report on ships' movements and offloads as well as NGS and Special Forces deployments, whereas the evening briefs would be more military in content as a result of the day's activities and would indicate the military requirements for the next day or so. That is not to say that there were no naval operations by day nor military ones by night.

By 30 May the Mount Kent Dropping Zone (DZ) was secured sufficiently for 42 Commando to fly in. During the previous night I had asked Sandy (because the gunline was outside my area of control) for *Avenger*, *Alacrity* and *Glamorgan* to bombard Mount Kent; they also gave Volunteer Bay some attention as a further diversion. During the day various close air-support missions were flown and, while successful in their actions, the delayed arrival of the aircraft was the cause of some irritation to Julian. The Harriers took thirty-five minutes instead of the twenty that Julian had been promised. He asked that the Carrier Battle Group be brought closer and that the unsatisfactory state of the communications be sorted out, but neither improvements occurred.

The Commando Brigade tasked ten sorties during the 30th. At Stanley airfield there was an unsuccessful attempt to use the laser-guided bomb but elsewhere more success attended strikes against Argentine positions on Mount Kent and Mount Challenger, Long Island Mountain, Mount Round and Mount Low. The 30th was also the day on which it was first indicated to me that 5 Infantry Brigade would definitely be used for the attacks against Stanley.

As a result thought had been given to landing the new troops straight into an area from where they could, with a minimum delay, close on the enemy in conjunction with Julian's men. Various plans were mooted, but the choices really numbered just three: to land within Salvador Waters, to land at San Carlos or to land at Goose Green.

Salvador and the surrounding area was now in our hands and the land had been seized into which the three new battalions could land by helicopter in slow time or by LCU in even slower time as the *Canberra* would have to anchor outside, which was not an option of which I approved. Nor did the ground forces, for this would put all the military eggs on to one axis of advance and would cause considerable overcrowding. The southern flank option's main drawback was that it was also the direction from which, we thought, Menendez was expecting us to come; it was far too far by sea from San Carlos and also by direct helicopter flight south of the main mountain range. A small advantage was that Goose Green was in our hands and the area was not overcrowded as an area in which the new brigade could shake itself out, organize and prepare for battle; but no large ship (including LSLs) could reach Goose Green for landing craft operations (from either direction – up Brenton Loch, too shallow, or along Choiseul Sound, too close to the enemy), so that was out. Even if they could be reached by large ship both these options suffered a common problem – lack of landing assets. We were desperately trying to get all the stores ashore, stockpiled in comparative safety, tabulated and sorted for easier distribution forward and until that task was completed any re-supply on either flank would be haphazard. To remove landing craft and medium support helicopters to offload the new Brigade outside San Carlos would slow this vital operation. We had two days before the first troops were ready to land, by which time we had to have made our decision.

Jeremy and his staff were carefully briefed on the options open to them and chose to land 5 Brigade straight into San Carlos. His sitrep for the 30th made the following points:

'We have this day closed elements of 42 Commando up into the Mount Kent area to join D Squadron 22 SAS. Operations there are finely balanced and I am wholly confident that if it is possible to hang on so far into the enemy forward area we have the right formation and units carrying out the operations to do so. We have taken casualties but I am hopeful that it will come off. Meanwhile 3 Para and 45 Commando are pushing forwards vigorously to support, and in due course to expand, these operations. It is also of significance that we have today fired into Moody Brook camp with land-based artillery.

'However, lest you be in any doubt, the difficult terrain and unpleasant weather have taken their toll, I know, of the units (3 Para and 45 Commando) who have made their long cross country marches.

'5 Infantry Brigade begin their offload tonight, albeit late because of weather and they will press forward with vigour.

'I have tonight issued my op order for closing up to Stanley and you will of course receive a copy.

'Prisoners of War remain a problem and not one often discussed at Staff Colleges.'

Clearly the plans laid by Julian and myself were not only working but were being reported as such by an officer trusted by those back in the United Kingdom.

The mass of prisoners was becoming a problem and Colonel Ian Baxter needed help. I was happy to assist, but hoped that my involvement would be temporary. We could not leave them ashore (shelter and food were in very short supply; even for our own men they were bad enough), so I arranged for 300 of them to be brought on board *Sir Percivale* until *Norland* or *Canberra* could take them off my hands and away from the war zone as required by the Geneva Convention. While both Julian and I had considered the problems of prisoners neither of us had expected quite so many.

It might be hoped that our attempts not to disturb the turtles and terns at Ascension or the King Penguin colony on Volunteer Bay would have built up some credit with Nature, but Neptune was still to stick his trident in uncomfortably. The problem was krill. These small red and foul-smelling shrimps choked the filters and even managed to jam open two of *Fearless*'s turbo alternator cooling water inlet valves so the filters could not be removed and cleaned. This took four days of strenuous diving by ship's and clearance divers, initially at night to avoid the risk of air attack, but then by day in poor visibility and very cold water. The risk of a bomb exploding nearby had to be taken. One bomb had exploded some yards off the *Fearless* and the noise was unimaginable inside the ship. It clanged like a badly tuned bell but I was told it had burst quite far away. The divers were undoubtedly taking a real and unpleasant risk.

Other 'normal' activities had to continue and, indeed, were now to increase in intensity with the opening of the second flank. At Divisional Headquarters' request I arranged, for instance, for *Avenger* to insert an SBS team into Volunteer Bay before bombarding Eagle Hill from off the beach. Sandy's tasking signal was typically short and to the point but at the same time allowed flexibility:

'Situation: UK forces are in area north of Stanley. Requirements exist to provide gunfire support.
Enemy forces: A. As in (. . . earlier signal) – SBS insertion.
B. As seen night 21/30 by *Avenger*.
Mission: To provide NGS in Eagle Hill area.
Execution: At 301900Z when detached, *Avenger* close Volunteer Bay area. Meet calls for fire from NGFO 1. Remain in area until 3 hours before sunrise then rejoin.'

In addition to all this I agreed with the General that San Carlos must remain strong, for I continued to expect (as had CTF in his earlier summary signal) the Argentines to conduct raids against us from West Falkland; or even direct from the mainland with paratroopers or chemical weapons. Since the beginning I was conscious of their underwater capability using the French- and Italian-built 'human chariots' that, before sailing, I had been warned they possessed.

We did not know then that the Argentines had no intention of breaking out against us from West Falkland but what we did know was that their Air Force was still capable of seriously disrupting our plans. With the arrival of the Divisional Head-quarters and the Infantry Brigade it was important to disabuse them of any complacency they might have had over any presumed air superiority they may have thought we had.

From the landing forces' point of view Julian was cynical of any claim that we were operating under a friendly air-umbrella. As an aviator, though, I believed that we had some form of air superiority, on the understanding that one can never achieve this totally. We would therefore be subject to attack, for any pilot determined enough will get through. While it was clear that a number of their pilots were intent on saving their own skins, there were obviously enough with the courage and skill to inflict serious harm. I was certainly not becoming complacent and nor, I believe, were my ships' Commanding Officers who had felt their lash.

Having said that, on 27 May the BMA at Ajax Bay had been attacked, destroying 45 Commando's Milan, plus netted loads of 105 mm ammunition and 81 mm mortar bombs waiting to be underslung by helicopter to Camilla Creek House in advance of 2 Para's raid. Pucaras attacked 2 Para during their advance to Darwin and later on, two days before our victory, four Skyhawks were to attack the 3rd Commando Brigade Headquarters and a Royal Artillery battery position supporting 2 Para's Wireless Ridge operation.

Before dawn on the 31st San Carlos was also bombed, this time by four high-flying Canberras, causing slight damage to 846 Naval Air Squadron's operating base. Luckily the Squadron had dispersed its Sea Kings well with some ashore but others at sea in *Intrepid* and *Fearless*. HMS *Minerva* managed to scramble a Sea Harrier from HMS *Hermes* but at a range of 210 miles and with the enemy warned by their own radar controllers in Stanley that they were now being intercepted, they escaped. The Harrier managed to close to five miles before being obliged to return the 300 miles home, which was all rather unsatisfactory.

Concerned that aircraft were still encroaching San Carlos, I asked for a Sea Dart ship in a second signal to Sandy on the subject (my first had been on the 29th). I was particularly concerned as the Sea Harrier standing-by for just such an event as the Canberra attack had actually been 210 miles to the east that day. By the time the 800 Squadron aircraft had been scrambled at 0355 it was too late to catch the invaders, thus (and not for the first time) making the whole operation rather pointless.

We were pretty certain that on East Falkland the mobility of Menendez's troops was becoming severely restricted as we whittled away at his helicopter-lift capability, but we remained fully aware that each night reinforcements of some kind or another were arriving in Stanley by C-130 and we seemed powerless to stop this lifeline of weapons, ammunition, spares, food – and even firewood.

The discovery of napalm at Goose Green was a serious concern. I flew down to be shown twelve 500-pound napalm tanks, leaking and scattered around the strip, plus fifty 220 pound 'homemade', napalm bombs, all designed to fit the Pucara. At times it had been a most uncomfortable visit as we tiptoed across taped areas which might or might not have marked minefields. It was clearly not naval officer country. It was also my first sight of Argentine troop positions and I noticed that hygiene was non-existent with human excrement inches from the side of the slit-trench, which itself was half full of water. We also found large pillow tanks for aircraft fuel which Mike Cudmore correctly commandeered before more of them were damaged. With Julian's agreement, we returned some 20mm anti-aircraft cannon to the ships. Flying back, I noticed the troops going about their sad duty of putting bodies in bags and preparing burial. Altogether it was an instructive visit for a naval officer and one which made me all the more determined to support the Land Forces who were now facing up to the enemy.

Yet another concern of mine at the time, which Sandy shared, was the possible use to which the Argentine hospital ship was being put, and so on the 31st, having obtained permission from the Red Cross I sent an inspection team. My main suspicion had been triggered by her rather strange manoeuvrings and I was anxious to find out what was behind them. Not only did the inspection team find nothing untoward but the flight-deck crew were well familiar with our procedures for receiving Lynx aircraft. The team was 'made welcome and given every assistance: the Commander spoke fondly of HMS *Dryad*!' I continued, with fair reason, to be suspicious of some of her activities as a ship in a war zone, if not of her 'on-board' work and this was confirmed when, later on in Stanley, I was given an eye-witness account of an Exocet missile being unloaded from the hospital ship. I remained convinced throughout that she was reporting our ship movements.

If Salvador was not to be used by 5 Infantry Brigade it was to be used by 3 Commando Brigade and that meant I needed to open up the anchorage for a regular resupply run of LSLs. For some days Julian had had an observation post on Centre Island watching the entrance to the Waters for mine-laying activities and fast patrol boats. They had nothing to report but Terry Peck (an earlier Chief of Police in Stanley who had escaped by motorcycle) reported that mines had been laid earlier across the entrance and to the north of Shag Island. As just one mine in the very narrow pass between Centre Island and Leopard Seal Bay would, if detonated, successfully block the entrance it had to be swept, but we possessed no sweepers.

Lieutenant-Commander Meatyard, my Clearance Diving Officer, was summoned to devise a method for improvising the eight-ton, plywood constructed LCVPs as minesweepers and this he was to do by towing (in addition to the AMSS Mk 1 sweep) various noise-making machinery such as a Black and Decker drill running in a waterproof box and towed astern.

Acoustic mines are one thing, contact and pressure mines are another and the LCVPs were certainly not likely to produce the same pressure waves as a 5000-ton, laden LSL: nor do they draw the same amount of water. On the night of 31 May/1 June *Intrepid* launched her LCVP minesweeping operation which was to earn each of the two young Royal Marine corporal-cox'ns a Mention in Despatches. An LCU actually preceded the LCVPs as they drew marginally more water, although, again, not as much as an LSL. Fortunately, nothing was found and the risk for an LSL was accepted.

On the 31st, with the new team in place and the move towards Stanley underway, I sent my Terms of Reference/Future Employment signal to my Task Group explaining the current position:

1. When the amphib landing of 3 Commando Brigade was complete the AOA technically ceased to exist and San Carlos became a 'Transport Area' (TA). This message addresses aspects of the defence of the TA, the coordination of transport shipping into/out of it and the interface between CLFFI (who needs support) and FOF1/COMAW (who both provide/control that support).

2. *Fearless*, with COMAW staff embarked and her comms fit, semi-permanently based in the TA, is uniquely suited for controlling and coordinating:
   a. Defence of TA by attached frigates.
   b. Amphib helos supporting the Division. Provision of night deck-landing in bad weather for amphib helos and, in extremis, Harrier. Fuel, workshops available.
   c. Landing craft assets and providing repair and maint of LC.
   d. The port of San Carlos (eg. harbour movements).
   e. FMG activities by *Stena Seaspread* detachment.
   f. Liaison between CLFFI and FOF 1. on transport ships movements.
   g. Certain Special Forces and NGS/surveillance activities in support of Division.

3. To achieve tasks at para 2, following would be necessary:

a. Move from *Intrepid* to *Fearless* of Special Forces command elements.
   b. Augmentation of COMAW staff by a Cdr (P), say, Cdr Yarker currently in *Canberra* (needed to control activities of four Commando Squadrons).

4. With *Fearless* tied for the most part to secure VHF Comms with San Carlos, *Intrepid* could retire to the deepfield, on call for any MCM or amphib op to be mounted.

5. Several of the tasks in para 2 could be performed by either the senior frigate present or a liaison team ashore but stumbling block is lack of secure voice comms from TA to *Hermes* and Northwood, the need for which points to *Fearless* as TA guardship.

6. Intend concept outlined above. Formal support of CLFFI and FOF 1 has been prepared and agreed with staffs and could be signalled if required.

From the Air Deputy in Northwood there was strong pressure to construct the Harriers' Forward Operating Base (FOB) ashore as soon as possible which was a sentiment that met with the full approval of Sandy, myself and the ground forces. The moment that we could control the CAP more directly and have them overhead within seconds could not come too soon for any of us inshore and ashore. Sandy, too, was keen so that he could (in his own words) 'unhook himself from a well-trodden stretch of water' and move his carriers to further safety.

Other improvements were noted and asked for: all STUFT and RFAs that sailed from the United Kingdom after 28 May were to be fitted with 20mm mountings and all RFAs and a selected number of civilian ships would be fitted with Chaff if they were likely to be employed within the Exclusion Zone. The laser equipment designed to dazzle pilots on their run-in to a target had been ordered and two sets initially dropped to the Carrier Battle Group during the first week of June. These were quickly fitted to *Plymouth* and *Yarmouth* with other sets being made available later earmarked for the two carriers and *Fearless*.

Seven sets of the more modern version of Chaff were accepted from the United States of America for ships due south after 27 May and the GR3 Harriers had been given the laser-guided bomb-delivery systems that they first used against Stanley on 30 May. In practice, this delivery method proved unsuccessful until a ground-based laser target marking system had been provided. On 13 June a Shrike missile capability was also introduced for the RAF Harriers – sadly a little late for operational use. Nevertheless all these improvements, and dozens more for all three services, were introduced quickly and smoothly thanks to a willingness on the part of our allies and the waiving of restrictions by our own Procurement Executive and Ministry of Defence. Under this general heading came the resupply of shortages, two of the most urgent being 3″ Chaff Rockets (which were so often used in San Carlos to put off a pilot rather than to divert radar guided weapons) and Seacat missiles with which so many ships were fitted and which were expended at a fast rate during the early air strikes in San Carlos. Lessons for the future here. 4.5″ shells were also expended at a much greater rate than previously calculated, particularly as the near demise of the United Kingdom's amphibious capability had also sounded the death knell for Naval Gunfire Support.

At the end of *Operation Corporate* we were to possess sufficient ammunition, throughout the Exclusion Zone, for just two more nights' bombardment at the rate required by CLFFI while the next resupply was then three or so weeks away. Failure to achieve victory was that close and if the military were to worry about their stocks of gunner ammunition available for the final battles we were equally worried about the naval equivalent. In fact, there was, contrary to rumour, plenty of gunner ammunition; there were just not the helicopters to lift it to the guns.

Meanwhile, at South Georgia, the arrival and cross-decking of the second Brigade had taken place without mishap. The *QE2* had arrived in the Grytviken anchorage during the early evening of 27 May – seven hours after *Canberra*: cross-decking began almost immediately. The transfer of men and stores went well and within twenty-four hours of the Cunarder's arrival the P & O liner was able to weigh anchor and head westwards. *Canberra* now had on board elements of a number of units: Divisional Headquarters; 2nd Battalion Scots Guards; 1st Battalion Welsh Guards; 656 Squadron Army Air Corps; 4th Field Regiment Royal Artillery; 9 Parachute Squadron Royal Engineers; 160 Provost Company; 36 Engineer Regimental Headquarters; 825 Naval Air Squadron; 63 Squadron Royal Air Force and 5 Infantry Brigade Headquarters and Signal Squadron. At the same time the 1/7th Gurkha Rifles were transferred to the *Norland* and the gallant ships' companies of HMS *Ardent* and HMS *Antelope* passed across from one liner to another for the sad journey home. The *QE2* also embarked the survivors from the equally gallant HMS *Coventry* brought out on board the RFA *Stromness*.

The RFA then received 300 'new' men from the homeward-bound liner plus bulk ammunition.

There should have been other transfers in Grytviken that day but the weather was so bad that the *Saxonia* had extreme difficulty transferring stores to *Resource*, indeed, it was to take five days.

What was not passed across from *QE 2* to *Canberra* was any food or beer, which *Canberra*'s purser had been led to expect. While neither I nor anyone else involved would wish to make too much of the issue this was one of a number of examples where simple luxuries of one sort or another never found their way to the front line where they were most needed and for where they were intended. With the MOD's blessing a well-known brewer sent, for instance, a large consignment of beer which travelled no further than Ascension Island before it was drunk. Dozens of copies of the magazine *Mayfair* did, though, reach the troops and ships' companies based in the Falklands; they might have preferred the beer! While well-meaning charitable organizations in the United Kingdom collected many 'goodies' for the men not all were welcome. Some of these caused logistic confusions and most did not get beyond the people stationed in the safety of the 'half-way halt'. It might have been better if the 'presents' had been kept back until victory had been gained before being issued. What disturbed me more was the insulting belief by certain members of the 'show business' community in the United Kingdom that a particularly nasty collection of specially produced pornographic and 'video nasty' tapes (which did arrive on the Islands and in the ships) were what our men wanted after battle.

The Great White Whale now had in her charge a very different collection of soldiers from those she had brought down earlier. These men were not used to the privations of life in the maritime world and, while their lack of military training during the journey from South Georgia to San Carlos was harshly commented upon, there were reasons why upper-deck fitness training, for example, did not take place. Dennis Scott-Masson, *Canberra*'s avuncular and amiable captain, reduced speed shortly after sailing from Grytviken describing the weather as 'tempestuous'. What the embarked force did do was to provide over forty machine-gun posts on the upper decks during what should have been a two day journey, but one that stretched to four and a half.

It was not a pleasant passage for anyone especially as all embarked, military and civilian, in *Canberra* and *Norland* knew that the enemy were aware of their movements and their load. In the same irresponsible manner over our departure from Ascension Island, our approach to landing and the move of 2 Para towards Darwin and Julian's HQ move to Teal, the BBC now broadcast that 5 Infantry Brigade was on the final leg of its journey in the *Canberra* and *Norland* to San Carlos. These ships could have become easy pickings for the submarine we believed was still sitting off the north east corner of the Islands. Due to government-sourced breaches of security we seldom achieved the most invaluable of military weapons, surprise. If surprise was lost then British lives would also be lost. This continual deliberate leaking of information was possibly the greatest threat to our morale.

If the Argentines could hit *Atlantic Conveyor* in the middle of the Carrier Battle Group they could hardly miss the great white *Canberra* (and the nearly as distinctive *Norland*) once she had left the protection of the Carrier Battle Group to begin her run into San Carlos.

In San Carlos Water a number of developments had been considered to make support of the enlarged land forces more complete and effective. The Harrier Forward Operating Base (FOB) had been recce'd by the Officer Commanding 59 Independent Squadron, Royal Engineers, as soon as D+1, on which day he chose a reasonably flat stretch of land immediately to the west of Port San Carlos. The old Auster strip marked on the charts at Little Rincon, San Carlos, had proved to be too soft, even if it was to have aluminium planks laid on top. *Stromness* had begun the offload of 11,000 planks on D+2, enough for a strip 850 feet long. She had also landed the emergency fuel-handling equipment and more planks to form the taxi area for refuelling. The strip was ready by D+9, which, by any standards, was an impressive effort, especially now that the full Aircraft Forward Operating Base was lying at the bottom of the South Atlantic. Delays followed while the pilots inspected the landing site and for repairs to be made after damage caused by the Chinook on the 30th. The first Harrier was to land on 5 June after bad weather had prevented fixed-wing flying for three more days.

This FOB was nicknamed HMS *Sheathbill* following the Fleet Air Arm practice of naming their air stations after birds. In this instance they had chosen well as a quote from Ewen Southby-Tailyour's *Reasons in Writing* explains. 'The Snowy Sheathbill is one of the less attractive Falklands inhabitants. All white, with a short, stout, green and brown bill and a permanent bleary look due to a patch of bare skin below the eyes, it scavenges for food and is especially attracted to the regurgitations of penguins and cormorants. With a fondness for eating seals' faeces and stealing eggs, it does not endear itself to many. Although its toes are unwebbed, it can swim well if pushed!'

The shortage of helicopters had to be resolved. I had continued to discuss this with Sandy until after Jeremy Moore's arrival when Sandy agreed that, with a lessening chance of submarines in the area, we should strip four of the Carrier Battle Group's anti-submarine Sea Kings, fly them ashore and use them as medium support helicopters with the ground forces. In fact we received four Sea King Mk 2s that had come down in *Atlantic Causeway* and, while they and their pilots were most welcome, their use highlighted the difference in flying practices between the 'pingers' and the 'junglies' (the anti-submarine pilots and those who fly in support of commando operations)! I hope it is not churlish to suggest that map reading, contour flying and military tactics are not the strong points of the former – and nor should they be – but they improved rapidly.

CHAPTER SEVEN

FINAL PREPARATIONS

... and the more I have reflected, the more I am
confirmed in opinion, that not a moment should be
lost in attacking the Enemy.

I am of opinion the boldest measures are the
safest.

Nelson in the *St George*, March 24, 1801,
to Admiral Sir Hyde Parker

JEREMY AND HIS staff began to concentrate on plans for a
Divisional attack against Stanley's outlying hills on 6 June, with
an assault on the capital itself by the 9th.

In San Carlos on Monday the 31st, *Elk* had come in, while
Atlantic Causeway and *Europic Ferry* had been prevented from
entering due to appalling weather offshore. This certainly did not
please Julian, desperate for fuel for his vehicles and for various
items of his War Maintenance Reserve which had been cross-
decked at South Georgia. Julian knew, as did I, that his Brigade
still had essential equipment on board four other RFAs,
(*Stromness*, *Fort Austin*, *Resource* and *Regent*) and he wanted
these stores ashore and forward. As always I had to consider the
choice of either cross-decking at sea, which took time but was
safer, or bringing ships in one at a time with small amounts of
stores embarked. As Ajax Bay would now service both Brigades
the quicker I filled it up direct from the individual ships the
better.

During the day *Elk* and *Sir Lancelot* continued to be unloaded by the LCUs (and damn the bombs) while POWs were embarked in *Sir Percivale*. The RFA *Tidepool* anchored close to Port San Carlos in a somewhat exposed position and filled the emergency fuel handling equipment (EFHE) that Major Roddy Macdonald, Julian's Sapper, had established at the Forward Operating Base (FOB). These consisted of large rubber pillow tanks ashore and sausages at sea, all interlinked with pumps and piping up to the landing strip. A first class piece of engineering done in very quick time. Out at sea with Sandy, 5 Infantry Brigade arrived in the loitering area (named more formally as the TRALA – or Tug, Repair and Logistics Area) also spread, with their equipment, across a variety of ships: *Canberra*, *Norland*, *Nordic Ferry*, *Baltic Ferry*, and *Atlantic Causeway*, all supported by the tanker *Blue Rover*. It was up to CLFFI to decide which units, and, therefore, which ships he wanted in first. He had, though, to take notice of the naval aspects of such an operation and thus accepted my guidance: San Carlos Water was still a dangerous place to be afloat.

The quickest and safest method of getting men ashore unhindered was to do it piecemeal and with care, and to this end 'troop' ships would only be brought in when there were assets available with which to unload them. It was all a balance and I did not have to argue loud and long, although ready to do so, that too many ships in the anchorage at once, just to give flexibility in unloading priorities, was a bad thing, particularly for merchant seamen's morale.

There was more to life than the offload of logistics. The night of 31 May/1 June was a busy one with the most important arrival being the submarine *Onyx* now giving us the ability to land the SBS with more chance of success than before. She was met off the Eddystone Rock by HMS *Avenger* and escorted to alongside *Fearless* shortly after midnight.

The first 'new' troops ashore in San Carlos were the Gurkhas from *Norland*, plus their heavy equipment in *Baltic Ferry*, both of which entered the anchorage during the night of 31 May/1 June. The battalion landed into Blue Beach Two along with three Army Air Corps Scout helicopters and a battery of Royal

Artillery light guns. Jeremy was keen to establish one of the battalions ashore and firm before bringing in the *Canberra* with the two others so the Gurkha Commanding Officer was ordered to march immediately to Goose Green and relieve 2 Para, still brushing themselves down after their battles.

I had also called in *Atlantic Causeway*, much to the military's relief, for she contained, among many other invaluable items, eight Sea Kings (four had flown ahead earlier) and twenty Wessex Mk 5s. The Wessex squadron (847) was short on pilots due to the lack of accommodation on board and so twelve aircraft were ferried ashore and 'laid up' in various small valleys until the rest of the Squadron pilots, in *Canberra* and *Engadine*, caught up with their machines, but at least it was progress. I privately thanked Ted Anson for these extra helicopters.

Atlantic Causeway also brought the RAF Regiment's Blindfire Rapiers giving us, in theory, the ability to engage targets at night and through cloud. Less welcome were the ninety (wheeled, not tracked) vehicles that accompanied them to manage just eight fire units – a fact that added emphasis to the argument for having a specialist Royal Marine tracked-Rapier unit within the Commando Brigade. Divisional Headquarters refused to land most of the RAF's caravans and test vehicles, without which, the RAF Regiment argued unconvincingly, they could not operate; but then they are largely static units not emotionally geared to commando-style operations.

All this unloading had to be conducted by six LCUs (the seventh and eighth had been delivered to Teal Inlet in order to unload the visiting LSL) and an assortment of Mexeflotes, some of which had been 'broken down', as experiments in north Norway had suggested over the years, to form ramp-support-pontoons for the stern ramps of the civilian ships. This was always a time-consuming operation when dealing with non-specialist ships and one that was never easy during air-raids, although the crews soon learned to ignore what was happening above their heads! My staff, planning ahead, had asked HMS *Hermes* for their Royal Marines Detachment to be cross-decked to *Norland* before she left the Carrier Battle Group. These men were to be ready as POW guards in *Norland*, once empty. I also asked for two of her LCVPs but we never received them or the Detachment.

By the end of the day it was clear that the three transport ships (*Norland*, *Baltic Ferry* and *Atlantic Causeway*) would not be emptied by dark and probably not until the following night. This worried me as our CAP protection remained sporadic and we had no Sea Dart. The Blindfire Rapier, now taking over the defence of San Carlos, would not be operational until after this particular offload had been completed, despite the many support vehicles that were allowed ashore.

Jeremy was anxious to bring in the remaining battalions of 5 Brigade and that meant the Great White Whale entering San Carlos again. During 2 June, with very crossed fingers for I was not happy with our air-defence capability, I called her in. In fact the poor weather made the decision easier, for she would be able to ride at anchor in San Carlos Water under a good, solid, low cloud base.

Those Gurkhas not moving by foot to Goose Green were flown forward by Chinook, while those who did march over Sussex Mountain did so without difficulty, leading me to expect great things of the Guards due in shortly.

This deployment of the Gurkha Battalion allowed 2 Para to plan for a future once again and this, combined with the arrival of Brigadier Tony Wilson clutching a promise made to him by Jeremy during their joint incarceration on board the *QE2* that his 5 Brigade would have parity with 3 Commando Brigade over the availability of assets, laid the first seeds of the later tragedy. Promises or not, and mostly it was 'not' as far as 5 Brigade was to discover; the 3rd Commando Brigade was committed to a series of moves that could not be stopped half way and which required the heavy use of air transport. This forced the energetic Wilson to take, or allow to be taken, a series of hasty decisions that culminated in my having to get them out of a jam into which they quite willingly seemed to walk, or fly.

On 1 June Jeremy and his three Brigadiers (he had now been joined by John Waters) had lunch with me in my cabin, during which Tony Wilson kept demanding every single helicopter that was available to move his Brigade. As these were not instantly forthcoming Tony had cause to believe that the Royal Marines were being given all priorities. The truth is that Julian simply had to complete his consolidation: it could not be halted half-accomplished. In an effort to calm him, I took Tony aside to explain that I appreciated his position and would do my best to bear his problem in mind, but the actual allocation of helicopters was in the hands of CLFFI's staff. I did not, though, feel it my right to remind him that men could walk forwards, but ammunition, food and fuel could, sensibly, only go by air.

Although I had passed Tactical Control of most of my helicopters to Divisional Headquarters I kept two back for upper-deck offloading and to be ready to protect our rear. People criticized us for fussing too much about West Falkland, but that is hindsight. I knew that CTF and Jeremy were worried and, knowing that the enemy was in strength in Fox Bay and Port Howard and had an observation post on Mount Rosalie watching our every move, so was I. It was quite feasible that the moment we embarked on our approach to Stanley they could have launched attacks against us in San Carlos at what would then be our weakest link in the logistic chain.

In the anchorage on 1 June the activity was mostly connected with unloading the shipping, while during the night before 3 Para had begun their move to Estancia House; 45 Commando was firm at Teal Inlet; 40 Commando guarded San Carlos and 42 Commando was in strength on Mount Kent and Mount Challenger. As most helicopter loads going forwards were ammunition, I was half aware that the forward troops might be short of food and that there was little that could be done about it.

I had agreed with Jeremy that all landing craft would remain under my operational control but that I would give tactical control to Julian for those in Salvador Waters. Despite requests, I was not prepared to give tactical control of the landing craft to 5 Brigade for I was never to trust their command to employ them sensibly. On the few occasions they managed somehow to purloin vessels or helicopters they failed to understand the operational danger of independent operations.

To task the landing craft my two Staff Officers, Majors Guy Yeoman and Tony Todd of the Royal Corps of Transport, remained on board while Ewen managed the execution of the task from his base on the beach at San Carlos. We made the best use we could of the landing craft and Mexeflotes, but their crews (who had no reliefs unlike the Helicopter Squadron's aircrew) had to be rested every twenty-four hours or so. Ewen took charge of this aspect by exercising great concern for his men and, in turn, for their efficiency, but his actions did not always meet with everyone's approval.

It was fascinating in a very fast-moving campaign of this nature to discover how impossible it was to please. Almost everyone, it seems, had a different idea of how fast things should move and how they should be done. Of course, almost everyone was only partly informed and so, probably, wrong! Clearly, on the passage down my impatience with the lack of long-term directives resulted from CTF being quite unable to give me them honestly while the political situation, of which I knew virtually nothing, changed daily. Now in San Carlos life was changing even more rapidly and it was all the more easy to blame others for misunderstandings, changes of plan, second thoughts, new intelligence and all the inevitable and unpredictable events of war which made one's life, if not impossible, certainly frantic. I tried to calm my staff by telling them to be slobs, let it all wash over them, but to keep a clear head and do what they believed best. It was probably of no help to them whatsoever but it helped me! I was extremely conscious that I was unable to get around the anchorage and encourage my people; there was simply neither time nor transport. Instead one had to get the answers right and thereby, I hoped, maintain their loyalty and trust. It would also save British lives and allow us to win.

One operation that was vital to the success of the northern flank's operations was the sailing overnight on 1/2 June of the laden *Sir Percivale* for Teal Inlet with the first consignment of 3 Commando Brigade's FBMA stores, she now proudly calling herself '*Sir Percivale* the First of All', having also been the first into San Carlos. Her loading had, though, taken up all the landing craft through most of the day and this in turn had delayed other important offloading serials; but priorities had to be made and at that moment she and her load were at the top. In fact, in consultation with Colonel Ian Baxter (a pragmatic, tireless breath of fresh air) we agreed that any LSL moved forward would contain just those stores that could be unloaded within one day using a short (sixty foot) Mexeflote and two LCUs. This was to ensure that at no time was an LSL to be exposed for more than one day at a time by herself in a largely undefended anchorage. I also reminded everyone that no ship of any size was to be on the move outside San Carlos, or any other anchorage, during daylight hours, and that included LPDs.

Having an LSL at anchor in Teal Inlet was a risk, but one that could not be avoided. There was no alternative and as always throughout the war I was determined that no matter what the land forces might accuse the Royal Navy of doing, or not doing, failing to 'engage the enemy more closely' would not be one of them. Longer-term support had been a point often discussed with Julian, for I knew well his fear, based on various peacetime amphibious exercises, that the Royal Navy, having landed the Brigade, would then push off, possibly taking much of his support with it, to chase submarines or simply play at manoeuvres.

As well as orchestrating the air and surface defence of San Carlos, the general offload of stores into Ajax Bay and the regular move forward of supplies to Teal Inlet, plus the very real problem of collecting and transporting prisoners of war, I had to help Divisional Headquarters plan the move eastward of the three new battalions. On the 31st Ewen Tailyour had been called across to *Fearless* to discuss the practicalities of such a move and the choice of destinations lying between Port Sussex and Bluff Cove that we could use depending on the developing situation. Interestingly, Ewen was now happy to conduct a transit of Brenton Loch in the dark, particularly as the Gurkhas were now due to clear Lafonia of any remaining enemy. The navigational problems still existed, of course, as did the possibility of being stuck high and dry on an unmarked shoal at dawn but with both 'banks' of the Loch in our hands the main danger would be attack by enemy aircraft. In practice, though, all Ewen was offering was a journey that took the men as far as Goose Green. There were still forty miles to go to Fitzroy, an area where Tony Wilson was already planning to set up his forward mounting base for operations into the hills south of those occupied by the 3rd Commando Brigade.

To meet both Jeremy's and Tony's plans Ian Baxter was becoming more and more desperate to move two battalions by sea, plus an immense amount of kit: at which point it became obvious that we had to think in terms of a second major seaborne operation and I was not convinced that was the right way to go about things. I did not like it one bit and demurred.

Up to this time I had not remotely considered the possibilities of a southern flank sea move other than for logistic reinforcement as far as the Goose Green garrison. Now I was asked by Jeremy to look along, and beyond, Choiseul Sound, but still only for stores. Men would either go by foot to Darwin or by helicopter if further, and only once Julian's men were forward and supplied.

Although we now needed to look as far as possible along the south we also studied beaches as close as Grantham Sound and Brenton Loch for use if the weather, or enemy, prevented us from conducting longer sea approaches. As far as the logistics were concerned, of course, the further I could transfer stores from San Carlos the better, but, as always, flexibility had to be uppermost in our minds. Swan Inlet and Mare Harbour were studied as likely logistic landing sites, as were Fitzroy and Bluff Cove.

Studying the chart, it was easy to see that confusion was likely to exist over names: Bluff Cove lies on the northern edge of Port Fitzroy whereas Fitzroy Settlement itself lies on the northern edge of Port Pleasant. There are, too, a few minor anomalies between names on the Admiralty charts and those on the 'land maps' issued to the ground forces.

At that stage I was not planning to take the battalions forward, although, had I been asked, and under happier circumstances I would have been able to allocate Chinook helicopters but all but one lay burnt-out on the sea bed. While moving the troops forward by sea would be one thing (and not yet in the strategy), I did need to ascertain whether or not logistic reinforcement by sea was feasible. Men do not need dry landings across prepared beaches but bulk stores on pallets or in the backs of vehicles do need jetties, slipways, or firm, reasonably shallow beaches. We would see what we could do.

Jeremy's direct contact with Northwood and, through Fleet Headquarters, to Ministers was invaluable. As the result of his work before he left England he knew what it was they wanted to hear, so his report covering the landing of the leading elements of 5 Brigade on 1 June was a typical example that at once eased tensions between 'us and them'. On the other hand it made me smile not only for its very un-naval style but for implying that he alone held command over ships, landing craft and helicopters. His view was that ...

Yesterday saw the first arrivals from 5 Bde in San Carlos ... Immediately it became light I visited TAC HQ 3 Cdo Bde in Teal ... Operations over the last few days have shown us that enemy has no stomach to fight us in this high and bitterly cold area and has withdrawn in the face of moves which threaten him ... (3 Commando Brigade Commander) has therefore pushed 42 Commando rapidly into the Mount Kent/Mount Challenger area and 3 Para onto Estancia Mountain and sought from me the assets to exploit what we perceived to be his advantage. I therefore took all the support helicopters off the unloading and allocated the whole lot to him. He is now moving his guns, ammo and infantry forward as fast as possible and is driving through the hills towards Mount Longdon, Two Sisters, and Mount Harriet positions which now appear to be forward enemy locations ...

Unfortunately the offloading of (5 Infantry Brigade) is inevitably delayed which is extremely frustrating for them ... I will bring them into battle as fast as my ... helicopter assets allow.

Meanwhile I am taking risks but have big prizes in view ... To support these operations an LSL, very rapidly loaded with 300 tons of combat supplies, is now moving to Teal Inlet. As soon as first-light move of 63 Sqn RAF (Rapier) into position is complete, a troop of T Battery will be moved to cover this area ... A day free of enemy air attacks upon us. Today (2 June) the anchorage will be very full, including *Canberra*, and our helicopters will be flying long distances without escort. I can keep my fingers crossed that our luck does not run out.

As I was the naval CTG on the spot helping to conduct these joint operations many of his claimed actions were the results of requests and not instructions. However, there was a war to be won, I was junior and once again it was not a good time to let such matters give offence. Both staffs knew the form and were working well together which was what I wanted. More importantly, I believe I knew Jeremy well enough to know he would have been mortified if any offence had been taken.

So now we reached 2 June with one Brigade well forward, another on its way and a definite feeling that we could begin the final phases that would wrap the whole thing up. We also received an appreciation from CTF which, although it told us much we knew already, helped us in the belief that, in most respects, we were all thinking along the same lines. He made these points:

Argentines apparently no longer see possibility of successful defence of Falkland Islands. Therefore assume their aim is to achieve a tolerable negotiating position. This could be achieved by a high profile success such as:

a. Hitting a carrier.
b. Attacking San Carlos.
c. Establishing an undisputed presence in some strength on West Falkland.

I was far from clear how these events would necessarily improve their negotiating position but the CTF went on to list a number of likely enemy actions as he saw them:

a. Feint by fast frigates/destroyers towards the Carrier Battle Group to draw off escorts.

b. Air attack on resultant weakly defended Carrier Battle Group and/or merchant ships.

c. Air attack on San Carlos allied to raid up Falkland Sound by southern-based Fast Patrol Boats.

d. Air/sea reinforcements of West Falkland Garrisons.

The CTF further assumed that any enemy action would be a brief, all out, effort during which our nuclear submarines would have to cope with their surface fleet while:

air defence will rest with AAA and such aircraft as you can leave ashore temporarily.

... all points that had been worrying Sandy, Julian and myself since before our arrival and which Jeremy had clearly understood since his arrival.

But CTF oddly went on to suggest that the carriers should be kept far to the east and that we should strengthen the sea and air defences of San Carlos; he also wanted us to establish a second Harrier FOB at Goose Green. San Carlos was to be emptied as far as possible, and we should task Special Forces for harassing attacks against West Falkland airstrips. Finally, he wanted us to deploy a small, overt presence on West Falkland with, he suggested, one company flying a prominent Union Jack at Pebble Island.

The signal came as something of a surprise. Not a few ideas were under way and had been since the early days. Having been left almost entirely and at times worryingly to ourselves, this now suggested a degree of back seat driving. The carriers were far to the east; our air and sea defences had been strengthened as far as our very limited assets allowed; we were trying to keep San Carlos as empty as possible; the FOB was completed and Special Forces were working flat out. We did of course appreciate the need to keep the carriers afloat, but tell that to a young marine under attack on the ground, or a young sailor hopelessly out gunned in a Type 12 Frigate hit by four bombs, knowing that their air-defence base is nearly two hundred miles away. In fact an educated assessment, later confirmed by the 'boffins' at Bath, showed that if one Exocet managed to get through the screen it was unlikely to be enough to hamper, seriously, the operational capabilities of a ship such as *Hermes*, but the risk could not be taken.

Interestingly, CTF's signal did not suggest that the loss of *Fearless* would also be a high-profile success for the enemy. This 'absence' gave me the feeling that, while the risk to the LPDs had all along been high, it was acceptable and that they, perhaps especially *Intrepid*, were regarded as the more expendable once their job had been done. I did not bother to jot down a list of ships in order of expendability but it was inevitably always in my mind.

The idea of flying a Union Flag at Pebble Island was strange. On the 3:1 ratio required for an attacking force over a defender this would have meant a Commando assault by air and sea merely to raise a Union Flag. We had Union Flags at Port San Carlos, San Carlos, Teal Inlet, Douglas Station, Goose Green and Darwin, so we put this suggestion aside. Pebble Island was, for Jeremy and me, off the line of march.

Goose Green, as a suggested additional FOB, was not a runner, as the provision of fuel would have been impossible from a ship even if we had managed to transport the thousands of aluminium panels across country: a rather unhelpful suggestion that continued to remind us that, while we welcomed their enthusiastic support, there were still huge areas of misunderstanding.

In fact (and, I suspect, partially to appease Northwood) Jeremy did consider, but on a small scale, two of CTF's suggestions as is seen in his daily report for 2 June: 'As the main body closes in, special forces will be released from this area and some will be switched to West Falkland. I intend to support these operations by earmarking a commando company for raiding at sub-unit level to the west whenever suitable targets offer.'

Intercepted radio transmissions between Menendez and Galtieri indicated that the Argentine Falklands Command now knew that they would be unable to match the British in what it saw as the possibility of further landings in strength by helicopter and landing craft in the vicinity of Stanley. We were not informed of this discussion; nevertheless we remained concerned that 'something' might be pulled out of the fanatical Argentine hat, even if it was not orchestrated by an increasingly defeatist, and defeated, Menendez. Attacks direct from the mainland had to be considered right up to, and beyond, victory ashore.

Thankfully 2 June was miserable with low cloud and drizzle and while this was bad for our own helicopter movement we could get on with unloading the shipping. *Canberra* anchored south of Fannings Island at 0617, the first LCU securing alongside at 0630 to begin the landing of the Scots and Welsh Guards. Captain Scott-Masson was anxious, naturally, to unload everything before dusk and get back to the safety of deep water; more so than most probably, for his command was unmistakable among so many grey or smaller ships. But this was not to be and she would still be with us on the 3rd, not sailing until late afternoon that day. The imperatives to get going were not in such evidence among her passengers, a fact that caused Beagle Burne to comment harshly.

I, too, was rather tetchy over the time it was taking to offload *Canberra*, which may, perhaps, be put down to the troops carrying out an 'administrative landing'. This is a meaningless expression often used for non-operational landings in peacetime, but one which has no place in war. 'Administrative' it might have been in the sense that the troops were being landed non-tactically onto secure beaches, but the ship herself and the ship-to-shore assets were all liable to air attack, a matter of which we and the ship were only too well aware, but something that had yet to impress itself on the newly arrived battalions. In fact a number of other issues also intervened which did not help the general air of unhurriedness: the fog prevented flying through much of the morning and there were not, as always, enough LCUs. So anxious was the ship to be rid of her passengers and on her way that four of her boats were willingly pressed into service to help with the offload. At one stage the *Canberra*'s crew formed a chain gang to move the Guards' first-line stores which they had not taken with them.

I had become very concerned at the lack of support helicopter expertise on my staff. My SAVO, Tim Stanning, and his assistant J. J. White had been transferred to Jeremy's Divisional Staff to control the naval helicopters. Flight Lieutenant Chubb, rejoicing in the title CLOT! (Chinook Liaison and Operational Tasking) was also working with Tim and JJ, leaving no one free to think ahead on behalf of myself or the squadron commanding officers or to assist Mike Cudmore. I decided to commandeer Commander Tim Yarker, an ex-Commando helicopter squadron commanding officer who was on board the *Canberra*, as, once 5 Brigade had landed, there would be little need for him to remain there. It was to be a wise decision.

A problem that had long diverted Sandy's and my attention was the possibility that Argentina had managed to obtain more Exocet missiles and had landed them in Stanley. One, as I was to discover, was probably landed from the 'hospital' ship. Despite sending Lynx helicopters on observation missions along the south coast we never found the one that we knew (courtesy of the SAS) existed on the back of a lorry in the Stanley area and which was trundled out from its hiding place each dusk to the area of Eliza Cove south of Stanley Common. What we suspected was that there might, just might, be an Exocet based at Pebble Island and capable of being launched perhaps from an Argentine Sea King. It was to remain a worry to me and to every departing or entering ship until after victory. *Canberra* did not want that attention and felt, quite sensibly, that the longer she was in sight of Mount Rosalie (cloud level permitting) at the northern end of the anchorage (for she could come no further south), the longer the Pebble Island Exocet team had to 'get its act together' to her possible disadvantage.

The 2nd of June was the day that the move along the south coast began in earnest, although the first phase was conducted with too much impetuosity and with too little consideration for longer-term plans. Those not used to joint or combined warfare and its requirement to dovetail events with great and precise care might have described the events as 'dashing', but as a direct result of actions that day I was forced to alter my plans for helping Divisional Headquarters move 5 Brigade.

During the afternoon a very small advance party of 2 Para moved to Swan Inlet house in a number of 656 Squadron (Army Air Corps) Scout helicopters. Once there it was ascertained by telephone that Fitzroy was clear of Argentinians and 5 Brigade, commandeering an asset for which they had not been given temporary tactical control, initiated a frantic ferrying operation using the overworked and otherwise fully-employed Chinook which just happened to be in the area on another task organized by the Divisional HQ. Part of 2 Para were flown forward to Fitzroy and Bluff Cove which they occupied by dusk.

Bold and dashing it might have been – and at that moment that is how it was seen – but it was to be the single most irresponsible act that led to the subsequent catastrophe. First, neither I nor, of more importance, Jeremy and his staff knew anything of this move and, secondly, the whole operation nearly ended in disaster as the Chinook was spotted by a Mountain and Arctic Warfare Cadre patrol high up in Winter Quarrie on Wickham Heights. The Royal Marine patrol commander, knowing that the Argentines had Chinooks, called a fire mission from 7 Battery of 29 Commando Light Regiment Royal Artillery – and then cancelled it just in time. The Cadre had earlier witnessed 2 Para's Scout helicopter moves and assumed, with every reason, that this Chinook was the prelude to an enemy counter-attack.

We now had a weak, unsupported battalion with no guns strung in penny packets for thirty miles across the southern flank. It possessed no defence against any Argentine counterattack by land or air, or even by sea had the enemy been prepared to brave the consequences. It was a most unsatisfactory position that CLFFI's staff found themselves in and which they now had to unscramble. They had, or should have had, better things to think about and organize, such as the coordinated move forward of mutually supporting and balanced forces. It can be argued that this was a military problem that did not affect me but the war was a combined operation from start to finish, with this just another phase needing my attention. It was clear that the only way to extricate 2 Para and tighten up the south coast was through some form of naval expedition involving the landing of men forward from ships or by marching them overland, supported by landing craft carrying their heavy kit, weapons and ammunition. I instructed my staff to consider the various 'naval' options for getting 5 Brigade out of the quicksand before the tide flooded in.

Warfare requires dash and initiative but what combined operations cannot accept are unknown, uncoordinated, unplanned moves along an open or sea flank – principles not understood by those whose concept of battle relies, conventionally, on strong, reliable, secure lines of communication and re-supply. Brigadier Tony Wilson must take (and indeed did take) much of the blame for this extraordinary move, a move that was to have dire consequences. Jeremy's daily report to CTF for 2 June praised Tony, for that initially is how many saw the action: 'However [5 Infantry Brigade], though their offload has not by any means been easy for them, have managed to get a leading element – part of 2 Para – into the Bluff Cove area ... Their task is now to close up and get themselves balanced so that I can pass them through [3 Commando Brigade] in due course.'

The comment about 'getting themselves balanced' might have been taken as a mild rebuke, for no such organization close to direct contact with the enemy should ever allow itself to become 'unbalanced'. Nor did the comment about passing the Army Brigade through the Commando Brigade go unremarked by those who had not been impressed by the standard of fitness and readiness of the new arrivals.

In the meantime 3 Para were patrolling forward to Mount Longdon from their secure positions on Mounts Vernet and Estancia while 42 Commando patrolled against Mount Harriet from Mounts Kent and Challenger and 45 Commando prepared for a helicopter move to the land between the two leading units. Special Forces patrolled the area around Berkeley Sound. These seemed to me to be sensible, aggressive, military preparatory tactics in advance of well-coordinated military actions. Julian's sitrep for the 2nd: '*Sir Percivale*'s safe arrival at 0900Z was excellent news and although her offload is only progressing slowly it will allow the FBMA to be established ... 40 Commando now reverted to Force Troops and temporarily (we hope) allocated for defence of the San Carlos bridgehead ... Atrocious weather conditions throughout most of the day however morale high ... Mountain and Arctic Warfare cadre ... possible contact at 2000Z, Bluff Cove, turned out to be insertion of 2 Para ... (expecting) *Sir Galahad* (next).'

Four Rapier had been moved forward to cover Teal Inlet and Julian's advance. Jeremy, John Waters and I visited him that day when I could see for myself just how 'high-risk' the Teal Inlet operation was, and yet, although the LSL was to be overflown it was never attacked. Julian was pleased with the success of this logistic operation so far. His Deputy Chief of Staff, Gerry Wells-Cole, very proud of his arrangements, showed me all his stores lined up along the beaches and hidden under small cliffs or in Jackass penguin or rabbit burrows. The helicopters would use the LSL as a forward fuelling point while the remainder of the fuel was pumped into barrels and taken ashore and so each time an LSL returned to San Carlos it would be absolutely empty of everything, which was the correct use of a logistic ship. Now that Julian had his men on Mount Kent we were able to calculate that no LSL in Teal Inlet could be seen from any known enemy position. The ships were still at high risk and I gained increasing respect for their Captains who fully realized that only they could carry out such a vital but unwelcome task.

I enjoyed my tour with Gerry Wells-Cole and visit to *Sir Percivale*. It would perhaps have been wiser if I had also attended Jeremy's discussions with his Brigadiers so that I could have a better understanding of their military requirements and be in a better position in my new role to act as official interpreter of the military requirements and passer of such information to Sandy. I still expected Jeremy to speak direct to Sandy from time to time, however.

If there was to be a particularly significant day in the planning for the final phases of the ground war then it is probably the 3rd June. The Gurkhas were at Goose Green, having relieved 2 Para. The Scots and Welsh Guards were ashore at San Carlos awaiting orders and 3 Commando Brigade (less 40 Commando, plus 3 Para) were patrolling forwards from their mountain positions on the north flank while, on board *Fearless*, Jeremy's and my staffs discussed the move of 5 Infantry Brigade. In the medium term the Brigade was to consolidate at Fitzroy (with a battalion there and another forward to Bluff Cove) while the Brigade's FBMA was to be established at Fitzroy prior to an advance to catch up with 3 Commando Brigade on the defensive ring of hills held by the Argentinians to the west of Stanley. Early that morning the Commanding Officer of the Welsh Guards, Lieutenant-Colonel Johnny Rickett, received orders from his Brigade Commander (with whom, in my cabin that lunch time, I was about to discuss the possible move of his Brigade by sea) to march southwards that night.

Johnny Rickett returned to his battalion HQ on the northern reverse slope of Sussex Mountain and gave his own orders at, I now know, about the same time that I was preparing my 'intention signal' for their move by sea. By first light the following morning he was (according to his 'land-move' orders) to be at High Hill (five miles to the north-east of Darwin and overlooking the Darwin-Bluff Cove track). This was not such a tall order for it was just fifteen miles along muddy and rutted tracks which, if not always conducive to swift 'yomping', would at least aid navigation in the dark and unfamiliar landscape. Unaware of this decision I continued to plan, with Wilson's concurrence, to get the two Guards battalions forward by sea.

After lengthy discussions in the joint planning room on 3 June a scheme was worked out that would relieve 2 Para from the dangers of being cut off and one that would at the same time bring up two of 5 Brigade's battalions. I had earlier looked hard at Ewen's suggestion that he could save them some time and effort by lifting them in LCUs from Port Sussex down Brenton Loch but, unknown to me, as I have said above, Tony Wilson had ordered the Welsh to start that night, on foot, direct for High Hill.

Jeremy had wanted one of 5 Brigade's battalions to take over 40 Commando's garrison duties, but I was relieved when he decided that those left behind in San Carlos should be Royal Marines who were used to helicopter and landing craft drills as well as being experts in amphibious warfare. Jeremy and I and also, clearly, CTF remained concerned about what might be happening behind our backs on West Falkland; if we needed to carry out a *coup de main* or to pre-empt any enemy action these specialists would be needed. I also trusted them to defend my anchorage and to use my assets with intelligence, but I don't think that Malcolm Hunt (40 Commando's Commanding Officer) would ever quite forgive me if he knew that I supported Jeremy Moore's decision. I have little doubt that it was the correct one and not an easy one for Jeremy, a Royal Marine, to take.

On the assumption that the Welsh Guards (and the Scots) would have to be transported by sea I sent a warning signal to Sandy, *Intrepid*, *Sir Tristram* and others with my intentions, the opening sentence of which read: 'Intend landing 2 × Bn 5 Inf Bde in Bluff Cove area at first light 6th June.' I used the term 'Bluff Cove area' as a general description; the actual destination had yet to be ascertained. I went on to say that the plan was to embark the whole of the Scots Guards and half of the Welsh Guards in HMS *Intrepid*, plus a reduced Amphibious Beach Unit (ABU) and four LCUs and two LCVPs. *Sir Tristram* would take the remaining half battalion of the Welsh Guards, some Rapier, some of the Brigade's War Maintenance Reserve and a sixty-foot Mexeflote. *Intrepid* was to return to the San Carlos anchorage overnight of the 6th/7th, giving her just one day at anchor to unload herself and to use her LCUs to unload the LSL. After the LPD's departure *Sir Tristram* was to continue unloading with the Mexeflote and return during whichever night she was empty.

The signal asked the Carrier Battle Group to allocate two escorts, anti-aircraft co-ordination, CAP and NGS and I wanted all this in place off, or above, the anchorage at a time yet to be decided. I was, too, relying heavily on the weather remaining bad; indeed it was at that time so bad we still could not, even if we had wanted, get helicopters across from the north to the south to assist.

This was the first plan and, as can be seen, required the two ships to be at anchor in the forward area throughout just one day, 6 June, guarded by two escorts and a permanent CAP. To guarantee that we could land men and stores across an unmined beach I warned Chris Meatyard, an SBS team and Royal Engineer mine-disposal experts, to fly eastwards on the night of 4/5 June with the task of choosing a beach adjacent to each settlement (Fitzroy and Bluff Cove) and then check for mines below, within and above the inter-tidal zone. Until they produced results I could not advise the ships' captains where they should anchor.

Only the LSL could fit into Port Pleasant due to a shallow bar across each of the two entrances, but nowhere, Ewen thought, could she actually beach – and certainly not at Bluff Cove. LCUs could land at both settlements from the LPD anchored off Port Pleasant with one-way journeys of about four miles from each 'beach'. The recce team worked all that night and flew back on the 5th to report. It was the first of several days when we never saw Chris out of his diving suit.

In San Carlos with very little in the way of transport to carry their heavy weapons, food, ammunition and large packs, from which the Commanding Officer was determined his Battalion would not be parted, the Welsh Guards set off across the hill during the night of the 3rd/4th, as instructed by their Brigadier. The attempt was a failure and by dawn on the 4th, instead of being well on their way to Bluff Cove and the beleaguered 2 Para, the Guards Battalion was back in its water-filled trenches to the north of Sussex Mountain. The Scots Guards were still at San Carlos.

The events of 3 June were covered by Jeremy in his daily report much as he had done for the previous days. Tony Wilson was still receiving praise in public:

I am not sure we got our prayers right. The weather today was better than yesterday but not as much as I would have liked. However, I have every hope that we will be well balanced on our present line which, it is now apparent, is at the doorstep of the enemy's intended main line of resistance, by 6th June which you will recall was the forecast date. As always, a period of rapid movement is having to be followed by one of logistic consolidation … After his daring dash to Fitzroy and Bluff Cove [Commander 5 Infantry Brigade] must now draw up his formation as I mentioned yesterday. [Commander 3 Commando Brigade] is probing the main enemy position and I am totally in agreement with his policy of now making full and detailed recce and preparation before he begins … this. I visited 42 Commando Royal Marines on Mount Kent and had a beautiful view of Berkeley Sound and Moody Brook, though to my chagrin the cloud rolled over Port Stanley as I reached the summit. The men are in excellent heart. 45 Cdo have now been marching to the sound of guns for some 40 miles and will I hope get into the front line tomorrow.

The logistic balance remains on a knife edge but I am hopeful that now all the men and most of the equipment are ashore we will get past having continually to go on running to keep up with ourselves.

This was not very accurate (much of the equipment was still at sea and it was I who was having to 'draw up' 5 Brigade) but, importantly, it was probably what the politicians wanted to hear.

During the morning of 4 June I summoned my team to discuss the details of the plan for using one LPD and one LSL to move the Guards Battalions forward direct to Fitzroy from where one of them could march to Bluff Cove. I was aware that the bridge joining the two settlements had been blown by the fleeing enemy turning the land route between the settlements from a relative easy going, (as far as the ground was concerned) seven mile 'yomp' into a boggy fourteen miles. I was prepared, somehow, to try to put the first wave straight into Bluff Cove, but not any subsequent body of troops, as the enemy might then be alert.

This tied-in neatly with Tony Wilson's wishes. He assured me any LSL in Fitzroy, where he wanted to establish the Forward Brigade Maintenance Area (FBMA), would be hidden from prying eyes in the Stanley direction by a ridge of low hills. It all sounded more sensible.

News from the northern flank indicated that time was short for the southern flank to 'catch up'; the Commando Brigade 'Sitrep' for the 4th stated: 'Atrocious weather ... resulted in little more than survival being achieved,' and the same report warned the Brigade's own units that, outside their area things were beginning to happen: 'First light 6th June 2 Battalions 5 Infantry Brigade (will) land Bluff Cove Area from HMS *Intrepid*. LSL *Sir Tristram* to provide forward BMA support.'

While this was good news for the men in the mountains it did not stifle comments about the time it was taking 5 Brigade to move out of San Carlos, especially as there was no opposition on the ground and all they had to do was move through friendly territory. Nor were comments about the move out of San Carlos restricted to the men of the Commando Brigade. Out at sea Sandy Woodward feared for the state of his ships which had been at intensive operations away from any form of shore support (or rest) for over two months. CLFFI himself was anxious but for different reasons: he had set 6 June for attacking the outlying Stanley defences, a date that was becoming swiftly and increasingly unlikely.

The movement of combat supplies along the northern flank was going well and so far unhindered. Julian's 'sitreps' for the 2nd and 3rd had repeated his delight with the establishment of an increasingly well-stocked BMA at Teal Inlet and the ability of his men to probe and patrol forward with good logistic and medical support was evident. His one concern (apart from the lack of helicopters and 40 Commando which he confidently expected to be returned to his command in the very near future) was fuel. This was despite the fact that he had an LSL pumping fuel ashore at Teal for helicopters and, herself acting as a floating fuel bowser when in the area. It was being used up almost as fast as we could deliver. All this, of course, had great relevance to what was in my and Ian Baxter's mind as we considered the move along the south: if our re-supply arrangements worked so well and uninterrupted on the north they could probably be made to work at Fitzroy – but Teal had been a long-planned move, executed by Royal Marines.

For landing troops Bluff Cove was attractive to 5 Brigade as it was close to the enemy, but not right under their noses, and it was the 'right side' of the bridge that linked it with Fitzroy and the west. It was, however, recognized as too close to the enemy for a Forward Brigade Maintenance Area.

What I did not appreciate, to begin with, was the lack of understanding of joint operations by the army Brigade nor the near non-existent communications that were to dog that Brigade. The blame for much of this inefficiency should not be laid at the door of Tony Wilson and his staff. Delaying the despatch of these reinforcements on the assumption that any plan to recapture the Falkland Islands was bound to fail suggests that the Army staff did not want to be part of that presumed disaster in the first place. Secondly, when the Brigade was despatched it was without two of its three original major manoeuvre units; it had no logistic back-up and little significant training, and certainly none in joint Navy/Army or Amphibious operations. That they were to fight and not garrison in one of the most complicated of military roles in a sub-Antarctic winter must have been a disagreeable surprise to the Army staff.

The Chinook that 2 Para hijacked had been tasked to bring forward the Brigade's communications equipment, only to be diverted from this task to push the Paras forward. Bearing in mind all we tried to do and fix, it is very difficult to sympathize with Tony Wilson over this and subsequent events. Even his own attempts to sort out the communications mess ended in disaster when he despatched a helicopter forwards without telling anybody. It was shot down by a British frigate waiting for the nightly Hercules flight whose probable flight path was similar to that taken by the helicopter.

I must stress that what I had in mind to attempt was not a full-scale amphibious operation. We were about to execute a perfectly normal move of troops and assets along a coastline that was already in our hands using an LPD (which Northwood had arguably implied was expendable) and LSLs. No one from CTF's staff sought my views by secure voice, although almost every morning I told them my availability and intentions; but I did discuss the subject at length with Sandy and received his full support: he gave me the clear impression that he was fully committed if this was the only way. I had only agreed to use this method of getting the men forward on the assumption, firstly, that the weather would remain bad in our favour, secondly, that we would have full-time CAP, and thirdly, that the loss of a ship, if that were to occur, would not alter the course of the war, providing that she had been unloaded. I was left in no doubt of the urgency of Jeremy's request in view of the state of some of his troops who, though Arctic-trained, were beginning to show the signs of undue exposure and trench feet. He clearly felt a stalemate could occur if he did not keep the impetus going. This would be disastrous both militarily and politically.

On the 4th I reconsidered the plans in order to look at ways in which I could use two LSLs instead of one LPD and one LSL or, alternatively, how I could conduct the move without having the LPD in the area over daylight: as a result I cancelled my signal of the 3rd. The disadvantage of using just LSLs was the lack of suitable places where they could beach. They would therefore need LCUs and Mexeflotes to land their men and cargo: they can carry the Mexeflotes but somehow would have to be accompanied by the landing craft. The LPDs could carry their own LCUs and launch them; they could also steam over five knots faster than the LSLs. There were only two ways of getting LCUs to the area: one was in an LPD the other was by steaming them independently at 9 knots – out of the question over such a long distance unless they were carried some of the way in an LPD. Thus we could not avoid using an LPD for part of, if not the whole of, the operation.

In the meantime the Guards had tried to march and failed. Hesitant to involve the Royal Navy, and still disparaging of the military efforts ashore, Sandy told me that they were to try again ggesting, naively, that it should only take them forty-eight urs – not, of course, that it was his decision. It had already ken just two hours marching to convince the Welsh Guards officers that enough was enough with the equipment they had to carry and with, in effect, no transport. I had listened sympathetically to their account as their Second in Command wrung out and dried his sleeping bag in my cabin. As a result I tried to explain to Sandy that marching was out of the question and that it was now up to us sailors – as I had always feared that it would be.

This, once again, highlighted the difficulties of communication, personalities and, I suspect, rank. While Jeremy was delighted with his clear secure voice conversations with Northwood, I don't recall that he ever tried the naval DSSS system to speak to Sandy himself. Perhaps *Fearless*'s kit was exceptional but besides making it sound as if one was talking to someone who spoke like an agitated Dalek, it had the infuriating habit of either cutting out their voice or one's own. Conversations on subjects of considerable concern inevitably were made extremely difficult, needing on both sides an enormous degree of patience – a virtue that was in increasingly short supply.

I began to regret offering to try to act as a messenger between the two Two Star Officers who inevitably saw themselves, correctly, as senior in rank and probably found it difficult to accept that I was a co-equal CTG, responsible, like them, to the CTF for my decisions. Nothing of this nature was ever said and I had no intention of complaining at this late stage. I did not at the time feel the need for acting Two Star rank but it might have helped my staff if that had been the case. Staff Officers who take on the mantle of their bosses' rank are, unfortunately, not uncommon but they were not around in this campaign at this stage as far as I was aware. The Divisional Staff and mine seemed to be pulling well together and I heard no complaints of our relationships with CTF's or Sandy's staff. There were, hopefully, only a few more days to go before it would all be over.

Although anxious to help the soldiers out, I had never liked the idea of such a move forward by sea for the men and hoped that it could be avoided; as it couldn't, I had a further discussion with Ewen over the use of LCUs as far as Brenton Loch. This short distance from San Carlos would hardly be worth the effort and I knew his views on LSLs unloading at Fitzroy or Bluff Cove, neither place having an ideal beaching point for such a large ship. If LPDs (and thus LCUs) were not to be involved then LCVPs (which lifted just four tons or about twenty-five fully-equipped men) could be carried as deck cargo on the LSLs in addition to one, or even two (if they could be spared from San Carlos) Mexeflotes. Each LSL could also carry, or be met by, Sea Kings. During the 4th I gave my staff the problem. David Minords came back to me time and again refining the options until we were satisfied that there was no better way of achieving the object.

'Normal' life continued and it makes sense to take stock of our position on the eve of this penultimate phase. My staff log for the day gives a fair impression of what else we were worrying about and what else my staff and I were involved in:-

'Low cloud and fog again restricted ops outside TA. Little Argentine air over TA, however, at 1915Z four contacts detected over West Falkland (possible supply run) and four over East Falkland – 3 Commando Brigade reported 3 bombs dropped Green Settlement (sic). In San Carlos Water *Elk* and *Nordic Ferry* continued unloading – *Arrow/Avenger* topped up with 4.5 ammo. *Sir Percivale* loaded for support of 3 Commando Brigade at Teal Inlet and *Sir Tristram* loaded for future 5 Infantry Brigade operations. Repairs continued on *Sir Lancelot*. Due to the weather the survey of prizes/jetty/gun at Darwin not carried out. Four aircraft overflew TA at 2115Z and attacked Mount Kent. The aircraft were at high level and remained within Seadart envelope for twenty-five minutes and Seaslug for ten minutes – ideal Type 42 targets. Ashore, direct contact with the enemy. Very limited movement of 3 Commando Brigade support elements achieved. Similarly, limited deployment of 5 Brigade, 3 Commando Brigade and 42 Commando. Patrolling to establish location of minefields in Two Sisters area. 45 Commando reached position at Estancia

House. Only one gun of 29 Commando Light Regiment RA at
Bluff Cove so far. 1/7 Gurkha Rifles complete at Darwin.'

In addition to those ships mentioned above, in San Carlos were
Fearless, *Intrepid*, *Plymouth* and *Penelope* while *Sir Galahad* was
unloading the second LSL-load of stores into the Teal Inlet
FBMA. We were expecting the arrival of *Blue Rover* and *Sir
Geraint*, due to meet up to the north of Macbride Head at 0230
the following morning. The submarine *Onyx* came and went,
after re-briefing for new tasks.

At sea, the Tug, Repair and Logistic Area (TRALA) was
under command of HMS *Glamorgan* with responsibility for at
least twelve assorted repair ships, tugs, RFAs and STUFT, while
120 miles east of Stanley seventeen ships from Carriers to
STUFT waited in the fog. Although operational, the Harrier
Forward Operating Base had yet to be activated.

To return to the move of 5 Brigade: at 1015 on the 4th Sandy
signalled that, although he was 'As keen as anyone to finish the
job fast ... Argentines are unlikely to repeat D-Day mistake of
going for the escorts ... by all means plan on 6th June but be
prepared for indefinite delay for weather ... Consider more
robust plan might be to move troops forward by foot/helo ... and
provide logistic support by one/two relatively inconspicuous
LSLs as at Teal ... Extremely reluctant to interfere your business
and will provide escorts you wish, but suggest you reconsider
first.'

This was a slightly surprising signal as I had discussed the move
with him on the secure voice circuit without him raising any real
objection: he knew my preference for a helicopter approach for
the men but he also knew the impossibility of achieving this
while there was low cloud. I had made it quite clear that this was
not an amphibious operation *per se* but a sea-move forwards
between areas held by our own troops. I had confirmed that an
LPD would not be risked at close quarters to the enemy and that
the operation would only be conducted with low cloud. I
reminded him that the men would take longer on foot and the

weather was at that moment perfect for our needs. I saw his signal as another yardarm-clearer. Hopefully, it was simply a matter of the usual communications difficulties and misunderstandings that appeared to be inevitable when colleagues are miles apart.

Five and a half hours later a signal from CTF threw us into even more disarray and was based, probably, on new political considerations; it may, also have been influenced by separate conversations between Sandy and Northwood and Jeremy and Northwood. If anyone at Northwood had asked me they would have understood that I was not intending to conduct a major operation, as they seemed to think, and that I was not intending to put any ship at undue, or unacceptable, risk – but they chose not to!

CTF's signal suggested that we should scrap the Bluff Cove option and put the two battalions into Teal Inlet. His concerns covered just about every eventuality that can be faced in joint operations and as such they had a ring of unrealism about them. We were, he argued, going to be attacked by air and ground artillery and if that did not stop us we would be sunk by mines. Our view was that to put the two Guards battalions into Teal Inlet was 'out' for it did not solve the problem with 2 Para being out on a limb: nor was it 'on' from the helicopter fuelling point of view nor was it possible in the mist. Fitzroy, though, was out of range of the heaviest enemy guns that we knew of (one of Northwood's concerns). As 2 Para had not been attacked we believed it was safe from this threat and we were reasonably confident (but not certain) that mines did not exist. From the military point of view there was no room for yet two more major units on the northern flank.

That night Jeremy Moore and I both sent signals to Northwood explaining that the move by sea along the south was the only sensible and tactical method to get the two battalions forward. With that said, and without waiting for an answer, Jeremy's and my staffs made plans that *Intrepid* should sail east at dusk, launch her LCUs in two waves with a battalion in each wave, straight into Fitzroy. This would ensure that she would only be at sea and away from San Carlos in the dark. If she loitered where I hoped she would between waves then her LCUs would only have a run of about one hour, five minutes to offload, a run back of an hour, half an hour to re-load the second battalion and then a final dash back to the beach by dawn at the same time that their mother ship steamed westwards.

While all this was going on in the afternoon of the 5th we received a firm signal from CTF saying that no LPD was to be risked out of San Carlos in daylight as the loss of such a ship would force Ministers to parley for a cease-fire. (There seemed to be a great deal of defeatist talk everywhere but in San Carlos.) At 1654 that afternoon I signalled back that while I recognized the political views over the LPDs the less-than-satisfactory and more time-expensive alternative would be to use at least one, and preferably two, 'expendable' LSLs to which Admiral Fieldhouse replied that that would not be vetoed by the politicians. He ended his signal with the words, 'The man on the spot must decide'! As 'that man' I decided to send two LPDs totally in the dark and over two nights, but an LSL would be needed and it would have to stay in daylight.

CTF's signal appeared to surprise both Sandy and Jeremy with Sandy saying to me that he had just *eaten his hat* and Jeremy non-plussed. Both appeared fully to support my decision.

In anticipation of my first plan being acceptable to Northwood Colonel Ian Baxter had ordered the Scots and Welsh Guards to embark in *Intrepid* throughout 5 June. Now, with CTF's latest signal to hand I had to ask that the Welsh Guards went back to their slit trenches. The Scots remained afloat.

It was now late in the afternoon of 5 June and my mind was made up. What I intended was to give Jeremy and his men my fullest support by a once-only venture to get them out of the hole into which they had tripped. It would only become a high risk venture if the cloud base lifted sufficiently for fixed wing air attack and from what we knew in San Carlos that seemed reasonably unlikely.

To avoid the off-chance through mechanical failure (for instance) of an LPD being at sea during daylight we would now offload one battalion in one wave of four LCUs straight into Bluff Cove and not wait for the returning landing craft to collect the remaining battalion who would not now be on board. There would be no possibility of *Intrepid* being out of San Carlos by daylight and that accorded with CTF's instructions and 'the man on the spot's' decision. We would repeat the performance the next night with one LPD but this time only as far as Fitzroy. 5 Bde would then be balanced.

Sandy told me that there would be no frigates on the southern gunline; The Met Officer briefed us that he believed, with very limited information, that the weather was not expected to moderate and I decided that speed and vigilance in everything that night from start to finish was vital, for I did not expect the Argentines to repeat their D Day mistakes. I summoned Ewen Tailyour from his beach headquarters to *Fearless* where the staff put various questions to him before sending him up to my cabin. I explained that the risk of sailing LSLs around the coast by night was not a problem but the inevitable daylight offloading before sailing back on the second night was. What could he do with just his landing craft on an independent passage? In my cabin he told me, as he had done before, that he could take men as far as the upper reaches of Brenton Loch and while they then marched he would lay up his craft in creeks and sail back under cover of the second night; but we both agreed that that was only solving a third of the problem as far as distance forward was concerned and only half the problem as far as the numbers of men were concerned.

The General and his 'southern' Brigade Commander wanted the men – all of them – at Fitzroy and Bluff Cove. Ewen said he could not do that unless the LPDs were involved. I thanked him by telling him that he had finally confirmed that the actions I and Divisional Headquarters were taking were the only ones that would solve the problem. He left for his beach, rather disappointed, I thought, at not being involved.

We planned for *Sir Tristram* to top-up with aviation fuel and to continue loading with Rapier firing points and Rapier and gunner ammunition to the level that could be unloaded in one day. Unfortunately in the event the Rapier firing points could not be lifted down from the hilltops because of the low cloud. She was also ordered to lift the Army's 16 Field Ambulance but they were disorganized ashore and failed to get there. These delays kept David Minords and my staff frantically busy. They also prevented us from sailing the LSL that night with *Intrepid*, and when she did sail the next night in company with *Fearless* she still did not have the Field Ambulance Team (surprisingly, still disorganized) nor the Rapier firing points. These were now to come on a second (originally unplanned) LSL, the *Sir Galahad*.

So the operation was 'on' with just one LPD (plus one LSL, if she was ready) during the night of the 5th/6th and with another LPD (plus the LSL if she had not been able to sail with *Intrepid*) the next night. The object was to deliver the Scots Guards to Bluff Cove on night one and everything else to Fitzroy the second night. I studied in detail the only two threats we, assuming the low cloud continued, thought existed: shore-based Exocet and air attack. Air attack we thought unlikely in the forecast weather conditions and, anyway, the first LSL in would be carrying sufficient Rapier – at least that had been the plan, but, as we have seen, cloud and delays generated by the Field Ambulance were to prevent this happening.

Somewhere at this stage Sandy put forward in a low classification signal the idea of steaming all six LSLs in through the narrows, at the entrance to Stanley Harbour, to land direct on to the Stanley waterfront as they were expendable. It was inevitably received by the LSLs and did little for their morale. We had to convince several of them that it was not a serious suggestion and certainly not one to which the Division or I would agree.

As far as the land-launched Exocet was concerned, intelligence suggested that there was an arc out from the coast south of Stanley Common within which this weapon could be aimed, but it was not something I took too seriously. I hoped that by creeping up the eastern edge of Lively Island there was every chance that the missile would be distracted by the coast if not by the chaff decoys fired by the LPDs. Being of shallower draught, an LSL could take a safe passage from south of Elephant Island to an anchorage off Fitzroy in Port Pleasant. This was perfectly possible, while at the same time keeping clear of the Exocet limits.

I expected *Intrepid* to take one of these courses but I knew that Peter Dingemans held the view that the LPD was a major war vessel and, as such, carried much the same political weight as an aircraft carrier. During my briefing for his night's task he had challenged me with the opinion that an LPD was too high risk to lose. I had gone through all the arguments many many times with Jeremy's and my own staff and the only risks I knew of were two enemy patrol craft (one was beached and the other holed up in Stanley), mines (which would affect the LCUs and LSLs not the LPD which could stand off-shore) and the weather suddenly changing for the better (not forecast) if he was still to be at sea in daylight (unlikely).

I replied that their Lordships 'Ought to be a damned-sight more unamused if we failed at this late hour to win the land battle and therefore only achieved a political stalemate because the Navy did not try and help.' Going through my mind was the not impossible thought that one good air attack in San Carlos could see the end of one or both LPDs in a matter of minutes. It was therefore wise to use them fully. The aim was still to repossess Stanley as quickly as possible.

All was now in place for the move of the two battalions. To navigate the LCUs from their launch position Ewen was again summoned from his beach, this time to be briefed by my SOO and GSO1. He was to travel in *Intrepid*, take the Scots Guards from the vicinity of Elephant Island to Bluff Cove, wait a day ashore with his boats then rendezvous with *Fearless* the second night at the same place – south of Elephant Island – and take the Welsh Guards to Fitzroy.

Later that afternoon I spoke at length to Sandy on the secure telephone and briefed him on the details: I was not seeking permission for the moves other than approval to pass my ships and craft through an area which he controlled. While he voiced the view that he still thought the Guards should march the distance in two days I disagreed, at the same time pointing out that no LPD would be out of San Carlos Water in daylight. I emphasized that the subsequent use of an LSL in Port Pleasant was a risk that we could unfortunately afford bearing in mind that the ship should not be seen from the Argentine hill-top observation points and that, additionally, we would achieve surprise while the weather remained foul. Any escorts supplied would return by night for, with so much land clutter, a frigate, unable to use its main armamant against aircraft, would merely be an additional target if it stayed in the area. A frigate's presence in the area in daylight would be hard to hide as it could do no good hiding under a cliff and could increase the Argentine conviction that a major landing was taking place.

To assist that night's other operations Sandy had earmarked HMSs *Cardiff, Yarmouth, Active* and *Arrow* to provide naval gunfire support for the 3rd Commando Brigade's night attack. This attack was postponed at 1600 by CLFFI who signalled his decision to, among others, the Carrier Battle Group at 1615; unfortunately Sandy did not appear to receive this cancellation and waited until 1940 to confirm that his ships were still needed. Shortly after this, the original signal was received in the Carrier Battle Group Flagship causing Sandy to order the withdrawal of two of his frigates at the same time allowing *Cardiff* and *Yarmouth* (already on their way) to continue to their station off Fitzroy (clear of the Exocet arc) as 'on call' NGS ships with the added and secondary task of keeping an eye out for any C-130 blockade runners. Unfortunately, during my telephone call Sandy confirmed, and promised, that there would be no ships in the area and, so suitably assured, I passed this news on to Peter Dingemans. I thought no more of it assuming that *Intrepid*, her LCUs and her own escorts, would be alone at sea that night off Lively Island with no risk of a blue on blue engagement.

In the event this was not so. The frigates had apparently already sailed by the time we spoke and, with all the other things that were happening, were not briefed about our venture. Sandy was uncharacteristically contrite when I spoke to him next day.

One snippet I did learn from Sandy that day was that he was

withdrawing *Hermes* further to the east for a routine boiler clean. While it was not my place to comment I did think it was a strange time to remove the largest 'airfield' we had in the war at such a critical time. He must have appreciated how badly we would need close air support and CAP over the next few days if the cloud-base lifted. He was possibly, quite simply, taking no chances on a longer term view.

On another topic relevant to frigate operations on the southern flank, Captain Hugo White of HMS *Avenger* agreed with me that night to enter Albemarle Harbour and investigate its use with a view to it being promulgated as an emergency hiding place. As he was due to carry out NGS duties into Fox Bay I agreed. We had considered Albemarle a likely safe haven for any LSL on the southern route that might be caught out at dawn or for a frigate delayed by engaging the enemy: it was deep-sided, narrow and winding and would give good, natural protection from air attacks. After *Avenger* had fired 133 high explosive shells and 38 starshells into Fox Bay her Lynx carried out a thermal-image recce to a ten-mile radius around Albemarle and, with no signs of enemy, she entered for a peaceful night with just the stars visible above the near crests. As a direct result I signalled my ships to consider using it as a bolt-hole or to prolong patrols around West Falkland.

This caused a small eruption. Sandy signalled that ships should not use it. This was the first and, if I recall correctly, the only occasion when he countermanded my orders. I did not agree with him and he had not consulted me. It was clearly better for the LSLs to know I was concerned for them and if they had to use it then I would probably have time to place a frigate to cork the bottle and provide some protection. I decided quietly to ignore Sandy's signal. I was in control of this area and would accept any consequences.

CHAPTER EIGHT

THE PRIZE

If anyone wishes to know the history of this war, I will tell them that it is our maritime superiority gives me the power of maintaining my army while the enemy are unable to do so.

The Duke of Wellington 1769–1852
Rear-Admiral T. Byam Martin reporting from the
Creole, *at sea, September 21, 1803, to Lord Keith, a*
conversation he had with the Duke.

THE STAFF LOG for the 5th reads:

'Early morning high-level bombing raid preceded a day in which the weather improved sufficiently to allow helos to try and catch up on inland tasks. Two battery lifts and redeployment of Rapier Troop in support of 3 Cdo Bde were achieved. However becoming obvious that political restraints, weather and military situation would necessitate the use of LCUs/LSLs for movement of Guards to Bluff Cove. To this end preparations for loading *Sir Tristram* principally with ammo were made: overnight 5th/6th *Intrepid* carried Scots Guards to Lively Island and then inserted them to Bluff Cove via LCUs. In San Carlos Waters FOB became operational during daylight hours and *Nordic Ferry/Elk* continued offload. *Sir Galahad* finished and *Sir Percivale* started offloading at Teal. *Exeter* arrived in TA to assume AAW duties.'

Jeremy Moore's sitrep for the same period suggested:

'A rather better day from the weather point of view so more progress was achieved with our flying programme ... I held a council of war with my Brigade Commanders ... we will make good use of the time while we build up our stocks to support offensive ops ... Life is returning to normal in parts of the Falklands ... in Lafonia today the rams were taken out to be put to the ewes some three or four weeks late.'

Intrepid sailed at 2030 on the 5th in company with HMS *Penelope* (Commander Peter Rickard) keeping loose station between two and three miles ahead. This duo was joined by HMS *Avenger*, ordered to make a fast passage even further ahead to bombard the Sea Lion Island air strip and generally keep the enemy from observing the movement forwards of the Scots Guards. I ordered the newly arrived *Exeter*, under Captain Hugh Balfour, to take up an anti-aircraft station also in the vicinity of Sea Lion Island. *Penelope* was in charge of co-ordinating the defence of the force until all were safely back in San Carlos, hopefully, by dawn. While the weather in San Carlos had improved it was basically a slight lifting of the cloud base sufficient for helicopter operations. Further east we, in San Carlos Water, believed that the cloud base was still likely to be lower.

In *Intrepid* Peter Dingemans opted for radio silence with no HF transmission while using radar only for navigation, and then strictly only when essential. A brief scare occurred ten minutes after the LPD sailed with three air contacts thirty nautical miles north-west but seven minutes later these were classified as spurious and the ships reverted to Air Raid Warning Yellow: the LPD relaxed from action stations to defence watches with just her port Bofors 40/60 mounting manned. (Facing the shore: port outward-bound – starboard homeward-bound – POSH!)

The journey to the LCU launch position was uneventful although there were a number of very minor alarms that kept the four warships on their toes. Vehicle lights ashore were spotted from *Intrepid* at 2120 and two minutes later *Avenger* reported lights and radar transmissions from an unidentified ship inshore, later confirmed as the Argentine hospital ship *Bahia Paraiso* which we had 'checked out' earlier. As I said at the time, while she may have been innocent as far as hospital ship duties were concerned I was suspicious that she was fulfilling a less legal role as a naval-manned vessel; she should not have been where she was, able to spot any traffic down the Sound for, by an agreement made, she should have sailed during that day for the open sea. It is probable that she reported the movement of the British warships down Falkland Sound that night allowing the Argentine command to make some not-very-difficult guesses. I doubt, however, if she could have identified the ships.

As *Intrepid* approached the southern entrance to the Sound, *Avenger* was sent further east to carry out her Naval Gunfire Support shoot. At 2130 the LPD was illuminated by what appeared to be a Tiger Cat fire control radar in the Carcass Bay area. However no enemy reaction was noted and by 0020 she had Sea Lion Island twenty miles on her port bow. We had been concerned that a Pucara and radar site were stationed on the Island, but there was no reaction and thus no proof. If there had been, *Avenger* was there to sort it out. This incident highlights a constant problem of the ships operating close to the Falkland Islands where there appeared to be unpredictable ducting of radar. This meant that many detections were made of Argentine radars at much greater ranges than would normally be expected. They had, of course, still to be inspected and checked out before they could be discounted.

Shortly after midnight a radar detection assumed to be a C-130 was reported in range, but *Penelope* was instructed not to engage with her 4.5 inch guns for fear of revealing the operation. The aircraft returned at 0103 on its way back to the mainland unmolested.

Peter Dingemans was in charge of the overall operation and had been personally briefed by me. He had clearly felt that the operation was somewhat risky, but I felt that he had not been involved in the day-to-day decisions of my Task Group where frigates and merchant ships were sailing every night and taking similar risks without such an important mission. I expected him to launch the landing craft not more than about four hours' steaming away from Bluff Cove, but exactly where he was to launch them I left to him to decide, depending on his view of the situation.

While providing close support for the group as a whole, I did not wish the escorts to go inshore with the LCUs as they were at considerable risk from Exocet and would almost certainly have drawn attention to the landing craft. Ewen, unfortunately, had not had such a full brief and had not had time to collect his own highly detailed charts from his tent ashore at San Carlos.

Peter dropped the four laden LCUs two miles off the west-south-west coast of Lively Island at 0230Z. On parting Peter confirmed to Ewen that there were no ships on the gunline that night and therefore no need for him to know the night's recognition signal. Surprisingly, he appears not to have given Ewen a launch position from which he could start his navigation. The weather at that moment was calm with low visibility, forcing the small flotilla to head, first, to the north-east to get a firm position from the nearest point of the Island before retracing its tracks southwards down the western edge of the two-mile kelp bank that extends off Reef Point. Only then could they turn to the east and, eventually, north-east.

Intrepid steamed quickly westwards with her escorts for a reasonably trouble-free return, enlivened only by the sighting of shell-fire ashore at 0407. *Penelope* was refused permission first to search Sea Lion Island for enemy aircraft and then again when she requested to search ahead. Peter was concerned lest the helicopter gave away their intentions. The LPD was back at her anchorage at 1027 just an hour after the Scots Guards landed at Bluff Cove drenched but at least safe and in the right place.

That morning I was about to fly off with Jeremy Moore to get a clearer idea of his requirements when Peter requested a meeting in my cabin; before I could reply that it was inconvenient he arrived on board in a rather agitated state to tell me that we were taking too great a risk with expensive ships like LPDs. I tried to explain Jeremy's and my reasons, not least of all that the General wanted all in place for the first attacks (now on the 9th) and that until the new Brigade was in the front line the physical

301

condition of the troops in the mountains would continue to deteriorate. I hoped that he understood this and that, in my view, there was a far greater risk to both LPDs as they lay in San Carlos Water in daylight under threat of air attack – but their presence was essential to the rapid offload of either 3 Commando Brigade's or 5 Brigade's store. I didn't like it but I had no choice if we were not to create delays by taking council of our worst fears. Our job was now to support the soldiery as best we could and his ship had not been at great risk. He had clearly had a very worrying night and two weeks in San Carlos was proving a strain. Privately I was far more concerned for the LSLs which would have to move forward and be there in daylight. The LPDs had well-trained teams and damage control experts and should have been able to absorb the odd bomb. This was not the case for the LSLs.

I too had remained up for most of the night until *Intrepid* was halfway home. There had been worrying reports of high-level flights which seemed to be reconnaissance but could have been bombing missions. Later we were to discover they had aircraft fitted with sideways-looking radar and this may be what they were up to. But so far the operation appeared to be going satisfactorily.

Throughout the 6th *Sir Tristram* continued to load with ammunition as requested by the Divisional staff. The four Rapier firing points and 16 Field Ambulance, Royal Army Medical Corps, plus gunner ammunition were directed to move on board but the weather continued to prevent the Rapier firing points from being lifted by helicopter and the Field Ambulance could still not get ready in time – which I considered a poor show as they had had plenty of notice. My orders to the staff had been to mirror the routine carried out with the Teal Inlet re-supply where the LSLs would only load with what could be unloaded in one day – thus lessening the chances of an OP observing, reporting and planning a raid for a second day. On this occasion *Sir Tristram* was well-laden; someone, I suspected later, had calculated that there would be more LCUs with which to offload her at Fitzroy than was ever available in Teal. They should have known, however, that I was about to remove four LCUs at the first opportunity (the night of the 7th/8th), and that we knew the beaches at Fitzroy were extremely limited in their ability to accept landing craft and loads.

With *Intrepid* back in San Carlos we now had to execute the planned move of the Welsh Guards. My last orders to Ewen had been to lie up his four *Intrepid* craft during the day at Bluff Cove before sailing to meet *Intrepid* again at a point just south of Elephant Island. *Fearless* was due to sea to refuel but Jeremy Larken, having heard of his sister ship's reluctance to go further east than Lively Sound, offered to take the next load. I agreed. So the plan was to offload two of *Fearless*'s pre-laden LCUs south of Elephant Island, bring in two of *Intrepid*'s LCUs, load these two and send the four inshore to Fitzroy. We would bring back to San Carlos the remaining two empty boats out from Bluff Cove. The four landing craft would then have a run of just twelve miles back in to Fitzroy and not, definitely not, Bluff Cove. Jeremy Larken assured me that he would be at the rendezvous point with Ewen at 0200.

My staff log for 6 June only tells a part of the story but continues to highlight what else we remained responsible for:

'Weather clamped down again over TA and inland restricting helo ops; no Argentinian air activity. The FOB was unusable due to the weather and only one CAP and one GR3 sortie all day. However there was no Argentine air/sea activity. Unloading *Elk*/*Nordic Ferry* continued. *Sir Tristram* completed load, *Sir Geraint* continued to load [for Teal]. *Sir Galahad* continued waiting to load. *Sir Percivale* unloading at Teal. *Sir Lancelot* repairing. *Blue Rover* fuelled *Elk*/*Plymouth* alongside but weather precludes *Fearless* and *Intrepid* refuelling at anchor. Support helo availability remains high although torrential rain is causing blade damage which is being contained. Overnight *Cardiff*, *Yarmouth*, *Avenger* fired 640 rounds into Bluff Cove area. *Argonaut* departed for UK. Overnight *Sir Tristram* to Fitzroy. Also *Fearless* attempted to land 1 WG at Bluff Cove but LCUs failed the R/V.'

Unannounced on the evening of the 6th, Ewen appeared on

board by Sea King direct from Bluff Cove to de-brief us on his previous night's adventures with the Scots Guards and to confirm the arrangements for the coming night: he was anxious to make sure one or two episodes were not repeated! Most of what he had to say was new to us but the staff were able to pacify him with details of gun-line ships, call-signs, recognition signals and, best of all from the Welsh Guards' point of view, Jeremy Larken's confirmation that Elephant Island would be the launching point.

In contrast to *Intrepid*'s return to San Carlos, we learnt that the LCUs' journey to Bluff Cove had been full of incident, not least of all having to complete this complicated passage from an uncertain start point, with no large-scale charts, with a probable compass error in excess of 30°, with an intermittent, unreliable and often unserviceable radar set and without log or depth sounder, apart from a lead line. They had been fired upon or possibly bombed from an unknown source before being starshelled by HMS *Cardiff* who had steamed unexpectedly out of the darkness thinking that they might be enemy patrol craft. She had drawn close, ordered the LCUs to heave-to (which they eventually did having at one stage decided to try and make a dash for shallower water) before flashing the single word '*Friend*'. This caused Ewen (believing that there were no friendly ships in the area) to reply, '*To which side?*' *Cardiff* did not answer and left the LCUs to continue their hideous voyage alone but now enlivened by gale force winds and heavy seas. They reached Bluff Cove at dawn with all hope of surprise, or even concealment that this move had taken place, destroyed by the frigates.

What nobody knew at the time was that earlier in the night *Cardiff* had detected an unidentified aircraft flying eastwards along the south of the Wickham Heights following the presumed flight path of the enemy C-130s. Having been given no indication of friendly air (or sea) movements and in accordance with his orders to intercept any C-130 that flew this route, Mike Harris (*Cardiff*'s captain) quite correctly engaged it with a Sea Dart missile. Later, when the LCUs were spotted, Mike decided (apparently on the toss of a coin) to check first this time – hence the starshells. For 600 men afloat in tiny, open, flat-bottom landing craft it had been an anxious seven hours.

While I was glad that the first insertion had been success___, despite some major misunderstandings, I was concerned that a number of factors had nearly combined to prevent this. What annoyed me immensely was that the craft had been dropped short by *Intrepid* and then 'sharpened up' by *Cardiff*, who, I had been informed, would definitely not be in the area. A horrendous blue-on-blue had only marginally been avoided.

But what failed to impress me more was the apparent lack of any communication either between my Flagship (which contained Jeremy's Divisional Headquarters) and parts of 5 Brigade: nor did the Brigade have communications forward from its own Headquarters at Goose Green to its units in the front. For instance, we were unaware for some time that the Army Scout helicopter was missing, and when we did eventually know, Jeremy asked me to see if any of the ships knew why. As a result we heard via Sandy that it had been shot down by *Cardiff* as it had been carrying forward, unknown to everyone except 5 Brigade, the Brigade Signals Officer with a relay station to sort out their communications mess.

I sent a happier Ewen back to Bluff Cove at dusk, expecting to see him again two hours after midnight (local time). Then, during my evening briefing with Sandy on the secure voice system, I asked why his ships had been on the gun line and briefed him on what we were now hoping to achieve.

Sandy's sitrep for the 6th mentioned *Cardiff*, *Avenger* and *Yarmouth* firing 640 rounds into the Bluff Cove area.

My sitrep to my own Task Group covering the twenty-four hours up to midday on the 6th was comprehensive:

'Both 3 Cdo Bde and 5 Bde have moved forward to invest Port Stanley. 3 Cdo Bde are being re-supplied by LSL through Teal Inlet ... and then ... by helicopter. This has been a most successful operation. The LSLs have not been molested by ... air or ... mines or patrol craft. 3 Cdo Bde ... now hold all ground from Mount Challenger through Kent to Long Island Mount and then east to Mount Low ... ready to attack when gun batteries with lots of ammo have caught up or been placed near Beagle Ridge and so be in a position to fire on selected targets in Stanley and its airfield.

'Main problem is getting 5 Bde forward into battle. Scots Guards landed last night ... Welsh Guards hopefully tonight with Gurkhas following. First LSL moves to Bluff Cove (area) tonight to start logistic support so that 5 Bde can advance on southern route ... Argentines ... possibly reinforcing West Falkland for political ends ... Not enough of us to chase them out while taking Stanley ...

'[Harriers] and nearly forty helicopters drink vast quantities of Avcat despite lousy flying weather. Tankers now common feature in San Carlos ...

'Any masters or captains who can spare time more than welcome to visit to get latest picture ... Military state clear but politically foggy and tending to gyrate ... Hang on tight we are actually doing very well but regrettably LSL's masters in particular need patience and perspicacity in large heaps as comms and telecomms not always sound and reliance must be placed on telepathy.'

While communications with the LSLs were poor for lack of equipment, it was even worse for ships like *Norland* where her Senior Naval Officer, Commander Chris Esplin-Jones received his instructions for a rendezvous on a bar chit lowered from a helicopter. While he made the meeting successfully, this incident shows the extent to which my staff had to go in order to control some of the ships. The daily situation report (SITREP) that I sent to my Task Group was an attempt to keep them up-to-date and ensure their morale remained high, but it was also the only means some of them had to work out where they might be needed next, hence telepathy!

Despite the possibility of the reinforcement in the Fitzroy area being compromised, the move of the Welsh Guards had to take place by sea if we were to make the General's start day of 9 June. With Argentinian activity the night before at a low level, and with no sign of mines, Jeremy Larken was prepared to take his ship further north and east to give the LCUs a short run round the corner into Port Pleasant and Fitzroy, still a risk worth taking providing the weather remained in our favour. During that evening the Welsh Guards were called on board *Fearless* and she sailed at 1930 with HMSs *Penelope* and *Avenger*, the latter was sent ahead to land an SBS party on Sea Lion Island where they were to find no signs of radar stations nor enemy aircraft. The LSL *Sir Tristram* followed at 2300 for Port Pleasant, which she entered before dawn. On board she carried a Mexeflote, Rapier and gunner ammunition and a few men for 5 Brigade's FBMA. For the reasons mentioned earlier, she was still not carrying the Rapier firing posts nor the Field Ambulance.

The agreed rendezvous position two miles south of Elephant Island was reached in clearing weather at 0250 with no sign of the LCUs from Bluff Cove. The two frigates and *Penelope*'s Lynx searched ahead and inshore but found nothing. We were then faced with a quandary: *Fearless* had embarked the only two LCUs available in San Carlos on the assumption that another two would meet us to take that half of the battalion that could be swiftly loaded, while *Fearless*'s two were pre-loaded with the heavy gear. Thus the Guardsmen and their equipment that were ready to sail were: Battalion Headquarters, Number Two Company, Recce Platoon, Anti-Tank Platoon, Machine-Gun Platoon, four communications Land Rovers and trailers, one section of Royal Engineers, various stores and compo rations.

The remaining two rifle companies and the Mortar Platoon, being lightly equipped, were ready to embark quickly into the two LCUs for which we were waiting: Jeremy Larken knew that he had to sail for San Carlos by 0415.

At about 0100 we received by a roundabout route a somewhat garbled signal from Ewen saying that the weather inshore was so bad that the LCUs were unable to sail to make the rendezvous. This contrasted with the rather pleasant conditions at sea. While *Fearless* waited for the landing craft either to appear from Bluff Cove or signal more positive news, Johnny Rickett sought the Divisional Commander to tell him that he was not happy with sending only half his battalion ashore, and, if only one half could go, it was the wrong half that was loaded in the LCUs. Jeremy Moore reassured him. 'Don't worry. I'll get the other half to Bluff Cove tomorrow night.'

In the Amphibious Operations Room, Major Guy Yeoman was told to call his assistant, Major Tony Todd, from his well-earned night's sleep to navigate the two LCUs inshore in Ewen's absence. Guy and Tony had both been flat out in San Carlos involved with the immediate offload of shipping and loading of *Sir Tristram* and had not been part of the planning group. When Guy heard the Welsh Guards wanted to go to Bluff Cove he briefed Tony Todd accordingly without, in his haste, checking, as he had not been informed that I had agreed with the Divisional Staff and Tony Wilson that I would only take them as far as Fitzroy Settlement. Tony Todd took his two LCUs which had been largely emptied of stores and loaded with two Companies of Welsh Guards in clear weather and with a satellite navigation set. For the first few of the nineteen miles they were escorted by HMS *Avenger*, sailing at 0415 and landing at 0700 without incident.

Meanwhile the LPD and two frigates had had to sail for San Carlos while *Penelope* was detached to deploy her helicopter in a search for the 'missing' LCUs. It scanned the coast from Elephant Island to Port Harriet but with no sign of them nor any enemy.

Apart from this one signal none of us knew the real reasons why the four *Intrepid* LCUs had failed to make the rendezvous but we were soon to learn part of the story. It would take several years before the full picture could be achieved. When Ewen returned by helicopter to Bluff Cove from San Carlos that night before (the 6th) he had found the gale still blowing and only one landing craft sheltering under the lee of White Point. Of the others there was no sign. In fact three had been 'hijacked' in his absence by a Parachute Regiment major briefly brandishing a pistol (the cox'ns preferring to stay put in accordance with Ewen's last orders) and sailed to Fitzroy (without charts or maps) taking 2 Para with them. The weather, which had moderated slightly, then worsened again making any return to

Bluff Cove for that night's operation impossible. As there were no reliable communications between Fitzroy and Bluff Cove nor between either of these places and *Fearless* none of us knew that the craft would not be able to meet us. Ewen, finding just one LCU sheltering offshore and unable to contact any of the others, had no choice but to send a signal via the Scots Guards (who could sometimes speak to the Gurkha Battalion – and even that was not guaranteed) saying that the weather was so bad he doubted (he was no more positive than that) that he would make the RV. Of course his unspoken reason was that he had no craft anyway but was hoping that by 'his' departure time from Bluff Cove to make the RV they would have shown up from whatever task or sheltering they were engaged in. That had to be by midnight to make Elephant Island but by that time none had materialized and Ewen had been obliged to remain ashore.

The Scots Guards could speak neither to their own FBMA nor their Brigade HQ at Fitzroy; if they had they could have told Ewen part of the story and a more positive signal might have been sent to Jeremy and me. If that signal had been received before we sailed from San Carlos we could not have brought more LCUs with us (there were now four in the Fitzroy/Bluff Cove area, two in Teal Inlet and two in *Fearless* – there were none remaining in San Carlos) but we might have had time to alter the load of the two we were to send ashore.

Shortly after dawn on the 7th, and now empty, the two *Fearless* LCUs sailed for Fitzroy from Bluff Cove to join the original four in unloading the newly-arrived *Sir Tristram*.

There were now, to my concern, six LCUs in the Fitzroy/Bluff Cove area and I wanted four of them back in San Carlos so that the offload of 5 Brigade stores could continue. Ships had been brought in to San Carlos for exactly this reason and now they were likely to have to sit there in daylight with only the air attacks to wait for – not pleasant or good. By sending *Intrepid* along the south coast, empty, to collect her LCUs and by loading *Sir Galahad* with the vital Rapier Firing Points and Field Ambulance plus the Mortar Platoon and two rifle companies of Welsh Guards there should have been enough landing craft (plus the

Mexeflote) to offload in Port Pleasant, remembering that I expected *Sir Tristram* to be empty and on her way to San Carlos at dusk. To help position the Rapier firing posts I sent a Sea King with *Sir Galahad*.

During the 7th the Welsh Guards were moved from *Fearless* to the LSL. They were indeed being messed about and I had full sympathy for them and their predicament, a sympathy that would have lasted but for the extraordinary behaviour of the men once afloat. Many of Jeremy Larken's sailors had moved out of their mess-decks in order that the soldiers might have a good rest on their way to and back from Elephant Island, only to find that this kindness was repaid by obscene vandalizing of the sailors' kit and in many instances of their private letters secured in their lockers. This was an unfortunate repeat of a similar event which had taken place while an LSL had been emptied and was having her bomb defused. In this case it was members of the Commando Logistic Regiments who should certainly have known better. Jeremy Moore was distressed enough to ask whose side they were on.

Earlier I had escaped the confines of my cabin and the Operations Rooms to wander around the tank decks to talk to the Guardsmen, many of whom were very young. They were surprised to hear that I was the equivalent to a Brigadier since Brigadiers apparently do not speak to private soldiers, but at one stage our conversation was broken up by two senior NCOs who told the guardsmen not to talk to me. It was a revealing incident that contrasted dramatically with the behaviour of *Antelope*'s ship's company when I went down to talk to them. This, to me, highlighted, once more, the vast differences between the naval and military.

As with *Sir Tristram*'s loading, *Sir Galahad*'s did not go as well as it should have done, but at least (and at last) we were able to get the Rapier firing points afloat. The wretched Field Ambulance, on their second attempt, was not embarked until seven hours after the Guardsmen. The Rapier's and Field Ambulances' destination was definitely Fitzroy which tied in with my instruction to Captain Phil Roberts of *Sir Galahad* to go no further than

310

Port Pleasant. There she might find *Sir Tristram* who should, by then, be empty. I have to say I was extremely reluctant to use *Sir Galahad* as she had survived some unexploded bombs and I felt she had had enough. Unfortunately for her, she was in San Carlos, just emptied and ready to join Sandy well to the east, when the need for an LSL arose. There was none other available.

At about 2030 that evening I received a signal from *Sir Tristram* saying that she would still be unloading throughout the daylight hours of the 8th and, thus, implying that she would still need some of the LCUs for part of the next day. This conflicted with my order that *Intrepid* would sail that night (7th/8th) to collect her LCUs, but the beaches were not good and she was therefore unlikely to be able to use all six together, so the collection made sense.

In the meantime, disturbed by the delays and the conflicting destinations demanded by his passengers, Phil Roberts asked me for a twenty-four-hour delay to his sailing of *Sir Galahad*, or, at least, firm clarification of his route. As I knew she could make Fitzroy by dawn and, as I had no reason not to believe that the visibility had not remained suitably poor, I told her to sail immediately for the settlement, a destination agreed by the Divisional staff and asked for by Tony Wilson. I was not aware, then, that the first half of the Welsh Guards had been taken direct to Bluff Cove by Tony Todd on Guy Yeoman's instructions.

Sir Galahad sailed later than I would have wished, at 0200, but arrived one hour before dawn to anchor two cables east of *Sir Tristram* in Port Pleasant.

All of this was of course only a small part of the activity being orchestrated by my staff over this period and it would be wrong, therefore, for this essentially quite 'normal' but disconcertingly exasperating move of two battalions to mask the other work being undertaken.

My staff diary for 6 June was full of military abbreviations. It explained that at Teal Inlet *Sir Percivale* was unloading, with her relief, *Sir Geraint*, loading at San Carlos: no problems there. Also loading in the TA was *Norland* with 491 prisoners of war, while *Elk* continued her lengthy task of ridding herself of gunner ammunition. There were no air attacks against either my ships or the troops ashore, although one high-flying Lear jet approaching on a reconnaissance mission with its side-ways looking radar, was engaged by HMS *Exeter's* Sea Dart and 'splashed' a few minutes after midday. The remains were later found on Pebble Island. I was in the Ops Room listening to Hugh Balfour's comments as he waited to engage the aircraft with his missile. We had managed to discover the Argentinian aircraft's frequency and I was horrified to hear the aircrew's screams as they plummeted to earth. Not one of us in the Ops Room enjoyed the experience, but war is war.

Hermes was cleaning her boilers and, with the rest of the Carrier Battle Group over 160 miles to the east and outside the TEZ, there were numerous gaps in the CAP cover despite the use of HMS *Sheathbill*.

Three of the trawlers converted to the mine-sweeping role entered the Exclusion Zone on their way to San Carlos bringing the number of ships under my operational control to twenty-six. We were anxious to employ the trawlers, as we could not be entirely happy bringing naval gunfire support ships into waters that had not been swept. I had always to take a rather more phlegmatic approach to the possibility of mines and had had to overrule my MCD Adviser, Chris Meatyard, who continued to maintain that certain sea approaches could be mined waters. I had largely had to ignore the possibility of mines on D Day and during our opening up of Salvador Waters and, indeed, for our advance along the south coast via the waters around Lively Island and Ports Pleasant and Fitzroy. I held the belief that a single pass of a frigate down Falkland Sound did not prove the absence of mines, nor (as I said in a signal to Sandy on the 7th) was the trawlers' wire sweep and 'limited acoustic capability' likely to prove much elsewhere. However, now that we had minesweepers it was wise to employ them. We certainly knew that the small Argentine patrol craft, the Argentine hospital ship plus the Falkland Island Government vessel MV *Forrest* and the

Falkland Island Company coaster MV *Monsunen* had, too, been plying their enemy's trade across waters in which we were interested. We could reasonably assume those areas were safe. Sandy knew, as did I, that the Argentinians had been experimenting with laying mines from the air but again there was no evidence of which I was aware that they had done so around the Falkland Islands. After an exchange of signals discussing the use of the trawlers Sandy rightly felt that, at least in Berkeley Sound, I deploy a mine sweeper in advance of frigates using the Sound for a gunline in support of the Divisional attacks. I agreed.

On the 11th June HMSs *Pict* and *Cordella* swept Berkeley Sound despite *Pict*'s machinery becoming inconveniently unserviceable on just about the only occasion it was needed. Nothing daunted, Lieutenant-Commander David Garwood, earned a Mention in Despatches for making the pass with all this auxiliary machinery running and his ship's company lying flat on the upper decks waiting for the bang. Thankfully, they waited in vain.

The Falkland Island Company's MV *Monsunen*, last seen in the kelp to the west of Lively Island, had been refloated by the Argentines and taken to Goose Green where she was found by 5 Brigade with a rope round her screw. I quickly took her away from the army after a discussion with Jeremy over the dangers of uncontrolled, random movements along the south. As I did not trust 5 Brigade to operate the ship within my area of control I sent aboard a Royal Navy Lieutenant and three ratings from *Fearless* to provide communications and to act as crew. They were officially designated Naval Party 2160 and were told not to operate by day and to accept instructions from 5 Brigade only if they were agreed, and, if not, to report back to me immediately before sailing on any mission about which they were doubtful. Tony Wilson probably found this difficult to accept but I remained adamant.

During the night HMS *Yarmouth* had been engaged by a 155 mm gun from the Sapper Hill area and returned the fire but with no known effect. She and HMS *Cardiff* had been supporting 3

313

Commando Brigade by targeting positions on Mount Harriet, Mount Longdon, and Wireless Ridge.

At dawn on the 8th, as I had done every day in San Carlos since our arrival, I stood on the bridge wing and looked towards Fannings Head, for that was the direction from which I expected the majority of the enemy air attacks. This preliminary glimpse each morning gave me a good indication of the cloud base I could expect. That day it had risen and while the sky was not wholly clear, the cloud, in my opinion, would allow the Argentinians to attack ships in San Carlos. What I was far from certain about, since we were 'up-weather' by some sixty-five miles, was the cloud base over the Fitzroy area.

A mixed day lay ahead, starting with Mike Goodman who came to me with considerable misgivings. Neither of us were happy that we had had to send the *Sir Galahad* on so late the night before and had been worrying whether she had arrived before dawn or not. We were also extremely concerned that *Sir Tristram* had not been unloaded and had had to stay another day. There was little we could do: we had committed ourselves to the action, but neither of us felt remotely comfortable that our luck would last. There had been far too many orders and counter-orders, some of which were so beyond our control that, despite our best efforts to avoid disorder, we feared a disaster could happen.

We had been trying to satisfy the needs of Divisional Headquarters since their arrival and had been going almost at a stampede rate well aware that this was the Navy's last throw in their support. If we could get this last LSL load through then there would be no need to send another into either Teal or Fitzroy. We knew the risks we were taking; we were convinced they were justified but we didn't like them, particularly since I had long felt the LSLs had borne with astonishing bravery far too great a part of the action.

I had a word with Mike Goodman and asked him to emphasize to *Plymouth*, tasked to bombard the enemy OP on Mount Rosalie, that she was not to leave San Carlos Water on any account while she did so. Mike assured me that he passed this message to *Plymouth*'s Operations Officer but Captain David Pentreath appears to have either not been informed or to have overruled it. In his Report of Proceedings he said that, once he was ready, he shot out from round Chancho Point at full speed heading for his chosen fire position two miles away and at that precise moment he received a warning of a possible air attack. It could be that he considered the spot he was heading for lay within my definition of being within the headlands. Either way he was lucky he did not suffer more than he did – and that looked dramatic enough from *Fearless*'s bridge!

Plymouth was hit by four bombs and, although none exploded, they caused considerable damage. She managed to return to San Carlos where a number of ships helped to put out fires and John McGregor's team patched numerous holes. This was the first day of air attacks in San Carlos since the Divisional Staff and 5 Brigade had arrived.

My staff report for 8 June covers most incidents:

'Good flying weather. Day of mixed fortunes in TA under heavy Argentine air attacks on different positions. *Plymouth* in San Carlos area; bomb damage to gun, mortar, magazine but fires/flooding under control. *Sir Tristram/Sir Galahad* in Fitzroy area severely damaged. *Sir Galahad* burning and abandoned, *Sir Tristram* possible unexploded bomb on board and abandoned. On plus side *Plymouth* splashed 1 × Mirage with Seacat in first raid. CAP splashed 1 × Mirage in second raid. Unconfirmed reports of 1 further splashed and possibly three damaged. In third raid land forces splashed 1 × A4 with ground fire. In fourth raid CAP splashed 3 × Mirage. Further one flew into sea. Last raid of 4 aircraft appeared to turn back before reaching target area. (Total 7 certs, 4 poss.) GR3 suffered engine failure when landing FOB and crashed. FOB expected to be fit for ops tomorrow. 2 × GR3 arrived *Hermes* from Ascension Island. NGS: *Cardiff*, *Yarmouth* onto Harriet, *Arrow* onto Stanley Airfield. Ashore good drying-out weather. Little change in own force position, no direct enemy action. Spasmodic enemy artillery fire. Own arty responded with good effect. Day of re-supply. 2024Z, 1 × LCU (F4) attacked by

4 a/c in Choiseul Sound and crippled. *Monsunen* attempted tow
but abandoned at approx 0300 and now believed to be drifting. All
4 a/c splashed by SHAR.'

It was not until the following day that we could piece together
the events in Port Pleasant during 8 June. *Sir Galahad* had
anchored just before dawn shortly after 1130Z two cables to the
east of her sister ship who was unloading with one LCU and her
small Mexeflote. The Welsh Guards were not amused to find
themselves unable to get ashore immediately and even less
amused to find that it was not Bluff Cove anyway. It was possible
to land men across the settlement jetty and with that in mind the
LCU and Mexeflote sailed from *Sir Tristram* to moor alongside
Sir Galahad's stern ramp. In addition to their part-loads of
ammunition (which could not be landed across the beach due to
high water) they were offering to carry the first load of men
ashore to the settlement jetty.

However, the Second in Command of the Welsh Guards (the
senior infantry officer afloat that day in Port Pleasant) was not
unreasonably determined that he would not be separated from
his kit and that, to him, meant continuing his journey to Bluff
Cove by sea. He would wait until dusk, if need be, to make that
journey by LCU. On the other hand the ship had to be emptied
of men to make the safe offloading of the heavy stores easier, and
to prevent any chance of loss through air attack. The Guards
officer's wishes, while understandable, could not be met, for
there was nothing available with which to move his men by day
other than the LCUs and the Mexeflote, and then only to Fitzroy
settlement. From here they could walk to Bluff Cove, the bridge
having been repaired sufficiently to take foot soldiers, or wait to
re-embark at dusk. By then the LCUs should have completed
offloading *Sir Tristram*. Fitzroy was, of course, the settlement
where I had agreed they should land.

Eventually a staff officer from 5 Brigade ordered the Guards
ashore but this instruction was countermanded by the senior
embarked officer, the RAMC Lieutenant-Colonel commanding
the Field Ambulance, who did need to get to Fitzroy and who

felt that he should therefore take priority. Further delays attended the embarked force as the landing craft, when it was finally able to accept the guardsmen for the short journey, developed a hydraulic failure in the ramp mechanism. The two Welsh Guards' rifle companies and the Mortar Platoon had now embarked for Bluff Cove in three different ships and were still some way short of their destination. Not only did they want to catch up with their colleagues but the Brigadier, the General, the whole of 3 Commando Brigade and myself (not to mention Sandy agitating, with every reason, for the 'military' to get on with the final battles) were all desperate for the infantry to consolidate forward and take their part alongside the Commandos.

Nevertheless it was not to be, and while a few vehicles and men of the 16 Field Ambulance managed to get ashore the guardsmen waited in the tank deck and the NAAFI. At 1710 the two ships were attacked by two waves of Skyhawks. The initial reports received by my staff spoke of over 200 men being killed. Naturally we could not, in *Fearless*, understand why the figure was so high, for we assumed that all passengers would have disembarked immediately on arrival.

Unfortunately the incident was immediately exaggerated by the press who 'happened' to be in the area at Tony Wilson's invitation to see his new forward HQ. The reactions were varied and fascinating on board. Jeremy, with his experience of Northwood, was concerned at the political implications and how the incident should be reported to Northwood. As far as I was concerned we had tried, largely succeeded, but now, not so surprisingly, had been caught. I could not believe the numbers involved and wanted more information. My main concern was what to do now. Would it be necessary to attempt further reinforcement by sea? I could rely on the system to look after the wounded and would need to send Staff Officers forward to assess the state of the two ships.

Happily, John Waters, Jeremy's Deputy, took much the same view as me and I was extremely grateful, as I had occasion to be before, for his quiet and professional support. What I knew of the load could be largely duplicated if that were necessary. I could not see that the loss of one or both LSLs anywhere near equated to the earlier loss of *Atlantic Conveyor*. I was also conscious that it was the first loss of a Royal Fleet Auxiliary that I had sustained in my forward and far more vulnerable area. I called Northwood on the secure voice system and told them that I would remain on board available for interview if required and prepared myself for the questions. Somewhat to my surprise I was never called.

While various discussions between Ewen, Tony Todd and the Guards officers had been taking place on *Sir Galahad*'s stern ramp the Sea King was lifting the Rapier into position. One of the four firing posts (by a terrible coincidence the one that covered the anchorage and its immediate approaches) was unserviceable due to a defect caused by the move from San Carlos. A spare had been sent for but it would not be until 1720 that it could be fitted – ten minutes too late.

Combat Air Patrol had been overhead until diverted (or were they decoyed?) by another wave of enemy aircraft. With a time-on-target of just ten minutes, due to the accident at HMS *Sheathbill* and the distance of HMS *Hermes* while she carried out her routine boiler cleaning, CAP was never going to be effective until after an attack – which they were, but by then the damage had been done.

I had asked to be informed if the weather lifted and would not have sent *Sir Galahad* forward if I had suspected that that was what was occurring. So far south we never received good quality 'met' information, despite embarking a Lieutenant-Commander (Met) with experience of South Georgia; he did his best as a single-station forecaster, but it was far from easy.

This operation had not been set up as an amphibious move with a Naval Officer in command, for I was simply transporting men and equipment into an area already held by us, much as we had been successfully doing at Teal. I regret that I placed too much trust on the new and inexperienced 5 Brigade which is really a complimentary reflection on my experience with the Royal Marines at Teal Inlet.

It has been suggested, after the event, that I should have sent in a warship to provide some form of air-defence but a frigate, for instance, only has two, 40 mm Bofors, the same as an LSL, while a few have only two 20 mm Oerlikons as close-range weapons. The 4.5 inch gun is no use close inshore as it largely depends on radar: with land all around them neither the gun nor the Seacat would have reacted in time. By sending in a frigate I would have provided another target without any increase in air defence. While this might have reduced the risk to an LSL, at that stage in the war frigates were more important for protecting the remaining shipping and providing naval gunfire support. Winning the land battle might not be the whole answer to the Falklands problem which could continue as a maritime war if the Argentinians chose. They had already claimed to have sunk the *Invincible* and may, possibly, have believed it. A victory at sea, given time and luck, could well be on their minds. It was not an attractive thought.

In other ways, though, I did regret not sending a warship because it might have interpreted the air raid warnings correctly and could have encouraged the RFA Captains to place as many small arms around the decks as possible at the appropriate time. I don't think the RFA Captains had been informed that we were getting our air raid warnings from submarines off the mainland coast and that they were therefore not specific on destinations. HMS *Exeter* called Air Raid Warning Red at 1658, but this was not received by *Sir Tristram* or *Sir Galahad*. Anyhow, they did not manage to close up their air defence teams until the very last minute. Communication with LSLs was always difficult.

For my part there was clearly a misunderstanding as I did not immediately appreciate that the first wave of Welsh Guards had been taken to Bluff Cove from *Fearless* – against my orders.

If the Welsh Guards had not been promised that the second half of the Battalion would also be taken to Bluff Cove, their Second-in-Command might have been less adamant about his destination and got his men off when advised to do so into Fitzroy. I could only risk the LCUs into Bluff Cove once and the Scots had taken that option. It was, in my view at the time, a risk worth taking once only and then with bad visibility. Anything that moved forward afterwards would be without the element of surprise, *Cardiff* or no *Cardiff*.

I felt dreadful as far as the LSLs were concerned as they were being asked to take the worst risks and had already had an unpleasant war with unexploded bombs lodged in most of them. Both Captain Robin Green and Captain Phil Roberts had been obliged to abandon their ships through fire. They asked to see me after they had been brought back to San Carlos. We sat in my cabin somewhat at a loss for words, staring at each other. There was very little any of us could say with both of them very shaken up. As they left, Robin turned and said, 'Thank you for seeing us. I don't envy you the decisions you have to make.'

I was immensely relieved and took that to mean that they still supported me. I could only reply, 'I'm terribly sorry, it didn't go at all as I had hoped. I expected the weather to have stayed in your favour and then you might have been OK. There is no way I could have protected you properly.' I still, of course, had no idea of the state of indiscipline and disorder that had come to exist with the soldiery.

In the end it all boiled down to three main aspects; the weather, the lack of communications within 5 Brigade and between 5 Brigade and Divisional Headquarters in *Fearless* and, perhaps most important of all, the shortage of support helicopters which arose from the loss of three Chinooks and six Wessex 5 in *Atlantic Conveyor*, the earlier loss of two Wessex 5 in South Georgia and two Sea Kings on a separate expedition. These two later tasks were arguably 'off the line of march' or, in other words, not essential to the maintenance of the aim. If these aircraft had now been available the move forward of 5 Brigade would have been very much more simple and safe – weather permitting.

There was a further disaster that day when one of *Fearless*'s LCUs despatched during the night to collect the communication Land Rovers of 5 Brigade's Headquarters and Signal Squadron, was attacked by Argentine aircraft in Choiseul Sound. She was lost with most of her crew. Her passengers escaped, but the

Brigade radios were also destroyed. The Colour-Sergeant cox'n (Johnston of *Antelope* fame) had been told not to sail in daylight but took the decision himself to do so once he realized the importance of his cargo.

With little alternative Jeremy postponed the Divisional attack by two days. The main attacks would now take place during the night of 11/12 June and in preparation for these the SBS and SAS would insert OPs north of Stanley and in sites on West Falkland from the submarine *Onyx* and the recently-arrived trawlers. The latter, with their stern chutes, were found to be ideal for launching raiding craft and rubber dinghies and relieved the Sea Kings with their night sights for work closer to the front line.

As a result of these earlier incidents I suggested to Sandy that the whole of the Falkland Islands should become my area of responsibility. I hoped that this might prevent possible misunderstandings between his and my group and I felt Divisional HQ had learnt a lesson and would now take greater steps to ensure no further misunderstandings took place between the Land and Naval forces. Sandy agreed and we sent a signal clarifying heights for aircraft to fly, etc, and generally tightening up the co-ordination.

During the nights of the 10/11th, 11/12th and 13/14th I kept my ships and landing craft busy with the move forward of ammunition along both flanks. I too had no alternative but to support Jeremy. In contrast to our earlier attempts, these reinforcement operations went without hitches. We even saved all the combat supplies from the tank deck of *Sir Tristram* and got them to the front line in time for the final assault.

With General Galtieri unable to accept that his position was now critical all was at last nearly ready for the final battles which would, we were all certain, lead to victory in Stanley. I never wished to play up our casualty figures as, heartless though it may sound, the loss of one mortar platoon was not going to affect the overall outcome whereas the loss of one of my frigates would be a much more significant setback. At the time we did not want the truth to come out as it was convenient to let Galtieri and

Menendez think we had suffered more than we had, but, thanks to the inevitable government-inspired press leaks the figures did get published. This caused the Land Force Deputy in North-wood to send a signal on these lines:

> 'News of *Galahad* strike and fact of casualties somehow blown. All press copy normally cleared by press release (MOD) but on this occasion slipped through. Deeply regret error. All here furious. Rather than wait for final list we have had to clear casualty notification ... Fully understand problem at your end.'

I remained sensitive towards the likelihood of an attack against San Carlos Water from either the mainland or from across Falkland Sound. I did not think that a victory on land would necessarily mean the end of hostilities at sea although I did not go so far as to think, as, I felt, Sandy did, that all hell would then be unleashed against us. We had to take a realistic view of the enemy's capability after all that they had suffered in the air and after all they had expended in the way of, for instance, Exocets. In *Fearless* we were almost cock-a-hoop over our success in the air. I considered that Sandy was handling his carrier battle group well, but had been surprised to hear that boiler cleaning was of such importance that it had to take place at a time when we had two Forward Base Maintenance areas being set up and still had San Carlos to defend, the General having already declared his aim to achieve success by the 12th. It was his problem, he was senior and it was not for me to question. I also agreed with him that, at this stage in the war, the risk of losing more escorts could be a long-term disaster if hostilities continued at sea long after the land battle had been won. We might easily find that it had all been a waste of time and effort. Their fleet, apart from the *Belgrano*, was very much in being.

During the final days of the land battles I, with my small and overworked staff, was in control of all coastal operations and, while some of my twenty-six ships continued to move supplies forward along both flanks, we remained nursing various problems in San Carlos Water, Berkeley Sound and Salvador. My worry over some form of retaliation attack or delaying tactics by the enemy were fuelled by intercepted reports on 10 June that 'Parcels would be shortly dropped in a lake.' which intelligence somehow deduced to mean a gas attack on the San Carlos anchorage.

We had suffered a delay but not one (apart from the human tragedy) as serious to our aim as that that had occurred with the loss of *Atlantic Conveyor*. There were now the final throes of the war to support logistically and practically and apart from a visit to the LSL *Sir Geraint* the day after the losses at Fitzroy to see how the LSLs were coping in the aftermath of the bombings I put the incident to the back of my mind. I had been helped in this by *Sir Geraint*'s Captain whom I visited with Brigadier John Waters who had kindly agreed to come with me to argue the military case should I find dissent. Together we flew on board the LSL and asked to be taken to the Captain's cabin where we found him asleep in his huge double bed in the middle of the day with a book across his stomach.

We woke David Lawrence (perhaps rather unkindly!) and asked him if he was a little frightened at being out in Teal largely unprotected. He made it quite clear that he fully appreciated the problem and understood the fact that only the LSLs could provide the transport necessary at this stage of the campaign. He understood the odds and the reason why we had to make the decisions we did. Brigadier Waters came away much encouraged, and so did I.

As we were expecting three replacement Chinooks, then at sea and approaching the Exclusion Zone aboard *Contender Bezant* steaming straight from Ascension Island, I sent Sandy a signal explaining how urgently we needed to lift the ammunition for a Divisional attack and asked that '(The ship) arrive TA earliest. Request direct routing to TEZ. Propose helos disembark when within range.'

Up to then all ships joining the Task Force had followed a track well to the east, but I felt that we were now able to straighten out the course a little to save time. This should have been a fact appreciated by the Carrier Battle Group in particular as Sandy's greatest complaints had been caused by (what he considered to be) the inordinate length of time the ground forces were taking to achieve success while, as he put it, his ships were deteriorating in the weather and being destroyed by the enemy. His reply to my request could have helped hasten the end for which he so desperately and intemperately kept calling – but it did not, and the *Contender Bezant* continued along her original track. I believed, but for his own reasons he did not, that the risk was now acceptable and certainly worth taking, and suitable escorts should be made available.

Another supply ship, the *Europic Ferry*, with RAF aircrew from 18 (Chinook) Squadron embarked, was sent east to meet the *Contender Bezant* which was then approaching a position 250 miles north of South Georgia, a long way from danger, so that they at least could be transferred to begin preparing their aircraft. It was a convoluted way of helping the 'war effort', especially as this method ensured that the vitally-needed aircraft would not reach their destination until 14 June, the day that Jeremy hoped to achieve victory with his land forces.

My staff diary for 9 June was very brief with no attacks in San Carlos. My secretary had to spend his day categorizing the survivors from the *Galahad* and *Tristram*, while *Intrepid* had to host the survivors of the 1st Welsh Guards and other military units. The two RFAs' ships' companies were to be given passage in *Atlantic Causeway*. As always, naval gunfire support continued with *Arrow* shooting at Stanley Airfield and *Yarmouth* at targets in the Two Sisters area. A particularly welcome guest was the RFA *Engadine* with her second and third line helicopter support.

Thanks to the FOB at HMS *Sheathbill*, fifty-eight CAP sorties were flown throughout 10 June, although a number of Argentine sorties also materialized. Three Pucaras from Stanley attacked 3 Para without causing casualties and nine Mirage 3s in three waves separated by only thirty minutes were launched, only to be turned back by the Harriers. The enemy, though, had success-fully diverted our attention and at least one C-130 reached Stanley that evening. At last, and not before time, my air defence ship, HMS *Exeter*, was able to report that the FOB was allowing good staying power and an 'alert CAP'. It was this business of being able to intercept, or being seen by the Argentine radar close to Stanley to be able to intercept much earlier than hitherto, that was now forcing the enemy fighters back. We still could not, though, stop the nightly C-130s re-supplying Stanley.

Exeter also did good work in sorting our problems of co-operation with the new RAF Regiment and their Rapiers. The staff diary read:

'Thursday, 10 June. A full anchorage unmolested. Force Replenishment at Sea (solids) from *Fort Grange* slow and will not be completed when she sails tonight. Progress with offload slow due to breakdowns in mechanical handling equipment. *Sir Geraint* who had gone to Teal progressed offload and minesweepers *Cordella* and *Pict* who had proceeded into Teal laid up there. Naval gunfire support – *Yarmouth* against Mount Harriet. Ashore a clear sunny day with no air attacks, a good helo flying day with much achieved. Little change in 3 Commando Brigade positions. 5 Infantry Brigade re-assessing position following *Sir Galahad/Sir Tristram* bombing. (Re-kit/re-group). Threat of gas attack develops. Task Group ordered to carry gas masks.'

Fears, real and imagined, flourished and, usually, died. For instance we received a signal indicating that as many as twelve enemy ships would be at sea that night (10th/11th) to add to the intercepted news of 'those parcels' being dropped in a lake. The first suggested a landing on West Falkland or possibly a determined attack on my ships in San Carlos. The second suggested the deployment of chemical weapons in, we guessed, San Carlos Waters. The meeting that night found Jeremy feeling very exposed, especially from the west, just as I had always felt. To counter any surface threat we promulgated a plan 'Porcupine'. The name seemed to fit the idea of being trapped in a cul-de-sac and having to retaliate or perhaps fight our way out.

The better news was that our support helicopter force had increased to eleven Commando Sea King 4s, ten partially stripped anti-submarine Sea King 2s, twenty-three Wessex 5s, and the one RAF Chinook. A problem, however, had been found and that was that the helicopter loads for 5 Brigade had been made up in bundles weighing 3,000 lbs, presumably for RAF Pumas as they were too heavy for our Wessex and uneconomically light for the Sea Kings. There was also a desperate shortage of strops and cargo nets which all added to the frustration.

Despite earlier experience of logistic ships overstaying their welcome in unprotected anchorages and an earlier prediction that this requirement would end, made before the date of the final attacks had been put back for the third time, I allowed *Sir Geraint* to spend a second day at Teal, while *Sir Percivale* loaded for her second run into that Inlet. *Sir Geraint* was reasonably well armed by now with two single Bofors guns, six general purpose machine guns, a Blowpipe detachment and a twin 20mm Rheinmetall anti-aircraft gun. This last, a desirable addition to our armoury, was one of a number captured at Goose Green and brought back to San Carlos.

On his arrival at Teal I had told *Sir Geraint*'s Captain that, if he thought it wise, he had my permission to put ashore some of his crew (those not directly involved in handling cargo, air defence or damage control) during daylight hours. However, following a request from Gerry Wells-Cole, the Head Logistician on Julian's staff, she was unloaded with everyone helping. Even so I had to accept, indeed insist, that she stay a second day for she too appeared to have been overloaded in their attempt to catch up with all the ammunition so vital to success. Loading a ship for one day's offload is not a precise science. So much depends on the speeds at which the LCUs can load, transport and off-load and how the cargo is stored, among many other uncontrollable factors such as weather, air attack and Murphy's law. It is really only possible to make an intelligent guess based on a few calculations and many other assumptions.

Continuing to operate at full stretch was MV *Monsunen* now with no civilians on board. We considered it too dangerous for them despite strict orders that she should operate only at night. She took, for instance, a company of the 1/7 Gurkha Rifles to Fitzroy from Goose Green on the night of the 10th/11th and returned immediately for more stores and vehicles. Her owners, the duplicitous Falkland Islands Company, behaved very strangely throughout and certainly seemed to plot how they could screw every last penny out of the Royal Navy for her use. The skipper was to claim that his ship had broken her back and the propellor shaft was bent but these claims were easily proved false after I sent *Fearless*'s engineer officer to check the story.

Although it was possible to launch as many Harriers as we needed during the day of the 10th this was in spite of rather than because of a good liaison between Divisional Headquarters who needed the close air support and Sandy who was providing it. There is a great deal of difference between CAP and on-call close air support for troops on the ground and we had not, even at this late stage, got it right. The Royal Air Force Liaison Officer on Jeremy's staff was moved to send a sharply worded signal expressing his clear view that the RAF GR3 operations of the day 'were something of a shambles'. What was needed was a Fleet Air Arm Officer detached from the Carrier Battle Group to Jeremy's staff. As a direct result Lieutenant-Commander Tim Gedge was sent ashore on the 12th to help with close air support during what were to be the final ground attacks. A useful lesson learned, but one learned very late.

During the night of the 10th/11th *Intrepid* sailed once again for Lively Island to deliver three LCU-loads of ammunition direct into Fitzroy and to collect one of *Fearless*'s LCUs that had been working non-stop in the area since arriving on 6/7 June. This journey was to ensure the ammunition in *Sir Tristram* was quickly and safely replaced in case we could not rescue it. The events on the 6th were now well behind us and all the supply runs went without further problems.

Fearless had been unable to deliver the LCUs herself since she had to go and replenish fuel at sea. It had been an exciting night as a radar intercept indicated a possible Exocet from the direction of Pebble Island. *Fearless* had been whipped into a shaking frenzy as they attempted to open the distance at full speed while firing chaff to decoy any possible missile before returning to the relative safety of San Carlos Water. During this time the Divisional staff had been completely out of touch with their troops ashore and, in particular, 5 Brigade because of the mountain range that stood between us. Major David Penny-feather, his Royal Marine Signals Officer, made the gloomy announcement at the morning brief, with the inevitable result that Jeremy decided to wait no longer and to move his Tactical Headquarters forward. The Divisional SATCOM system direct to Northwood was far superior to our DSSS and so he was already relying less on *Fearless* for communications. In addition he, quite rightly, wanted to be in closer touch with his troops. John Waters, Jeremy's excellent deputy, remained behind as the invaluable linkman. This state of affairs was to be better than I found when Julian went ashore but nevertheless the loss of direct contact with Jeremy was a little worrying. At least we knew what the military plans were for the next three days and if all went well there would be no further demands.

The staff diary reads:

'11 June. Naval gunfire support area 5 nautical miles long and 1000 yards wide swept overnight in Berkeley Sound. *Intrepid* inserted, recovered 3 LCUs from Fitzroy. CAP SHAR confirmed *Bueno Suceso* still at Fox Bay. Fine sunny winters day with no air activity. *Sir Geraint* finished offload at Teal. Counter mined *Antelope* upper deck ordnance. Support helo point with 70,000 pounds of fuel established at Fitzroy. Elements of helo squadrons moved forward for duration of Operation. Ashore, a day for battle procedures and final preparations. Reasonable weather and lack of air strikes aided our activities. HQ LFFI Tac HQ deployed to Fitzroy at 1830Z assuming command at 2100Z. Main HQ remains in *Fearless*. Just prior to midnight report first fighting. 3 Para fighting on Mount Longdon, 42 Commando in contact on Mt Harriet, 45 Commando crossing their start lines.'

The figure of the fuel established at Fitzroy mentioned in my staff diary above hides the astonishing work achieved by my Air Engineer Officer, Mike Cudmore, and others. On a visit to Darwin he had found large rubber pillow tanks, some of which had been slashed but others were serviceable. These had been taken forward to Fitzroy and filled with fuel from *Tristram* and *Galahad*. This was to be of inestimable value over those dramatic last few days of the battle. Mike Cudmore and Tim Yarker helped mastermind the movements of the helicopter squadrons forward, and together helped ensure the Squadron Commanding Officers were free for operations and their engineers were well supported.

Mine-clearing of the fire support area down the length of Berkeley Sound during the night of the 10th/11th had required HMS *Pict* to put all but fourteen of her crew on board her near-sister *Cordella* before proceeding down the Sound with her remaining crew gathered above the waterline and lying flat on their backs. The acoustic hammer failed during the second of six runs so the captain, David Garwood, switched on all auxiliary machinery as a substitute. I was able to signal about midday that, 'No mines found. Consider low risk to NGS ship in swept area and indications are mines not present in general area of MCM Ops.'

With the move forwards of ammunition still critical, and knowing that a significant amount was unexploded onboard the LSL *Sir Tristram*, I despatched, on the 11th, a small team from HMS *Fearless* consisting of her Engineer Officer, two RFA officers and five Royal Navy ratings. They had a number of tasks: to report on the state of each ship; to give whatever assistance was required to enable the offload of *Sir Tristram* to be re-started; to search for crypto material and to collect personal effects before any unauthorized removal was made.

A significant passage from the *Fearless*'s Marine Engineer Officer's report on *Sir Tristram* read:

> 'The whole of the aluminium bridge (and superstructure) ... has been consumed in an intense fire. Some of the outer structure is still standing but the centre part has collapsed into a pile of molten metal and debris down to steel deck level ... The hull structure which is steel is still intact. The fire did not spread forward of the bridge and the vehicle deck and all army stores on it are undamaged as are the messdecks and stores either side of the vehicle deck ... The engine room is still whole ... The engines and generators themselves are undamaged ... a fortnight's work ...

assuming the shafts are straight ... The switchboards are apparently intact ...

'The hull has three holes in it: bomb entry hole starboard side aft three foot above the waterline and exit hole port side aft two foot above the waterline ... Bomb entry hole starboard side aft one foot above the waterline. The second bomb went down the tiller flat and exploded, severely damaging the steering gear compartment which has become 'oval'. The vehicle deck above the tiller flat is rounded upwards by one foot.'

This was encouraging, especially as the report went on to tell me that the offload of *Sir Tristram*'s stores was continuing now that the stern gate's securing chains had been blown, thus lowering the ramp and allowing access to her interior, a decision made on the spot by the clearance divers which had had the MEO's full support but which caused some comment at the time. If this action had not been taken the ground forces could not have reaped the benefit of the unexploded ordnance. Its effect was, however, to make the LSL unserviceable for immediate sea-going operations, though as far as I was concerned these seemed some days away. A bonus for the inspection team in their thoroughly unpleasant duty was the discovery of *Sir Tristram*'s wine store: 'This had been cooked but some wine bottles were intact ... We drank (a bottle) with no ill effects – a slightly mulled taste.'

The report concluded that *Sir Tristram* was, perhaps surprisingly (given the import of the first eyewitness accounts) salvageable and would be very useful as a POW ship with 300 good bunks available and a 'massive amount of space on the vehicle deck ... [she] will be a secure prison anchored off Fitzroy settlement.' The news on *Sir Galahad* was rather more as expected, '... a total write-off and it is unlikely that much will be salvaged from her.'

Sir Galahad had been found to be a rather different matter with only the mine clearance officer (Lieutenant Bernie Bruen) and his Leading Hand boarding her. She was still burning at the time with occasional small explosions occurring at unexpected intervals. The fire was reported to have 'Spread from stem to stern,' devouring almost everything that was not solid steel. Some bodies could be seen caught in hatchways.

Other reports received included a Special Forces' statement that military headquarters 'of a sorts' existed in Stanley Town Hall and the Police station. This prompted Jeremy's staff to request a heli-launched missile attack on these pin-point targets. This was met with concern by Tim Yarker who sought my approval. It certainly seemed a bit wild to me but if the General really wanted it and believed that it would assist his efforts and the aircrew were prepared to try, then I would approve it. I was assured that they did and that was good enough for me. It was, of course, impossible in San Carlos to visualize clearly what the task entailed or what the risks were. The General had tactical control of the helicopters but I still retained operational control and could have vetoed it. The Divisional staff detailed an 845 Squadron Wessex 5 based at Teal Inlet to engage with AS 12 missiles. This it attempted to do from a position behind Cortley Hill at a range of about 4,000 yards. This first missile malfunctioned and fell short (close to the Argentine hospital ship which might have raised an eyebrow or two) but the second hit the upper floor of the Police Station. The aircraft then came under sustained small-arms fire before making its escape below cliff height up the Murrell River. This 'escape' manoeuvre had not been seen by the second helicopter, flying shot gun, who assumed the worst when his leader disappeared from view 'below ground level' amid a stream of tracer!

Shortly before this the Harriers had again attacked Stanley Airport causing structural damage, including a Pucara, but still leaving the runway intact for C-130s.

For the land forces' night attacks I had been asked to provide four naval gunfire frigates operating from the south coast and Berkeley Sound gunlines. Each of the ships, *Arrow* to the north and *Avenger*, *Yarmouth* and *Glamorgan* to the south, were to prepare 300 rounds and be ready by midnight 11th/12th for 'on call' tasks. Between them, by dawn, they had fired 788 rounds and had set fire to a fuel dump close to the racecourse, destroyed a 155mm gun and harassed numerous enemy troop positions. Most importantly, they had kept the enemy's heads down at crucial moments of our land-force attacks.

It might be useful here to explain Julian Thompson's views on 'fire support' as this is an expression not well understood by many, until they have suffered it or handed it out. To paraphrase parts of a passage from a paper written by him after the war:

> 'Neither light artillery nor NGS 4.5 inch guns are heavy enough to destroy static defensive positions. Although some fire may kill, wound or demoralize some of the enemy it can be relied upon only to keep the occupants' heads down while the rounds are actually falling; in gunner parlance, to neutralize them ... Therefore all fire support, unless followed by an assault (while the enemy is still reeling from the onslaught and is disorientated) will be wasted ... Although assaults on Argentine defences were immediately preceded by bombardments by 105mm, 81mm mortars and NGS no positions were destroyed ... In some cases fire support was brought down within 100 metres of our own troops to minimize time for enemy recovery.
>
> 'I discounted the enemy being forced to abandon permanently defensive positions because of gunfire or air attack alone. For this reason and to conserve ammunition before the main attacks anything other than harassing fire by 105 guns or mortars or in support of patrols was forbidden by me ... With hindsight this is an important lesson because a good deal of NGS was wasted in harassing fire before the main attacks. It should have been reserved to give the enemy an almighty, concentrated crack in the immediate run-up to, and during, the Brigade attacks. I should, have suggested this at the time ... It would have avoided the threat of a shortage of 4.5 inch high explosive that ensued.'

HMS *Intrepid* carried forward yet more ammunition along the south coast and recovered the previous night's ammunition-run LCUs. Before dawn the frigates broke off their engagements and headed back to their respective daytime areas; in particular HMS *Avenger* returned to her favourite spot in Albemarle Harbour, the one so thoroughly disapproved of by Sandy, and *Glamorgan* headed towards the outer reaches of the Exclusion Zone. While cutting a corner (of which she had been warned) to save time she was hit by a shore-launched Exocet suffering thirteen dead and severe, but containable, damage.

Shortly after dawn on 12 June we received reports that Julian's Brigade had broken the outer ring of Menendez's defence and was occupying its objectives with the end truly, and physically, in sight. At the time, though, nobody, least of all Julian, was counting chickens. We were all keeping our fingers and toes crossed. The campaign had gone on long enough and we could not wait for it to end.

The 'breaching' of Menendez's defences signalled the beginning of the end and was the result of the most significant land fighting of the war. By dawn that day (12 June) the Argentines knew exactly what faced them and how inadequate they were when confronted by men of the quality of the Commandos and Paras at night. From this moment the future of the land battle was, finally, not in doubt but was now merely a function of how long Menendez could delay the inevitable. Three decisive commando/battalion attacks (including, later, a spirited and hard assault by the Scots Guards onto Mount Tumbledown) ending in the shambolic withdrawal and capture of dispirited Argentine soldiers (and suspiciously few of their officers) were to prove our ability once and for all.

My staff war diary again:

'12 June. Offload continued overnight. *Intrepid* inserted 3 recovered 2 LCU from Fitzroy. *Sir Geraint* came out of Teal, *Sir Percivale* went in. By day consolidation of *Sir Geraint* from *Elk*. Began *Sir Bedivere* offload. Drained AVCAT from *Blue Rover* – *Sir Geraint* topped up for Teal, EFHE took what was left. NGS fired against enemy positions by *Glamorgan*, *Avenger*, *Yarmouth* and *Arrow*. During the course of this *Glamorgan* hit by Exocet. Vulcan raid against Stanley airport (14 of the 20 1000 lb bombs failed to explode). 3 Cdo Bde carried out highly successful night attack on Mt Longdon, Two Sisters and Mt Harriet. All objectives secure. Phase 2 involving 5 Bde capturing Tumbledown and Mt

William takes place overnight 13/14 June. 3 Cdo Bde silent night attack commenced 112359Z went noisy approx 0200Z. Support by NGS from 4 ships and arty of both Bdes with concurrent Vulcan strike on Stanley Airfield. 42 Cdo established on Mt Harriet. 200 POWs. 45 Secure on Two Sisters. 3 Para after stiff fight secure on heavily defended Mt Longdon. During 12th became evident that more time required to position 5 Infantry Brigade for next attack. Therefore postponed until night of 14th/15th.'

By Sunday, 13 June we understood that all was nearly in position for the final assault on the enemy's inner ring to the west and south of Stanley. The 3rd Commando Brigade had achieved all its objectives – Mount Harriet, Two Sisters and Mount Longdon, with the Mount Harriet battle considered to be one of the more outstanding infantry successes of the war, although it is often overlooked as such due, paradoxically, to the professionally low number of own-casualties compared with other battles of less complexity. Now the Commandos had to wait a further twenty-four hours than planned for the infantry to capture Mounts William and Tumbledown before Julian could press on to Sapper Hill and the outskirts of Stanley with an assault on Wireless Ridge timed to take place concurrently with that of the Scots Guards onto Tumbledown.

From then on we learnt much from John Waters through his personal reports to Ian Baxter, Jeremy Larken and me: Julian intended to attack Stanley from the south and rear; indeed in his 'O' Group covering his plans for the night of the 14/15th his Brigade mission was simply to 'Capture Port Stanley'.

5 Brigade's attacks were scheduled for the night of 12/13 June but for good reasons Tony Wilson asked for, and was granted, a delay so that he could 'recce' previously unseen ground.

My part during this peak of activity, expectation and hope was (on the 13th) to get *Sir Geraint* safely into Teal Inlet, which we did, although she was overflown by 'spent' A4s going home unmolested after an air attack on the forward troops. Rapier was reported to be 'off the mark' which was a further disappointment to add to that of the Sea Harriers failing to make contact due to their distance from the Forward Operating Base in San Carlos and the poor warning. *Sir Percivale* came back to the apparent safety of San Carlos while the RFA *Olna* pumped fuel all day to various ships and installations within San Carlos Waters. Both *Fearless* and *Intrepid* did the same for two Sea Harriers when HMS *Sheathbill* was temporarily unuseable. The two Type 21 frigates HMSs *Arrow* and *Active* provided covering naval gunfire support onto Sapper Hill and Moody Brook from the Berkeley Sound Gunline while, ashore, 3 Commando Brigade consolidated all of its forward units. The helicopters allocated to 5 Infantry Brigade spent a very busy day moving the Scots Guards towards Mount Tumbledown and the Gurkhas forward from Goose Green.

The most important battle of this final phase was 2 Para's attack on Wireless Ridge during the night of the 13th/14th. They had reverted to 3 Commando Brigade's command for this operation and were due to secure the start line for the Brigade's advance into Stanley. After the battle the Commanding Officer (now Lieutenant-Colonel David Chandler) stood and watched the enemy retreating into Stanley, and on his arrival Julian Thompson was shown this exodus. He immediately informed the Divisional Commander who ordered him to 'get the Brigade moving in a general advance'. This he did.

Then, almost suddenly, on the 14th with the Scots Guards victorious on Tumbledown and 45 Commando aborting their attack onto Sapper Hill after they discovered it occupied (unplanned) by the Welsh Guards, someone reported that white flags could be seen flying over Stanley. Whether or not this is true nobody has ever confirmed, but it was good enough for most of us to accept as a long-awaited fact. The Argentines were reported to be running into town while Captain Rod Bell (the Royal Marines' Spanish interpreter) and Mike Rose flew forward to Menendez to negotiate the surrender which Jeremy Moore was prepared to accept – unconditional or conditional. The wording might have been an important piece of national pride and semantics to the Argentine commanders but to the British a surrender was a surrender and that was that.

Later that evening I took a copy of Jeremy Moore's signal to the wardroom and read it out ending with the quoted words that 'The Islands are once more under the Government desired by their occupants.' I privately thanked God, and had my first drink for many weeks and hoped that my eldest daughter had enjoyed her sixth birthday.

I then handed the copy of the signal to Brian Hanrahan who was in the wardroom at the time and told him I had no objection to it being released. I understand that Mrs Thatcher heard it on the news early the following morning and had to wait for confirmation from the Secretary of State!

CHAPTER NINE

THE AFTERMATH

Much, if not most of the Navy's work goes on
unseen.

Sir Winston Churchill, April 20, 1943,
at a Conference of Ministers

EARLY ON THE morning of 15 June I received an invitation
from Jeremy Moore to fly up to Stanley and attend the formal
surrender. He asked me to contact Sandy since he was unable to
do so, but by the time I received his message there was not
enough time for Sandy to fly in and join us. John Waters and I
jumped into a helicopter and flew up together. We walked up to
the Secretariat where the signing was to take place and waited
outside for the Argentine Higher Command to arrive.

The whole scene was one of chaotic mess. We had passed
burnt-out, damaged and fully serviceable helicopters, large
containers which I was told were full of food and all the
paraphernalia of a beaten army hastily moving on. Everywhere
was mud. Of islanders we could see few.

We had not long to wait. Staff cars appeared with outriders
and out stepped impeccably turned-out, well-washed and, I
thought, rather well-fed officers, still carrying arms. They looked
more like victors than victims and contrasted strongly with the
dirty camouflaged battledress most of our military were still

wearing. They seemed, however, to enjoy the sense of occasion, but the impression was of an army of almost medieval style with officers and men remote from each other.

The ceremony was short and I attempted to find out if the Argentinians would admit total defeat and not molest our shipping or aircraft, or whether they would simply acknowledge that they had lost the land battle alone. I could get no immediate reply but pressed for information later. It seemed that those in the Falklands clearly had no authority on this point – vital to us at sea – and the signing had, therefore, simply been a surrender of their forces ashore on the Islands, both in Stanley, West and East Falklands. Hopefully, it was enough.

Flying back, I asked the pilot to stop at an abandoned observation post which seemed to be the highest in the ridge of hills running west from Stanley. Standing on top of the highest rock with my binoculars, I looked towards Fitzroy to see if the range of hills had indeed hidden the LSLs as I had been promised. It was possible to just pick out the top two to three feet of *Sir Galahad*'s mast and I felt that at least that piece of information had been reasonably accurate, and the cause of the attack was unlikely to have been a visual sighting, certainly not of *Sir Tristram* who was tucked in closer to the high ground and who had, of course, arrived the day before the attack. Much later I was told that our intelligence had intercepted messages highlighting the increased activity in the Fitzroy/Bluff Cove area and calling for an air attack, but this information was never passed on to me. Whether it would have been possible to react in time and change the plans which had been agreed by, and indeed involved, all three CTGs I do not know. The seeds of that unsatisfactory day were sown years before when Joint Army/ Navy warfare training was abandoned along with so many other aspects of inter-Service co-operation. The importance of the event in military terms was grossly over-exaggerated in the public eye by the unfortunate attention of so many of the media who had been invited to the area for quite a different reason.

My Air Engineer Officer, Mike Cudmore, summed up some of the problems immediately facing all of us:

'Half the Divisional Staff is in Stanley and half in San Carlos. There is much to do with the military having to get the town going, with the whole of the Falklands to be visited and aided, with 10,000 POWs to round up and organize – an unknown air threat – Argentina politically not contactable. Mines, unexploded bombs, ships' programmes, etc, etc, etc.'

My staff diary for 15 June is again, self-explanatory and, (from memory) naturally, contemporary in tone:

'Clear evidence of effect of airborne re-supply with stocks of rations for five days in many places. Ammo dumps considerable. Began clearing POWs into *Canberra* in wintry conditions of gales from the south and driving snow. *Cardiff* at Port Howard, *Avenger* Fox Bay. Senior Mine Clearance Diving Officer quick survey Port Stanley and met Argentine Naval Captain who gave him detailed charts of minelay – believed contact (mines) only. SAEO visited Stanley airfield found serviceable Pucaras and one hole in runway. Other holes simulated by earth; handling equipment, tower, and hangars all badly damaged. G2/COMAW visited Port Stanley harbour and inspected jetties, berths and landing slips. All looked useable. PC 82 *Islas Malvinas*, MV *Forrest* and *Yehuin* all Argentine manned and believed serviceable ... (Falkland Islanders) opinions of Argentinians vary. Many pitying conditions of those not supplied with rations. Tales of eating bones and chicken food. Others near airdrop relatively fat with several days of reserves in kit bags. Clear evidence of effects of NGS. While not always accurate, devastating to (Argentine) morale. Blizzard conditions over Falklands are making logistic problems the most pressing. 11,000 POWs reported in Stanley. Laying down arms, moving to airfield for processing and awaiting movement. 2,000 reported West Falkland. Food for only two days. 3 Cdo Bde in Stanley area. 5 Bde 50% Fitzroy, remainder move by 16th June. (Arty) Btys remain in place. CLFFI TAC HQ at Government House. *Fearless* remains in San Carlos until air threat reduced. Own troops in good spirit but present conditions make early provision of shelter important.'

What was my Group to do now? Sandy clearly had to continue to keep his Carrier Battle Group in safety and in being, ready in case the Argentinians should attempt to continue the maritime war. He would need to be able to continue to provide CAP until we felt reassured there would be no more air attacks. The General had all the problems of prisoners of war and controlling troops who had just been through several days of intense battle. He also had to consider the Islanders who lacked a civilian government and do what he could to provide for their immediate needs. I still controlled the assets needed to send supplies around the Islands and also remained concerned for the protection of my merchant ships and RFAs and the Islands as a whole. We had, therefore, to take no chances and, despite the possibility of surrender, I had ordered four frigates on to the northern gunline just in case the Argentinians tried any trickery and the ground troops needed our immediate support. With the prisoners of war out of the way, there would be no need for such concerns, but we would still need to protect ourselves in the Islands.

We therefore decided that we would continue to operate as before; no ships away from San Carlos, Teal or Fitzroy by day where they could hope to gain some protection from Rapier and ground forces. All coastal movements must continue at night only; ships remained darkened and at a high state of readiness for action.

A high priority would be to establish and open Stanley Airfield but this was where vast numbers of prisoners had been moved to get them away from the town and their arms dumps.

Jeremy returned to *Fearless* later in the morning and we decided to visit Port Howard and Fox Bay together that afternoon. This was a marvellous moment and I can scarcely remember a more welcome cup of tea than we were given that day in the kitchen at Port Howard while we sat there in scruffy battledress without our boots on. We heard more of the Argentines and how the SAS patrol had been treated. Malcolm Hunt, the Commanding Officer of 40 Commando, was sitting outside beside an enormous pile of weapons, bayonets, steel helmets and clothing, with a huge grin, having taken the surrender of Port Howard forces with *Cardiff* lying offshore. We then flew down to Fox Bay for a similar brief visit to find *Avenger* well under way with their surrender.

At Fox Bay was a small group of doctors who had been moved out of Stanley. Rather to my surprise, one turned to me (having previously just asked me to ensure he was flown immediately to Stanley) and asked what the Navy had been up to. All we seemed to have done was lose ships while the Land Forces had achieved marvels and a great victory. This biased and uninformed view was to be met many times, not just in the Falklands but back at home. While it astonished me at the time, I was not wholly surprised as I knew the Navy had not got its press relations anywhere near right.

Jeremy and I discussed the immediate future. He would now stay ashore at the Governor's Residence and set up a permanent Headquarters. The logistic element of his staff would remain in *Fearless*, at least for a few more days. He asked if I would ferry forward the stores now dumped in San Carlos and Teal to more permanent dumps near Stanley, and I decided to bring *Fearless* up closer to Stanley to improve liaison with a longer term view of my Staff and I moving ashore and releasing the ships to return home. This could not of course be done until we had suitable office accommodation earmarked. We still also had to think of the Islanders.

I therefore detailed *Intrepid* to remain in the San Carlos area. Despite the removal of military stores, we believed it sensible to maintain San Carlos as a forward naval and air operating base. *Intrepid* was to control helicopters and provide a list of all the Islanders in his area of influence and tabulate their needs and conditions. At the same time he was to co-ordinate the removal of prisoners or war. *Fearless* was to do the same for East Falklands. Here the job was made slightly more easy because the Gurkhas, already well established in Darwin, could cover much of Lafonia and their immediate area. Both would work in conjunction with the ground troops so that a picture could be quickly painted as to the overall state of the Islanders and, hopefully, their economy. We also needed to confirm the immediate prisoner-of-war problem since it rapidly became obvious that the Senior Argentine Officers had little idea how many troops they had in the Islands or where they were based. Nor, it seemed, did they have much knowledge of where onshore they had laid mines.

While these plans were being hatched, Admiral Fieldhouse called me on the DSSS for an update and to thank my Staff and me for our efforts. I tried to describe the scene at the airport and the problems of the prisoners of war in increasingly unpleasant and even blizzard conditions. We could soon have a further catastrophe on our hands as these dispirited and unsheltered men would have little resistance to the elements. CTF clearly wanted a world statement and asked me to gather as many of the press as I could and brief them of our concern. I did so, but clearly most of the reporters already knew the story.

It was an interesting request, since shortly after Jeremy Moore's arrival the three CTGs were forbidden to talk directly to the press. The signal had not been rescinded. I had found this a very disconcerting order. If we could not talk to the press, then it was essential that one of our Staffs was delegated to do so, which was really much the same thing as us talking. If this was not done, then the press would quite naturally follow their instincts and find any story which, to some extent, is what happened. I had quietly agreed that Jeremy Larken, as my Chief of Staff, should talk 'off the record' to try and ensure that a sensible slant was achieved, but it was not easy. With the Divisional Staff and my own on board, I personally kept to the order as it would have been seen to be disloyal not to do so. I thought that best in the circumstances. I believe the original instruction was issued after Sandy had given two interviews which were reported differently, one interviewer suggesting he believed the campaign would be easy while the other suggested he felt it would be difficult. Few Naval Officers are trained to cope with the press and interviews or interrogations of this kind, and we can be easy meat for the unscrupulous as a result. Nevertheless, a more imaginative approach to press relations would have been sensible. Someone had agreed to a large number coming with us but someone else seems to have decided they should not be properly briefed or informed. Not good, and no doubt part of the reason for those odd remarks at Fox Bay.

Fearless, with my staff and I still embarked, was sailed at 2100 on Wednesday, 16 June to Port William just outside Stanley. It felt odd to be away from San Carlos and not particularly comfortable to be anchored where one could feel the swell, but the move made sense. Several ships came to anchor nearby and several members of my Staff and I went ashore to see what was to be done and what we could do.

There was a clear need to set up an organization to control the harbour and so we started negotiations with Northwood to create a legal Queen's Harbourmaster (QHM), which duty we then took on until an appointed officer arrived. It was to be several days before this was formally approved. Once ashore, we met Sandy who had flown in to see the situation for himself, and we discussed how we saw the future, the prisoner-of-war problem and the roulement of ships as well as the longer term threat from Argentina. Like the military ashore with the 3rd Commando Brigade Troops, we had no wish to retain the RFAs or merchant ships longer on station than necessary but realized that until we knew how naval and air operations would go, we must retain the warships, but possibly not the two LPDs *Fearless* and *Intrepid*.

Later on the 17th we heard that Galtieri had been removed from the Junta so we had achieved more than a simple thrashing of their occupation forces. We also heard that the Argentines had no objection to *Canberra* and *Norland* proceeding to the mainland to land the prisoners of war, and so we continued to load both ships as fast as we could.

Canberra sailed for Puerto Madryn on Friday, 18 June, while *Norland* topped up and sailed on the following day, taking most of the remaining prisoners. About five hundred Special Category prisoners were retained in Ajax Bay in case we needed a bargaining chip with Argentina. These were mostly officers and I spent an uncomfortable time walking through them one afternoon. None admitted to speaking English but there were rather too many grey-eyed Teutonic blonds there for my liking. At least they were camped in full sight of an unexploded 1,000lb retard bomb stuck in the wall of the building waiting to be defused. I hoped they would reflect on it and keep quiet. Menendez himself had been embarked in *Fearless* where he occupied the Landing Force Commander's cabin, recently vacated by Jeremy Moore and earlier on by Julian Thompson.

Life continued at a slightly slower pace than the gallop we had been moving at over the past few weeks. It was time to reduce my Staff and get as many home as possible. It was already becoming obvious that discipline was breaking down ashore and I was glad we were on board ship. There was an element of anarchy and self-interest which I disliked. It was frustrating and very disappointing and was caused, to a large extent, by the incredible filth that was difficult to clear for fear of mines and booby traps, and the sudden aimlessness of the troops. One of my Staff (a Royal Navy Commander) was moved to write the following in his personal diary:

'17th June. Off at first light into Stanley with Colonel Preston – a nice man. Overlapped with Admiral Woodward who is visiting for the first time ... I find Stanley utterly depressing. The troops are in a post war mood and very selfish. Grab, grab – transport, houses, equipment, food etc – gone is the spirit of selflessness in the field. It will return but at present all is filth, squalor and [the] looting instinct prevails. Quite the worst aspect of the whole campaign. How different from yesterday when the Paras were on parade for a church service in disciplined lines and when 45 Commando marched into town carrying their rucksacks in a line a mile long. Very impressive.'

On Sunday, 20 June Jeremy Larken and I flew into Stanley to attend the Reverend Bagnall's excellent Service of Thanksgiving in the Cathedral which ended with the three verses of the National Anthem, including that marvellous one, 'Confound their knavish tricks.' It was down to earth soon after as I stood outside by the whalebone arch with Jeremy Larken. One of the more intelligent reporters came up to us – or rather he approached Jeremy Larken. He seemed to be quite wound up and started quizzing Jeremy about the distance away from the action that Sandy had kept the Carrier Battle Group. Luckily I had firmly briefed Jeremy Larken but every time I tried to chip in to support the view that Sandy was quite correct in his desire to preserve the aircraft carriers, the reporter made it clear he did not want to know my opinion! He obviously had a bee in his bonnet and no amount of comment from me was going to swat it. It was unfortunate that Sandy had been unable to make this Service or he would have been able to see for himself the quite extraordinary opinions that were being bandied around, partly because of the previous instruction that people like myself were not allowed to speak to the Press and partly because the Press had inevitably tended to go where they thought the action was most likely to be and that, of course, was ashore. The Press had ready access to troops and opinionated Junior Officers but sadly little access to those who were actually doing the thinking and making the decisions. It would be a little time before Jeremy and Sandy were to be allowed to talk directly to the Press. The ban on my speaking was not lifted.

The next day we returned in *Fearless* to San Carlos and felt at home again. More discussion took place with Sandy, Jeremy, Peter Dingemans of *Intrepid* and myself on how the QHM should operate and interface with the military and what was needed for the future. The naval war could well, of course, continue. Everything was taking longer to agree than anything that had occurred before and we finally hoped to have the QHM properly set up by midnight on the 25th as there were clear signs that the job was essential. Fortunately Commander Willis came fresh from the UK to set it up, but he was to have his difficulties.

On the 23rd Jeremy Moore and I attended the sad Service I had arranged on board the *Tristram* for those who had been killed in her and in the *Galahad*. I found it extremely moving. I was still by no means sure of the sequence of events that had taken place. Shortly after this, the *Galahad* was towed out to sea to be sunk by a torpedo while the *Tristram* was towed round to Navy Point for repairs and subsequent use as an accommodation ship.

It was decided that the 3rd Commando Brigade would return home in the *Canberra* as soon as her prisoner-of-war run was completed. Some would travel in *Fearless* as I was slowly getting established on shore and wanted her homeward bound as soon as possible. I would miss her as we had lived through an adventurous time, but she and her crew deserved a rest. She sailed on 25 June, ten days after the surrender while *Sir Bedivere* was placed alongside the Falkland Island Company jetty in Port Stanley as an accommodation ship for Jeremy, his Divisional Staff and my Staff.

I had also hoped to release *Intrepid* as well but we had first to make sure communications between Jeremy's new shore-based headquarters and Sandy were operating well. Clearly if I was ashore I could use the Army communications system but until then we needed a ship like *Intrepid* with a good naval communications fit. In addition it was becoming obvious that some of the LCUs would still be needed and we were not clear if they could be lifted home by other means or whether an LPD would need to stay.

These and many other problems continued to exercise my reduced team as we established ourselves in the Secretariat on 25 June in the offices vacated by Julian and his 3rd Commando Brigade Headquarters.

On that day Sandy came ashore again and I stood back with John Waters while Sandy and Jeremy, the two two-star Commanders, welcomed Rex Hunt, the late Governor and now Civil Commissioner, back to the Islands. From that day our discussion on civilians took on more meaning and I much enjoyed the Joint Rehabilitation Committee which Rex Hunt chaired, and through which he formally sought help from the Services.

By 26 June *Canberra* had returned and finally loaded up with Julian and his Brigade, and sailed for home chasing *Norland* and *Europic Ferry* who had sailed the day before with more of his men, mostly the Paras. I was sad to see all these people leave and longed to get home myself with my exhausted Staff but it was not to be, despite an agreement with FOF3's Staff that we should be relieved early. Meanwhile problems of all sorts continued, such as the Falkland Island Company, making difficulties over their jetty and refusing to accept *Monsunen* back. They claimed it was not up to Board of Trade regulations. They of all people stood to gain from our victory, but it was clear their Stanley staff had been ordered to squeeze the last drop out of the Government if they could.

Happily, the snow fell thickly and hid most of the more obvious indications of unwelcome occupation. The Falkland Island Company jetty had been covered with human excrement before it was hosed down by *Sir Bedivere*'s Chinese crew.

The Islanders appeared to need to go back into their shells and adjust to what was to be an entirely different existence. Never before, I imagine, had they seen so much mess and chaos and so many British Troops. The sooner hutted accommodation could be provided and our Troops could move out of Stanley the better.

We had a moment to take stock. Despite being under fairly regular conventional air attack, my task group had lost only one of my precious LSLs and two frigates out of twenty-six ships. We had lost one LCU. Yes, we had had a fair number of other LSLs, RFAs, frigates and destroyers damaged but all of them would return home safely. The merchant ships had largely survived unscathed but had been as exposed as any to the risks and air attacks. Astonishingly we had not lost one support helicopter from enemy action or through lack of spares or maintenance problems since we arrived at San Carlos all those weeks before. One Commando Sea King had its rotor blade damaged by a 20mm bullet and one Wessex 5 had received 7.62mm bullets through its windscreen and fuselage. Three of the anti-submarine Sea Kings had been damaged, two by 7.62mm bullets and another from shrapnel. All were able to continue their missions. Nor had we lost through enemy action any of the 3rd Commando Brigade's equipment apart from the two Gazelles on D-Day. The only loss which we all felt strongly was the Welsh Guards mortar platoon and equipment in the *Galahad*. Otherwise all of 5 Brigade's gear had also been landed and moved forward safely. We could also claim a number of Argentine aircraft shot down.

My Commando Helicopter Squadrons had wisely taken themselves to Navy Point and set up camp there. The base was still surrounded by minefields, but they were able to operate helicopters and we were able to bring *Tristram* alongside their jetty while she was being repaired for her tow homewards. They too deserved to get home but they were in too great a demand and some would have to wait.

The next few weeks were therefore spent trying to move the army's stores, allow the Islanders some degree of movement and continue to defend the Islands. All the while old friends would leave for home and new fresh faces would appear. Many of the newcomers would repeat the Fox Bay Doctor's message and some would add that the Navy had had a comfortable time with regular meals and hot showers, while their men (actually the men they had relieved) had lived for weeks in fear and squalor. It was an uncomfortable experience to find the Director of Army Public Relations along with 'war artists' and many others filling the Falklands while not one Naval officer flew down to find out what had or was happening.

I was intrigued also, in talking to the Naval Staff at Northwood on the Army's excellent satellite communications system, to hear they too appeared exhausted and even small problems were taking an unimaginably long time to solve. I gained the firm impression that we in the Royal Navy were all like salmon that had just spawned and hoped we would have a chance to mend before we got to sea again. It was the most frustrating time, enlivened only by the thought that we were slowly helping the Islanders return to normal.

With the first RAF C-130 came two bags of mail and low-priority signals that had not been able to come by radio. Amongst them were signals telling me Sandy intended to visit us off Ascension! We looked at the pile and decided not to investigate further, but it told its own story.

We moved out of the Secretariat to let Mr Baker back into his office and shifted all our papers to the old school, a little further out of town and now sterilized and clean. We were closer to Jeremy and his new staff but the liaison was never to be as good as it had been in *Fearless*. Finally, my task group was disbanded and I became the naval Chief of Staff to the Commander British Forces Falkland Islands or ComBFFI with Derek Refell now at sea in command of the Carrier Battle Group and all offshore naval forces.

It was not to be until 13 July that I was able to bring all but one of my Staff home with me for what I considered was more than a well-earned rest. I had been intensely pleased with what they had achieved and their cheerfulness throughout the campaign. I felt that my merchant ships, RFAs and naval vessels had done an excellent job and deserved all the rest they could get.

The story would not be complete without mentioning two signals received at the war's end; one from the defeated military dictator, and the other from the victorious political leader. The loser made no apologies for the misery to which he had subjected many of his people.

'From the Head of the Army to the Commanders of all districts and units of the army. Farewell message from the Commander in Chief of the Army at the moment when I hand over command of the army. For the last time I address myself to all members of the army, in order to express to them some of the concepts which I hope to be fundamental. My career began full of hopes developed from an absolute conviction and now, today is the culmination, the wheel has turned a full circle. I leave the way open for other men to correct my mistakes and to benefit from our achievements, if indeed there were any, to lead this institution to its glorious destiny. I assume complete responsibility for the crucial circumstances in which the Republic is living, as Commander in Chief of the Army, member of the Military Junta and President of the Republic, whilst taking that unusual historic and momentous decision, convinced that we did everything possible to achieve an objective long pursued by the nation and that we Argentinians will persist until its achievement. We have suffered a military setback, even if only partial, which, however, will not affect in any way the permanent values which are the very essence of the Army I commanded, the highest honour to which a soldier can aspire. These difficult moments in its life will affect it because its deep roots are fed from the most holy and pure, the country in whose service it had dedicated its existence, the antibodies allow it to rejuvenate itself and the pain to fortify itself in the face of adversity. An army which has carried the peace of the nation eradicating the threat of subversive violence promoted by policies of political slavery and indignity. An army which has placed its men to defend the homes and permanent interests of the nation, offering the lives of its officers, non-commissioned officers and men for its territorial integrity, its greatness and the liberty and dignity of all its sons. An army which has fought bravely under all circumstances, which had to act and which could only be overcome when it was faced by an unequal struggle against an enemy superior because of the advanced technology of its resources, which endowed it with a military might impossible for our army to equal however great their courage and professional aptitudes.

'Throughout the whole of my professional life I have seen all those acts which are the sublime fighting spirit of the Argentine soldier. I know full well his fighting spirit and capacity. I have total knowledge of the quota of blood which has redeemed his oath of total allegiance to the flag of the fatherland, which conjures up so many heroes and martyrs. With the whole force of my spirit as a soldier, I pay homage to them and feel for all those no longer with us and for those who have suffered pain. Above that blood, that pain, those deaths and that heroic conduct surges that force which enjoins men at arms, which tempers their spirit and which cherishes their dreams. We must renew our hopes for a better future with spirit and vigour, with eyes fixed firmly on the glorious future, but without forgetting the glorious past. At the same time we must affirm the internal cohesion of the forces and of the other armed forces as an indispensable base from which to well serve the interests of the fatherland.

'To your hands I deliver this testimony of my efforts, to your hearts the cherishing of my dreams. I pledge the remainder of my life to be used in the most useful way, to improve the wellbeing of the fatherland and of the army. My successors have the great tenacity, energy and fortitude necessary to assume a great responsibility, the knowledge to guide the forces in these dangerous times and the humility which will allow them to accept the advice of wise men who without doubt will come to their aid.

'At the end of this message my career as a soldier will end a full career with intensity in each one of its multiple facets. I have exercised control and obedience. I have done my duty.'

(Thank goodness he wasn't making a victory speech!)

What a load of drivel, I remember thinking, no wonder they lost for they had, in fact, much equipment that was far in advance of our own but as always one volunteer is better than ten pressed men.

... and the short, no-nonsense message which says more than the whole of the above:

From CTF 317. Personal for CTGs 317.8, 317.1, 317.0. The Prime Minister has asked me to pass to you her personal congratulations on your outstanding victory.

On passing by Ascension Island on his way home the Captain of *Avenger* was reported to have said: 'The war was fun, the peace hell'. A fair summary, I feel. I hoped that my First Sea Lord, Admiral Sir Henry Leach, would now agree that he had retrieved the Falkland Islands satisfactorily and that the spirit of the old 'can do' navy had once again triumphed, if only just. I was certainly proud to be a Royal Navy Officer and, having seen how my people performed, was very glad to be British.

The Captain duly appreciated my valour, and patted me on the back.

'There,' said he, 'you are fairly a sailor now; been drunk, been aloft, and been in action. Take your hands out of your pockets, youngster, or I shall order the sailmaker to stitch them up.'

Captain Frederick Chamier, Royal Navy 1796–1870

APPENDIX I

The Principles of War

There are a number of versions but this is the British one. They have been developed and refined over centuries of warfare and I was delighted to notice that Julian Thompson and, later, Major General Jeremy Moore had them pinned above their desk in their cabin in HMS *Fearless*.

Their relevance to this story will be obvious, bearing in mind the difficulties in developing clear political objectives and then translating these into military aims at all levels, a problem that will undoubtedly be repeated in the future. They are:

1. The selection and maintenance of the aim.

2. The maintenance of morale.

3. Offensive action.

4. Security.

5. Surprise.

6. Concentration of force.

7. Economy of effort.

8. Flexibility.

9. Co-operation.

10. Administration.

There are, perhaps, also principles of fighting, although these are not, as far as I am aware, laid down. They were fortunately taught to most small boys of my time. It was explained as the gentlemanly art of self-defence against bullies and thugs. My mentor was Sid Collet who had survived WWI and still had a bullet in his skull. Nevertheless he was a remarkable gymnast and boxing instructor. I owe him a very great debt. He was one of my few heroes. Sid explained that even people like myself with a well-developed sense of self-preservation could, if we kept our tempers under control, refused to panic and thought hard, survive or even beat a bully at his own game.

Later I boxed for my public school and narrowly avoided boxing for the Royal Navy. Ivor Paine, Mr Stenbridge and Mr Bishop drummed in the same message at Marlborough and throughout the Falklands campaign I kept telling myself, 'If they fight, box them; if they box, fight them'.

Jeremy Moore described our battle as more akin to prize-fighters boxing toe to toe. There was considerable truth in this as we had chosen San Carlos, knew it was well within their aircrafts' radius of action and quite simply had to take them head on. I do believe, however, that we boxed them!

The Staff of CTG 317.0

1. At the start of Operation Corporate:

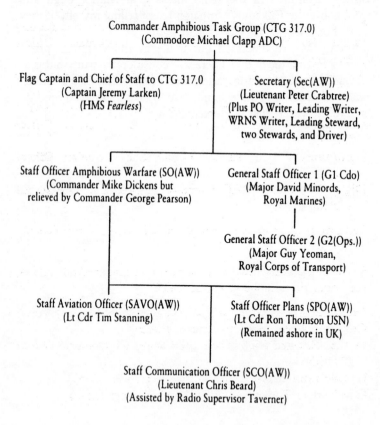

Commander Amphibious Task Group (CTG 317.0)
(Commodore Michael Clapp ADC)

Flag Captain and Chief of Staff to CTG 317.0
(Captain Jeremy Larken)
(HMS *Fearless*)

Secretary (Sec(AW))
(Lieutenant Peter Crabtree)
(Plus PO Writer, Leading Writer,
WRNS Writer, Leading Steward,
two Stewards, and Driver)

Staff Officer Amphibious Warfare (SO(AW))
(Commander Mike Dickens but
relieved by Commander George Pearson)

General Staff Officer 1 (G1 Cdo)
(Major David Minords,
Royal Marines)

General Staff Officer 2 (G2(Ops.))
(Major Guy Yeoman,
Royal Corps of Transport)

Staff Aviation Officer (SAVO(AW))
(Lt Cdr Tim Stanning)

Staff Officer Plans (SPO(AW))
(Lt Cdr Ron Thomson USN)
(Remained ashore in UK)

Staff Communication Officer (SCO(AW))
(Lieutenant Chris Beard)
(Assisted by Radio Supervisor Taverner)

2. Supplementary Staff included:

Lt Cdr Mike Goodman Staff Warfare Officer (SWO (D))

Lt Cdr Chris Meatyard Staff Mine Countermeasures and Diving Officer and, inititally, Staff Intelligence Officer (SMCDO & SINTO)

Instructor Lt Cdr A. K. Manning Assistant to SMCDO (ASMCDO)

Lt Cdr Peter Ambler Assistant Warfare Officer (AWO (A))

Lt Cdr J. J. White Assistant Staff Aviation Officer (ASAVO)

Lt Cdr Dobbinson Staff Intelligence Officer (SINTO)

Major Tony Todd, RCT General Staff Officer 2 (G2 (Ops.))

Flight Lt White RAF Staff Air Intelligence Officer (RAFINTO)

Instructor Lt Cdr A. C. M. Wood Staff Metereological Officer (SMETO)

Surgeon Capt J. M. Young on loan from CTG 317.8 (SMO)

Commander Mike Cudmore Staff Air Engineer Officer (SAEO)

Commander Tim Yarker Group Staff Aviation Officer (GAVO)

Flight Lt Chubb RAF Chinook Liaison and Operational Tasking (CLOT)

Leading Radio Operator Maynard, who acted as my Yeoman of Signals.

3. From *Fearless* there were numerous co-opted assistants, the most prominent of whom were:

Cdr John MacGregor Staff Marine Engineer Officer (SMEO)

Cdr John Kelly MBE Executive Officer

Lt Cdr Edward Richardson Staff Weapons Electrical Officer (SWEO)

Lt Cdr John Prime Staff Navigating Officer (SNO)

Cdr Robert Thompson Staff Supply Officer (SSO)

Both **John Kelly** and **Robert Thompson** also helped fly support helicopters.

4. From my own staff the Petty Officer Writer and WRNS Writer were left behind with Cdr M Dickens and Lt Cdr R. Thomson USN while the following came:

Leading Writer Weir
Leading Steward Baistow
Leading Airman (Met.) Park
Steward Leech
Steward Millward

APPENDIX 3

Task Group 317.0

During the Amphibious Phase

HMS *Fearless* (Capt E.J.S. Larken) with CTG 317.0 embarked
(Commodore M.C. Clapp) and CTG317.1
(Brigadier J.H.A. Thompson, Royal Marines)

HMS *Intrepid* (Capt P.G.V. Dingemans)
HMS *Broadsword* (Capt W.R. Canning)
HMS *Brilliant* (Capt J.F. Coward)
HMS *Antrim* (Capt B.G. Young)

HMS *Plymouth* (Capt D. Pentreath)

HMS *Argonaut* (Capt C.H. Layman LVO)
HMS *Coventry* (Capt D. Hart-Dyke)
HMS *Yarmouth* (Commander A. Morton)

HMS *Ardent* (Cdr A.W.J. West)

HMS *Antelope* (Cdr N.J. Tobin)

RFA *Fort Austin* (Commodore S.C. Dunlop CBE)
RFA *Tidepool* (Capt J.W. Gaffrey)
RFA *Stromness* (Capt J.B. Dickinson)
RFA *Resource* (Capt B.A. Seymour)
RFA *Sir Percivale* (Capt A.F. Pitt)

RFA *Sir Geraint* (Capt D.E. Lawrence)

RFA *Sir Lancelot* (Capt C.A. Purtcher-Wydenbruck)

RFA *Sir Galahad* (Capt P.J.G. Roberts)

RFA *Sir Tristram* (Capt G.R. Green)

SS *Canberra* (Capt D.J. Scott-Masson)
Naval Party 1710 (Capt C.P.O. Burne RN)

MV *Norland* (Capt M. Ellerby)
Naval Party 1850 (Commander C.J. Esplin-Jones RN)

MV *Elk* (Capt J.P. Morton)
Naval Party 2050 (Commander A.S. Ritchie)

MV *Europic Ferry* (Capt C.J.C. Clark)
Naval Party 1720 (Lt Cdr C.E.K. Roe RN)

845 Naval Air Squadron (Lt Cdr R.J. Warden)

846 Naval Air Squadron (Lt Cdr S.C. Thornewill)

FCDT1 (Lt Cdr B.F. Dutton QGM)

FCDT3 (Lt N.A. Bruen)

Later additions:

825 Naval Air Squadron (Lt Cdr H.S. Clark)

847 Naval Air Squadron (Lt Cdr M.D. Booth)

848 Naval Air Squadron (Lt Cdr D.E.P. Baston)

18 Squadron, RAF (Wing Cdr A.J. Stables)

Minesweeper Support Ship *St Helena* (Capt M.L.M. Smith)

Naval Party 2100 (Lt Cdr D.N. Heelas RN)

Minesweeping Trawlers
Pict (Lt Cdr D.G. Garwood)
Junella (Lt M. Rowledge)
Cordella (Lt M.C.G. Holloway)
Arnella (Lt R.J. Bishop)
Northella (Lt J.P.S. Greenop)

RFA *Engadine* (Capt D.F. Freeman)

Offshore Patrol Vessels
Dumbarton Castle (Lt Cdr N.D. Wood)
Leeds Castle (Lt Cdr C.F.B. Hamilton)

Others on temporary attachment to TG 317.0 included:

HMS *Exeter* (Capt H.M. Balfour LVO)
HMS *Avenger* (Capt H.M. White)
HMS *Minerva* (Cdr S.H.G. Johnston)
HMS *Penelope* (Cdr P.V. Rickard)
HMS *Arrow* (Cdr P.J. Bootherstone)
RFA *Blue Rover* (Capt J.D. Roddis)
RFA *Olna* (Capt J.A. Bailey)
RFA *Tidespring* (Capt S. Redmond)
RFA *Fort Grange* (Capt D.G.M. Averill CBE)
RFA *Sir Bedivere* (Capt P.J. McCarthy)
SS *Atlantic Causeway* (Capt M.H.C. Twomey)
Naval Party 1990 (Cdr R.P. Seymour RN)

SS *Baltic Ferry* (Capt E. Harrison)
Naval Party 1960 (Lt Cdr G.B. Webb RN)

SS *Nordic Ferry* (Capt R. Jenkins)
Naval Party 1950 (Lt Cdr M. St J.D.A. Thorburn RN)

MV *Monsunen* (Lt I. Mclaren RN)
(Naval Party 2160)

APPENDIX 4

A Ministry of Defence Amphibious Discussion

Unknown to us in the Fleet, in December, 1981, some thought was being given in the Ministry of Defence to an 'out of area' amphibious capability rather than an almost purely NATO-orientated Royal Navy and Royal Marines as we have described in the prologue.

The following exchange of paper actually took place and gives an amusing insight into the thinking, and the working of the Ministry, at that time.

First, from the Director Naval Operations and Trade (DNOT) to his naval and civilian counterparts:

WORLD-WIDE AMPHIBIOUS CAPABILITY

1. I have recently cleared two papers which subsequently have had additions implying that the RN possesses substantial amphibious capabilities. An example is as follows:

'Additionallly, the UK retains at present the ability to deploy a brigade of two commandos with full combat and logistic support in specialist amphibious ships world-wide, without reliance on ports, airfields or overflying rights.'

2. As the wretched Director of Naval Operations (and of course *Trade*) who would have to put flesh on such a skeleton, I can't visualise such an operation. Please let the first *victorious* battle of the Falkland Islands remain the only one – otherwise Ministers will be led to believe that we can repulse Argentina et al.'

This caused the Royal Marines' department, who had not been

addressed on the original Memorandum, to reply:

'1. It is not clear to me whether, in Reference A, DNOT is querying the capability itself, or the likelihood of that capability being exercised. If it is the former, the details are spelled out clearly in 'X,Y,Z' and in other UK position papers on out-of-area capability connected with the Rapid Deployment Force. If it is the latter, then I would have thought that the one thing we should have learned in the last 35 years is to expect the unexpected, particularly with a Prime Minister and a Cabinet that are clearly more prepared to look beyond the boundaries of NATO than their predecessors.

2. The UK currently possesses an impressive ability to undertake amphibious operations, and I find it surprising that anyone on the Naval Staff should wish to decry, or perhaps not appreciate, what is one of the Royal Navy's more significant capabilities.'

This robust, if somewhat huffy, Royal Marines' challenge was clearly drawn to the attention of the Assistant Chief of Naval Staff (Operations), Rear Admiral Whetstone, who, probably to calm the waters, replied in verse, highlighting the delays expected by the regular use of a L.P.D. as a Cadet Training Ship:—

> 'Hey diddle-de-dee; Amphibiosity
> If a crisis arises in Timbuctoo
> And a Minister asks what can we do,
> It's a helluva lot — in a month or two.
> Hey diddle-de-dee.
>
> Hey diddle-de-dee. Where is our L.P.D?
> In Curacao on a training cruise.
> Then call her back, there's no time to lose
> If our bootnecks' skills we want to use.
> Hey diddle-de-dee.
>
> Hey diddle-de-dee, high capability.
> If a coup d'etat occurs today

> *On the other side of Bengal Bay*
> *By mid July we'll be on our way*
> *With Amphibiosity!'*

This caused the Chief of Staff to the Commandant General Royal Marines, Major General Wilkins, to put the matter to sleep by further verse, but clearly showing there appeared to be a change of direction in the Cabinet policy.

> *'If trouble brews in distant lands*
> *We heave a sigh and wring our hands*
> *Forgotten are the lessons learnt*
> *(Afraid of fingers getting burnt?)*
>
> *But now it is too plain to see*
> *That Nott wants 'Boots' in the L.P.D.*
> *If we had played this vital card*
> *We would not have been hit so hard*
>
> *Invincible's role we found too late*
> *And sadly this has sealed her fate*
> *An L.P.D. she could have been*
> *And stayed in service for the Queen*
>
> *The Aussies now have seen the light*
> *And we have sadly lost the fight*
> *Invincible will sail away*
> *And live to fight another day*
>
> *The lesson's clear, we should have known*
> *We might have kept her for our own.*
> *"Out of area" operations*
> *Should have been our aspiration*
>
> *We clearly need more Boots, not less*
> *To save us from this frightful mess*
> *A.S.W. is not the same –*
> *Power Projection is the game!'*

And there the matter was, as far as we know, allowed to rest – until!

INDEX

Ranks are those held at the time.

369

371